POETRY ON ART

Renaissance to Romanticism

Edited by

THOMAS FRANGENBERG

SHAUN TYAS
DONINGTON
2003

© 2003, The Contributors

Typeset from the disc of the editor by the publisher

Published in 2003 by

SHAUN TYAS
1 High Street
Donington
Lincolnshire
PE11 4TA

ISBN
1 900289 56 3

Printed and bound by the Alden Group, Oxford

Poetry on Art
Renaissance to Romanticism

CONTENTS

LIST OF PLATES

49. Heinrich Dannecker, *Friedrich Schiller*, 1794, marble, Staatsgalerie, Stuttgart (photo: Conway Library, Courtauld Institute [neg. no. 832/60 (30)]).
50. *The Dying Gaul*, 241–197 B.C., marble, Museo Capitolino, Rome (photo: Conway Library, Courtauld Institute [neg. no. L73/1 (24)]; photograph by Dr Nicholas Penny).
51. Francis Chantrey, *The Sleeping Child, Harriet Acland (?),* plaster model (?), Sir John Soane's Museum, London (photo: Copyright of the Trustees of the Sir John Soane's Museum).

INTRODUCTION

From the sixteenth century onwards, poetry was one of the most widely used genres of literature in polished social exchange. This ubiquity of poems in everyday life chronologically coincided with, and to some degree was generated by, the proliferation of academies as one of the principal arenas of entertainment, learning and literary exertion, most notably in Italy, but to varying extents also in the rest of Europe. Nobody with a reasonable education was excluded from the use of poetry when dispensing praise or blame or exchanging information, a custom that has waned only in the last two centuries. Countless poems are extant today, in manuscript or in published form, the vast majority written by authors who were not professional writers. Any subject could be addressed in poems, including the visual arts.

Poetry on art is, of all genres of art literature, the least well known. This observation continues to hold in spite of a considerable amount of literature devoted to this subject;[1] the vast number of poems preserved in archives and libraries is, for the time being, beyond the reach of comprehensive reconnaissance, and in art historical monographs poems do not attract attention as frequently as they might, either as historical sources[2] or as literary

---

[1] Apart from numerous more narrowly focused analyses in articles and books, many of which are referred to in the papers in this volume, see G. Kranz, *Das Bildgedicht in Europa. Zur Theorie und Geschichte einer literarischen Gattung*, Paderborn 1973; M. Albrecht-Bott, *Die bildende Kunst in der italienischen Lyrik der Renaissance und des Barock. Studie zur Beschreibung von Portraits und anderen Bildwerken unter besonderer Berücksichtigung von G. B. Marinos 'Galleria'*, Wiesbaden 1976; G. Kranz, *Das Bildgedicht. Theorie, Lexikon, Bibliographie*, 3 vols, Cologne, Vienna 1981–7; L. Gent, *Picture and Poetry 1560–1620: Relations between Literature and the Visual Arts in the English Renaissance*, Leamington Spa 1981; C. E. Gilbert, *Poets Seeing Artists' Work: Instances in the Italian Renaissance*, Florence 1991; J. Dundas, *Pencils Rhetorique: Renaissance Poets and the Art of Painting*, Newark, London 1993; A. Golahny (Ed.), *The Eye of the Poet. Studies in the Reciprocity of the Visual and Literary Arts from the Renaissance to the Present*, Lewisburg, London 1996.

[2] The usefulness of poetry as art historical source material was highlighted as early as 1904; see A. Colasanti, 'Gli artisti nella poesia del Rinascimento. Fonti poetiche per la storia dell' arte italiana', *Repertorium für Kunstwissenschaft*, 27, 1904, pp. 193–220.

1

works in their own right, suggesting a widespread doubt that historical information can be gleaned from such material.

The present volume contains seven papers read at a Leonardo da Vinci Society symposium at the Warburg Institute in London, convened by the editor in 1998, and three that were written for this book. The selection of papers is intended further to document the great variety of insights art history and literary history may gain from the study of poetry; it aims to convey the diversity of responses to art in poetry and the subtlety of the interrelation between art and poetry. Poetry and poetic theory informed artistic practice, and in particular portrait painting; books containing poems represented in portraits may comment on the respective painting or offer a key to its interpretation; numerous artists wrote poetry on a variety of subjects, including art; some art theory was written in verse; a number of distinguished poets chose art works as their subject; lastly, men – and women – who were not artists or writers by profession resorted to poetry more than to any other literary genre when wishing to comment in writing on works of painting or sculpture. Thus poetry can function as one of the most illuminating gauges of contemporary reactions to and attitudes towards the visual arts.

The volume reflects the fact that poetry on art was, at least initially, more common in Italy than elsewhere, gaining increasing degrees of popularity north of the Alps, not least due to the spread of Italian culture across Europe during the sixteenth and seventeenth centuries.

The majority of sustained analyses of art and any other subject were, and continue to be, written in prose. Expositions of complex arguments are found in didactic poetry, an example being provided by a section of Karel van Mander's *Schilderboeck* studied by Charles Ford in this volume. Such lengthy poems, however, are greatly outnumbered not only by prose texts; within the genre of poetry they are likewise rare when measured against the number of poems adopting more condensed formats, in particular that of the sonnet. The concision characteristic of most poetic texts accounts for the fact that poems usually focus on a select number of issues, evoking their wider context through spirited allusion.

The extremely widespread recourse to commonplaces sets poetry apart from other literary genres; nonetheless, poetic responses to art can be seen as having their own kind of specificity, a specificity that may be recognized in the choice of artists, art works or art theoretical issues, in the way an art work's iconography is verbalised, or in the selection of artistic characteristics of individual works to be addressed in a poem. The essays in this volume aim to demonstrate that an engagement with this specificity can make the study of poetry as rewarding as that of any other text in the history of art literature.

My thanks go to the Humanities Research Board of the British Academy for a travel grant, and to the Foundation for Intellectual History for most generous financial support both of the symposium and this volume.

Poems by Bolognese Painters from the Renaissance to the Late Baroque

GIOVANNA PERINI

To the best of my knowledge, the earliest example of a poem written by a Bolognese painter is a sonnet in Italian by 'Hercule depintore bolognese', printed in the famous collection of Greek, Latin and Italian poems by various authors mourning Serafino Aquilano.[1] The booklet was published in 1504 with a dedication to Elisabetta Gonzaga, Duchess of Urbino. Other contributors include its editor Giovanni Filoteo Achillini, famous and fashionable poets like Girolamo Casio, Antonio Tebaldeo and Scipione Carteromaco, and a very peculiar specimen of *letterato* and university professor, Tommaso Sclarici del Gambaro, portrayed by Leandro Alberti in his *Descrizione di tutta Italia* as 'canon of S. Petronio who was not only a singular lover of antiquities and medals, but also had the knowledge to divine from the lines of the hand and also of the face. He was furthermore a most subtle sculptor of precious things'.[2] His name is entered in the Bolognese goldsmiths' guild in the year 1486 together with seven other members of his family and over 100 people (often entire families) who had apparently failed to register before or, like Francia, had probably omitted paying their fees since the time of their earlier registration.[3] As no work is attributed to

---

[1] G. F. Achillini, *Collettanee Grece-Latine e Vulgari per diversi auctori moderni nella morte de l'ardente Seraphino Aquilano*, Bologna 1504, sig. I 2v [= fol. 74v]. On this collection of poems, see G. Romano, 'Verso la maniera moderna: da Mantegna a Raffaello', in *Storia dell'arte italiana*, V/1, *Dal Cinquecento all'Ottocento: Cinquecento e Seicento*, Turin 1981, pp. 5-85 (esp. pp. 35, 47) and, more recently, C. Franzoni, 'Le raccolte del Theatro di Ombrone e il viaggio in Oriente del pittore: le Epistole di Giovanni Filoteo Achillini', *Rivista di letteratura italiana*, 8, 2, 1990, pp. 287-335 (esp. pp. 305-10).

[2] 'canonico di San Petronio, che non solamente fu singolare amatore de l'antiquitati et di medaglie, ma anche hebbe cognitione di divinare secondo le linee della mano et etiandio della faccia. Fu parimenti sottilissimo scoltore de cose pretiose'; L. Alberti, *Descrittione di tutta Italia*, Venezia 1551, fol. 274v. See also G. Fantuzzi, *Notizie degli scrittori bolognesi*, 9 vols, Bologna 1781-94, vol. 4, pp. 50-3, and most recently S. De Maria, 'Artisti, "antiquari" e collezionisti di antichità a Bologna fra XV e XVI secolo', in M. Faietti and K. Oberhuber (Eds), *Bologna e l'Umanesimo 1490-1510*, Bologna 1988, pp. 16-42 (esp. pp. 25-6).

Tommaso Del Gambaro, his name has escaped the attention of Giovanni Romano, who instead emphasises the presence, among the contributors to the *Collettanee* for Serafino Aquilano, of a much better-known sculptor from Central Italy, Gian Cristoforo Romano, the son of Isaia da Pisa, much employed by the Gonzaga and Sforza courts in the North. [4]

Regarding the identity of 'Hercule depintore', Giovanni Romano and, following him, Vincenzo Farinella, have suggested that he might be Ercole Banci or Banzi. Little is known about this artist, apart from his probable connection with either Francia's or Costa's workshop and a questionable corpus of rather mediocre works assembled in the past twenty years around a couple of signed pictures. [5] In an unpublished contract written in the year 1515 'Hercules, an eloquent man, the son of the late master Bartholomew the painter, Bolognese citizen from the parish of St Isaiah, public *nuncius* of the *comune* of Bologna', together with his wife Rosa sells a house to 'the most eminent doctor in arts and medicine, *dominus* Jacopo the son of Faustinus Bottrigari, nicknamed da Carpi', [6] i.e. Jacopo da Carpi, the famous owner of Raphael's *Saint John* and a lecturer at the University. [7] Although the general index of the Public Records' Office lists the seller as 'Hercules pictor' (not as a 'nuncius'), he seems to have been only a part-time artist, in order to conform to family tradition. While it is clear that he was a public officer, the nature of his office is harder to define, for 'nuncius' is neither 'praeco, tubicen' (the

3   Archivio di Stato, Bologna, Fondo Capitano del Popolo, series 'Liber Matricularum Artium', vol. 5, fol. 161r.

4   Romano 1981 (as in n. 1 above), pp. 35, 47 and most recently A. Bacchi, 'Da Gian Cristoforo Romano ad Alessandro Menganti: note sulla scultura del Cinquecento a Bologna', *Nuovi Studi*, 1, 1996, pp. 65–91 (esp. pp. 66–7).

5   See Romano 1981 (as in n. 1 above), p. 35 and V. Farinella, *Archeologia e pittura a Roma tra Quattrocento e Cinquecento. Il caso di Jacopo Ripanda*, Turin 1992, pp. 28, 51, n. 8. Specifically on Banci see the entry by S. P., in *Allgemeines Künstlerlexikon*, Munich, Leipzig 1992, vol. 6, p. 555, with earlier literature, unfortunately omitting F. Filippini, 'Ercole da Ferrara e Ercole da Bologna', *Bollettino d'arte*, 11, 1917, pp. 49–63, where the poem is discussed on p. 58, n. 5, and most recently S. Stagni, 'Alcuni ampliamenti per Ercole Banci', *Paragone*, 479–81, 1990, pp. 93–9.

6   'disertus vir Hercules quondam magistri Barth[olome]i pictoris Bononiae civis capellae Sancti Isaiae nuncius publicus Communis Bononiae'; 'Eggregio artium et medicinae doctori Domino Magistro Jacobo quondam Faustini de Botrigaris de Carpo'; Archivio di Stato, Bologna, Ufficio del Registro, Copie degli atti notarili, no. 107, fol. 386r, notary Giacomo di Giovanni Francesco Borgolotti, sale dated 16 July 1515.

7   On Jacopo Berengario (or Barigazzi or Botrigari) da Carpi, see the entries by A. Castiglioni, in *Enciclopedia italiana*, Rome 1929–39, vol. 6, p. 693 and by T. Ascari and M. Crespi, in *Dizionario biografico degli Italiani*, Rome 1960–, vol. 6, pp. 360–4. For his Raphael, see the entry by G. Chiarini, in *Raffaello a Firenze. Dipinti e disegni delle collezioni fiorentine*, Florence 1984, pp. 222–8, entry no. 19.

town crier: in fact, his name is not among those in office in or around 1515), nor 'orator' (the ambassador or official diplomatic envoy, always a nobleman). His qualification as 'eloquent', however, seems to fit well a man who was officially engaged in a verbal activity and therefore might have enjoyed writing poems such as the one printed in 1504. This Ercole cannot be identified with Banci, whose father was called Giacomo. He may well be either of the two persons named Hercules mentioned by Achillini in his *Viridario* published in 1513, but written in 1504.[8] The records of the painters' guild, however, offer no support for this identification, because the only 'Hercules' ever mentioned there (an Ercole Coltellini registered in 1507) is the son of one Francesco,[9] while 'Hercules pictor' of 1515 is the son of 'magister Bartholomeus' and a 'magister' must be registered in the guild. Thus his father must be the 'Bartholomeus quondam Magistri Zanobii de Florentia' registered in 1490, the son of Zanobi Del Migliore, a little-known student of Filippo Lippi's and a collaborator of Pesellino's.[10] His activity in Bologna in the year 1461 or after, recorded in the guild's book, has been little noticed and is furthermore disputed by some.[11] A son of master Bartolomeo, called Zanobi after his grandfather, was registered in the guild in 1501.[12] It is therefore possible that Ercole deliberately avoided registration either because he was both a part-time artist and a public officer, or simply to avoid fees and obligations. (The rule that prevented members of the same family from being registered simultaneously in the guild may date from later years.)[13] Even

[8]   The part of Achillini's poem referring to Bolognese artists is reprinted in Farinella 1992 (as in n. 5, above), pp. 203–5. Farinella (ibid., p. 51, n. 8) suggests that 'il dopio Hercole' refers to the Ferrarese painter Ercole Grandi and to the Bolognese Ercole Banci.

[9]   Archivio di Stato, Bologna, Fondo Capitano del Popolo, series, 'Liber Matricularum Artium', vol. 6, fol. 253r.

[10]   Archivio di Stato, Bologna, Fondo Capitano del Popolo, series 'Liber Matricularum Artium', vol. 6, fol. 252r.

[11]   Ibid. On Zanobi del Migliore in Bologna, see F. Filippini, 'Notizie di pittori fiorentini a Bologna nel Quattrocento', in *Miscellanea di Storia dell'arte in onore di Igino Benvenuto Supino*, Florence 1933, pp. 417–28 (esp. pp. 420–5); see also the more recent discussions of a painting attributed to him in the Collezioni Comunali d'Arte, Bologna in A. Bacchi, 'Vicende della pittura nell'età di Giovanni II Bentivoglio', in B. Basile (Ed.), *Bentivolorum Magnificentia. Principe e cultura a Bologna nel Rinascimento*, Rome 1984, pp. 285–335 (esp. p. 302, n. 33) and K. Lippincott, 'Chaos and the Egg: New Evidence from a Fifteenth-Century Bolognese Altarpiece', in G. Perini (Ed.), *Il luogo ed il ruolo della città di Bologna tra Europa continentale e mediterranea. Atti del Colloquio C.I.H.A.1990*, Bologna 1992, pp. 135–52 (esp. p. 141, n. 22), where recent literature challenging the attribution is reported.

[12]   Archivio di Stato, Bologna, Fondo Capitano del Popolo, series 'Liber Matricularum Artium', vol. 6, fol. 252v.

[13]   On this rule, see G. Feigenbaum, 'Per una storia istituzionale dell'arte bolognese,

Francesco Francia was registered in the painters' guild only as late as the end of 1503.[14] Obviously, registration was no prerequisite for obtaining work at the Bentivoglio court, whose patronage may have been sufficient to get commissions from public institutions as well. It looks as if registration was considered a matter of private choice and interest, on grounds we cannot fathom. It also looks as if the guilds (or at least some of them) hardly ever had the power to enforce membership when applicable. Apparently, some guilds, like the blacksmiths', were more powerful and careful in such matters than others, such as the carpenters', which registered no members for decades and even centuries. However, the history of the Bolognese guilds in the fifteenth through to the seventeenth centuries is still largely unexplored.[15]

Whoever 'Hercule depintore' may have been (Banci, Coltellini, the son of Bartolomeo, or any of the three homonymous contemporary painters identified by Filippini),[16] and whatever the style of his paintings may have been, if his sonnet in memory of Serafino Aquilano is anything to go by, he was not very gifted in the art of versification, although he had studied his Petrarch enough to borrow a few phrases, rhymes and rhetorical devices.

> Più volte Seraphin col dolce canto
> Havea confuso Morte e il fiero Amore.
> Subito l'empia e il crudo con furore
> Deliberorno haver la gloria e il vanto.
> Sdegnato ognun di loro in ogni canto
> Con tutta la sua forza e il suo valore
> Lo circondorno con tanto terrore
> Che per pietà ciascun ne fa gran pianto.
> Così finì soa vita, o crudel atto,
> Non già la fama soa, che vive in charte,
> Benchè 'l mondo senza el resti disfatto.
> Adesso Amore e Morte in ogni parte
> Se dogliono di tanti errori a un tratto
> Che'l canto e suon sia perso, il stile e l'arte.

> Serafino had confounded Death and fierce Love
> Several times with his sweet song.
> Suddenly pitiless Death and cruel Love decided

1399–1650: nuovi documenti sulla corporazione dei pittori, i suoi membri, le sue cariche e sull'Accademia dei Carracci', in *Il restauro del Nettuno, la statua di Gregorio XIII e la sistemazione di Piazza Maggiore nel Cinquecento: contributi anche documentari alla conoscenza della prassi e dell'organizzazione delle arti a Bologna prima dei Carracci*, Bologna 1999, pp. 353–77 (esp. p. 357).

[14] Archivio di Stato, Bologna, Fondo Capitano del Popolo, series 'Liber Matricularum Artium', vol. 6, fol. 253r.

[15] The most recent and comprehensive survey is in G. Roversi, 'Le arti per l'arte. Le sedi e il patrimonio artistico delle antiche corporazioni di mestiere bolognesi', in *La Mercanzia di Bologna*, Bologna 1995, pp. 83–167, with earlier literature.

[16] See Filippini 1917 (as in n. 5 above), p. 58.

Out of rage to conquer glory and something to boast of.
Each of them angry, with all their strength and valour
Surrounded him in every corner
With such a terror
That everybody weeps abundantly out of compassion.
Thus his life came to an end, oh what cruelty,
But not his fame, which lives on in papers,
Although without him the world is lost.
Now Love and Death all of a sudden
Repent everywhere because of so many errors,
For his song and music are lost, just like his style and art.

I should like to stress three facts: firstly, the standardised quality of the language, which shows very little evidence of regional influence, with the exceptions of the possessive pronoun 'soa' for 'sua' – a form which is also used in the poem – and of the pronoun 'el' for 'ei, egli'. Secondly, the total absence of any reference to the visual arts, unless such a reference is obscurely implied in the poet's fame 'which lives on in papers' and therefore outlives any more material monument. This is a contrastive topos in the tradition of Horace much favoured in Baroque poetry, but probably less common in the early Renaissance, despite some instances in Petrarch's letters. Thirdly, the taste for allegory and personifications, while essentially medieval in origin, does not exclude more modern (or classical) figures of speech such as hyperboles in praise of the deceased ('without him the world is lost').

The principal reason why this rather unremarkable poem should be discussed here at some length is that it is nearly contemporary with another well-known eulogistic sonnet, the authenticity of which has been hotly disputed. The latter was allegedly written by another Bolognese painter in honour of a famous but younger living artist. I am referring to Francia's sonnet in honour of Raphael published in Malvasia's *Felsina Pittrice*.

All'excellente Pictore Raffaello Sanxio, Zeusi del nostro secolo, di me Francesco Raibolini detto il Francia

Non son Zeusi nè Apelle e non son tale
Che di tanti tal nome a me convegna,
Nè mio talento, nè vertude è degna
Haver da un Raffael lode i[m]mortale.

Tu sol cui fece il Ciel dono fatale
Che ogn'altro excede, e so[v]ra ogn'altro regna
L'excellente artificio a noi insegna
Con cui sei reso ad ogn'antico uguale.

Fortunato garxon, che nei primi anni
Tant'oltre passi, e che sarà poi quando
In più provecta etade opre migliori?

Vinta sarà Natura e da tuoi inganni
Resa eloquente, dirà te lodando

Che tu solo il pictor sei de' pictori.

To the excellent painter Raphael Sanzio, the Zeuxis of our age, by me,
Francesco Raibolini called il Francia

I am neither Zeuxis nor Apelles, and I am not such
That such a name owed to so many others is owed to me,
Nor are my talent and virtue worthy
To receive immortal praise from a Raphael.

You alone, on whom Heaven has bestowed this fateful gift,
Exceeding and reigning over all others,
Teach us excellent art
Which made you the equal of all ancients.

Fortunate youth, who in his first years
Advances so much, what will be when
At a more advanced age [you produce even] better works?

Nature will be conquered, and made eloquent
By your deceptions, she will say in your praise
That you alone are the painters' painter.[17]

For external as well as internal reasons, this poem cannot be earlier than 1506
or later than 1516, and is generally dated around 1508.[18] Just like the better-
known sonnet ascribed to Agostino Carracci, 'Chi farsi un buon pittor cerca e

[17] C. C. Malvasia, *Felsina Pittrice*, 2 vols, Bologna 1678, vol. 1, p. 46. A slightly
different version from the one published in 1678 is preserved in the Biblioteca
Comunale, Bologna, MS B 16, unnumbered fol. before fol. 297r: 'Copia d'un
sonetto trovato tra le carte del Francia ch'erano del Lamberti etc. | Non son
Xeusi nè Apelle e non son tale | Che di tanti tal nome a me convegna, | Nè mio
< ?..?lento > talento, nè virtute è degna | Aver da un Raffael lode immortale. |
Tu sol cui < diede il > fece il Ciel dono fatale | Ch'ogni altro excede, e sovra
ogn'altro regna | L' < ?ecc? > excellente artefitio a noi insegna | Con cui sei rexo
ad ogni antiano eguale. | Fortunato graxon, che ne'i primi anni | Tant'oltre passi,
< che sarà > e che sarà poi quando | In età più provecta opre migliori | Vinta sarà
Natura e da < te.. > tuo inganni | Resa eloquente dirà te < sol > lodando | Che
< Raffel sei > tu solo pict < t > or sei tra pictori'.

[18] Cf. incidental remarks in E. Camesasca (Ed.), *Raffaello. Gli scritti. Lettere, firme,
sonetti, saggi tecnici e teorici*, Milan 1993, pp. 107–17, 323, and more specifically, C.
Dempsey, 'Malvasia and the Problem of the Early Raphael and Bologna', in
Raphael before Rome (Studies in the History of Art, 17), J. Beck (Ed.), Washington
1986, pp. 57–70. This sonnet is discussed in G. Perini, 'A proposito di critica
positiva e verità storiografica: la vera data di morte del Francia e la presenza di
Raffaello a Bologna', appendix to eadem, 'Carmi inediti su Raffaello e sull'arte
della prima metà del Cinquecento a Roma e Ferrara e il mondo dei *Coryciana*', in
Römisches Jahrbuch der Bibliotheca Hertziana, 32, 1997-8, pp. 367–407 (esp. pp.
402-3, n. 208). A very different view will be presented in J. Shearman, *Raphael in
Early Modern Sources (1483-1600),* Rome 2002 (in press), with a full chronological
account of the different opinions on this sonnet. I am grateful to the author for
sharing this part of his typescript with me.

desia' ('Whoever tries and wants to become a good painter'), Francia's has been considered a forgery written by Malvasia since at least 1911, although doubts had been raised by Grimm as early as 1872.[19] I have no intention of discussing Agostino's sonnet here, nor shall I comment on the other compositions in verse by the Carracci transmitted by Malvasia, Bellori or others, for I have already done so elsewhere and have not changed my opinion.[20]

As regards Francia's sonnet, a comparison with Hercules's helps to establish some basic facts. First of all, a sonnet written by a painter is not unprecedented or extraordinary in Bologna in the age of the Bentivoglio or immediately afterwards. If Francia was an amateurish versifier, he was most certainly not an exception in his environment. Vasari's statement on the exchange of correspondence between Francia and Raphael should not be considered suspicious, nor should Malvasia's documentation regarding it be distrusted in principle. Secondly, Francia's hyperbolic praise of his rival is neither surprising nor anachronistic. Praise always tends to be hyperbolic if it is devised to please unreservedly. That his sonnet is much more effective and modern than Hercules's may well be because Francia's was a better and more original talent, not only in painting but also in verse. Thirdly, the content of Francia's poem has nothing uncharacteristic of its period and ambience, especially if it is compared with Filippo Beroaldo's and Bartolomeo Bianchini's prose in praise of Francia. If the latter is 'in painting not to be considered second to anybody',[21] why should Raphael not be flattered with the address 'tu solo il pictor sei de' pictori' ('only you are the painters' painter')? Such praise does not necessarily imply any real acknowledgment of Raphael's artistic qualities, nor do I see its form as 'flagrantly anachronistic'. This kind of superlative could easily be found in a variety of other texts, including the Bible.

Francia's rhetorical denial of being Zeuxis or Apelles is not surprising when one remembers that in 1494 Niccolò Burzio had stated that Phidias, Praxiteles, Parrhasius, Zeuxis, Apollodorus and even Apelles, if alive, would consider Francia superior to them.[22] Had not Strazzola mockingly compared the notorious dauber Ombrone da Fossombrone to Apelles?[23] Why should

---

[19] See Shearman 2002 (as in n. 18 above) and Dempsey 1986 (as in n. 18 above), pp. 57–8, on the dating of this literary exchange.

[20] G. Perini, *Gli scritti dei Carracci*, Bologna 1990, pp. 55–69 and eadem, 'Aggiunte e postille a Gli scritti dei Carracci', *Accademia Clementina. Atti e Memorie*, 32, 1993, pp. 127–40 (esp. p. 133).

[21] 'in pictura nemini posthabendus': B. Bianchini, in M. Baxandall and E. H. Gombrich, 'Beroaldus on Francia', *Journal of the Warburg and Courtauld Institutes*, 25, 1962, pp. 113–5 (esp. p. 113, n. 3).

[22] N. Burzio, *Bononia illustrata*, Bologna 1494, sig. b 7r–v.

[23] See V. Rossi, *Scritti di critica letteraria dal Rinascimento al Risorgimento*, Florence 1930, pp. 146–50.

Raphael himself not have used such a common topos in his earlier, lost sonnet, to which Francia's allegedly replies? The claim that the young Raphael equalled the ancients and with his art conquered nature herself is not unusual in contemporary art literature in general, and in the poetry on Raphael surviving from the Cinquecento in particular. (Incidentally, we have no evidence that Malvasia was conversant with other early poems on Raphael.) The personification of Nature in Francia's sonnet may remind the reader of those of Love and Death in Hercules's. As for the forecast of Raphael's triumph in his later years, it does not need to be seen as a retrospective construction on the part of a possible seventeenth-century forger, nor as a hardly-believable early prophecy of Raphael's artistic merits. It is simply one more eulogistic topos that could easily have been applied, even to a scarcely talented young artist, if literary praise was to be bestowed upon him. Such a prophecy ever coming true was objectively irrelevant. This verse's resemblance to the similar statement in the distich on Raphael's tomb often attributed to Bembo, but more likely by Tebaldeo, can hardly be surprising, because they are only twelve years apart and originate from related intellectual backgrounds.[24]

Ultimately, the only obvious and remarkable difference between the two Bolognese sonnets is their respective linguistic and stylistic pattern, or rather patina. Francia's Italian, unlike Hercules's, has a strong local flavour, thanks to its fairly consistent Padanian spelling and choice of words, interspersed with Latin reminiscences. These characteristics, however, do not provide evidence of forgery, but rather of a difference in the literary qualities and milieu of the two artists. Francia's Italian reflects a type of regional language close enough to Giovanni Sabadino degli Arienti's *Porrettane* in prose, while Hercules's may well have been polished by the editor of the volume, Giovanni Filoteo Achillini, a strenuous advocate of the so-called 'lingua cortigiana' (courtly language) in the context of the early debate about Italian.[25] His Italian was basically Tuscan, although he maintained that regional terms from Bologna as well as from other cities could be employed freely, to add to the precision, beauty and expressiveness of the language.

Francia's and Agostino's sonnets are by no means the only poems by Bolognese painters recorded in Malvasia's *Felsina Pittrice*: several more appear in the second volume, devoted to seventeenth-century artists. Unlike the previous compositions, their authenticity has never been drawn into question,

[24] See G. Perini, 'Raffaello e l'antico: alcune precisazioni', *Bollettino d'arte*, 80, 1, 1995, pp. 111–44 (esp. p. 116) and V. Golzio, *Raffaello nei documenti, nelle testimonianze dei contemporanei e nella letteratura del suo secolo*, Città del Vaticano 1936, pp. 119–20.

[25] M. Vitale, *La questione della lingua*, Palermo 1978, p. 59. For editorial interventions in Cinquecento presses, see N. Maraschio, 'Grafia e ortografia: evoluzione e codificazione', in *Storia della lingua italiana*, 3 vols, Turin 1993, vol. 1, pp. 137–227 (esp. pp. 183–205).

even though only part of them appear in other seventeenth-century publications, or have been studied in depth.[26] They are ascribed to Lionello Spada and Giovanni Luigi Valesio, two artists who may be characterized as marginal in the context of Bolognese painting for their style as much as for their rank. Both were members of the literary academy, 'dei Selvaggi', established by the noted physician and man of letters Giovanni Capponi from Porretta.[27] It seems that Valesio was a member also of other literary academies, such as the – aptly enough – obscure Tenebrosi from Ferrara.[28]

Beside Spada's and Valesio's, Malvasia also published a couple of poems by Agostino Mitelli in his biography of the painter. Like Malvasia himself and Agostino Carracci earlier on, Mitelli was – or at least seems to have been – a member of the Accademia dei Gelati.[29] The only trait the three artists have in common is their political allegiance to Spain, which may be particularly relevant in the discussion of Spada's literary oeuvre, as we shall see presently.

In general, their poems contain little or no reference to the visual arts. They all fit well in the tradition of occasional poetry which was so common in seventeenth-century Italian literary academies and of which Hercules's sonnet is a very early example; most of such poetry was written for aristocratic weddings, births, deaths or theatrical events. References to the visual arts are almost totally absent in the works transcribed by Malvasia. Apparently his selection, based on aesthetic criteria, was intended to provide samples of the authors' literary styles and was meant both to complement his verbal accounts of their artistic qualities and further to enhance the portraits he provides of them.

The poems' place in Malvasia's work may help to explain why, in the case of Valesio, he ignored the few sonnets from *La cicala* of 1622 alluding to Valesio's activity as a painter. Malvasia depicts him as a tolerable poet, a decent engraver and a dauber, and Malvasia's literary selection supports his verdict, generally accepted also by present-day art historians.[30] Admittedly, in his printed poems, Valesio refers mostly to a genre he is not known to have

26 For Valesio's poems see Malvasia 1678 (as in n. 17 above), vol. 2, pp. 147–9, 151–2; for Spada's ibid., pp. 113–4, 124–5.
27 M. Maylender, *Storia delle Accademie d'Italia*, 5 vols, Bologna 1926–30, vol. 5, pp. 152–3 and R. Zagnoni, 'Accademie porrettane fra Cinquecento e Settecento', *Il Carrobbio*, 17, 1991, pp. 325–42 (esp. pp. 326–8).
28 Maylender 1926–30 (as in n. 27 above), vol. 5, p. 297.
29 See V. Zani, *Memorie, imprese e ritratti dei Signori Accademici Gelati di Bologna*, Bologna 1672, sig. + +4r and G. Perini, 'Ut Pictura Poesis: l'Accademia dei Gelati e le arti figurative', in D. S. Chambers and F. Quiviger (Eds), *The Italian Academies of the Sixteenth Century*, London 1995, pp. 113–26 (esp. pp. 113–6).
30 Benati, 'Valesio, Giovanni Luigi', in *La pittura in Italia. Il Seicento*, 2 vols, Milan 1989, vol. 2, p. 908 and N. Roio, 'Giovan Luigi Valesio', in E. Negro and M. Pirondini (Eds), *La scuola dei Carracci. Dalla bottega all'Accademia di Ludovico*, Modena 1994, pp. 335–44.

practised (portraiture); but he also mentions a *Cleopatra* he painted for Cardinal Maffeo Barberini, the Legate in Bologna from 1611 to 1614. This work is recorded in the Barberini inventory of 1623 together with a *Head of David with a sling* which, unlike the *Cleopatra*, is also found in later inventories.[31] It may be significant that both pictures were originally unframed, and that the *Head of David* eventually obtained a cheap plain black frame: apparently, they were not treasured possessions and their presence in the gallery was surely due to an unsolicited gift from the artist, who was as ambitious as he was untalented, rather than the result of a commission. Such apparent lack of esteem of his works fits in with the image, fashioned by Malvasia after the Vasarian Pinturicchio, of a deviously diplomatic artist whose social graces make up for his lack of talent and account for his acceptance and survival in the art world.[32] Further evidence for the accuracy of this assessment is provided by the epithalamium *La pittura* Valesio wrote in 1622 for a Ludovisi wedding, and by the dedication of his booklet *La cicala* to Cardinal Ludovico Ludovisi, the Cardinal Nephew of Gregory XV with whom he left Bologna for Rome to make a successful career at court.

Despite the pervasive influence of Marino on Bolognese poetry, it is clear from what we have seen so far that the situation in Bologna was at odds with the spirit in which the *Galleria* was written.[33] The poetry of local artists may be seen as the counterpart of the diffident attitude towards the visual arts displayed by Bolognese men of letters during the early years of the Accademia dei Gelati.[34] The lack of a local intellectual tradition among artists comparable to Michelangelo's, Bronzino's or Lomazzo's literary efforts can partly be blamed for this absence of interest in the visual arts, the only notable exception being the one sonnet by Agostino Carracci already referred to. It is therefore no coincidence that in 1614 Valesio alone took part in the well-known literary dispute between Ludovico Tesauro and Ferrante Carlo, generated by a poem by Marino dedicated to Raffaele Rabbia, a member of the Accademia dei Selvaggi.[35] It soon grew into a more general debate about artistic practice in contemporary art academies, fuelled by the notion of 'ut

[31] M. Aronberg Lavin, *Seventeenth Century Barberini Documents and Inventories of Art*, New York 1975, p. 68, nos 82, 86, p. 249, no. 446, p. 269, no. 100.
[32] Cf. Malvasia 1678 (as in n. 17 above), vol. 2, pp. 140, 150 and G. Vasari, *Le Vite de' più eccellenti pittori, scultori e architettori nelle redazioni del 1550 e 1568*, 6 vols, Florence 1966–1987, vol. 3, esp. pp. 571, 575.
[33] On Marino's *Galleria*, see M. Pieri, 'Capriccio ma non troppo (introduzione)', in G. B. Marino, *La Galeria*, 2 vols, Padua 1979, vol. 1, pp. XXV–XLV, and, from an art historical point of view, E. Cropper, 'The Petrifying Art: Marino's Poetry and Caravaggio', *Metropolitan Museum of Art Journal*, 26, 1991, pp. 193–212.
[34] Perini 1995 (as in n. 29 above), pp. 113–26. For later interest of the Gelati in the visual arts, see A. Colantuono, *Guido Reni's Abduction of Helen. The Politics and Rhetoric of Painting in Seventeenth-Century Europe*, Cambridge 1997, esp. p. 137.
[35] Zagnoni 1991 (as in n. 27 above), p. 326.

pictura poesis'. Giampiero Cammarota has stressed the importance of Valesio's testimony regarding the Carracci academy and its practices.[36] Indeed, Valesio's position in the Bolognese art world is unparalleled.

In 1949 Frances Yates drew attention to the British Library Add. MS 25,596, containing 'a collection of academic *rime*' allegedly from the Bolognese Academy dei Selvaggi. A brief survey of its contents led her to the conclusion that 'such gatherings should more properly be regarded as social clubs than as in any sense learned institutions. The Selvaggi were simply a group of friends whose doings were very important to one another, though the literary historian dismisses their *rime* with not undeserved contempt'.[37] The British context of this disparaging assessment is revealed by the ensuing comparison, based on a suggestion in Baretti, of Italian academies to the clubs in Dr Johnson's England, a somewhat ungenerous simplification. First, it should be stressed that only a minority of artists were members of such 'literary clubs', suggesting both success and limitation of the artists' claims to a better social status in modern societies, wherever court ethics and politics could not intervene on their behalf.

Secondly, a closer look at this manuscript reveals that it is a fat miscellaneous volume of over 300 folios, containing specimens of Bolognese poetry from the thirteenth to the seventeenth centuries. Some of the earlier compositions (such as Honesto da Bologna's and Guinizelli's) are late copies in a seventeenth-century hand (possibly Montalbani's), but others (such as a fragment from a longer poem)[38] are original fourteenth-century texts on parchment bound with early to mid sixteenth-century works, including poems from Cesare Nappi's entourage or compositions in Cesare Rinaldi's style. Whoever assembled the collection, copying out most of the *Collettanee* in memory of Serafino Aquilano, was a man of letters interested in preserving the local literary heritage of Bologna from its earliest and most illustrious examples to his own day. I suspect that this volume tallies well with a comparable and still little-studied collection in the Biblioteca Universitaria di Bologna known as 'Palladium eruditum', based on Cesare Nappi's manuscripts and later assembled by Ovidio Montalbani. This manuscript stands in the tradition of another seventeenth-century collection put together by Antonio Lamberti, which is now lost but was well known to Malvasia.[39]

---

[36] G. P. Cammarota, 'I Carracci e le Accademie', in A. Emiliani (Ed.), *Bologna 1584. Gli esordi dei Carracci e gli affreschi di Palazzo Fava*, Bologna 1984, pp. 292–326 (esp. pp. 323–4).

[37] F. Yates, 'The Italian Academies', in eadem, *Renaissance and Reform: the Italian Contribution* (Collected Essays, 2), London 1983, vol. 2, pp. 6–29 (esp. p. 23).

[38] British Library, Add. MS 25,596, fols 187r–188v.

[39] The so-called 'Palladium eruditum' is Biblioteca Universitaria, Bologna, MS 52, busta II/1. As for Lamberti, see Perini 1990 (as in n. 20 above), pp. 68–9 and n. 71 below.

The 'Rime degli Accademici Selvaggi di Bologna raccolte nel Principato del Signore Oldrado Garganelli detto il Desioso' discussed by Yates is only a small section of the manuscript and is clearly a fair copy prepared for publication by a professional scribe.[40] The inclusion of this manuscript may indicate that the whole volume was assembled by a member of that academy. In this section 14 out of a total of 49 poems (mostly sonnets and madrigals) are by Giovanni Valesio, l'Invescato,[41] while three are dedicated to him by fellow academicians, such as Giovan Filippo Certani, il Palustre, and Raffaele Rabbia, l'Agitato.[42] The former was a nobleman who hosted the Selvaggi academy in his house.[43] Unlike Rabbia, he praises Valesio for the 'doppio stil' ('two-fold style'), that is, 'i colori e la favella', painting and poetry, with which he portrays his beloved.[44]

Valesio prefers to cast himself in the role of a man of letters, writing sonnets for the deaths of illustrious and beautiful gentlewomen like Barbara Casali or Smeralda Rinuccini Marescotti or of noblemen like Francesco Maria Caccianemici.[45] He also congratulates Lorenzo Pietramellara on his joining the Academy and Cardinal Orazio Spinola, a former deputy Legate in Bologna, for his activity as the Legate of Ferrara.[46] Sharing a deeply held belief of the

[40] British Library, Add. MS 25,596, fols 28r–63r.
[41] See Appendix. It must be noted that, according to O. Montalbani (*Minervalia Bononiae*, Bologna 1641, p. 212, reprinted in Zagnoni 1991, as in n. 27 above, p. 327), there were two Giovanni Valesio who were simultaneously members of the Selvaggi Academy: The painter, with the academic penname of 'l'Invescato', and a nearly homonymous character (Giovanni Luigi Valesio) using the academic name of 'lo Stridolo'. Giovanni Luigi, though, was the complete name of the painter, while his brother's name is known to have been 'Hernando' (Malvasia 1678, as in n. 17 above, vol. 2, pp. 139–40) and Fantuzzi records but one Valesio. I should therefore think that Valesio may have changed his academic name at some point, or that Montalbani got confused and attributed to the same person in the same academy names belonging to different literary academies where he was a member.
[42] British Library, Add. MS 25,596, fols 48v and 57r respectively. See Appendix.
[43] On Certani see Fantuzzi 1781–94 (as in n. 2 above), vol. 3, p. 170 and on Rabbia ibid., vol. 7, pp. 146–7.
[44] The nickname of Rabbia's beloved is 'Clotho': see Rabbia's sonnet in British Library, Add. MS 25,596, fol. 30r. Certani shows some penchant for painting also in his other sonnet on St Luke as a painter (ibid., fol. 51v: see Appendix).
[45] On Caccianemici see n. 50 below. On Barbara Casali, see below, ibid. On Smeralda Rinuccini Marescotti, a Florentine, the wife of Senator Ciro Marescotti, see Biblioteca Comunale, Bologna, MS B 698/II, n. 76 (B. Carrati, 'Alberi genealogici'), no. 76. The date of her death is not recorded in the relevant Carrati MSS: Biblioteca Comunale, Bologna, MSS B 910–914 (B. Carrati, 'Li morti sì nobili che civili e di famiglie antiche della città di Bologna').
[46] On Spinola's career, see L. Pastor, *Storia dei Papi dalla fine del Medioevo*, 17 vols, Rome 1958–64, vol. 12, pp. 46, 235. For his years in Bologna as deputy legate of Pietro Aldobrandini, who never resided in Bologna, see A. Masini, *Bologna perlustrata*, 2 vols, Bologna 1666, vol. 2, pp. 231–2 and M. Ferretti and M.

Spanish community in Rome, the poet hails him as the next Pope and volunteers to celebrate the day of his future accession as a painter rather than a poet ('dirò più col pennel che con l'inchiostro', 'I shall say more with the brush than with ink'). Other sonnets deal with religious subjects (Christmas Eve), or the feelings of a lover who has to leave his beloved or greets the birth of his beloved's daughter, or is angry with his rivals, or hopeful when the cloak of his beloved who contemptuously passes by gets caught in a splinter of the church bench where he is kneeling in prayer and this makes her stop, albeit unwillingly. A significant part of these poems have found their way into *La cicala*, most often in an edited form with stylistic variations and improvements.[47] They help focus Malvasia's evaluation of Valesio's poetry: 'for he wrote and composed poetry in a manner that may afford delight and pleasure, if for nothing else, at least for a certain degree of sweetness, for some easy and clear natural talent. Surely if he had not been faced with the most productive and perfect century in Tuscan prose and poetry and if in Bologna, his home, he had not been faced with Claudio Achillini, Girolamo Preti, the Marquess Malvezzi, Matteo Pellegrini, the Manzini brothers and other such authors, he would have been held in higher esteem.'[48]

It is intriguing to observe that Lionello Spada has not contributed one single line to this particular manuscript collection of poems, despite being a founding member of the academy. Although the London manuscript is undated, the election of Orazio Spinola as Cardinal in September 1606 is an obvious *terminus post quem*, while Oldrado Garganelli's appointment as the supervisor of the Franciscan convent in Todi in 1620 is an equally obvious *terminus ante*, because after that date he would no longer live in Bologna. In fact, the collection can be dated even more precisely: Spinola died in 1616, five years earlier than Pope Paul V Borghese whom he was expected to succeed; he left the Legation of Ferrara at the end of 1615, after which date he could no longer be addressed as Legate.[49] Moreover, both Francesco Maria Caccianemici

---

Pasquali, 'Cronotassi critica dei Legati, Vicelegati e Governatori di Bologna dal secolo XVI al XVIII', *Atti e Memorie della Deputazione di Storia Patria per le Province di Romagna*, 23, 1972, pp. 117-301 (esp. pp. 211, 213). For his years in Ferrara, see *La chiesa di San Giovanni Battista e la cultura ferrarese del Seicento*, Milan 1981, pp. 12, 25, 44 and passim and J. Southorn, *Power and Display in the Seventeenth Century. The Arts and their Patrons in Modena and Ferrara*, Cambridge 1988, pp. 101, 111–4, 174, n. 8 and 9.

[47] See Appendix.

[48] 'avendo egli scritto e composto in modo che può dilettare e piacere, se non per altro, per una certa dolcezza, per una tal qual vena naturale, corrente e pulita. Certo che se non incontrava in un secolo il più ferace e perfetto sì nella prosa che nella poesia toscana, ed in Bologna sua patria non avea a fronte un Claudio Achillini, un Girolamo Preti, un Marchese Malvezzi, un Matteo Pellegrini, i Manzini e simili, erasi per farsi più di lui conto'; Malvasia 1678 (as in n. 17 above), vol. 2, pp. 146–7.

and Barbara Casali died in 1609.[50] Spada's whereabouts between 1608, when he writes a sonnet for an Este wedding, and November 1614, when he signs a contract in Reggio Emilia, are uncertain, and it is generally assumed that his trip to Malta and his stay in Rome occurred during this period.[51] Thus his absence in this collection of poems is most probably accidental and may further confirm the proposed dating.

Spada's sonnet for the Este wedding is not among those dating from the period 1607–08 published in the *Felsina Pittrice*.[52] They were printed to corroborate Malvasia's assessment of Spada's poetry: 'And if his Muse was not one of the most sublime, she was not one of the lowest, and one could bear her'.[53] Spada's most striking poem published by Malvasia is the otherwise undocumented composition in ottave rime entitled 'Per la morte del gran Gioannin da Capugnano'.[54] It is a merciless satire on a fourth-rate country craftsman with no notions of either design or painting.[55] His lack of mimetic

[49] See n. 46 above.

[50] For Caccianemici's death on 17 June 1609 and his funeral and burial at Sant'Andrea degli Ansaldi, see Biblioteca Comunale, Bologna, MS B 911, p. 80 (B. Carrati, 'Li morti e seppelliti in varie chiese di Bologna'). For Casali, see Biblioteca Comunale, Bologna, MS B 914, p. 16 (idem) recording two masses in her memory at San Giovanni in Monte. She was the wife of Curzio Pannolini: see Biblioteca Comunale, Bologna, MS 698/II, no. 33 (B. Carrati, 'Alberi genealogici').

[51] F. Frisoni, 'Lionello Spada', in Negro and Pirondini (Eds) 1994 (as in n. 30 above), pp. 266–7.

[52] Malvasia 1678 (as in n. 17 above), vol. 2, pp. 113–4.

[53] 'E se la sua Musa non delle più sublimi, non fu dell'infime e potè tollerarsi'; ibid., p. 113.

[54] Ibid., pp. 124–5. The biography of Giovannino is ibid., pp. 122–6.

[55] For an instance of his production, see F. Varignana, in A. Emiliani (Ed.), *Le collezioni d'arte della Cassa di Risparmio in Bologna. I dipinti*, Bologna 1972, pp. 357–8, entry no. 18 and pl. 28. Two more 'masterpieces' are published by P. Biavati, 'Giovannino da Capugnano "il pittoraccio"', *Nuèter*, 1975, pp. 18–23. For his engraved portrait by Mitelli see F. Varignana, *Le collezioni d'arte della Cassa di Risparmio in Bologna. Le incisioni, I, Giuseppe Maria Mitelli*, Bologna 1978, p. 355, no. 374. Although undated, this print is most probably contemporary with the *Felsina Pittrice* and posterior to the death of Giovannino, who was contemporary with the Carracci and Spada. I think that it is a sort of ideal pendant to the satirical print of the 'Accademici Scontornati' ('Academicians without outlines'; ibid., p. 354, no. 369), which must have been at the back of Giovanni Ludovico Bianconi's mind when he wrote his notorious criticism of Piranesi's life studies in the obituary of the artist published in the *Antologia romana* (1778–9, no. 34, pp. 265–7; no. 35, pp. 273–5; no. 36, pp. 281–4). Both prints were designed by Pietro de' Rossi in Rome, ruling out any possibility of actual acquaintance between the authors of the print and Giovannino. Given that Gaetano Giordani thought he was a member of the Giovannini family in Capugnano (C. C. Malvasia, *Felsina Pittrice*, Bologna 1841, vol. 2, p. 86, n. 1), he was related to the Dominican Father

and drawing skills was so great that his inventions could be understood only thanks to captions stating what was portrayed. Malvasia could find a detailed account of his artistic deeds in Ottonelli's *Trattato della pittura e della scultura, uso et abuso loro* (1652), in the chapter concerning 'pitture ridicole', pictures that move to laughter.[56] As Casale has shown,[57] Pietro da Cortona was responsible for most, if not all contemporary artistic examples in the *Trattato*, and may have heard of Giovannino from Bolognese painters in Rome. Yet the Jesuit Ottonelli was from Fanano, a village in the Apennines only a few miles away from Capugnano, and could very well have been aware of this dauber thanks to local traditions or a possible acquaintance with the noted Dominican theologian Fra' Girolamo Giovannini who was Giovannino's brother.[58] In fact the Giovannini, also known as Zannini, had been a prominent family in Capugnano since the fifteenth century.

Giovannino was the modern incarnation of a type of artist already condemned by Aelian and, more recently, Paleotti, namely 'so stupid a painter, and so inexperienced in his art, that he did not paint anything that preserved some resemblance and he was forced to add the name of everything, saying: "this is a horse, this is a tree, this is a book", and everybody laughed about him'.[59] Accordingly, in his ottave rime Spada states that

> Se mai di suo pensiero contornava
> Qualche inventione in fondo a un orinale,
> Era bisogno, a farla manifesta,
> Scrivergli sotto: la tal cosa è questa.

> Whenever he drew the outline
> Of some invention on the bottom of a chamber pot
> It was necessary, to make it plain,

Girolamo Giovannini who edited Schott's *Itinerarium Italiae* (1600) and was later plagiarised by Thomas Coryate; see E. Chaney, 'The Grand Tour and the Evolution of the Travel Book', in A. Wilton and I. Bignamini (Eds), *Grand Tour. The Lure of Italy in the Eighteenth Century*, London 1996, pp. 95–7 (esp. p. 95). On Giovannino see most recently G. Perini, 'Giovannino da Capugnano: leggenda biografica e realtà storica', *Gente di Gaggio. Storia e luoghi d'Appennino*, 9, 18, 1998, pp. 110–20.

[56] G. D. Ottonelli and P. Berrettini, *Trattato della pittura e della scultura, uso et abuso loro*, (Florence 1652) Reprint Treviso 1973, pp. 244–5.

[57] V. Casale, 'Ragione teologica e poetica barocca', ibid., pp. XV–CXLI (esp. pp. XVI–LII), and idem, 'Poetica di Pietro da Cortona e teoria del Barocco nel "Trattato della pittura e scultura"', in A. Lo Bianco (Ed.), *Pietro da Cortona 1597–1669*, Milan 1997, pp. 107–16.

[58] See n. 55 above.

[59] 'un pittore [...] sì sciocco et imperito nell'arte sua, che non dipingendo cosa che s'assomigliasse, era sforzato di aggionger il nome alle cose, dicendo: "questo è un cavallo, questo è un arbore, questo è un libro", onde ognuno se ne ridea'; G. Paleotti, *Discorso intorno alle imagini sacre e profane* (1582), in P. Barocchi (Ed.), *Trattati d'arte del Cinquecento*, 3 vols, Bari 1960–2, vol. 2, p. 390.

To write underneath: This is such and such a thing.[60]

Malvasia's life of Giovannino, an amplified paraphrase of Ottonelli's account, is apparently a humorous appendix to the Life of Spada, very much in the early humanist tradition of comic artistic characters such as Boccaccio's Calandrino and Buffalmacco, or Brunelleschi in Manetti's *Novella del Grasso legnaiuolo*.[61]

In Spada's poem, however, Giovannino's literary model is much closer in time, albeit distant in space: Don Quijote, in the second part of his adventures (1615), recalls 'Orbaneja, the painter from Ubeda, who, when asked what he painted, would answer: "Whatever will come of it". Sometimes he painted a cock of such forms and appearance that it was necessary to write nearby in gothic letters: "This is a cock".'[62] As Emilie Bergmann has shown, this is a well-established topos in Spanish art literature of the Golden Age and remains popular well into the following century.[63] Two undated epigrams reprinted in Pacheco's *Arte de la pintura* (1649), instances in Lope de Vega's works (1632) and in Calderon's *La devocion de la Cruz* (1635) show the diffusion of this topos in the decades immediately following Spada's death. In his own days, however, apart from Paleotti quoting Aelian, his only possible source was Cervantes, and this sounds extraordinarily appropriate for the only Bolognese artist who had the opportunity of spending some time in close contact with Caravaggio and his followers, many of whom were active in the Spanish colony of Naples.

Still, it is not clear whether Spada read Spanish: the *Don Quijote* was translated into Italian only as late as 1622, the year of his death. Given Malvasia's early poetic training and fame for Bernesque comic poetry,[64] it would probably make some sense to question the authorship of these ottave rime. Malvasia had better literary equipment and training for forging these

[60] Malvasia 1678 (as in n. 17 above), vol. 2, p. 125.

[61] As G. Tanturli has shown, Manetti's *Novella* should not be separated from his *Vita* of Filippo Brunelleschi, together with which it was composed; see G. Tanturli, 'Introduzione', in A. Manetti, *Vita di Filippo Brunelleschi preceduta da la Novella del Grasso*, Milan 1976, pp. XI–XLIX (esp. pp. XXIII–XXIV, XXVIII–XXIX, XLI–XLIII).

[62] 'Orbaneja, el pintor de Úbeda, al cual preguntándole qué pintaba, respondió: "Lo que saliere". Tal vez pintaba un gallo, de tal suerte y tan mal parecido, que era menester que con letras góticas escribiese junto a él: "Éste es gallo"'; M. de Cervantes Saavedra, *El ingenioso hidalgo Don Quijote de la Mancha*, M. de Riquer (Ed.), Barcelona 1990, pp. 584–5 (see also p. 1081, where the same episode is repeated in slightly different phrasing).

[63] E. Bergmann, *Art Inscribed: Essays on Ekphrasis in Spanish Golden Age Poetry*, Cambridge, Mass. 1979, pp. 168–70, n. 14.

[64] G. Perini, 'Carlo Cesare Malvasia's Florentine Letters: Insight into Conflicting Trends in Seventeenth-Century Italian Art Historiography', *The Art Bulletin*, 70, 1988, pp. 273–99 (esp. pp. 275, 279).

verses than any other poem by Bolognese artists included in the *Felsina Pittrice*. Thus a pun like: 'Quella del vino sol fu la sua bozza', where 'bozza' means both sketch and flask or bottle (according to the regional form of 'bozza' for 'boccia'), is very much in the taste of Malvasia's unpublished early poems, packed with double meanings, mostly of an erotic nature. [65] Even a hyperbole like the following might be somewhat suspicious:

Se pingea qualche casa a un tanto il giorno
E ch'il padron foss'ito a pranzo, a cena,
La trovava fornita al suo ritorno,
E la cantina di spegazzi piena.

When he painted some house at a daily fee
And its owner had gone out for lunch or dinner
When he was back it was all done
And even the cellar was full of daubs. [66]

The term 'spegazzi' has an illustrious Venetian and Bolognese tradition, as I have illustrated elsewhere. [67] However, its usage is not the monopoly of art critics such as Malvasia and Boschini, for in 1663 it is adopted in his private correspondence by Salvator Rosa, a painter-poet bred and born in Southern Italy. [68] I am therefore inclined to consider the ottave rime on Giovannino da Capugnano as probably authentic, trusting Malvasia's premise that 'In comic compositions, then, and even better in satirical ones he could equal anybody else who had entered this particular road. I regret that I cannot transcribe the original versions of the capitolo in triplets against Denis Calvaert and another one praising a pretty lady confectioner, for I have already committed them to fire, for they would clearly document how exceedingly excellent he was in this genre.' [69]

Apparently the ottave rime on Giovannino da Capugnano are the only extant specimen of a 'lower' poetic genre which was widely practised in Bolognese workshops. [70] Malvasia's book thus becomes a sample collection of

---

[65]   Biblioteca Universitaria, Bologna, MS 1204/I, fols. 18r–27v.

[66]   Malvasia 1678 (as in n. 17 above), vol. 2, p. 124.

[67]   G. Perini, 'Il lessico tecnico del Malvasia', in *Convegno Nazionale sui lessici tecnici del Sei e Settecento*, 2 vols, Florence 1981, vol. 1, pp. 219–53 (esp. pp. 234–6).

[68]   B. Migliorini, *Storia della lingua italiana*, Milan 1994, p. 43.

[69]   'In stile giocoso poi, ma più nel satirico, star potette al pari d'ogni altro che questa ardita strada giammai battesse, e spiacemi che di un capitolo di terzetti contro Dionigio Calvarte e di un altro in lode di bella pasticciera non mi sia lecito trascrivere gli originali, che ho già destinati al fuoco, che ben'apparirebbe quanto in questo genere pur troppo fosse eccellente'; Malvasia 1678 (as in n. 17 above), vol. 2, p. 114.

[70]   Perfectly believable is the story of a satire written by Spada against Calvaert: it is very much in the tradition of Bolognese workshops, for it should be remembered that Agostino had been charged with writing a satirical sonnet against Passerotti (Malvasia 1678, as in n. 17 above, vol. 1, p. 364).

poetic efforts by Bolognese artists through three centuries, very much a counterpart in print to Antonio Lamberti's famous manuscript collection of local poetry, from which Malvasia allegedly extracted some of his published materials.[71] Others were gathered through Malvasia's own painstaking activity as a collector of drawings and prints.[72] The four lines by Agostino Mitelli transcribed by Malvasia from a drawing in his collection and a sonnet of his sent to some friend in Spain are the only extant documents of Mitelli's poetic activity that justified his membership in the Accademia dei Gelati.[73] The fact that the quatrain is a moral commentary on the subject of the drawing done by Mitelli's son Giuseppe Maria (*Apollo and Marsyas*) and effectively provides an alternative, improved version of the verses prepared by the young draughtsman himself explains why Malvasia was confident in attributing rhymed captions in prints to their inventors, especially if they were the Carracci. It also proves how, by the mid-seventeenth century, versification had become a common feature in family workshops.

When, at the turn of the century, Giovampietro Cavazzoni Zanotti gave ample evidence of being a man of letters as much as a painter, he would simply bring the long-term process documented in Malvasia's book to completion.[74] Unlike most of his predecessors, however, he would not refrain from writing about art, both in verse and in prose. However, it would probably be fair to say that, all in all, he was a man of letters rather than a painter.

---

[71]   Ibid., sig. b3v, pp. 46, 49.

[72]   Perini 1988 (as in n. 64 above), pp. 286–8 and B. Bohn, 'Malvasia and the Study of Carracci Drawings', *Master Drawings*, 30, 1992, pp. 396–414 (esp. pp. 396–8).

[73]   Malvasia 1678 (as in note 17 above), vol. 2, pp. 413–4.

[74]   On Zanotti, see M. G. Bergamini, 'G. P. Zanotti', in M. Saccenti (Ed.), *La Colonia Renia. Profilo documentario e critico dell'Arcadia bolognese*, 2 vols, Modena 1988, vol. 1, pp. 88–9, 242–50; G. Perini, 'Letteratura artistica e società a Bologna al tempo di Giuseppe Maria Crespi', in A. Emiliani and A. B. Rave (Eds), *Giuseppe Maria Crespi 1665–1747*, Bologna 1990, pp. CXCIII–CCVI (esp. pp. CXCV–CCVI), and E. Grasman, *In de schaduw van Vasari. Vijf opstellen over kunstgeschiedschrijving in 18de-eeuws Italie*, s.l. 1992, pp. 49–82.

APPENDIX
POEMS FROM BL MS 25,596

(1) Al Signor Giovanni Valesio del Palustre Selvaggio
[i.e. Giovanni Filippo Certani]

Da lo stame non pur ch'avolge al Fato
Questa Parca d'Amor pende il tuo Fato,
Gentil Valesio: un sol suo sguardo irato
Porria di vita ancor renderti escluso.
Ma non convien ch'in ciò resti deluso
Lo tuo sperar dal merto sol guidato,
Ch'il caro nome e 'l bel sembiante alzato
E' homai, la tua mercè, fuor d'uman uso.
Però se doppia vita a lei procacci
Trattando il doppio stil, dritt'è ben ch'ella
Doppia corona alla tua fronte allacci.
E mentre opri i colori e la favella
Onde il tempo e l'oblio vinci e discacci
Cloto cortese fia, non men che bella.
(fol. 48v)

(2) Per la sacra Imagine di Nostra Signora dipinta da San Luca,
del Palustre Selvaggio

I colori da l'alba e dal più vago
Serenissimo Ciel Luca prendea,
Luca pittor divin, mentre pingea
De la Donna del Ciel la bella imago.
Nè solo in quella di ritrar fu vago
Mortal sembiante di celeste dea,
Che gl'interni desiri anco esprimea,
Ond'ha l'affetto in Dio contento e pago.
Quinci divinità dal volto spira,
Santi desiri imprime e sente ardore
Di celeste desio chi la rimira.
E fra la riverenza e fra 'l timore
Mentre l'occhio e'l pensier s'avolge e gira
Null'altro brama, e 'n lei s'acqueta il core.
(fol. 51v)

21

(3) Al Funerale della stessa Signora [Smeralda Rinuccini Marescotti] del medesimo [i.e by l'Agitato, Raffaele Rabbia]

Vanne Valesio, che già intorno è cinto
D'accese faci l'honorato sasso,
Quel sasso, oimè, quantunque humile e basso
Di *smeraldi* bellissimi dipinto.
Per la pietà vedrai lo stuolo accinto
Quasi per gran dolor di vita casso;
Io per me nel languir son fatto lasso.
Offri tu almeno il pianto al corpo estinto.
Poi che cruciosa con perversa guerra,
Volge sossopra il mondo ebra di sangue
L'Arcera micidial ch'ogn'alma atterra.
E quel volto divin per cui si langue
Quivi si giace, e freddo marmo il serra,
Fatto carcere eterna al corpo essangue.
(fol. 57r)

SONNETS BY GIOVANNI LUIGI VALESIO

(4) In morte della Signora Barbara Casali

Di questa saggia e generosa estinta
Non sapea il mondo celebrar le lodi,
Mentre del mondo in tra fallaci nodi
Giacea sepolta e nel suo frale avvinta.
Hor che di stelle su nel cielo è cinta
E non teme del tempo inganni e frodi,
Giust'è ben ch'ogni lingua il canto snodi
Ond'a posteri sia chiara dipinta.
A quest'alma sì bella hor queste note
Meste col pianto onde s'asperge il viso
Sieno essequie umilissime e divote.
Che già a lettre di sol veder m'avviso
Su i margini del ciel, fra l'auree rote
Che Barbara risplende in Paradiso.
(fol. 29v)

(5) Partenza

Là dove s'alza quasi al cielo il monte
Dov'ha sua reggia l'aquilone algente,

22

Dove l'alto Appennin s'erge possente,
Cinto di nubi la superba fronte,
Là dove il picciol Reno ha cuna e fonte,
Ov'ha le luci il sol fra nembi spente,
Dove poco più su s'erge la mente
E di poco più su cadde Fettonte,
Donna, là su poggiai colmo d'ardore
Del grave ardor che mi consuma il petto
Per trovar refriggerio al mio dolore.
Ma, lasso, del mio seno antico letto
E tirannia del cor s'ha fatto Amore,
Ond'è ch'in van freddo soccorso aspetto.
(fol. 33v)
(printed in G. L. Valesio, *La cicala*, Rome 1622, p. 29)

(6) Nel medesimo soggetto

Sol per veder del picciol Ren la culla
E del padre Appennin la cima altera
Lasciai di Voi, mio Sol, l'imago vera
In cui l'alma si nutre e si trastulla.
Donna, tanto m'alzai, che poco o nulla
Vidi sopra di me l'ardente sfera,
E vidi il tergo a l'aquila leggiera
E dove il sole ogni gran nembo annulla.
Poggiai tant'oltra per provar se'l foco
Ch'arde lassù s'agguaglia al grave ardore
Che per Voi mi consuma a poco a poco.
O fallace pensier, disse il mio core,
Disegual paragone, ahi quanto è poco
Calor di sfera ov'ha sua fiamma Amore.
(fol. 34r)
(printed as 'Comparatione d'arsura', ibid., p. 30)

(7) In morte del Signor Francesco Maria Caccianemici

Di quest'umide stille il vivo fonte,
I sospiri ardentissimi e i lamenti
Queste mie note e funerali accenti
A te, Caccianemici, ornin la fronte.
Potess'io penne haver veloci e pronte,
Per seguirti la sù fra i giri ardenti,
Com'ancor fra li spirti almi e lucenti,

23

Le palesi direi tue lodi e conte.
Ma forse perchè tu, cantor di Delo,
Rapisti l'alme che l'oblio raccolse,
Rapito fosti, e tolto al mortal velo,
E poichè il ciel la tua bell'alma accolse,
Posso dir (s'abbellir si puote il cielo)
Ch'ornar se stesso di te stesso ei volse.
(fol. 46r)

(8) All'Illustrissimo e Reverendissimo Signor Cardinal Spinola,
Legato di Ferrara

Signor, s'avvien giammai (come si crede)
Che meco il mondo un dì V'adori in Roma
Con fregio d'or su l'onorata chioma,
Del sacro manto e de le chiavi erede,
Vedrassi alhor a la Vostr'alta sede
Venire il Trace e tutta l'Asia doma,
Con grave incarco e tributaria soma
Ad inchinarVi et a baciarVi il piede.
Et io, che tento hor con la penna sola,
Fatto presago del gran merto Vostro,
AlzarVi là dove il desir sen vola,
Alhora potrò lodarVi al secol nostro
Che mutando in color senso e parola,
Dirò più col pennel che con l'inchiostro.
(fol. 46v)

(9) [untitled]

Esci, vaga fanciulla, alma gentile,
Parto di Lei che riverente onoro.
Appresti a te sua bella cuna d'oro
Amor, che femmi a chi ti fece umile.
E lo stuol de le gratie, aureo monile,
A te cinga, e d'illustre, alto lavoro
Qual non vide giamai l'adusto Moro
Virtù fregi, te sola, a te simile.
Esci, ch'onor già ti prepara il letto
E fia bellezza che t'involga e fasci,
E ti fia l'onestà corona e tetto.
Hor sì felice e gloriosa nasci,
Perchè forma prendesti in sì bel petto,

Ed hor ti nutri in sen bel latte e pasci.
(fol. 47r)
(printed as 'Parto di bella donna', ibid., p. 40]

(10) [untitled]

Di voi fuggendo, o cittadine mura,
Il grave incendio e 'l più cocente ardore,
Ov'è più fresca l'aura e vago il fiore
Rivolgo ogni pensiero, ogni mia cura.
Qui mia vita trarrò lieta e sicura,
Passando men noiosi i giorni e l'hore,
E se'l petto ritien foco d'Amore
Men cruda fia lungi da Voi l'arsura.
Ma (lasso) i' fuggo, e pur la fiamma mia
S'accese lungi ancor dal bel sembiante
Che vive in me, benchè tra Voi pur sia,
E ben ch'io vada fra bei colli erranti,
Prova < Nutre > il mio petto, ovunque stia,
Più ch'estivo calor, fiamma d'amante. < Amore >
(fol. 48r)

(11) Sepolcro della nobilissima estinta la Signora Smeralda Rinuccini

Sia d'alabastro il bel sepolcro, e sia
Di *Smeraldo* finissimo il lavoro
Pari al nome a la fede; e poi sia d'oro
Il pavimento in cui si fermi e stia.
Da scultore eccellente a fantasia,
Sculto sia delle Parche il Concistoro.
La men cruda sia Cloto: Amor fra loro
Pianga l'atto crudel d'Atropo ria.
In fronte a l'edificio a bei colori
La Gioventù si pinga e la Bellezza,
ch'esprimano acerbissimi dolori;
Ma stia nel mezzo in rigida alterezza
Morte tiranna de' mondani onori,
In atto ch'interrompa ogni dolcezza.
(fol. 52v)
(printed as 'Sepolcro per la signora Smeralda Rinuccini', ibid., p. 54)

(12) Epitaffio per la Signora Smeralda Rinuccini

Smeralda è già nel quarto lustro estinta
Che nobile e gentile al mondo visse,
Gemma la cui bellezza il ciel prescrisse
Fra' gloriosi smalti esser avvinta.
Tu ch'hai già per pietà l'alma convinta,
C'hai nel bel nome suo le luci affisse,
Se lagrimò il pastor che qui lo scrisse,
Tu fagli ancor di pianto umida cinta.
Il sasso ond'ella è chiusa anch'ei l'onora,
Ch'irrigando d'umore il pavimento
Per l'occulta beltà s'ange e scolora.
E se formar sapesse un solo accento
(Ma gliel vieta Natura) udresti ancora
Favellar per pietade un monumento.
(fol. 53r)
(printed as 'Epitaffio per la medesima Signora Smeralda Rinuccini',
ibid., p. 55)

(13) Manto trattenuto da una panca in chiesa

Divoto in atto riverente e pio
Mentr'io chiedea mercè del mio fallire
(Non so se per pietade o per martire)
Comparve il mio bel sol, l'idolo mio.
A sì rara beltà mi volsi anch'io
E vidi al suo splendor mill'occhi aprire.
Ella, ch'a gioco prende il mio morire,
Passommi accanto e non pur disse addio.
Pietose più di lei sue spoglie alhora
Col soglio ov'io languia per mia fortuna
Fer con nodo gentil breve dimora.
Alhor tacito dissi: "Amor raguna
Forse per me più dolce laccio ancora,
Se'l manto di costei anco s'aduna".
(fol. 53v)
(printed with minor variations as 'Donna crudele e manto pietoso',
ibid., p. 24)

(14) Nell'ingresso del Signor Lorenzo Pietramellara nell'Accademia

Lorenzo, Voi che per le vie d'onore

Sicuramente accelerate i passi
E per dove sicuro a gloria vassi
Saggio splendete de' prim'anni il fiore;
Voi, che sul primo giovenil furore
Risvegliate prudenti i pensier lassi,
E con veri d'onor fregi non bassi
La fronte ornate e d'immortal sudore
Hor che di Voi, ne le Selvagge piante
Innesto nobilissimo s'asconde,
Pur di gloria maggior Cupido amante,
Fra me parlando dico: "Apollo infonde
Ne' Vostr'alti pensier gratie cotante
Perchè diate a' Selvaggi e frutti e fronde".
(fol. 54r)

(15) Tenebre bramate

Ahi, troppo sol per me tua luce pura
Per le piagge serene hor si rinfranca,
Ahi, troppo sol per me lucente e bianca
Ti scopri ov'eri dianzi e bruna e scura.
Ahi, quanto fatta hor sei per mia sventura
Cortese, ond'io la via sicura e franca
Calchi col piè notturno; Ahi, che non manca
A me, senza la tua, scorta sicura.
Deh, poi ch'a tuo piacer tre forme prendi
Chiara nel ciel, casta ne' boschi e nera
Ne gl'abissi, hor pietosa a me ti rendi.
O se cangiar non voi tua forma vera,
Almen fra' nembi esser cortese apprendi,
E sì vedrò il mio sol ne la tua sera.
(fol. 54v)

(16) La Notte di Natale

Questa, Selvaggi, è la gran notte a cui
S'inchina il Sol ch'in Oriente nasce,
Questa è la notte in cui ristretto in fasce
Il gran Verbo divin si mostra a nui.
O madre felicissima di Lui,
Che nel suo parto Vergine rinasce,
O bel figlio ch'in lei si nutre e pasce,
O noi felici ancor per ambedui.

Avventurosi poi selve e pastori
C'hebber gratie sì care, onde fur degne
Di prima vagheggiar sì bei splendori.
Deh, se portiam pur de' Selvaggi i segni,
Perchè di lane invece, e rozzi onori
Non presentiamo al gran Bambin gl'ingegni?
(fol. 55r)
(a somewhat similar poem is printed in *La cicala*, p. 70)

(17) Al fiumme Reno

Fiume gentil, che l'onda tua vagante
Drizzi colà, dov'il mio ben risiede,
Deh, ferma per pietà l'umido piede
A' preghi, ohimè, di fuggitivo amante.
O, sè fermar non degni il corso errante,
Concesso almen Vi sia (la tua mercede)
Sul cristallino tergo la mia fede
Recar cortese a la mia Cloto avante.
S'in te non è l'umanitade estinta,
Se'l mio pregar tu non ascolti in vano,
Saluta lei, ch'ho dentro al sen dipinta.
Questa fede (dirai) benchè lontano
Ti sia, ti serba intatta, al core avvinta
Là dov'io nacqui il tuo Pastor montano.
(fol. 61r)

(18) Amanti importuni

Sciocca turba d'amanti a lo splendore
Del Vostr'almo e gentil volto sereno,
Donna, talhor io veggio, e poco meno
Che farfalle aggirarsi al Vostro ardore.
Ma incrudelirsi ancor lo stesso Amore
Contro lor ne' Vostr'occhi io scorgo a pieno,
Et in vece d'ardor vibrar veneno,
E in Voi d'ira formarsi un bel rossore,
Carattere di sdegno, e manifesti
Per difesa di Voi taciti accenti
E segni evidentissimi son questi.
Ma che legger non sanno, e solo intenti
Ai volgari pensier, volanti e presti,
Corrono incauti a i Vostri raggi ardenti.
(fol. 61v)

28

To Loosen the Tongue of Mute Poetry: Giorgione's Self-Portrait 'as David' as a Paragone Demonstration

PAUL HOLBERTON

The grandiloquent title of this paper is designed to recall, first and obviously, Simonides's 'painting is mute poetry; poetry is vocal painting';[1] secondly, more obliquely, a phrase from the Codex Urbinas, in which Leonardo, polemically contrasting painting to the other arts, pits it in particular against poetry:

> Ma per non sapere li suoi operatori dire la sua ragione, [la pittura] è restata longo tempo sanza advocati, perché essa non parla, ma per sé si dimostra e termina ne' fatti; e la poesia finisce in parole, co le quali come briosa sé stessa lauda.

> But because its practitioners do not know how to state its case, painting has remained a long time without advocates, because painting does not speak, but shows itself through itself and goes no further than the facts; but poetry's end is words, with which, and vigorously, it praises itself.[2]

That 'per sé si dimostra, e termina ne' fatti' rings down to the present, for in the absence of 'parole' the interpretation we choose to place upon Renaissance paintings has as its only evidence the paintings themselves, uncorroborated; and even when we give them their lines to speak, obdurately mute is what the paintings themselves remain. The interpretation I wish to put upon a certain painting by Giorgione is more than can be proved, and perhaps more than may be found likely, despite some circumstantial evidence to assist it. It may even not be accepted that the work is so anomalous as to demand an interpretation. However, Leonardo's remark may support the idea that the work might have been painted deliberately in order to 'rival' poetry and the intention, not being sympathetic to later viewers, might subsequently have been lost – or obscured, for Giorgione's interest in the *paragone* between the arts is a fact of the sources, and has been accepted and further investigated by current scholarship.[3]

---

[1]   As from Plutarch, *De Gloria Atheniensium*, III, 346f-47c.

[2]   Codex Urbinas 1270, fol. 28v; Leonardo da Vinci, *The Literary Works*, J. P. and I. A. Richter (Eds), 3rd edition, London 1970, item 20.

[3]   For Giorgione and the *paragone*, see most recently G. Helke, 'Giorgione als Maler

In some ways this is a diversion from the central theme of this collection of papers, which is rather poetry about art than art 'about' poetry. However, Giorgione's 'demonstrations' (I believe *dimostrazione* is a term that might appropriately have been applied at the time to these pictures) belongs *pari passu* with the increasing articulacy and discussion about art that was a phenomenon of the Renaissance, and in particular beside the kind of poetry about portraiture that has been assembled and analysed by John Shearman in Chapter 3 of his book *Only Connect.* Shearman, indeed, underlines the stimulative, competitive interaction of poet-spectators' demands and artists' achievements. This interaction can be traced back to the interest at the turn of the fifteenth century, following contact with Byzantium, in the rhetorical 'exercise' of *ekphrasis*: *ekphrasis* evidently invited rivalry in 'describing' not only between poets and other poets, but between poets and painters. Initially, Guarino da Verona implicitly reserved to poets and denied to artists the possibility of *ekphrasis* – in a letter of 1417, in which, reading Pausanias, he claimed he found his evocation of the monuments of Corinth 'more vivacious' ('vivacior') in words even than the image ('effigies') itself. However, as soon as artists had once again 'brought alive' works described in classical authors – above all, but not only, Lucian – this position was inevitably weakened; in the generations following Guarino there was some argument about it.[4] Conspicuously, Leonardo was polemical on the part of artists, or specifically painters, in seeking to vindicate the range of possibilities and effects of art vis-à-vis poetry (even if much critical debate that falls under the heading of *paragone* keeps within the field of art, most commonly contrasting painters and sculptors). It was largely accepted by the mid-sixteenth century, in the Florence of Benedetto Varchi and Giorgio Vasari, that painters could not paint – or 'ekphrasize' – the 'inner' nature of living beings, but earlier and in northern Italy others under Leonardo's influence, such as Giorgione, might have been as combative as Leonardo himself in seeking to push back the perceived limits of art. What an artist thought he could show in art (or through art) surely deserves to be considered beside what his audience thought they could read in (or into) art.

My speculation is that Giorgione painted his self-portrait deliberately in order to set up a *paragone* to poetry, but because the picture 'termina ne' fatti', because the *paragone* is stated in purely pictorial terms, this artistic intention has never been recognized by posterity. The circumstantial evidence I have been able to marshal may be summarized as follows: there are signs

---

des Paragone', *Jahrbuch des Kunsthistorischen Museums Wien*, N.F. 1, 1999, pp. 11–79 (published after this article was written).

4 For the early humanist approach to art, see M. Baxandall, *Giotto and the Orators*, Oxford 1971, esp. pp. 78ff. Guarino's letter is *Epistolario di Guarino Veronese*, R. Sabbadini (Ed.), Venice 1915, vol. 1, p. 125, no. 59. For later 're-materializations' of ancient works of art, see M. J. Marek, *Ekphrasis und Herrscherallegorie*, Worms 1985.

that Giorgione was influenced by Leonardo and his ideas; there are other
pictures of his circle which may be interpreted as referring to the *paragone*;
the sources give some oblique support to an interpretation along these lines;
and precisely the interpretation put forward here for Giorgione's self-portrait
is later claimed by Aretino in 'parole' for a work by Titian.

Before turning to the intellectual context, we must first consider the
self-portrait itself, which is, unfortunately, by no means straightforward. By
contrast to the *paragone* painting of a soldier attributed to Giorgione by
Vasari, there is no doubt that the work once existed, and probably we may
infer it was known to *cognoscenti*. To his contemporaries, Giorgione was
better known for his portraits and half-lengths than for other kinds of
paintings, such as landscapes ('... e per lo più non faceva altre opere, che
mezze figure e ritratti', according to Ludovico Dolce).[5] The self-portrait was
in the most important collection of art in Venice of the time, that of the
'patriarchal' branch of the Grimani (it may have been acquired by Giovanni
Grimani in Giorgione's lifetime; it is documented in 1528 in the inventory
taken of his heirs' collections).[6] It was surely known to Michiel, even though
the notes he presumably also made on the Italian works in the Grimani
collection, as opposed to his extended list of the Netherlandish and German
works there, which does survive, have been lost. The self-portrait is also
reported by Vasari, in his second edition;[7] in so far as it survives, it is actually
the only genuine work by Giorgione, excepting the almost entirely destroyed
frescos on the Fontego de' Todeschi, known visually both to Vasari and to
modern scholarship. In his second edition, Vasari opened his Life of
Giorgione with the very same three works in the Grimani collection, the
self-portrait, 'un generale di esserciti' and a 'putto', that are listed together in
the 1528 inventory, and among these the self-portrait was the most ambitious.

The woodcut portrait of Giorgione appended to his Life in Vasari's
second edition (Pl. 1) is evidently based on the Grimani self-portrait, and so,
with independent knowledge of the original but adapted after the example of
Vasari's woodcut, is the portrait in Ridolfi's Life of Giorgione.[8] By the time
Ridolfi was writing, the self-portrait had left Venice, and, according to
Ridolfi, was in the collection of the brothers Van Veerle in Antwerp, still

[5] Ludovico Dolce, *Dialogo della pittura intitolato l'Aretino*, in *Trattati d'arte del Cinquecento fra Manierismo e Controriforma*, P. Barocchi (Ed.), Bari 1960-2, vol. 1, pp. 141-206 (esp. p. 202).
[6] P. Paschini, 'Le collezioni archeologiche dei prelati Grimani del Cinquecento', *Atti della Pontificia Accademia Romana di Archeologia, Rendiconti*, 5, 1926-7, pp. 149ff. (esp. p. 170); idem, *Domenico Grimani Cardinale di San Marco (†1523)*, Rome 1943, pp. 153-4.
[7] Giorgio Vasari, *Le vite de' più eccellenti pittori, scultori ed architettori*, P. Barocchi and R. Bettarini (Eds), Florence 1966-, vol. 4, p. 41.
[8] Carlo Ridolfi, *Le Maraviglie d'Arte*, D. von Hadeln (Ed.), Berlin 1914-24; T. Pignatti, *Giorgione*, London 1971, pl. 218.

together with the 'general of armies' and the putto.[9] Hollar made engraved copies of nine of the Venetian works in this collection, including the *Self-portrait*, dated 1650 (Pl. 2);[10] his others, where they can be compared to the originals, are accurate in the detail if not in the proportions, and this copy agrees with Vasari's woodcut and description, although Hollar's engraving is fuller and more precise, featuring a 'stepped' sill of the kind peculiar to pictures of Giorgione's circle. Thereafter, the picture itself disappears from view (along with its companions). The painting in the Herzog Anton Ulrich-Museum in Brunswick with which it has been identified (Pl. 3) is first recorded in 1744, as a copy after Giorgione.[11] There is a further derivation in Budapest;[12] there is also a copy in Hampton Court (Pl. 4), which is already mentioned in 1628.[13] One's immediate impression is surely that the Hampton Court picture (though it, too, is not complete) agrees with the Hollar engraving very closely, and that the Brunswick picture is a less accurate version.

The claim of the Brunswick picture to be the original portrait by Giorgione rests predominantly on X-ray evidence published in 1959.[14] X-rays revealed beneath the present surface a Madonna holding a child in an individual composition very like one by Catena. However, even if the Madonna dates from Giorgione's period, the present surface need not do so; indeed, the earlier composition is incomplete, and the support must therefore have been reduced before the present image in its supposed original form was painted over it. If the two complete compositions are reconstructed, they do

---

[9] See further K. Garas, 'Giorgione e Giorgionisme au siècle XVIIe, I', *Bulletin du Musée Hongrois des Beaux-Arts*, 25, 1964, pp. 51ff. (esp. p. 54).

[10] Indexed under Verle in G. Parthey, *Wenzel Hollar. Beschreibendes Verzeichnis seiner Kupferstiche*, Berlin 1853, p. 309.

[11] G. Adriani, *Herzog Anton Ulrich-Museum, Braunschweig: Verzeichnis der Gemälde*, Brunswick 1969, p. 65; Pignatti 1971 (as in n. 8 above), cat. C1; *Selbstbildnisse und Künstlerportraits von Lucas van Leyden bis Anton Raphael Mengs*, exh. cat., Brunswick 1980, cat. 1, pp. 38–42; C. Hornig, *Giorgiones Spätwerk*, Munich 1987, cat. 24, p. 213; M. Lucco, *Giorgione*, Milan 1995, p. 140; J. Anderson, *Giorgione: Peintre de la 'brièveté poétique'*, Paris 1996, pp. 306–7.

[12] Garas 1964 (as in n. 9 above), p. 78, suggested that Vasari's woodcut might have been based on this work (Pignatti 1971, as in n. 8 above, cat. C2; Anderson 1996, as in n. 11 above, p. 324), also recorded by Hollar; but though the costume agrees with Vasari's woodcut, the pose of the head, the facial expression and the hair do not; if Vasari knew and used another version, would he not have mentioned it? The attribution to Giorgione of the Budapest picture remains highly dubious.

[13] See J. Shearman, *The Early Italian Pictures in the Collection of Her Majesty the Queen*, Cambridge 1983, cat. 112.

[14] C. Müller-Hofstede, 'Untersuchungen über Giorgiones Selbstbildnis in Braunschweig', *Mitteilungen des Kunsthistorischen Institutes in Florenz*, 8, 1957–9, pp. 13–34 (esp. p. 14). In May 1995 the curator Sabine Jacob kindly confirmed to me that no new technical examination had been undertaken since that time.

not fit together (Pl. 5). There is, furthermore, a marked difference in technique and medium (tempera as opposed to oils) between the Madonna beneath and the portrait above. It seems more likely that a picture of the Madonna contemporary to Giorgione was cannibalized at some later time in order to create the Brunswick *Self-portrait* than that Giorgione had been involved in reproducing or inspiring another artist's composition, then, deciding to make a portrait of himself, cut the canvas down and changed the medium he was using. It is coincidental that Vincenzo Catena, the author of the composition beneath, has been revealed by an inscription on the back of Giorgione's '*Laura*' in Vienna to have been Giorgione's 'cholega' (Pl. 8). [15]

The crucial argument against the originality of the Brunswick picture, even if one were to rationalize its discrepancies with the Hollar engraving, is that the Hampton Court picture cannot have been copied from it. The Hampton Court figure is clearly more youthful, has a more pronounced frown (these furrows at the bridge of the nose are still more marked in the Hollar), and distinctly more elongated proportions; its handling in general is more timid, more restrained, less painterly. Then in the Brunswick canvas there is no trace of Goliath's head – neither on the surface nor in X-rays nor in infra-red photography – at the position at which both the Hollar print and the Hampton Court copy show it; the proportions of all three images differ, but the head and the hand holding it should appear at a level with the end of the lace that falls forward free against the shirt. Instead, in this area in the Brunswick picture, there is only a vague dash of white paint, presumably meant to correspond to the highlit vertical ridge of the cuirass that is clear in the other two images. [16] Not least, there is a red drape over the Brunswick figure's left shoulder that has no counterpart in the other copies, and, as far as can be seen, it is all of a piece with the rest of the picture. [17] The Brunswick

[15] J. Wilde, 'Ein unbeachtetes Werk Giorgiones', *Jahrbuch der preuszischen Kunstsammlungen*, 52, 1931, pp. 91–100 (esp. p. 93). The inscription reads: '1506 a di primo zugno fo fatto questo de man de maistro Zorzi da Chastel fr[anco] cholega de maistro Vizenzo Chaena ad istanzia de miser giacomo ... [veniziano?]'. Instead of transliterating the last word, Giacomo's surname, Wilde put an ellipsis, implying, as appears to be generally believed, that the last word is lost. It is not, as can be seen from Wilde's photograph; but it is very difficult to read. At the Kunsthistorisches Museum, Sylvia Ferino kindly had the back re-examined, whereupon the inscription was discovered to have faded; but it reappeared under infra-red light. The lettering readily corresponds with no known Venetian family name.

[16] Müller-Hofstede 1957–9 (as in n. 14 above) supposed that Hollar had distorted the proportions of the portrait, but neglected to observe that in the placement of the head, as in other aspects, the Hampton Court picture agrees with the Hollar engraving. He observed in the Hollar a misunderstanding of the end of the lace with which the armour is tied, correct in the Brunswick picture, as in the Hampton Court copy, and therefore demonstrating the independence of both images from the engraving.

portrait has a ruddiness in the face for which there is no counterpart in accredited works by Giorgione or his circle, the impasto'd highlights on the armour at the shoulder stand up flat in a manner foreign to Giorgione's softer, more measured shading (but typical of the handling of oil-paint in the advanced seventeenth century), and it is odd that the figure's undershirt is not the lead-white white so typical of Giorgione's circle but rather a warm grey. Doubts have accompanied the Brunswick picture from the earliest record through all the scholarly literature, and they must be permitted at last to prevail.[18] Its poor condition makes the Brunswick picture hazardous to date, but the omission of Goliath's head suggests a post-Vasari, historicizing motivation for the copy's creation.[19]

The importance of the Royal Collection copy is that, though certainly cruder than the original, it restores to us a more schematic physiognomy, resembling the stylized ovals of the faces of the *Boy with an arrow* in Vienna or the *Venus* in Dresden; more typically of the sixteenth century, it shows a more laborious *contrapposto* within a more constructed spatial recession, with a more painstaking lighting and modelling and foreshortening. Unfortunately the picture remains disfigured by overpaint (the features and hair are reinforced, the mouth repainted), otherwise abraded, and heavily obscured by varnish. It has very little freshness or colour.[20] Though otherwise agreeing fairly well, it suggests that the neck of Hollar's figure is too squat, and the foreground arm too perpendicular.

On this better basis, one can be more precise than hitherto about the iconography of Giorgione's lost picture and about the way in which a number of surviving early sixteenth-century Venetian works relate to it.

[17] Müller-Hofstede (ibid.) was forced to suppose that the red cloak might be an addition by a restorer, but advanced no evidence for this. His claim that minor changes in the composition revealed by the X-rays prove it could not be a copy is not convincing.

[18] Pignatti 1971 (as in n. 8 above) held out against Robertson (who had earlier wavered) and others that the Brunswick picture was a copy. In Hornig 1987 (as in n. 11 above), p. 213, the verbal opinion of the conservator Knut Nicolaus that there were grounds for believing the picture a copy is quoted, though Hornig chooses not to endorse them and elsewhere Nicolaus has accepted the picture's originality (K. Nicolaus, *Gemälde untersucht, entdeckt, erforscht*, Brunswick 1979, p. 219). J. Anderson, reviewing Hornig in *Kunstkronik*, 42, 1989, pp. 432–6 (esp. p. 432), and in her own book of 1996 (as in n. 11 above), pp. 306–7, has also supposed the picture original; Lucco 1995 (as in n. 11 above), p. 140, reports opinion divided.

[19] For the seventeenth-century reception of Giorgione, see P. Holberton, 'La critica e fortuna di Giorgione: il conflitto delle fonti', in *La pittura nel Veneto: Il Cinquecento*, M. Lucco (Ed.), vol. 3, Milan 1999, pp. 1115–40.

[20] These comments incorporate those of Viola Pemberton-Pigott of the Royal Collection Trust, who kindly examined the picture at my request (letter to the author, 4 April 1995).

Directly derivative, as may now be more clearly seen, is a male portrait by an anonymous artist closely contemporary to Giorgione now in the Kress Collection in the National Gallery, Washington (Pl. 6).[21] This picture borrows the *Self-portrait*'s entire compositional scheme, and specifically the pose of the head, the foreshortening from below, the relationship of the body to the similarly split parapet, and the position of the grasping hand, for which, as X-rays show, this artist struggled to invent a suitable alternative attribute. The X-rays have been supposed to reveal a clutched sword or dagger,[22] but the shadow taken to be a sword-hilt was in fact created by a stretcher-key below the support.[23] The kerchief and the book have little apparent meaning, though the clenched fist goes well with the domineering pose and expression of the head. This forcefulness also fits the inscription 'VVO', assuming that this should be expanded to 'Virtus Vincit Omnia', a motto found among other similar protestations in the frieze of the so-called Casa Giorgione in Castelfranco, a widely-accepted attribution to Giorgione.[24] The Casa Giorgione frieze carries not only the message 'Virtus vincit omnia' but the connected mottos 'Sola virtus clara eternaque habetur' and 'Tempus territ' (*sic* for 'terit', 'wears away') – the latter directly recalling the *Col Tempo* inscribed on Giorgione's '*La vecchia*' in the Accademia in Venice. A still

---

[21]   Pignatti 1971 (as in n. 8 above), cat. 31; R. F. Shapley, *Catalogue of the Italian Paintings in the National Gallery of Art, Washington*, Washington, D.C., 1979, pp. 213–7; *Le Siècle de Titien*, exh. cat., Paris 1993, cat. 41; Lucco 1995 (as in n. 11 above), p. 141; Anderson 1996 (as in n. 11 above), p. 345. Although Müller-Hofstede 1957–9 (as in n. 14 above) (for the first time, to my knowledge) related this picture to Giorgione's *Self-portrait*, the two paintings are usually discussed without reference to each other.

[22]   R. Pallucchini, 'Il restauro del ritratto di gentiluomo veneziano K. 475 della National Gallery of Art di Washington', *Arte Veneta*, 16, 1962, pp. 234–7.

[23]   Examination summary, February 1990, curatorial records, National Gallery of Art, Washington.

[24]   G. Padoan, 'Il mito di Giorgione intellettuale', in *Giorgione e l'umanesimo veneziano*, 2 vols, R. Pallucchini (Ed.), Florence 1981, vol. 1, pp. 425–55 (esp. p. 430, n. 10); *Siècle de Titien* 1993 (as in n. 21 above), cat. 41. The idea advanced by N. T. Grummond, 'VV and Related Inscriptions in Giorgione, Titian and Dürer', *Art Bulletin*, 47, 1975, p. 346, that the Vs stand for 'vivus' and 'verus' and derive from inscriptions beneath classical epitaphs has several weaknesses: for example, the word 'vivus' is used in the epitaphs to indicate which of those represented or responsible for the monument was alive rather than dead, and not to comment on the nature of the portraiture. There is no Renaissance case (that she cites or I know) in which the message supposed to be borne by these initials is expanded. Further arguments against are given in *Siècle de Titien* 1993 (as above), cat. 41. The mottos of the Casa Giorgione are set in their cultural context by M. Pastore Stocchi, 'G. B. Abioso e l'umanesimo astrologico a Treviso', in *La letteratura, la rappresentazione, la musica al tempo e nei luoghi di Giorgione*, M. Muraro (Ed.), Rome 1987, pp. 17–38.

closer connection between this frieze and Giorgione's paintings is provided by
the crude diagrams of solar and lunar eclipses (with their labels the wrong way
round!) which Giorgione used again, shuffled, on the parchment held by the
right-hand of the *Three Philosophers*.[25] Simply 'V V', or 'Virtus Vincit', is
found on the parapet of Giorgione's accepted male portrait in the Staatliche
Museen, Berlin.[26] Initials or emblems of similar or broadly similar intent
occur on several other portraits of the time, often on parapets before the sitter
that appear to have been 'stepped' specially in order to accommodate it or
them (notably one of good quality, unconvincingly attributed to Cariani, in
the Brera; Pl. 7).[27] Again, the laurel of Giorgione's Vienna '*Laura*' (Pl. 8) is a
visual emblem of victory. Reasonably, one could suppose that Giorgione's
portrayal of himself in the figure of David makes the same comment about his
own portrait, visually and allegorically, namely that virtue conquers.

This is not what Vasari tells us: he describes Giorgione's *Self-portrait* as
'fatta per Davit – e per quel che si dice, è il suo ritratto', reflecting an
incomprehension of Venetian allegory that is more obviously apparent in his
disingenuous remarks about the frescos on the Fontego de' Todeschi.[28]

[25] These derive from the elementary astronomical textbook by Johannes Engel, of
which there were many similar editions: see V. Masséna, prince d'Essling, *Les
Livres à figures vénitiens de la fin du XVe et du commencement du XVIe siècle*,
Florence, Paris 1907-14, vol. 1, p. 387, nos 432-5. The sun is half-hidden by the
philosopher's hand, but above it the crescent shape of the earth with the circle of
the moon projected over it and the moon to the left, small, are clear. By way of
comparison, the same schematic diagram appears on the disc beside Giulio
Campagnola's '*Astrologer*' (Hind 9; see now P. Holberton, 'Notes on Giulio
Campagnola's Prints', *Print Quarterly*, 13, 4, 1996, pp. 397ff.).

[26] Pignatti 1971 (as in n. 8 above), cat. 11; Hornig 1987 (as in n. 11 above), cat. 14;
Siècle de Titien 1993 (as in n. 21 above), cat. 16; Lucco 1995 (as in n. 11 above), p.
74; Anderson 1996 (as in n. 11 above), p. 296. Despite the consensus of these
writers, this picture has also been attributed to Titian, and this view is still held.
The inscription, though not now original, seems more likely to have been
retouched together with other parts of the canvas than to have been a later
interpolation.

[27] Inscribed CE on the raised parapet; see *Musei e Gallerie di Milano: Pinacoteca di
Brera: Scuola veneta*, Milan 1990, p. 212. The present lettering may well not be
original, but the area is unlikely to have been blank. For the pictures by Titian in
the National Gallery inscribed 'T.V.' and for a derivative of the male portrait
dated 1512 and known in three versions, and also for the picture known in several
versions of a woman in white called *Violante*, inscribed with a 'V' on the parapet,
see below in the text and related notes. There is a problematic portrait of '*Alvise
Crasso*' with 'V.V.' on the sill and the date 1508 (Pignatti 1971, as in n. 8 above,
cat. A25, whereabouts unknown); a portrait in Budapest of '*Antonio Brocardo*',
with a philosopher's hat inscribed V. and a *triceps*, perhaps meaning prudence; see
Pignatti 1971 (as in n. 8 above), cat. A7; *Siècle de Titien* 1993 (as in n. 21 above),
cat. 25; Lucco 1995 (as in n. 11 above), p. 94; Anderson 1996 (as in n. 11 above), p.
307, and others.

However, he reproduces, in this questioning tone, the very words of the 1528 inventory: 'Ritratto di Zorzon di sua mano fatto per david e Golia'. In the most basic terms, this clearly was seen as a self-portrait; but it was also seen as something more, as allegorizing. Though Vasari claimed not to recognize the significance of the *Judit fatta per Giustizia* above the entrance on Titian's façade of the Fontego de' Todeschi, that significance is pretty clear; even though he does not unquestioningly accept the combination involved of a representation of the artist as David, its significance is again pretty clear: it is a visual representation of virtuous victory. There is no doubt that that is how David's conquest of Goliath was seen at the time, notably as depicted by Donatello, whose bronze *David* is reflected in the pose of Giorgione's own *Judith* in St Petersburg.[29]

In the original Giorgione's illusionistically confrontational figures, caught in the instant, have an elusive, meditative reticence, and one can imagine something similar when standing before the Brunswick picture. However, the melancholy that the Brunswick copy has conveyed to several observers really is not appropriate to Giorgione's original.[30] Rather, the furrows on the brow (attested by Hollar and the Hampton Court copy) should be referred to those on Colleoni's in the monument by San Zanipolo, or possibly to the 'ciglia basse e strette' Leonardo recommended for an angry figure.[31] This David bears no harp; his armour marks him as a warrior, or rather as a knight,[32] and the blood still drips from Goliath's severed artery.

[28] A fuller analysis of the Fontego 'programme', including a discussion of Vasari's reaction to it, can be found in P. Holberton, 'Poetry and Painting in the Time of Giorgione', PhD diss., Warburg Institute, University of London 1989.

[29] See C. M. Sperling, 'Donatello's Bronze "David" and the demands of Medici politics', *The Burlington Magazine*, 134, 1992, pp. 218ff., and M. M. Donato, 'Hercules and David in the Early Decoration of the Palazzo Vecchio: Manuscript Evidence', *Journal of the Warburg and Courtauld Institutes*, 54, 1991, pp. 83ff. See also J. Białostocki, 'La gamba sinistra della Giuditta: il quadro di Giorgione nella storia del tema', in *Giorgione e l'umanesimo* 1981 (as in n. 24 above), vol. 1, pp. 193ff.; I have not found S. Smith, 'A Nude Judith from Padua and the Reception of Donatello's Bronze David', *Comitatis*, 25, 1994, p. 59, but it may well be germane.

[30] Cf. Müller-Hofstede 1957–59 (as in n. 14 above), p. 30, followed by J. Anderson, 'The Giorgionesque Portrait: From Likeness to Allegory', in *Giorgione. Atti del convegno internazionale di studio ...*, F. Pedrocco (Ed.), Asolo 1979, pp. 153ff. (esp. p. 154). S. Jacob, in *Selbstbildnisse* 1980 (as in n. 11 above), observed that such a melancholic interpretation would have been unique, and J. Woods-Marsden, *Renaissance Self-Portraiture: The Visual Construction of Identity and the Social Status of the Artist*, New Haven, London 1998, p. 118, related the work rather to Mantegna's self-portrait.

[31] Leonardo, Richter (Eds) 1970 (as in n. 2 above) , item 584 (BN 2038, fol. 29r).

[32] For David as a figure of the perfect knight, see M. Keen, *Chivalry*, New Haven, London 1984, pp. 119–23.

The triumph of virtue over adversity was a platitudinous Renaissance theme, hardly less so than the transience of the flesh. Giorgione would seem to have taken up both themes and to have begun devising iconographies involving them early in his career[33] – illustrating the former probably for the first time in his surviving oeuvre in the still crudely foreshortened *Warrior* in Vienna.[34] This painting appears to depend on the well-known drawing by Leonardo of *Five heads* in the Royal Library at Windsor, on the back of which there is an inscription opposing good and evil.[35] If in the Giorgione a young man is the protagonist rather than an old one, this is not likely to have been the only work by Leonardo Giorgione had seen. Giovanni Grimani was the probable owner within their lifetimes not only of three works by Giorgione but also of at least two by Leonardo: 'Uno quadro una testa con girlanda di man di lunardo vinci' and 'Uno quadro testa di bambocio di lunardo vinci' ('A picture [of] a head with garland by the hand of Leonardo Vinci'; 'A picture [of] a head of [a] putto by Leonardo Vinci').[36] These offer striking precedent in general for the 'subjectless' heads and half-lengths for which Giorgione became known, but the 'bambocio' in particular was presumably a direct precedent for Giorgione's lost Grimani putto and similarly the 'testa con girlanda' for the Vienna *Warrior* (owned by Zuanantonio Venier).[37] The Grimani inventory of 1528 also includes 'six bizarre heads on paper' which are likely to have been by Leonardo as well.[38] It is, further, difficult to suppose that Giorgione's '*Laura*' was painted without some knowledge of Leonardo's *Ginevra de' Benci*, commissioned by Bernardo Bembo,[39] whose son Pietro owned a copy by Giulio Campagnola of a design

[33] See P. Holberton, 'Varieties of *giorgionismo*', in *New Interpretations of Venetian Renaissance Painting*, F. Ames-Lewis (Ed.), London 1994, pp. 31–41.

[34] Pignatti 1971 (as in n. 8 above), cat. A64; *Leonardo and Venice / Leonardo e Venezia*, exh. cat., Venice 1992, cat. 67; *Siècle de Titien* 1993 (as in n. 21 above), cat. 26. For the provenance and identification of the Vienna *Warrior*, overlooked in Anderson 1996 (as in n. 11 above), p. 304, see P. Holberton, 'La bibliotechina e la raccolta d'arte di Zuanantonio Venier', *Atti dell'Istituto Veneto di Scienze Lettere ed Arti*, 144, 1985–6, pp. 173ff.

[35] Windsor RL 12495; the inscription is Leonardo, Richter (Eds) 1970 (as in n. 2 above), vol. 2, p. 340, item 1355. See now M. Clayton, article forthcoming in *Apollo*, August 2002, on this drawing and Giorgione's picture.

[36] Paschini 1926–7 (as in n. 6 above), p. 174; this item, missed by the contributors to the 1992 *Leonardo and Venice* exhibition catalogue (as in n. 34 above), was pointed out by J. Anderson, in 'Leonardo and Giorgione in the Grimani Collection', *Achademia Leonardo Vinci. Journal of Leonardo Studies and Bibliography of Vinciana*, 8, 1995, pp. 226–7 (esp. p. 226).

[37] For whom see Holberton 1985–6 (as in n. 34 above).

[38] Paschini 1926–7 (as in n. 6 above), p. 181; for Leonardo's caricatures, see M. Kwakkelstein, *Leonardo da Vinci as a Physiognomist: Theory and Drawing Practice*, Leyden 1994.

[39] J. Fletcher, 'Bernardo Bembo and Leonardo's portrait of Ginevra de' Benci', *The*

by Giorgione.[40]

A further possible means of contact between Giorgione and Leonardo is provided by the engineer and architect Giorgio Spavento, *proto* to the city of Venice from 1486. He was assigned with two others in March 1500 to inspect defences against the Turks in the Friuli,[41] an inspection with which Leonardo by one means or another was also involved.[42] Spavento is further documented along with Giorgione on a job in the Doge's Palace in 1507,[43] and is likely to have brought Giorgione in to paint frescos the following year on the Fontego de' Todeschi, for which as *proto* he was responsible.[44] There is also, of course, the report by Vasari introduced into his second edition of Giorgione's Life that Giorgione had seen work by the hand of Leonardo; while this may have been an invention designed to support the notion in Vasari that all pioneers of what he called the 'terza maniera' worked in a style derived from the Tuscan master, it may also be a piece of information picked up at the same time as and together with the notice of the three Grimani pictures by Giorgione.

Evidence that contact between Giorgione and Leonardo may not simply have involved sight of Leonardo's work but also embraced reception of his ideas, particularly about contrasts between art, poetry and music, comes from the well-known passage in Paolo Pino's treatise of 1548, repeated in what appears to be an independent variation in Vasari, that Giorgione painted a picture *in paragone* with sculpture.[45] A *St George* in Pino, a nude in Vasari, the picture may well not have existed as either of them described it, since the germ of the story seems to be the picture of a bathing scene by Van Eyck known to Bartolomeo Facio, who comments on its reflections, and to Vasari, who reports it in Urbino.[46] It is not the *paragone* itself that recalls Leonardo,

---

[40] Marcantonio Michiel, *Notizia d'opere di disegno*, G. Frizzoni (Ed.), Bologna 1884, p. 51.

[41] See G. Padoan, 'Leonardo and Venetian Humanism', in *Leonardo and Venice* 1992 (as in n. 34 above), pp. 97–110 (esp. p. 104 and n. 54).

[42] See P. C. Marani, 'Leonardo in Venice and the Veneto. Documents and Evidence', ibid., pp. 23–36.

[43] G. B. Lorenzi, *Monumenti per servire alla storia del Palazzo Ducale di Venezia*, Venice 1868, item 141; R. Maschio, 'Una verifica dei documenti dell'archivio', *Antichità Viva*, 17, 4–5, 1978, pp. 5ff.

[44] See further J. McAndrew, *Venetian Architecture of the Early Renaissance*, Cambridge, MA, 1980, p. 426.

[45] Barocchi (Ed.) 1960–2 (as in n. 5 above), vol. 1, p. 131; Vasari, Barocchi (Ed.) 1966– (as in n. 7 above), vol. 4, p. 46.

[46] Vasari, Barocchi (Ed.) 1966– (as in n. 7 above), vol. 1, p. 133; M. Baxandall, 'Bartholomaeus Facius on Painting. A Fifteenth-Century Manuscript of the *De Viris Illustribus*', *Journal of the Warburg and Courtauld Institutes*, 28, 1965, pp. 90ff. (esp. pp. 102–3); G. T. Faggin, *L'opera completa del Van Eyck*, Milan 1968, nos 58, 61. See further A. J. Martin, *Savoldos sogenanntes 'Bildnis des Gaston de Foix': zum Problem des Paragone in der Kunst und Kunsttheorie der italienischen*

but the terms in which it is conceived: in both Pino's and Vasari's versions
the painting with reflections rivals sculpture in the totality and instantaneity
of the impression it makes on the beholder, which is very much in accord
with Leonardo's repeated argument that art delivers more immediately and
effectively than words (or music), which work through time, and is therefore
superior to poetry.[47]

This evidence in turn makes it more likely that one painting Giorgione
really did paint, his '*Laura*', was also intended to function in the terms of a
paragone, this time as a challenge to poetry. This damaged painting has caused
much confusion and speculation, which this paper cannot hope to resolve, [48]
but the notion that the '*Laura*' was an intended 'rival' to poetry is buttressed
by the existence of a contemporary poem by Girolamo Bologni, doubting
whether Petrarch in his poetry or Jacopo Bellini in his painting ' *The archetype
of Laura*', otherwise unrecorded, had depicted a more praiseworthy Laura. [49]
Published apparently for the first time in Degenhart and Schmidt's catalogue
of Jacopo Bellini's drawings, this poem is evidently not widely known and so
is worth repeating here:

> In archetypa Laurae effigies in pictura Jacobi Bellini:
>
> Si tali facie fuit puella
> qualem mira refert tabella: per te
> vix laudata satis fuit Petrarca:
> sin talis fuit ipsa Laura, quale < m >
> laudas carminibus tuis Petrarca
> est pictura minor; proculque distat < . >
> Atqui munus utrumque tam decorum est
> ut vos non homines ratus fuisse < m, >
> o par gloria pictor et poeta.
> Divinum ingenium utriusque mirer
> sed quae materiam dedit canendi
> caeli sydera lucet inter alta
> iam non Laura suae invidens Dianae

Renaissance, Sigmaringen 1995; and Helke 1999 (as in n. 3 above).

[47] Passages by Leonardo contrasting painting to the other arts are gathered together
in *La letteratura italiana. Storia e testi*, XXXII, 1, *Scritti dell'arte del Cinquecento.
II. Pittura scultura poesia musica*, P. Barocchi (Ed.), Milan, Naples 1971; but see C.
J. Farago, *Leonardo da Vinci's Paragone: A Critical Interpretation with a New
Edition of the Text in the Codex Urbinas*, Leyden 1992.

[48] For bibliography see Anderson 1996 (as in n. 11 above) and Helke 1999 (as in n. 3
above).

[49] See B. Degenhart and A. Schmidt, *Corpus der italienischen Zeichnungen 1300–1450*,
II, 5–8, *Venedig. Jacopo Bellini*, Berlin 1990, vol. II, 5, p. 20, n. 17. For Girolamo
Bologni see notably A. Gentili, *I giardini di contemplazione*, Rome 1985, ch. 1.

On the archetype of Laura a likeness in painting by Jacopo Bellini

If the girl was with such a face
as the marvellous tablet reports: by you,
Petrarch, she was hardly sufficiently praised.
But if Laura herself was such as
you praise her in your poetry, Petrarch,
the picture is the lesser, and a long way short.
However, the talent of both is so fitting
that I would not have thought you mortals,
o painter and o poet equal in glory!
Let me admire the divine genius of both,
while the woman who provided the matter for singing
shines among the high stars of heaven
not now with any envy for her own Diana

Presumably, though it was specifically Petrarch's Laura, this was not a straightforward portrait of Laura, like the one recorded by Michiel in Pietro Bembo's collection[50] – Bellini's painting conveyed something more than the mere features, so as to suggest Laura's virtuous chastity ('her' Diana because she was devoted to the chaste goddess), and justifying the contrast between the 'archetype' of Laura of the title and the 'matter', or flesh, of the historical Laura. One would expect some kind of symbolism, even if it were no more than a framing device like that surrounding Jacopo's portrait of Mehmet II in the National Gallery, London. However Girolamo may have justified Bellini's equal status to Petrarch, the basis on which Giorgione's 'Laura' competes with the poet's is surely, by contrast, its eroticism. Giorgione's painting may not come across today as particularly voluptuous, but the woman is undeniably nude, showing her breast. In Leonardo's writings, art's trump over words is its ability immediately to inspire concupiscence, whereas poetry takes time, at best, to inflame.[51] Giorgione's laureate, i.e. victorious, woman is not a portrait of Petrarch's material Laura (who was well known to be blonde, for example, and, besides, chaste), but she is a paradigm of female beauty and male desire, and as such a challenge to the vision that Petrarch depicts of his own desired. Implicit in Giorgione's conception may be a kind of *paragone* that is found occasionally in poetry before the *Canzoniere*, including Dante, then commonly in the *Canzoniere* itself and in other love poetry after it – the metaphor of the lover 'painting' (or 'writing' or 'sculpting') the image of his beloved in his heart.

The idea that Giorgione may have depicted a 'Laura' of the kind that the lover would find written, sculpted or painted in his own heart may even be necessary to understanding the painting, because the image in the heart might be, indeed usually was, blatantly erotic, regardless of the real comportment of

---

[50]   Michiel, Frizzoni (Ed.) 1884 (as in n. 40 above), p. 50.
[51]   This point has now also been made in Helke 1999 (as in n. 3 above). She sees the *'Laura'* as a kind of Muse.

the beloved. One might say that the painting's sexual nudity marks it precisely as a vision of the heart (an erotic fantasy) and not as a real woman. Petrarch's visions of Laura are sometimes clearly erotic, without of course Laura herself, the material Laura, being unchaste. Petrarch also, not in his two sonnets on Simone's portrait of Laura, but in sonnet no. CXXX, himself had made the *paragone* that the image Love painted in his heart was more beautiful than the work of the artists of antiquity: [52]

...
E sol ad una imagine m'attengo
che fe' non Zeusi o Prasitele o Fidia
ma miglior maestro e di più alto ingegno

And only to one image I attach myself,
made not by Zeuxis or Praxiteles or Phidias,
but by a better master and one of higher genius

this 'better master' being Love, often invoked as the writer, painter or sculptor who impresses the beloved in the poet's imagination. (I have not undertaken a wider search specifically for this metaphor, but the notion is as extensively developed as one could wish at one point in Lorenzo de' Medici's *Comento*, and also utilized in Philip Sydney's *Arcadia*: see Appendix).

A context of *paragone* suggests the imputation of a further motivation to Giorgione's self-portrait as David. As we have seen, showing himself as David visually encapsulates what had been stated in an inscription – 'virtus vincit' – in previous portraits, and by this device represents an invisible quality there intimated by a label. To represent the inner, invisible quality, however, is to trespass on the sphere of poetry and words, which alone are meant to be able to convey such abstractions in the discussion of the *paragone* conducted in the academy at Florence in the mid-sixteenth century. [53] This does not appear to be an idea that Leonardo had come across or argued against, although it is clearly anticipated in the inscription beside Ghirlandaio's 1488 *Portrait of Giovanna Tornabuoni* in the Thyssen Collection, and flirted with in humanist epigrams on portraiture particularly in Rome. [54] Given, though, that *paragone* was a topic in vogue, and that the same patron demonstrably had contacts to Leonardo, it is a reasonable hypothesis that in depicting himself as David Giorgione intended to 'demonstrate' that painting could in fact represent the inner, supposedly unrepresentable quality of virtue. It is even possible that Giorgione's *Vecchia* in the Accademia in Venice was in 1567 called 'Giorgione's mother' by analogy with his self-portrait; [55] and, just as *La Vecchia*

[52] Text from the Garzanti edition, E. Rigi (Ed.) (1966), Milan 1974.
[53] Most obviously Benedetto Varchi in the third *disputà* of his 'Della maggioranza delle arti', in Barocchi (Ed.) 1960–2 (as in n. 5 above), vol. 1, pp. 55–8.
[54] Thyssen Collection; see for the epigram from Martial and for early sixteenth-century contemporary comment on portraiture J. Shearman, *Only Connect: Art and the Spectator in the Italian Renaissance*, Princeton 1992, ch. 3, 'Portraits and Poets'.

42

herself seems actually to regret personally the universal of her aging condition, so, if we had the original of Giorgione's self-portrait, we should surely see his virtuous character and spirit expressed pictorially as well as embodied iconographically.

If there is no direct precedent for such an enterprise by Giorgione, there is no precedent, either, for an allegorizing self-portrait, [56] and further circumstantial evidence that it once bore the weight I have suggested can be found in certain surviving works painted immediately afterwards, supplemented by hints in the sources. Above all, even if the capacity of painting to reproduce inner qualities was denied, without counter-argument, in later discussions in Florence, Aretino in Venice would assert for Titian in 'parole' exactly the pictorial reach that I have surmised Giorgione's self-portrait was intended to attain.

Sebastiano Veneziano, subsequently known as Del Piombo, seems to have emerged from Giorgione's studio around or very shortly after 1506, [57] and his *Salome* (also called *Judith*) in the National Gallery, London, dated 1510 (Pl. 9), may be seen as a development both of Giorgione's ' *Laura*' and of his self-portrait. The facial type or the actual model is the same as the ' *Laura*', and the motif of the severed head is taken up from the self-portrait. The woman's victory is clear, although its meaning is different if she is read as Judith – virtue conquers lust – or as Salome – beauty conquers resistance. [58] Titian painted the same subject, giving Salome (or Judith) the features of Giorgione's *Venus* and the severed head apparently his very own – the Cupid pointing his arrow from the keystone rendering the conquest by the woman

[55] A. Ravà, 'Il camerino delle anticaglie di Gabriele Vendramin', *Nuovo Archivio Veneto*, 39, 1920, pp. 155ff. (esp. p. 178).

[56] For artists' self-portraits see Woods-Marsden 1998 (as in n. 30 above), and for the 'isolation' of Giorgione's 'experiment', for which this paper hopes to provide in fact a context, p. 117.

[57] This view, though it cannot be properly argued here, depends on two cardinal suppositions: that Michiel's notice that he completed Giorgione's *Three Philosophers* (evidently not a late work by Giorgione, so unlikely to have been finished after his death) is correct and implies Sebastiano's assistance; and that Sebastiano painted the highly Giorgionesque Accademia *sacra conversazione* with St Catherine (M. Lucco, *L'opera completa di Sebastiano del Piombo*, Milan 1980, cat. 248): for this view see especially M. Hirst, *Sebastiano del Piombo*, Oxford 1981, pp. 4–6, pls 1–3. However, the 'early' half-length of a young girl in Budapest (Lucco 1980, as above, cat. 4; Hirst 1981, as above, pp. 4, 93–4) seems inconsistent with this development and would have to be denied to Sebastiano.

[58] For the idea that the painting represents Judith, see P. Joannides, 'Titian's *Judith* and its context: the iconography of decapitation', *Apollo*, 135, 1992, pp. 163ff.; however, the woman bears no sword, a standard attribute of Judith, and the head resides on a platter, a standard attribute of St John the Baptist (frequently occurring as a depicted object of devotion by itself), so where is the ambiguity? See also the next note.

of the man explicit.[59] As now inverted, the idea was taken up in the next century, notably by Allori,[60] and then others: indeed, the conquered artist's severed head had a greater *fortuna* than Giorgione's original invention, even if Giorgione initiated the conceit of the self-portrait with a message.

Again, on Titian's female portrait with a profile bust on the parapet in the National Gallery, London, known as '*La Schiavona*' (Pl. 10), the letters 'T.V.' surely refer back to earlier portraits bearing the inscription 'V.' or 'V.V.'[61] and constitute a pun, meaning both 'Titianus Vecellius' and 'Titianus Vincit'. Not simply the painter, but Titian the painter vanquishes sculptors, since his portrait is so much more life-like than the relief bust, and by extension antiquity; he also vanquishes fellow artists.[62] Titian's *Man with a blue sleeve* in the National Gallery (Pl. 11) has the same two initials, which are still more likely to bear this latter meaning if the picture may be supposed, as has frequently been claimed,[63] a self-portrait. If it is a self-portrait, then surely Titian painted it with conscious reference to Giorgione's self-portrait, reducing Giorgione's presentation of his art's 'superiority' to a simpler rivalry – with Titian claiming greater impact, greater *colorito*.[64] That there was sharp

[59] H. E. Wethey, *The Paintings of Titian*, I, *The Religious Paintings*, London 1969, cat. 137; see previous note on the iconography. The idea that the woman is Judith had previously been advanced in E. A. Safarik, *Galleria Doria Pamphili: I capolavori della pittura*, Florence 1993, p. 12, and was rebutted in *Tiziano: Amor Sacro e Profano*, exh. cat., Rome 1995, cat. 11.

[60] See J. Shearman, 'Cristofano Allori's "Judith"', *The Burlington Magazine*, 121, 1979, pp. 3–10 (esp. p. 9). Shearman supposed that Goliath rather than David constituted Giorgione's self-portrait.

[61] Possibly Titian's *Schiavona* shows reference to a painting known in three versions, in Modena, Budapest and formerly a private collection in Boston: Lucco 1980 (as in n. 57 above), cat. 193; R. Pallucchini and F. Rossi, *Giovanni Cariani*, Bergamo 1983, cat. A27, A42, A54; P. Rylands, *Palma Vecchio*, Cambridge 1992, cat. A12; *Tiziano: Amor Sacro e Profano* 1995 (as in n. 59 above), cat. 26. The version in Budapest suggests the authorship of Sebastiano, though not his autography, in the brilliance of the white, the crinkling of the drapery, and the character and foreshortening of the face, recalling other females by the young Sebastiano. The discreet but unmistakeable flower in her hair marks the woman as an invention rather than a portrait.

[62] See L. Freedman, '"The Schiavona". Titian's Response to the Paragone between Painting and Sculpture', *Arte Veneta*, 41, 1987, pp. 31–40.

[63] See C. Gould, *The Sixteenth-Century Italian Schools, The National Gallery, London*, repr. London 1975, p. 281; H. E. Wethey, *The Paintings of Titian*, II, *The Portraits*, London 1971, cat. 40; C. Hope, *Titian*, London 1980, p. 30.

[64] Titian's portrait is not usually dated before 1510, but seems to be proved to be before 1512 by the date of the portrait deriving from it known in three versions: K. Garas, 'Giorgione et Giorgionisme au XVIIe siècle, III', *Bulletin du Musée Hongrois des Beaux-Arts*, 28, 1966, pp. 69–93 (esp. p. 70); Pignatti 1971 (as in n. 8 above), cat. V15. The version in Munich (R. Kultzen and P. Eikemeier, *Bayerische Staatsgemäldesammlungen. Alte Pinakothek/München: Venezianische Gemälde des*

rivalry between artists in Venice around this time is suggested by the inscription complaining of envy by Jacopo de' Barbari on his *Madonna* in the Louvre[65] and by Dolce's report, taken up in Vasari's second edition, that Giorgione was extremely miffed to have been praised for Titian's work on the Fontego de' Todeschi.[66] (The knife in the wound was that Titian's work was on the less prominent and prestigious side, the landward entrance to the Fontego, arousing the implicit query, why should you have painted the minor façade better than the main one?) There seems, too, to have been another portrait by Titian, according to Vasari representing a member of the Barbarigo family, which from his description was evidently similar both to *The man with a blue sleeve* and to Giorgione's Berlin portrait,[67] and which we may deduce probably again bore his T.V.: Vasari's comment, that 'se Tiziano non vi avesse scritto in ombra il suo nome, sarebbe stato tenuto opera di Giorgione' ('if Titian had not written his name in shadow, it would have been taken as a work by Giorgione') has generally been taken simply to mean that Titian imitated Giorgione's style very closely, something that he does not in fact appear to have done. Another explanation is that Vasari, no more comprehending the *enjeu* here than when reporting Giorgione's self-portrait, adapted an original piece of information explaining Titian's 'T.V.' as a swipe at Giorgione to his own notion of the similarity of the two artists' styles (into which he had been led by the misinformation of his 1550 edition).[68]

Aretino, in his letters and sonnets addressed to Veronica Gambara on Titian's portraits of the Duke and Duchess of Urbino (now in the Uffizi), claimed that Titian had conveyed the 'virilità de l'animo' of the former and 'virtuti interne' of the latter. He did not, by contrast, believe that Apelles had been capable of depicting more than the outer form of Alexander:[69]

> ...
> non finse già [Apelle] del peregrino subietto
> l'alto vigor, che l'anima comparte,
> Ma Tizian, che dal cielo ha maggior parte,
> fuor mostra ogni invisibile concetto ...

---

[65] *15. und 16. Jahrhunderts*, Munich 1971, p. 208, no. 2276) bears the date MDXII, making it likely that the MDXI on the St Petersburg version is defective.

See J. A. Levenson, *Jacopo de' Barbari and Northern Art of the Early Sixteenth Century*, PhD diss., New York University 1978, cat. 2; the inscription reads: *pascitur in vivis Livor, post fata quiescit | Tum suus ex merito quemque tuetur honos*; Ovid, *Amores*, I, xv, 39–40.

[66] Barocchi (Ed.) 1960–2 (as in n. 5 above) vol. 1, pp. 201–2; Vasari, Barocchi (Ed.) 1966– (as in n. 7 above), vol. 6, p. 157.

[67] Ibid., vol. 6, p. 156.

[68] See Holberton 1999 (as in n. 19 above) for further discussion of Vasari on Giorgione.

[69] Pietro Aretino, *Lettere*, F. Nicolini (Ed.), Bari 1913, Book I, no. CCXXIV, 7 December 1537, to Veronica Gambara.

[Apelles] did not convey of his extraordinary sitter
the high vigour, in which the soul has a part,
but Titian, who has a greater share from Heaven,
shows outwardly every invisible idea ...

The masculine, martial qualities of the Duke, corresponding to the standard, 'Petrarchan' virtues of the Duchess, are exactly those we might once have been able to detect in Giorgione's lost self-portrait:

Egli ha il terror fra l'uno e l'altro ciglio,
l'animo in gli occhi e l'alterezza in fronte.

He has havoc between his brows,
spirit in his eyes and pride in his frown.

APPENDIX
Pictures in the Heart

The relevant part of Lorenzo's sonnet, on which he comments in his *Comento*, is as follows:

> Quanta invidia ti porto, o cor beato,
> che quella man vezzosa or mulce or stringe,
> tal ch'ogni vil durezza da te spinge;
> e poi che sì gentil sei diventato,
>   talora il nome, a cui t'ha consecrato
> Amore, il bianco dito in te dipinge,
> or l'angelico viso informa e finge
> or lieto or dolcemente perturbato

Lorenzo's comment is as follows:

> Debbesi adunque presupporre che degnissima pittura fussi quella, della quale era ornato il cor mio; perché tre cose, secondo il giudizio mio, si convengono ad una perfetta opera di pittura, cioé il subietto buono, o muro, o legno, o panno, o altro che sia, sopra al quale distenda la pittura; il maestro perfetto e di disegno e di colore; ed oltre a questo le cose dipente sieno di lor natura grate e piacevoli agli occhi: perché, ancora che la pittura fussi perfetta, potrebbe essere di qualità quello che è dipinto, che non sarebbe secondo la natura di chi debbe vedere. Conciosiaché alcuni si dilettano di cose allegre, comè animali, verzure, balli e feste simili; altri vorrebbono vedere battaglie o terrestri o maritime e simili cose marziali e fere; altri paesi, casamenti e scorci e proporzioni di prospettiva; altri qualche altra cosa diversa; e però, volendo che una pittura interamente piaccia, bisogna adiungervi questa parte: che la cosa dipinta ancora per sé diletti. Era il mio cuore materia e subietto molto atto a ricevere ogni impressione ....

E. Bigi (Ed.), Lorenzo de' Medici, *Scritti scelti*, Turin 1965, repr. 1977, p. 362.

In Sydney's *Arcadia*, Book 1, there is a tournament, Philandrus having challenged all comers to try by battle whether his lady, whose portrait he displays, is the fairest of all. Contenders bring one after another pictures of their own ladies, except for an ill-apparelled knight (who turns out to be Zelmane/Pyrocles), who has none, but declares: 'Certainly', said he, 'her liveliest picture, if you could see it, is in my heart ....' Sir Philip Sydney, *The Countess of Pembroke's Arcadia*, V. Skretkowicz (Ed.), Oxford 1987, p. 103.

'e nuovi Omeri, e Plati':
Painted Characters in Portraits by Andrea del Sarto and Agnolo Bronzino[1]

WOLF-DIETRICH LÖHR

> Dann lese ich einen Dichter der Vorzeit,
> und es ist mir als sähe ich mein eignes Herz.
> Goethe, *Die Leiden des jungen Werther*

> cantare d'amore non basta mai,
> [...] ci vuole passioni.
> Eros Ramazzotti

Don't we often want to read someone's mind like a book? When we look at a portrait, the stillness of the sitter looking back at us seems an invitation to such a reading. Unavoidably, though, our scrutiny is but skin-deep, and we easily interpret ugliness as moral deficiency and deem mere beauty to be virtue. But one should not judge the book by its cover, they say. This truism harks back to a central point of the old quarrel about the precedence of poetry or painting. That one cannot judge people by their external features was maintained by the poets, who always claimed as their domain the penetration to the essence of a human being, the definition of character. [2] In

---

[1] This essay is a shortened version of my 1998 M.A. dissertation at the Freie Universität Berlin, 'Bronzinos 'erlesene' Kundschaft. Zum "Bildnis des Ugolino Martelli" in Berlin'. I am grateful to Thomas Frangenberg for help with the translation. I would also like to thank Ulrich Pfisterer and Claudia Lanfranconi for their critical reading, and Martin Dönike and of course Karin Müller for continuous motivation. The quotation in the title is from a sonnet by Bronzino addressed to Cosimo I; see *Sonetti di Angiolo Allori detto il Bronzino e altre rime inedite*, D. Moreni (Ed.), Florence 1823, p. 32, 'Al Duca di Firenze e Siena', v. 10.

[2] The competition between these two arts has a long tradition and the solution suggested in Simonides's famous phrase (as related in Plutarch, *De gloria Atheniensium*, III, 346f–47c) of poetry as 'articulate painting' and painting as 'mute poetry' is obviously disadvantageous for the painter (all the more so at a time when poetry was habitually read aloud), since poetry is claimed not only to possess all the qualities of painting but also to provide what painting cannot, speech. This partiality was criticised by Leonardo. In his opinion poetry should be considered as 'blind painting'. See C. Farago, *Leonardo da Vinci's Paragone. A Critical Interpretation with a New Edition of the Text in the Codex Urbinas*, Leiden 1992, p. 216. On the *paragone* debate in the Cinquecento see L. Mendelsohn,

the sixteenth century, the Florentine humanist and poet Benedetto Varchi claimed that the writer represents 'il di dentro', meaning 'the concepts and passions of the spirit', while the painter's ability is restricted to the imitation of 'il di fuori', meaning 'the body and the appearance of all things'.[3] Varchi compared the difference between the two arts with the difference between body and soul.[4] In the poet's opinion, it is nothing but the body, the cover of the soul, that the painter's work can show us.

Pandora

The open book in Andrea del Sarto's *Portrait of a man* in London[5] (c. 1517; Pl. 12) suggests that here an artist takes on the challenge of poetry and, in his

---

Paragoni: Benedetto Varchi's 'Due Lezzioni' and Cinquecento Art Theory, Ann Arbor 1982, and E. Cropper, 'The Beauty of Woman: Problems in the Rhetoric of Renaissance Portraiture', in N. J. Vickers et al. (Eds), *Rewriting the Renaissance. The Discourses of Sexual Difference in Early Modern Europe*, London, Chicago 1986, pp. 175–90 (esp. p. 189). The development of the *paragone* during the Quattrocento is discussed in K. B. Lepper, *Der 'Paragone'. Studien zu den Bewertungsnormen der bildenden Künste im frühen Humanismus: 1350–1480*, Bonn 1987. A fundamental study of the relationship between poetry, portrait and spectator is found in J. Shearman, *Only Connect ... Art and the Spectator in the Italian Renaissance*, (1988) Princeton 1992, ch. III. The changing interpretations of Horace's famous dictum *ut pictura poesis* (*Ars Poetica* 361) are reviewed in U. Pfisterer, 'Künstlerische Potestas Audendi und Licentia im Quattrocento. Benozzo Gozzoli, Andrea Mantegna, Bertoldo di Giovanni', *Römisches Jahrbuch der Bibliotheca Hertziana*, 31, 1996, pp. 107–47 (esp. pp. 109–18). See also his article 'Paragone' in *Historisches Wörterbuch der Rhetorik*, G. Ueding (Ed.), s.v.

[3] '[...] i poeti imitano il di dentro principalmente, cioè i concetti e le passioni dell'animo, e bene molte volte discrivono ancora e quasi dipingono colle parole i corpi e tutte fattezze di tutte le cose, così animate come inanimate; et i pittori imitano principalmente il di fuori, cioè i corpi e le fattezze di tutte le cose'; Benedetto Varchi, 'Lezzione nella quale si disputa della Maggioranza delle Arti e qual sia più nobile, la Scultura o la Pittura', in P. Barocchi (Ed.), *Trattati d'arte del Cinquecento. Fra Manierismo e Controriforma*, vol. 1, Bari 1960, pp. 1–82 (esp. p. 55). See also Mendelsohn 1982 (as in n. 2 above), pp. 61ff.

[4] '[...] pare che sia tanta differenza fra la poesia e la pittura, quanta è fra l'anima e'l corpo.'; Varchi 1960 (as in n. 3 above), p. 55. On the problematic relationship between body and soul with regard to portraiture, see Hannah Baader's comment on Cicero in R. Preimesberger, H. Baader and N. Suthor (Eds), *Porträt*, Berlin 1999, pp. 91–4.

[5] For long, this portrait has been considered to be that of a sculptor, interpreting the object in the man's hands as a block of stone. For Alessandro Cecchi, on the other hand, it is a brick, and he therefore proposes the identification of the sitter as Paolo da Terrarossa (see A. Natali and A. Cecchi, *Andrea del Sarto. Catalogo completo*, Florence 1989, cat. no. 33, with further literature). Judging by the domestic ambience evoked by the chair, the attention the sitter seems to have paid to the object before turning his head, the way he holds it, and the clearly visible

painted representation, enables the viewer to read the sitter's inner values as well. The man's head is turned dramatically over his shoulder, his eyes critically viewing the beholder; thus the figure is charged with emotion and spontaneity, indicating the sitter's inner life. A generation later, Varchi would write: 'The painters show what they can of the inner [values], namely the emotions [affetti]'.[6] In contrast with the confrontational manner of the young man's pose, the pages of the open book in his hand remain mute.

The motif of the book gained a more central rôle some years later, in Andrea's *Girl with the Petrarchino* in the Uffizi (c. 1528; Pl. 13).[7] The young lady, glancing at us out of the darkness with inclined head, refers with her gesture to the volume, half-hidden, half-shown, that rests on her thigh. The right half of her face approaches the picture plane; raising her eyebrows slightly, she scrutinizes us with an intimidating, imperious gaze. If we follow the hint of her finger, her demand seems to be directed towards the book in her lap, a then-common edition of Petrarch's *Rime sparse*, called the *Petrarchino*. It is opened to pages 67/68, the latter displaying the two sonnets 'Ite caldi sospiri al freddo core' (no. 153) and 'Le stelle il cielo e gli elementi a prova' (no. 154), whereas the preceding page with the poems 'Non d'atra e tempestosa onda marina' (no. 151) and 'Questa humil fera, un cor di tigre o d'orsa' (no. 152) is concealed by the book's cover.[8]

The emphasised intimacy of the eye contact forces the beholder into a rôle of which the script is dictated by the painted sonnets of Petrarch. It is necessarily a male part, the part of the unrequited lover. Antithetical topoi like 'hot sighs' and 'cold heart',[9] crying and laughing, fear and hope[10] dominate Petrarch's relation with Laura. Oscillating between the appeal of

---

      separation of the two pages, emphasised by the different degrees and gradation of the illumination, it is much more likely to be a book than a brick.

[6]   'Bene è vero che, come i poeti discrivono ancora il di fuori, così i pittori mostrano quanto più possono il di dentro, cioè gli affetti'; Varchi 1960 (as in n. 3 above), p. 55.

[7]   See Natali and Cecchi 1989 (as in n. 5 above), pp.121f., cat. no. 48.

[8]   For the sonnets see F. Petrarca, *Canzoniere*, M. Santagata (Ed.), Milan 1996, p. 719 (no. 153); p. 722 (no. 154); p. 713 (no. 151); p. 716 (no. 152). In art-historical scholarship, these texts have so far received little attention. For J. Pope-Hennessy, *The Portrait in the Renaissance*, New York 1963, p. 235, the name of the girl, Laura, must be 'the accident [...] responsible for the pose'. He sees no relationship between the content of the poems and the painting. J. Shearman, *Andrea del Sarto*, 2 vols, Oxford 1965, vol. 1, p. 123, suggests that the painting is the portrait of a mistress commissioned by her lover, and that the contrast between the lady and sonnet 152 that calls her a 'tiger-hearted beast' was intended by the patron.

[9]   Cf. the beginning of sonnet 153, found on the upper half of the visible page: 'Ite caldi sospiri al freddo core [...]'; Petrarca 1996 (as in n. 8 above), p. 719.

[10]   Sonnet 152 on page 67 of the *Petrarchino*, opposite the poems visible on the painting: 'In riso e'n pianto fra paura e spene | mi rota [...]'; Petrarca 1996 (as in n. 8 above), p. 716, v. 3f.

conspicuous sensuality and denial of any proximity, the discourse of Petrarchism shaped much of contemporary literature, for example the work of Pietro Bembo. The Venetian poet composed just in these years the last poems of his *Rime*, which proved to be the Cinquecento's most influential response to Petrarch's *Canzoniere*.[11]

When trying to penetrate the body's shell in the act of description, both Petrarch and his imitators adopted the figure of *pars pro toto*, focussing on a single feature of the body from which an image of mind and character is built up.[12] Laura's eyes are thus frequently seen as a threshold between outward beauty and the virtue it enshrines.[13] The sonnet 'Non d'atra e tempestosa onda marina' (no. 151), the topmost on page 67 of the *Petrarchino*, not legible in the portrait, but still implicitly there, amplifies this topic. Laura's eye is described – as if there were only one – as divine light ('luce divina'), as dignified ray ('raggio altero') and as Cupid's forge. It is even considered as the inspiring 'text' in which the poet is able to read what he is saying and writing about love.[14]

In Andrea's painting, the posture of the girl and the spotlight illumination bring about a similar accentuation of one eye. On the central axis of the composition, it corresponds, connected through the neckline of the dress, with the indicating gesture of the hand. The eye, as most speaking feature of the image, thus finds its counterpart in the text that the beholder is invited to recall, or better, to speak.

[11] On Bembo see C. Dionisotti's useful introduction in P. Bembo, *Prose della volgar lingua – Gli Asolani – Rime*, C. Dionisotti (Ed.), (1966) Milan 1997, pp. 7–54 (esp. p. 47). The paradigms of Petrarchism are discussed in K. W. Hempfer, 'Probleme der Bestimmung des Petrarkismus. Überlegungen zum Forschungsstand', in W.-D. Stempel and K. Stierle (Eds), *Die Pluralität der Welten. Aspekte der Renaissance in der Romania*, Munich 1987, pp. 253–77. Vasari likewise chooses a Petrarchist vocabulary when describing the love-relationship of Andrea del Sarto and his wife, culminating in the phrase: '[...] ancora che egli vivesse in questo tormento, gli pareva un sommo piacere'; G. Vasari, *Le vite de' più eccellenti pittori, scultori e architettori nelle redazioni del 1550 e 1568*, R. Bettarini and P. Barocchi (Eds), vol. 4, Florence 1976, p. 357.

[12] For Petrarch's patterns of description and their reception in sixteenth-century poetry see N. J. Vickers, 'Diana described: Scattered Woman and Scattered Rhyme', *Critical Inquiry*, 2, 1981, pp. 265–79.

[13] For example, in the sonnet 'Io temo sì de' begli occhi l'assalto' (no. 39), cf. also 'I begli occhi ond'i' fui percosso in guisa' (no. 75), and 'Io avrò sempre in odio la fenestra' (no. 86); Petrarca 1996 (as in n. 8 above), pp. 215, 394, 430. On this topic see M. Martelli, '"Ascendit mors per fenestras nostras" (Nota a RVF, LXXXVI 1–2)', *Quaderni Petrarcheschi*, 7, 1990, pp. 53–64.

[14] Petrarca 1996 (as in n. 8 above), p. 713, v. 5–8: 'Né mortal vista mai luce divina | vinse, come la mia quel raggio altero | del bel dolce soave et nero, | in che i suoi strali Amor dora et affina'; v. 13–4: 'ch'a parte a parte entro a' begli occhi leggo | quant'io parlo d'Amore et quant'io scrivo'.

But what exactly does the lady's gesture indicate (Pl. 14)? Her hand partly covers Petrarch's sonnet 'Le stelle e il cielo e gli elementi a prova' (no. 154). Again, Laura's eye is its protagonist, only this time more distinctly aestheticised. As 'living light' ('vivo lume') and 'singular mirror of nature', it is explicitly claimed to be the product of an artistic competition of the elements, a 'work' of superhuman beauty.[15] The concluding lines of the poem take a step beyond a merely aesthetic appreciation: they evoke the moral effect of the eye on its beholder, consisting in the kindling of 'honour and virtue' and the annihilation of 'vile desire' through the 'highest beauty'.[16]

It will not have escaped the attentive beholder, at least if we suppose he is male, that the poem describes nothing but his own situation vis-à-vis the painting. Petrarch's writing on beauty finds a visual counterpart here. The beholder, as a new Petrarch, sees the beloved, who is, as was Laura herself, a 'work' of 'art'. Seen – and read – in this manner, del Sarto's portrait offers through the poem a description of itself. Phrases like 'mirror of nature' and 'living light' provide concise and current metaphors expressing on the one hand the lifelike imitation of nature, and on the other the sublimation of the painter's lifeless pigments.[17] Furthermore, for the reader/beholder the

[15]   'Le stelle, il cielo et gli elementi a prova | tutte lor arti et ogni extrema cura | poser nel vivo lume, in cui natura | si specchia e'l sol, ch'altrove par non trova. | L'opra è sì altera, sì leggiadra et nova, | che mortal guardo in lei non s'assecura; | tanta negli occhi bei, for di misura, | par ch'Amore et dolcezza et grazia piova.'; Petrarca 1996 (as in n. 8 above), p. 722, v. 1–8.

[16]   The beautiful eyes and their effect create an aura capable of converting the lover's vices into virtues: 'L'aere percosso da' lor dolci rai | s'infiamma d'onestate, et tal diventa | che'l dir nostro e'l penser vince d'assai. | Basso desir non è ch'ivi si senta, | ma d'onor, di vertute. Or quando mai | fu per somma beltà vil voglia spenta?'; Petrarca 1996 (as in n. 8 above), p. 722, v. 9–14.

[17]   Alberti, for example, refers to nature as model for the artist ('ciò che voremmo dipingere piglieremo dalla natura [...]'), but also to the mirror as a means of correcting the image: 'Adunque le cose prese dalla natura si emendino collo specchio.'; L. B. Alberti, *Opere Volgari*, in *Trattati d'Arte*, C. Grayson (Ed.), vol. 3, Bari 1973, p. 82. For nature as point of reference and the mind of the painter as a mirror in the writings of Leonardo see F. Fehrenbach, *Licht und Wasser. Zur Dynamik naturphilosophischer Leitbilder im Werk Leonardo da Vincis*, Tübingen 1997, pp. 60–76. Liveliness as crucial to painting is a topos current throughout art literature; it may suffice to cite Vasari, who describes Andrea del Sarto's self-portrait on the *Assumption* for B. Panciatichi with what seems to be the highest formula of praise, as 'vivo vivo'; Vasari (as in n. 11 above), vol. 4, 1976, p. 370. For Leonardo's opinion that painting works with light itself, see Leonardo da Vinci, *On Painting. A Lost Book (Libro A)*, C. Pedretti (Ed.), Berkeley, Los Angeles 1964, p. 71: 'La pittura à composizione di luce e di tenebre insieme mista [...].' The term 'lume' used by Petrarch is central also to Alberti's advice on the use of light in a composition; see, for instance, Book II, ch. 46 ('[...] resta a dire del ricevere de' lumi'); Alberti 1973 (as above), p. 80. The correct disposition of the 'lumi' leads, Alberti points out, to a sculptural three-dimensionality: 'Io [...] loderò quelli visi

emphasised 'moralising' effect of Laura's beauty proves to be a power of the image itself, thus referring to a feature of painting very much discussed in these years.[18]

As one looks closer at the gesture of the girl, the transference from described to depicted eye is sustained more explicitly: her index finger covers verses 4 and 5 of the sonnet, and its tip should point exactly to the first word of verse 5, just occluded by the cover of the book: 'l'opra' - the work. [19] The beholder, though, cannot simply read this line, he has to reconstruct it from the remaining text of the poem, easy to decipher on the painting even today. The delayed encounter with the verse - when the poem is recited in its entirety - charges it with all the more importance: 'The work is so dignified, so graceful and new' ('L'opra è sì altera, sì leggiadra et nova'). This phrase sounds like a eulogy of the painting, put into the mouth of the beholder who addresses not the heavenly but the earthly work, not Laura's eye but its visual description.[20] The verse is loaded with terms common in Cinquecento and earlier art literature. 'Altero' - 'dignified' or 'sublime' - frequently appears in poems on paintings by Aretino or Varchi, characterising the self-assuredness of the sitter or the corresponding mode of representation employed by the artist.[21] 'Leggiadria', 'grace', in art theory is almost synonymous with 'grazia'.[22] Some years later, Vasari and his co-authors established *leggiadria* as a crucial feature of the 'maniera moderna', the progressive art of the sixteenth century, connecting it not only with criteria such as 'grazia' and 'sveltezza', but also with abilities owed to the 'natura' of the artist, such as 'artificio', 'giudizio' and 'disegno'.[23] The last word of Petrarch's verse is the epithet

---

quali come scolpiti parranno uscire fuori della tavola'; ibid., p. 82.

[18] See Mendelsohn 1982 (as in n. 2, above), p. 47.

[19] In John Shearman's opinion, however, the girl points at the opposite page; see Shearman 1965 (as in n. 8, above), vol. 1, p. 123. The book's cover occludes all the first words of the verses; therefore the word just before her fingertip must be 'l'opra'.

[20] Already Caterina Caneva has mentioned the emphasis placed on the metaphoric image of the eye, also present in the verse the girl points at (which Caneva does not comment on); see *Andrea del Sarto 1486–1530. Dipinti e disegni a Firenze*, exh. cat., Florence 1986, p. 158.

[21] See, for example, Varchi's poem addressed to Bronzino (Appendix 10., v. 1) , or the sonnet by Aretino on Titian's *Portrait of Francesco Maria della Rovere*, discussed below.

[22] See, for example, Alberti 1973 (as in n. 17, above), p. 86 (II, 48) on the effect of colours: 'Sarà ivi grazia quando l'uno colore appresso, molto arà dall'altro differente; [...] Sarà per questa comparazione ivi la bellezza de' colori più chiara e più leggiadra.' Cf. L. Grassi and M. Pepe, *Dizionario della critica d'arte*, 2 vols, Turin 1978, vol. 1, p. 276.

[23] Vasari (as in n. 11 above), vol. 4, 1976, p. 5, in the proem to the third part of the *Lives*, writes about the *maniera* of the Quattrocento: '[...] mancava una leggiadria di fare svelte e graziose le figure e massimamente le femmine et i putti con le

'novo' – 'new'. It foreshadows the demand for originality frequently reiterated in fifteenth- and sixteenth-century art literature, the fundamental artistic merit of 'invenzione' ('invention' or 'inventiveness'). [24] Within the aesthetics of *imitatio*, 'invenzione' denotes both the conception of any artistic product and the specific contribution of a particular author. [25] Alberti advises the painter to acquire 'new inventions' through familiarity with men of letters and poets and in this way to increase praise and fame of his art. [26]

When one approaches the painting to read the characters in the book, the rest of the work can be examined. Andrea's 'vivo lume' willingly gives away its facture, the brushstrokes reveal the hand of the master and his 'art'. The beholder's attention has to switch from painting to (painted) text, from seeing to reading. When he then compares originality and effect of these two elements, he engages in a performance of the *paragone* of poetry and painting, [27] explicitly provoked through the thematic affinity, even congruence

---

membra naturali come agli uomini, ma ricoperte di quelle grassezze e carnosità, che non siano goffe, come i naturali, ma arteficiate dal disegno e dal giudizio'; Sharon Fermor ('Poetry in Motion: Beauty in Movement and the Renaissance Conception of *leggiadria*', in F. Ames-Lewis and E. Cropper (Eds), *Concepts of Beauty in Renaissance Art*, Aldershot 1998, pp. 124–133) discusses this term with a different emphasis. In 1591 Francesco Bocchi describes Andrea's *Madonna del sacco* with the words 'ne si puote imaginare, quanto in ogni parte sia leggiadra, et graziosa'; F. Bocchi, *Le Bellezze della Città di Fiorenza*, (Florence 1591), J. Shearman (Ed.), Amersham 1971, p. 229. As the following lines of the poem cited in the portrait also adduce the terms 'dolcezza' and 'grazia', this sonnet contains much of the vocabulary used by later critics to praise del Sarto's colouring and art; see R. Williams, 'A Treatise by Francesco Bocchi in Praise of Andrea del Sarto', *Journal of the Warburg and Courtauld Institutes*, 52, 1989, pp. 111–39. For Alberti 'leggiadria' was mainly an effect of a certain use of colours, when dark and light colours connected by 'a certain friendship' ('certa amicizia') are subtly balanced; Alberti 1973 (as in n. 17 above), p. 87 (II, 48). We do not have many written documents by Andrea's hand regarding his use and understanding of colours. But on the preparatory drawing for the *Girl with the Petrarchino* he did leave notes on colour, which have so far attracted little attention; he mentions precisely those colours which were, in Alberti's eyes, best friends: 'bigio', 'verde' and 'bianco'; see D. Cordellier, in *Hommage à Andrea del Sarto*, exh. cat., Paris 1986, p. 71.

[24] For the importance of 'novitas' as a criterion of artistic production see the famous verses of Horace, *Odes*, II, 1, 2–4: 'carmina non prius | audita [...] canto.' Cf. also *Epistles*, I, 19, 21ff.: 'Libera per vacuum posui vestigia princeps, | non aliena meo pressi pede. qui sibi fidet, | dux reget examen. Parios ego primus iambos [...]'.

[25] See Grassi and Pepe 1978 (as in n. 22, above), vol. 1, pp. 262–4, and the discussion of the term *invenzione* in R. W. Lee, *Ut pictura poesis. The Humanistic Theory of Painting*, New York 1967, pp. 16–23.

[26] Alberti 1973 (as in n. 17, above), p. 94: 'Pertanto consiglio ciascuno pittore molto si faccia famigliare ad i poeti, retorici, e agli simili dotti di lettere, già che costoro doneranno nuove invenzioni, o certo aiuteranno a bello componere sua storia, per quali certo acquisteranno in sua pittura lode e nome'.

of both. Text and image are meant to be matched against each other an eye for an eye, proving in the end the priority of the communicative force of painting, already emphasized in the theory of Leonardo.[28] Whereas John Shearman saw a deliberate paradox between the painted girl and her description in sonnet no. 152 as 'beast with a tiger's heart', I suggest that both of these media follow a parallel antithetical structure. For Petrarch's Laura is a beauty 'in the form of an angel', but she is cruel as well; she is chaste but still in no way conceals her sensuality. The young lady in del Sarto's portrait shows the same ambiguity of ideal grace dressed in demure clothing and challenging coquetry.[29] Whereas the reader of Petrarch only successively discovers the contrary traits of Laura's character, they appear simultaneously, at first glance, in the painting.

Confronting the viewer/reader life-size, the image provides not just an adequate visual idea of the fictional character, but also an interpretation of the text.[30] In the first line of Petrarch's sonnet pointed out by the lady one finds echoes of the myth of Pandora, who is said by Hesiod to have been, like much later Laura's eye, a creation of the elements and the gods (the stars). The painting seems to focus on this dark side of the beloved Laura. As his mythical colleague Hephaestus did in Hesiod's words, Andrea 'fashion[s] a sweet, lovely maiden shape', not even forgetting the flowers in her hair.[31] Yet

---

[27] Already the first line of the poem refers to a competition ('prova'), see n. 15 above.

[28] 'La pittura ha il suo fine comunicabile a tutte le generazioni dell'universo, perché il suo fine è subietto della virtù visiva, e non passa per l'orrecchio al senso commune col medesimo modo che passa per il vedere.' Here cited as in Grassi and Pepe 1978 (as in n. 22 above), vol. 2, p. 644 (*virtù visiva*). See Fehrenbach 1997 (as in n. 17 above), pp. 39–51. Cf. also F. de Hollanda, *Vier Gespräche über die Malerei. Geführt zu Rom 1538*, J. de Vasconcellos (Ed.), Vienna 1899, pp. 42f.

[29] This ambiguity of the painting has been observed by a number of scholars, however, without reference to the sonnets; see, for example, R. Monti, *Andrea del Sarto*, Milan 1965, p. 114.

[30] Plazzotta, on the other hand, sees in Andrea's depiction a 'coy Laura', an entirely positive 'wish-fulfilment, making the physical charms of the Lady available'; C. Plazzotta, 'Bronzino's Laura', *The Burlington Magazine*, 140, 1998, pp. 251–63 (esp. p. 259).

[31] See Hesiod, *Works and Days*, 60–79: 'And he bade famous Hephaestus make haste and mix earth with water [...], and fashion a sweet, lovely maiden shape, [...]. [...] and the rich-haired Hours crowned her head with spring flowers.'; cited after Hesiod, *The Homeric Hymns and Homerica*, transl. H. G. Evelyn-White, Cambridge, London [1914] 1977, p. 7. The crocus in the hair of the girl is a spring flower. Cf. the more overtly misogynous version of Pandora's origin in Hesiod, *Theogony*, 570–612. Hesiod's works were available in a Latin translation by Nicolaus Valle since 1471; see D. and E. Panofsky, *Pandora's Box. The Changing Aspects of a Mythical Symbol*, New York 1956, p. 14, n. 1. The parallels of the myth of Pandora with the sonnet (and more generally Petrarch's image of Laura)

WOLF-DIETRICH LÖHR

her gaze and gesture, more than Petrarch's verses, reveal the disastrous talents of this primeval woman, her ability, endowed by Venus, to provoke 'cruel longing', and her 'shameless mind and a deceitful nature' given by Mercury.[32] Whereas the speaker of the sonnets never falters in his praise of Laura and finds any 'vile desire' eventually overcome by her beauty, the painted visualisation acutely questions the lover's distance and his Platonising elevation of his beloved by accentuating her sensuality, enhanced by bright illumination and her proximity to the picture plane.[33] The flirtatiousness of Laura/Pandora acts as a warning, because she is the 'beautiful evil' gladly embraced by the unknowing man.[34] Her raised eyebrow hints to the analogy, often stressed by Petrarch, with the bow from which Amor's 'lethal shot' is dispatched.[35]

---

are numerous; sweetness and grace as central to her effect on the lover are also found in Hesiod.

[32] Zeus begs Aphrodite 'to shed grace upon her head and cruel longing and cares that weary the limbs. And he charged Hermes [...] to put in her a shameless mind and a deceitful nature.' (*Works and Days*, 65–70; translation as in n. 31 above, p. 7).

[33] 'Basso desir non è ch'ivi si senta' (as in n. 16 above, v. 12) rhymes with the amplified repetition of the same notion at the end of the poem: 'vil voglia spenta' (v. 14). This effect of the painting may have encouraged Enea Vico to take up aspects of Del Sarto's depiction in his engraving of *Fiammetta del Boccaccio*, another literary object of love. Perhaps still in the Cinquecento, Archduke Ferdinand II fittingly pasted this engraving in a volume next to one of Petrarch; see S. Ferino-Pagden, *Vittoria Colonna. Dichterin und Muse Michelangelos*, Vienna 1997, cat. I, 61. The splayed fingers of the girl, just in front of her lap, may have erotic connotations, comparable to what von Flemming observed regarding Bronzino's *Portrait of Laura Battiferra* (see also below); see V. von Flemming, 'Harte Frauen – weiche Herzen? Geschlechterverhältnis und Paragone in Bronzinos Porträt der Laura Battiferri', in idem and S. Schütze (Eds), *"Ars naturam adiuvans". Festschrift für Matthias Winner zum 11. März 1996*, Mainz 1996, pp. 272–95 (esp. p. 283). Even more overtly erotic seem the connotations triggered off by the crocus in the hair of the girl, as it is the kind of flower expected – at least by some contemporaries – to decorate the graves of prostitutes. An epitaph-poem by Michele Marullo addressed to a member of this old profession ends with the words: 'And may the crocus grow on your grave' ('et crescat tumulo spica Cilissa tuo!'). The poem was first published in his *Epigrammaton libri*, Rome 1489, I, 42 ('Epitaphium Pholoes'). Here cited after the *Antologia della poesia italiana, 2, Quattrocento-Settecento*, C. Segre and C. Ossola (Eds), Turin 1998, p. 65, v. 44.

[34] In Hesiod, *Works and Days*, 57f. Zeus speaks: 'But I will give men as the price for fire an evil thing in which they may all be glad of heart while they embrace their own destruction.' In *Theogony*, 585, Pandora is called 'the beautiful evil'; Hesiod 1977 (as in n. 31 above), pp. 7, 123.

[35] See, for example, Petrarca 1996 (as in n. 8, above), p. 646, no. 133, v. 5: 'Dagli occhi vostri usció 'l colpo mortale'; ibid. 731, no.157, v. 10f.: 'et gli occhi eran due stelle, | onde Amor l'arco non tendeva in fallo'. In any case the eye seems to be where the beauty and lethal danger of Laura coincide most explicitly; see ibid. p.

56

There is a commentary on Andrea's art which sheds light on at least one contemporary's understanding of the *Girl with the Petrarchino*. Antonfrancesco Grazzini in his epitaph for the artist used a remarkably Petrarchan vocabulary. But he did not refer, as usual, to Petrarch's poems on Simone Martini, but cited the beginning of sonnet no. 154, the poem to which the girl points in her *Petrarchino*. As has been suggested for the deployment of the poem within the painting, Petrarch's words are in Grazzini's epitaph adapted to the praise of art. Petrarch, looking at Laura's beauty, describes her eyes as an object of divine artifice – 'Stars and heaven ... expended all their arts and every utmost care'. Grazzini, entranced by Andrea's beautiful works, describes the artist with a variation on Petrach's words: 'Andrea del Sarto, on whom stars and heaven expended every care so that art might attain the highest honour of painting'.[36] The painting does not present itself as only a portrait, but it acts as stimulus for the discourse of the *paragone*, here to be understood as an intellectual game of variations on common themes, rather than the struggle for status among the arts. Through the poems, the painter engages the beholder directly; both the poems and the beholder reading or reciting them are integral components of the intellectual structure of the painting.

'Lauro'

Andrea del Sarto may have been inspired to experiment with a combination of image and text by another artist, who, more than Andrea himself, was also active as a poet: Agnolo Bronzino.[37] Bronzino, of a younger generation,

---

683, no. 141 ('Come talora al caldo tempo sòle'), v. 5f: 'fatal mio sole | degli occhi onde mi vèn tanta dolcezza'.

[36] 'Per Andrea del Sarto | L'ossa qui son, ma l'alma in altra parte | vive, d'Andrea del Sarto, ove ogni cura | poser le stelle e'l cielo, acciò che l'arte | giungesse al sommo onor della pittura. | Costui nel colorir parte per parte | fe' spesso invidia e scorno alla natura; | e s'ei viveva più tanto o quanto, | agli antichi e moderni toglieva il vanto.' Cited after A. Grazzini, detto il Lasca, *Le Rime Burlesche edite e inedite*, C. Venzone (Ed.), Florence 1882, p. 667. For Petrarch's text see n. 15 above.

[37] A stylistic influence of Bronzino on del Sarto's late period has been observed by P. Costamagna, *Pontormo*, Milan 1994, p. 81. A similar use of a text, drawing the beholder into the painting, can be found in Pontormo's double-portrait in Venice (Collezione Cini), usually dated around 1525 (ibid., cat. 40). This work seems to be the first to establish an explicit relation between text and image, as both of the sitters turn outward towards the spectator, while the lines, taken from Cicero, *De amicitia*, VI, 22, speak of friendship that is found 'wherever you turn', ' quoquo te verteris'. On this and related double-portraits, see H. Baader, *Die Sprachen der Freundschaft und die Kunst des Porträts* (forthcoming). There is, of course, a strong Quattrocento tradition in which portrait and text are combined, especially as far as medals are concerned. Furthermore, in book illumination, authors are often shown with their own works, sometimes opened and turned towards the

showed an early interest in poetry, perhaps inspired by Benedetto Varchi. With Varchi he held a lifelong dialogue in sonnets and his friend judged the painter competent enough to correct his verses.[38]

A portrait in Milan, now almost unanimously attributed to Bronzino, in all probability marks the starting-point of their relationship (c. 1527, Pl. 15).[39] A boy dressed in black looks at the beholder with large eyes. He holds an open book with two Italian sonnets. Whereas the one on the left is taken – not unexpectedly – from Petrarch's *Rime*,[40] the one on the right was

spectator. But only rarely the text of these books is legible, and where it is, it gives no more than general information about the literary work. This is the case, for instance, in a Cicero manuscript illuminated around 1470 in the studio of Francesco d'Antonio del Chierico. On fol. 1r within the initial it shows the author holding a book containing the incipit line of which the miniature itself forms part; see *Matthias Corvinus und die Bildung der Renaissance*, exh. cat., Vienna 1994, cat. 5, fig. 5. As an early example of a close text-image relationship in an autonomous portrait one may cite Boltraffio's fine portrait of Gerolamo Casio (Milan, Brera, ca. 1500). After an alteration which apparently took place after Casio's laureation in 1523, it shows the sitter with a laurel-wreath and a poem in his hand, apparently by himself; see M. Reggiana Rajna, 'Un po' d'ordine fra tanti Casii', *Rinascimento*, 2, 3–4, 1951, pp. 337–83 (esp. pp. 337f.). The few barely legible lines refer to Leo X and the laurel that now adorns his head. It should be observed, though, that in this case the text is not turned invitingly towards the onlooker, but remains inside the self-contained fictional world of the image. I hope to deal in more detail with this and related examples in a study on portraits of poets.

[38]   In a well-known letter of 1539 Varchi praises Bronzino's knowledge of poetry and sends to him and to Tribolo a translation of Ovid which they are to correct and comment on. A new transcription of this letter, a survey of Bronzino's poetical production and a discussion of his relation with Varchi are found in D. Parker, 'Towards a Reading of Bronzino's Burlesque Poetry', *Renaissance Quarterly*, 50, 1997, pp. 1011–44, passim. In his letter (Parker, as above, p. 1041) Varchi writes: '[...] la poesia non è altro che una dipintura che favelli, così la pittura non è altro che una poesia mutola.' Three years before, B. Daniello had written in his treatise on poetry: '[...] e detto essa pittura altro non esser che un tacito e muto poema, et allo'ncontro pittura parlante la poesia.'; B. Daniello, *Della Poetica*, Venice 1536, in B. Weinberg (Ed.), *Trattati di Poetica e Rhetorica del Cinquecento*, vol. 1, Bari 1970, pp. 227–318 (esp. p. 242). The friendship between Bronzino and Varchi, important and lasting as it obviously was, might still not deserve the idealistic characterisation of R. W. Gaston, 'Love's Sweet Poison: A New Reading of Bronzino's London Allegory', *I Tatti Studies*, 4, 1991, pp. 249–88 (esp. p. 265). The exchange of sonnets, where the *risposta* always had to use the same vocabulary and rhyme-scheme, was a common form of literary conversation throughout the Quattro- and Cinquecento, and certainly not the sign of a 'vero amore'.

[39]   Already with this early work, Bronzino had found his way into the academic elite from which most of his later clients were to come; see A. Cecchi, 'Il Bronzino, Benedetto Varchi, e l'Accademia Fiorentina: Ritratti di Poeti, Letterati e Personaggi Illustri della Corte Medicea', *Antichità Viva*, 30, 1–2, 1991, pp. 17–28.

composed, as Alessandro Cecchi has shown, by Benedetto Varchi. It is
dedicated to the precociously talented humanist Lorenzo Lenzi, allowing the
initiated onlooker to identify him as the sitter of the portrait. [41] Already with
the first words, 'famous branches', the text paraphrases the sitter's name (Pl.
16). When the menace of the plague loomed over Florence in 1527, Varchi
and Annibale Caro took refuge in Bivigliano, there enjoying the 'beauties
found in Petrarch and Cicero'. [42] Lenzi not only accompanied but also inspired
the older men, serving as a kind of male muse. Alluding to Petrarch's mistress,
Lorenzo's own name and the poet's laurel, already earned by the boy, he was
nicknamed 'Lauro'. [43]

Not unlike del Sarto in his *Girl with the Petrarchino*, Bronzino assigned a
descriptive function to the texts in making his pictorial work their equivalent.
In a first, merely literary step, the coupling of the sonnets fuses Laura's
legendary beauty with that of Lauro/Lorenzo, praised in Varchi's poem. The
textual descriptions are both, of course, coined in visual terms. In their new
context, they cannot be read without the painting as their shared point of
reference. The image must be seen as congruent with the 'beautiful face, [...]
that shines more than any other in the world' [44] celebrated by Petrarch.

[40] Petrarca 1996 (as in n. 8 above), p. 701, no. 146. See A. Cecchi, '"Famose frondi de
cui sancti honori...": un sonetto del Varchi e il ritratto di Lorenzo Lenzi dipinto
dal Bronzino', *Artista*, 2, 1990, pp. 8–19.

[41] The text of the poem reads as follows: 'Famose frondi de cui santi honori | Per
non so qual del ciel fero Pianeta | Rado hoggi s'horna Cesare o Poeta | Mercè del
guasto Mondo, et pien d'errori | Chi sarà mai, che degnamente honori | Il bel che
in voi si dolcemente acqueta | I venti, & le Tempeste, e'n ciel i lieta | Ogni
Anima gentil del volgo fuori? | Et chi fia poi, che degnamente ancora | Adorare
possa, et quanto si conviene | L'alta Vertù: ch'è nel bel vostro involta | Io da chè
prima nasce l'Aurora, | Fin che di nuovo a l'oriente viene, | V'adoro, e'nchino
solo Una volta.'; cited after Cecchi 1990 (as in n. 40 above), pp. 8f. A portrait of
Lenzi is referred to in Vasari's life of Bronzino, see Vasari (as in n. 11 above), vol.
6, 1987, p. 232.

[42] Varchi's biographer Giovanni Battista Busini records their devotion to the
'bellezze che si trovano nel Petrarca et in Cicerone'; cited after Cecchi 1990 (as in
n. 40 above), p. 11. See also A. Cecchi, *Agnolo Bronzino*, Florence 1996, p. 6.

[43] Cecchi 1990 (as in n. 40 above), pp. 10f. A reference to the evergreen leaves of
laurel might also be seen in the green colour of the background. Poems as agents
of fame are the subject of a sonnet by Petrarch, where the speaker says (v. 9–14):
'del vostro nome, se mie rime intese | fussin sì lunge, avrei pien Tyle e Battro, | la
Tana e'l Nilo, Athlante, Olimpo et Calpe. | Poi che portar non posso in tutte le
quattro | parti del mondo, udrallo il bel paese | ch'Appenin parte e'l mar
circonda et l'Alpe.'; Petrarca 1996 (as in n. 8 above), p. 701.

[44] Ibid., v. 7f.: 'o piacer, onde l'ali al bel viso ergo | che luce sovra quanti il sol ne
scalda'. Also the verses (5f.): 'o fiamme, o rose sparse in dolce falda | di neve [...]'
can be read as descriptions of Lorenzo's fair complexion and the red of his lips
and cheeks.

Varchi's sonnet suggests a deeper level of interpretation to the beholder, as it speaks of the 'high virtue, enclosed in your beauty'. [45] Those inner qualities, which in the discourse of the 'paragone' tended to be the domain of poetry alone, are here said to be in direct connection to outward beauty and thus available for pictorial description. Again, the moral force of beauty is emphasized; it 'sweetly soothes winds and storms'. [46]

Reading the poems in front of the portrait suggestively imparts such poseidonic power to the painting itself. The image that the sonnets evoke in the mind of the reader is replaced by a product of the painter's art, a visual image of the sitter who can thus be read as clearly as the book in his hand.

Letters

It is not surprising that Bronzino's boy as well as del Sarto's girl kindle our attention with sonnets by Petrarch, as this poet had laid the foundations of the modern literary discourse on images. The new genre of poems on paintings, though based on ancient roots, was inaugurated by him with two famous, most likely fictional, descriptions of Simone Martini's portrait of Laura. [47] These reveal the extreme poles of judging a painting: While one sonnet laments that the depicted Laura fails to answer to the wooing of her lover, the other attests to Simone a heavenly merit: he was able to show Laura's soul through the veil of her body. [48] Petrarch's poems became archetypes alluded to wherever the topic of portraiture was addressed in Quattro- and Cinquecento poetry. The threshold of the impossible painting that speaks or breathes and lets the sitter's spirit shine through, remains the most current topos of praise, sometimes reached, sometimes crossed, mostly just missed. [49] As Mary Rogers has shown, poets were far from ignorant regarding the recent technical developements of painting and its increased illusionism. Thus Pietro Bembo, to give due emphasis to his eulogy of Giovanni Bellini, engages in a dialogue with the portrait of his 'donna', adressing it with 'O immagine'. [50] As the Cinquecento progressed, the edition of Bembo's *Rime* (1530) came to constitute a point of reference for the

---

[45]   See n. 41 above, v. 11.

[46]   See n. 41 above, v. 6f.

[47]   See the groundbreaking work of M. Albrecht-Bott, *Die bildende Kunst in der italienischen Lyrik der Renaissance und des Barock*, Wiesbaden 1976, pp. 67–129. See also G. Kranz, *Das Bildgedicht*, 2 vols, Vienna 1981.

[48]   Petrarca 1996 (as in n. 8 above), pp. 400–3, no. 77, pp. 404–6, no. 78. See the commentary of Hannah Baader in Preimesberger et al. 1999 (as in n. 4 above), pp. 179–88.

[49]   Again it may suffice to cite Vasari; see, for example, his judgements on some portraits by Bronzino, cited below, n. 134.

[50]   See Bembo 1997 (as in n. 11 above), pp. 512f., sonnet 19; cf. M. Rogers, 'Sonnets on Female Portraits from Renaissance North Italy', *Word and Image*, 2, 4, 1986, pp. 291–305 (esp. pp. 291f.).

imitation of Petrarch, and the renewed debate about the 'paragone' stimulated poets and painters alike.[51]

Pietro Aretino opened up new ground with his sonnet on Titian's portrait of Francesco Maria della Rovere, on which he was able to trace, one by one, the virtues and intellectual abilities of the duke. Titian did not have to raise the body's veil, because he understood, so Aretino maintains, how to make these inner values visible in the depiction of the outer shell: 'But Titian [...] shows on the outside every invisible concept'.[52] During the period when Aretino wrote this poem, Benedetto Varchi, acting as the tutor of the Strozzi family, was forced to flee the anger of the Medici and settled in the Veneto.[53] On 9 October 1536, during a pilgrimage to Bembo in Padua, he wrote to Aretino: 'If Your Highness possess that sonnet on the portrait of the duke of Urbino in print, I would very much like to have it and send it to Florence'.[54] Varchi must refer to the poem cited above. His letter documents both the attention paid to Aretino's poetry on art and Varchi's own function as a transmitter of literary news of this kind to Florence.

We do not know to whom exactly he might have sent the sonnet, if it ever reached him. But keeping in mind the widespread interest of the Florentines in sonnets on art,[55] and considering that letters, especially those including prominent poetry, were meant to pass from hand to hand,[56] Aretino's poem would probably have arrived, earlier or later, in the hands of

[51] See Mendelsohn 1982 (as in n. 2 above), p. 38 and Cropper 1986 (as in n. 2 above), p. 189.

[52] 'Ma Tiziano [...] | fuor mostra ogni invisibile concetto; | però'l gran duca nel dipinto aspetto | scopre le palme al suo cuor sparte.' (v. 5-8); cited after Rogers 1986 (as in n. 50 above), p. 303. The poem, together with its famous pendant on the portrait of the duke's wife, Eleonora Gonzaga, has come down to us in a letter to Veronica Gambara dated 7 November 1537, but was written as early as 1536. Both portraits are today in the Uffizi. On Aretino's contribution to the genre of poetry on painting see Albrecht-Bott 1976 (as in n. 47 above), p. 77.

[53] See Mendelsohn 1982 (as in n. 2 above), pp. 4, 30.

[54] 'Se vostra Signoria ha quel sonetto sopra il ritratto del Duca d'Urbino, in stampa, l'arei carissimo per mandarlo a Firenze.'; cited after *Lettere scritte a Pietro Aretino*, 4 vols, [1560], Repr. Bologna 1968, vol. 2, p. 187. The date is surprisingly early, given that the portrait was not completed at this time and arrived in Pesaro only in 1538. But as early as 17 July 1536 the duke asked Titian to send back the armour, lent to the artist for the painting; see A. Natali, in *Tiziano*, Venice 1990, p. 227, cat. 28; see also V. von Rosen, *Mimesis und Selbstbezüglichkeit in Werken Tizians*, Emsdetten, Berlin 2001.

[55] See D. Heikamp, 'Rapporti fra accademici ed artisti nella Firenze del '500', *Il Vasari*, n.s. 1, 1957, pp. 139-63.

[56] In June 1541, for example, Ugolino Martelli thanked Aretino for a sonnet he had sent to him and asked for another copy, as the first was so much in demand that he feared he might never see it again; see *Lettere scritte a Pietro Aretino* 1968 (as in n. 54 above), vol. 3, p. 114.

Varchi's friend, Bronzino. One may assume that his curiosity was excited by the literary fame of Titian, inaugurated by this sonnet. Furthermore, Bronzino himself had worked for Francesco Maria della Rovere in the early 1530s, before he began his career as court painter to the Medici. [57] In Florence he later acquired fame comparable to Titians's, both internationally and in Venice.[58] It is hardly conceivable that Bronzino should not have engaged in an artistic *paragone* with his Venetian colleague.[59] The look that Titian had taken into the soul of the sitter, according to Aretino's words, is a specifically poetic concept that must have appealed to the *poet* Bronzino.

In the years preceding the foundation of the Accademia Fiorentina that he was to join later, Bronzino could find like-minded interlocutors among Varchi's friends. In November 1536, Varchi thanked Aretino on behalf of the young poet, Ugolino Martelli, for his portrait, which Varchi had passed on to Martelli.[60] Varchi might also have been involved when, some time later, his

[57]   See C. H. Smyth, *Bronzino as a Draughtsman. An Introduction*, New York 1971, pp. 80f. Bronzino might have seen portraits by Titian, or replicas, in Pesaro. His *Portrait of Guidobaldo della Rovere* (Florence, Palazzo Pitti) shows traces of a dialogue with Titian's works.

[58]   In Paolo Pino's *Dialogo della Pittura* of 1548, the Florentine 'Fabio' and the Venetian 'Lauro' engage in a dispute about Titian and Bronzino, who represent the art of Florence and Venice respectively. Fabio enumerates the most important contemporary masters and then adds: '[...] ma se Bronzino seguita all'ascendere, egli verrà un eccellentissimo maestro, et ardisco ch'el mi par el più bel coloritore che dipinga à giorni nostri.' Lauro replies: 'Bronzino è un perito maestro, e mi piace molto il suo fare, e li son anco parzial per le virtù sue, ma a me più sodisfa Tiziano.'; cited after P. Barocchi (Ed.) 1960 (as in n. 3 above), vol. 1, pp. 93 – 139 (esp. pp. 126f.). Cf. Smyth 1971 (as in n. 57 above), p. 81. Mary Pardo suggests that Benedetto Varchi might have informed Pino about contemporary painting in Florence; see M. Pardo, 'Testo e contesti del "Dialogo di Pittura" di Paolo Pino', in *Paolo Pino. Teorico d'arte e artista. Il restauro della pala di Scorzè*, Angelo Mazza (Ed.), Treviso 1992, pp. 33 – 49 (esp. p. 43).

[59]   Smyth 1971 (as in n. 57 above), p. 81, points out that the portrait of Guidobaldo was executed 'in a spirit of emulation and also of competition' with Titian. The practical consequences of this competition can be traced, as has recently been shown by Mozzetti, in the hide-and-seek Pierfrancesco Riccio played with Titian's portrait of Aretino. The painting, which Aretino had sent to Cosimo to promote his friend Titian, was kept away from the duke in spite of several requests, obviously to strengthen Bronzino's position as a court painter; see F. Mozzetti, *Tiziano. Ritratto di Pietro Aretino*, Modena 1996 and von Rosen 2001 (as in n. 54 above), p. 332.

[60]   On 17 November 1536 Varchi wrote to Aretino: 'Messer Ugolino Martelli a chi ho dato una delle teste di V.S. si raccomanda infinitamente, e la ringrazia.'; *Lettere scritte a Pietro Aretino* 1968 (as in n. 54 above), vol. 2, p. 190, no. 306. It is unlikely that the term 'teste' here refers to painted portraits; probably Aretino had sent the engraving executed by Carraglio before 1538 (see *The Illustrated Bartsch*, vol. 28, *The Italian Masters of the Sixteenth Century*, S. Boorsch and J. Spike (Eds), New

disciple, Ugolino, had Bronzino paint the sophisticated likeness that Wilhelm Bode added to the Berlin art collection in 1878 (Pl. 17). [61]

Ugolino

The portrait shows the courtyard of a palace, where Ugolino, dressed in fine black clothing, is sitting at a table. In the background a statue of David responds to his pose; the original, known as the Martelli *David,* is today in the National Gallery, Washington. [62] The sculpture had been a well-known property of the Martelli family since the fifteenth century. From the painter's signature and Vasari's reference to a portrait of Ugolino Martelli in his life of Bronzino, Bode was able long since to identify the sitter. [63]

When the likeness was painted, the statue was still regarded as a work of Donatello and later, in Vasari's historiographic construction, it helped to prove the crucial rôle of the Martelli as patrons of the young sculptor. [64] In the portrait, it assumes the semantic function of a coat-of-arms, assigning the sitter to his family, whereas the books surrounding him – works of Virgil, Homer and Pietro Bembo – reveal his humanist leanings.

Ugolino Martelli (1519–1592) was the offspring of a well-to-do family of silk merchants with a taste for art; members of the family had obtained an impressive number of prestigious offices since the fifteenth century, thanks to the family's allegiance to the Medici. [65] Ugolino was destined for an ecclesiastic career; he studied Latin and Greek with two of the most respected Florentine scholars, Francesco Verino the Elder and Piero Vettori. The exuberant praise of his teachers portrays him as a talented boy, 'beautiful', says Vettori, 'through honesty and virtue'. [66] Like his friend Lorenzo Lenzi, Ugolino

---

York 1985, p. 203, no. 64) or the engraving by Raimondi, by this time already more then ten years old (see I. H. Shoemaker and E. Broun, *The Engravings of Marcantonio Raimondi,* Lawrence 1981, cat. 46).

[61] See R. Wildmoser, 'Das Bildnis des Ugolino Martelli von Agnolo Bronzino', *Jahrbuch der Berliner Museen,* 31, 1989, pp. 181–214 (esp. p. 183).

[62] On this statue, see D. Lewis, 'David di casa Martelli', in A. P. Darr and G. Bonsanti (Eds), *Donatello e i suoi. Scultura fiorentina del primo Rinascimento,* Florence 1986, pp. 232f.

[63] See Vasari (as in n. 11 above), vol. 6, 1987, p. 232. The signature 'BRONZO FIORENTINO' can easily be deciphered on the edge of the table. See J. Meyer, *Königliche Museen zu Berlin. Beschreibendes Verzeichnis der Gemälde,* Berlin 1878, p. 50. On the provenance of the statue see K. Lydecker, 'The Domestic Setting of the Arts in Renaissance Florence', PhD diss., Johns Hopkins University, Baltimore 1987, p. 197.

[64] See Vasari (as in n. 11 above), vol. 3, 1971, p. 212.

[65] A short life of Ugolino is found in Wildmoser 1989 (as in n. 61 above), p. 183f. New documents in A. Civai, *Dipinti e Sculture in Casa Martelli. Storia di una collezione patrizia fiorentina dal Quattrocento all'Ottocento,* Florence 1990. The following survey is based predominantly on S. Salvini, *Fasti Consolari dell'Academia Fiorentina,* Florence 1717, pp. 29f.

followed northwards their common mentor Varchi, who, still in exile, settled in Padua in 1537. There both disciples lived in their teacher's house.[67] The three Florentines soon belonged to Pietro Bembo's inner circle. From this fertile ground, the Paduan Accademia degli Infiammati emerged not long after the Venetian poet was called to Rome to be elevated to the rank of cardinal in 1539. The academy's founding fathers are reported to be Daniele Barbaro, Leone Orsini and, last but not least, Ugolino Martelli, then just twenty years old. Famous names joined this academy, among others Lodovico Dolce, Alessandro Piccolomini and Sperone Speroni. All shared the same interest in poetry in their native language and its theoretical foundations. The academy's predominant task was the production of new poetry in *volgare*. The members met on Thursdays and Sundays for recitation of their compositions.[68] Through the criticism and corrections of two *censori* the texts were meant to reach a state of the greatest possible perfection. In 1541 Ugolino was chosen for the office of *censore*,[69] as he was already counted among the prominent poets in *volgare*.[70] Some of his few poems that have come down to us are dedicated to the courtesan-poetess Tullia of Aragon, who in turn praises the 'learned and adorned verses' of the Florentine.[71] His theoretical interests in

---

[66] Salvini 1717 (as in n. 65 above), p. 29. See also Cecchi 1991 (as in n. 39 above), p. 20.

[67] Salvini 1717 (as in n. 65 above), p. 28. Cf. Mendelsohn 1982 (as in n. 2 above), p. 191, n. 8.

[68] On the academy in Padua see F. Cerreta, 'An Account of the Early Life of the Accademia degli Infiammati in the Letters of Alessandro Piccolomini to Benedetto Varchi', *The Romanic Review*, 48, 1957, pp. 249–64; R. S. Samuels, 'Benedetto Varchi, the "Accademia degli Infiammati", and the Origin of the Italian Academic Movement', *Renaissance Quarterly*, 29, 1976, pp. 599–634.

[69] Samuels 1976 (as in n. 68 above), p. 616 and n. 73.

[70] Aretino in 1537 ranked him among the most important poets of his time; see P. Aretino, *Lettere sull'arte*, E. Camasesca (Ed.), vol. 1, *1526–1542*, Milan 1957, p. 110. Cf. Wildmoser 1989 (as in n. 61 above), p. 184. In 1539 Varchi sent to Lodovico Dolce 'un [sonetto] di quel Martello, che è un giovanetto nobile, & molto letterato, Greco, & Latino di suo tempo, & di nuovo si è dato al Toscano.' This comment obviously refers to Ugolino's poetic production, which Carlo Strozzi has likewise in mind when he writes to the young Martelli in 1542: 'O veramente felice, anzi felicissimo, & più tosto beato voi, il quale in quegli anni, che gli altri sogliono appena incominciare, havete, si può dire, compita l'opera vostra [...].'; cited after Salvini 1717 (as in n. 65 above), pp. 29f.

[71] See *Le Rime di Tullia d'Aragona Cortigiana del Secolo XVI*, E. Celani (Ed.), Bologna 1891, p. 27, sonnet XXIII, v. 1. Tullia's collection of poetry was published in 1549 and includes a dialogue of sonnets between her and Ugolino. Varchi characterised Ugolino's poetic talent several times with phrases such as 'quelle dolci vostre rime | Onde già conto al mondo sete e caro.'; cited after *Opere di Benedetto Varchi con le lettere di Gio. Battista Busini*, 2 vols, Milan 1834, vol. 1, p. 548, sonnet 'Voi ch'alla prima...', v. 5f. As this poem refers to the death of Luca Martini, it must date from 1561. In numerous sonnets Varchi emphasizes

poetry resulted in a number of lectures at the academy. Having recovered from a grave illness, Ugolino returned to Florence in 1542, where on 12 May he became a member of the recently founded Accademia Fiorentina, modelled on its Paduan predecessor. In the same year he was elected *censore*, and, in 1544, consul. He delivered numerous lectures, mostly on the poetry of Petrarch and Bembo.[72] The latter he seemed to imitate also in the modesty of his ecclesiastic ambitions, a late fruit of which was the episcopate of Glandèves in southern France, obtained in 1572. Soon, however, he resided in his home town, where he could give his undivided attention to his diverse scholarly interests. He was regarded as an exemplary 'learned bishop' and died in 1592.[73]

So far Bronzino's ambitious portrait has – with few exceptions – been dated to the years around 1536/37, for reasons of style and history.[74] On the one hand, Ugolino left Florence for Padua in November 1537, and on the other, affinities with the style of Pontormo have often been stressed, above all regarding the face and hands.[75] Berlin being remote for American and Italian

---

Ugolino's precocious abilities: 'Felice Ugolin, voi ch'avete donde | Non temer, nato apena, il tardo obblio, | Tal grazia e tanta in voi l'altero Dio | Di Delo infin del quarto cielo infonde.'; ibid., p. 566, v. 5–8.

[72] He also wrote a book on the *Odes* of Horace, as is reported by his biographer Marco Antonio Romoli in the eighteenth century; see Wildmoser 1989 (as in n. 61 above), p. 185.

[73] He is ranked among the 'Vescovi dotti' by F. Verino the Younger in his *Discorsi delle maravigliose opere di Pratolino* of 1576; see Salvini 1717 (as in n. 65 above), p. 36. Salvini also lists further books and manuscripts by Ugolino.

[74] H. Schulze, *Agnolo Bronzinos Werke*, Strasbourg 1909, proposes the dates 1534 (p. 8) and 1535 (cat. IV); Smyth 1949 (as in n. 57 above), p. 184: 1535–8; K. W. Forster, 'Probleme um Pontormos Porträtmalerei I', *Pantheon*, 12, 1964, pp. 376–84 (esp. p. 380): the late 1530s; S. J. Freedberg, *Painting in Italy: 1500–1600*, [1971] Hongkong 1993, p. 431: around 1536; E. Bacheschi, *L'opera completa del Bronzino*, Milan 1973, cat. 24: 1535–8; E. Schleier, 'Bildnis des Ugolino Martelli', in *Katalog der ausgestellten Werke des 13. bis 18. Jahrhunderts* (Staatliche Museen Preußischer Kulturbesitz Berlin, Gemäldegalerie), Berlin 1975, p. 65: 1537–8; C. McCorquodale, *Bronzino*, London 1981, p. 51: 1535–6 or 1537–9 (on p. 52 he describes the sitter as 18–20 years old); E. Cropper, 'Prolegomena to a New Interpretation of Bronzino's Florentine Portraits', in A. Morrow et al. (Eds), *Renaissance Studies in Honour of Craig Hugh Smyth*, 2 vols, Florence 1985, vol. 2, pp. 149–62: 1540; Wildmoser 1989 (as in n. 61 above), seems to accept her dating.

[75] The date of his departure is given by Cecchi 1991 (as in n. 39 above), p. 20, as 15 November 1537. He does not, however, cite any document. See also Cecchi 1996 (as in n. 42 above), p. 6. A dating of the portrait before his departure has recently been accepted by E. Schleier, *200 Meisterwerke* (Gemäldegalerie Berlin, Staatliche Museen zu Berlin Preussischer Kulturbesitz, 1), Berlin 1998, p. 346. The proximity to the style of Pontormo has been stressed by J. Alazard, *Le portrait florentin de Botticelli à Bronzino*, Paris 1924, p. 229; A. Venturi, *Storia dell'arte italiana*, vol. 9, pt. 6, Milan 1933, pp. 36f; Forster 1964 (as in n. 74 above), pp.

scholarship alike, the panel's rather bad state of conservation has hardly ever been mentioned.[76] Some of the better preserved parts, for example the left hand of Ugolino or the sleeve-band, still show a three-dimensionality and smoothness of surface that would be unusual for Bronzino's work of the 1530s. To find parallels for the vivid movement of the figure, its helical rotation, continued up to the turned eyes, one has to look to the works of the early 1540s, the frescoes of the Cappella di Eleonora or the Budapest *Nativity*.[77] Furthermore, the extreme foreshortening of the architecture, framing the sitter and pushing him towards the beholder, is closely related to the *Portrait of Bartolommeo Panciatichi* in the Uffizi, datable to the early 1540s.[78] In addition, some years ago John Kent Lydecker discovered documentary evidence in the books of Ugolino's father that allowed Elizabeth Cropper to date the painting to 1540. A close reading of the expense accounts of Luigi Martelli gives the following picture: on 26 May 1540 Luigi confirmed to the carpenter Giuliano di Baccio d'Agnolo that he would receive 12 scudi for 'a cut panel [quadro] of willow for the portrait of my son Ugolino'. The money was handed over on 25 June, obviously by Ugolino himself.[79] The term 'quadro' in the Cinquecento refers to a panel for a

---

380f.

[76] The topmost layer of paint is badly worn in many places, making the skin seem pale and flat and reducing the garment's brilliance, attested by some better preserved areas, to a flat black area. The state of conservation has so far been commented on only by Wildmoser 1989 (as in n. 61 above), p. 181, n. 3.

[77] On the dating of the frescoes for Eleonora, see J. Cox-Rearick, *Bronzino's Chapel of Eleonora di Toledo in the Palazzo Vecchio*, Berkeley, Los Angeles, Oxford 1993, pp. 60–2. For the *Nativity*, see Baccheschi 1973 (as in n. 74 above), cat. 26.

[78] Ibid., cat. 34. Likewise, the abbreviated form of the signature which recurs only on the Panciatichi *Holy Family* (ibid., cat 31), points to the years around 1540. Vasari mentions the portrait of Ugolino Martelli immediately after reporting Bronzino's return from Pesaro, datable to the middle of the 1530s, but he then continues with the paintings for the Panciatichi; see Vasari (as in n. 11 above), vol. 6, 1987, p. 233. In addition, on the right book, the name of Pietro Bembo (see below) is preceded by an 'M.'. This letter is probably not an abbreviation of 'Messer', but of 'Monsignore'. If this contention is correct, it provides a *terminus post quem* for the painting, or at least for the inscription on the book, as Bembo was elevated to the rank of cardinal in 1539.

[79] Archivio di Stato di Firenze, Carte Strozziane, serie V, 1481, fol. 15r. The text is only partially cited in Lydecker 1987 (as in n. 63 above), p. 299. Here it is given in its entirety, and following as closely as possible the orthography of the secretary: 'Giuliano dibaccio dagniolo Legniaiuolo de[ue] aue|re addi 26 dimaggio 1540 12 [then follows the symbol for 'scudi'] e sono p[er] 1° qua|dro di siglio intagliato p[er] il ritratto d'ugholino mio figlo auuto sino addi 25 giuglio posti [?] ughol|ino mio figlo dare [there follows a reference to fol. 16].' Ibid., fol. 16r, the corresponding entry reads: 'Ms. Ugholino mio figlo de[ue] dare addi 25 giugnio 1540 | 12 [scudi] p[er] tanti fatti buoni p[er] lui a giul dibaccio da|gniolo Legniaiuolo [per?] auere [there follows a reference to fol. 15] 1° quadro disiglio

painting, on occasion together with a frame; in the present case, the latter seems to be referred to in another entry.[80] If the 'ritratto di Ugholino' listed in Luigi's books was indeed the Berlin portrait, the carpenter's delivery of the panel in June 1540 would provide a *terminus post quem*, dating the portrait exactly to the year and months when Ugolino was involved in the foundation of the Paduan Accademia degli Infiammati.

The Muses' Fathers[81]

On close inspection, the painting proves to be the complex, yet explicit *image* of a young poet in *volgare*, developed, as the *pentimenti* suggest, in close collaboration between client and artist. The revisions predominantly concern the statue in the background.[82] Initially, it must have been planned as much larger, but as a result of the reworking it has become the focus of the zoom-like perspectival construction, relating directly to the protagonist in the foreground.

---

intagliato p[er] ornamento alla sua testa.' The payment is noted a third time (ibid., 1482, fol. 5r): 'giulo dibaccio dag[no]lo legn[a]i[uo]lo | 72 [scudi] e sono p[er] piu legna mi auti da Lui da di 13 dap[ri]le 1537 sino addi giugo 1540 in [there follows an illegible word] datemi | 1° quadro disig[li]o della testa dug[olin]o 12 [scudi] [...].' Apparently, the money was handed out to Ugolino, who personally paid the carpenter. He must have been present in Florence at least on this occasion; the assumption that 1537 is the *terminus ante quem* for the portrait is thus undermined. It is, furthermore, questionable that the departure for Padua was a sufficiently important event in Ugolino's life to have occasioned the making of a portrait. If it was, the painting in the National Gallery, Washington, identified by Charles Seymour as another likeness of Ugolino because of the family coat-of-arms it displays, might date from this early period. See F. R. Shapley, *Paintings from the Samuel H. Kress Collection. Italian Schools XVI – XVIII Century*, London 1973, pp. 14f. Shapley dates this portrait as late as 1545–50; Costamagna 1994 (as in n. 37 above), cat. A134, observes a dependence on the painting in Berlin and suggests 1540 as the most likely date.

80 Cropper 1985 (as in n. 74 above), p. 152, only refers to a frame, not a panel; Lydecker 1987 (as in n. 63 above), p. 299, n. 31, translates the line as 'a panel and a frame for a portrait'. In fact, the term 'ornamento' in the second quotation could point to a frame. However, Giuliano di Baccio d'Agnolo worked for the Martelli predominantly as a carpenter, not as a woodcarver, as documented by the list of his work in ASF, Carte Strozziane, serie V, 1482, fol. 5r. The *Vocabolario degli Accademici della crusca*, [Venice 1611] Repr. Florence 1974, p. 669, defines the meaning of 'quadro' by providing as synonyms the Latin words 'quadratum' and 'tabula picta', not specifying if the panel is framed or not. The wood is referred to as 'siglio' (Latin 'siler', i.e. willow); the scribe appears to have used this term loosely, since modern analyses have shown that the Berlin portrait is painted on poplar.

81 Ugolino Martelli in a sonnet calls Pietro Bembo the 'gran padre delle Muse'; cited after Varchi 1834 (as in n. 71 above), p. 566, 'Voi ve n'andate...', v. 2.

82 See Wildmoser 1989 (as in n. 61 above), p. 210f.

Bronzino not only 'modernised' the posture of the famous sculpture by giving it a soft curve,[83] but also assimilated the face of David, originally of an oval form in the tradition of Donatello, to Ugolino's with his long, straight nose. In contrast to the model, David's head is turned to the same side as the sitter's. Thus, the young hero of the Old Testament in the background seems to be the visualised *type* of the young poet in the foreground. And indeed, David was not just a champion and commander, but above all a singer, a Christian poet *avant la lettre*: 'He loved his creator wholeheartedly, each day he praised him with songs'.[84] He was regarded as the author of the psalms, one of the most important texts for private devotional reading, available in numerous translations and reinterpretations, one composed by Pietro Aretino.[85] David's power of poetical creation is explained through Divine inspiration, for which reason Marsilio Ficino counts him among the *vates*, the prophetic, visionary poets. As 'trumpet of Almighty God',[86] he is the Christian mirror image of the pagan Orpheus and, with him, the archetype of the poet in general.

Poetic activity defines the sitter of this portrait, as is suggested by the books around him. On the left, hardly visible, we see a work of Virgil; on the right, a volume bearing Bembo's name supports Ugolino's left hand, and, on the table, the *Iliad* of Homer lies open.[87] At first glance, the choice of texts in Greek, Latin and Italian might seem unsurprising; Castiglione in his *Cortegiano*, for example, recommends that the courtier should be versed in these three languages.[88] In Bronzino's portrait, Bembo represents the poet in *volgare*, whereas Homer and Virgil mark the peaks of the history of literature as it was construed by Quintilian. For him, the works of these two authors, treasure houses of 'moral' qualities, should be the starting point of any study of literature, as they fill the reader's mind with the noblest thoughts and

[83]   Ibid., pp. 197 ff.; here, however, David is interpreted as a martial figure with negative connotations. Ugolino, Wildmoser claims, indicated his lack of affinity with the warrior by means of the perspectival construction of the painting.

[84]   Ecclesiasticus, 47, 8.

[85]   See n. 177 below.

[86]   Ficino calls him 'sacer ille vates David, omnipotentis tuba dei' and 'poeta sacer'; see *De vita libri tres*, I, vii, 116 and I, x, 51.

[87]   The volume on the left shows the inscription [Publius Vergilius] MARO, the name 'M. P. Bembo' on the cover of the right book is today legible only in raking light. On the *Iliad*, see the following section.

[88]   B. Castiglione, *Il libro del Cortegiano*, in C. Cordié (Ed.), *Opere di Baldassare Castiglione, Giovanni della Casa, Benvenuto Cellini*, Milan, Naples 1960, pp. 5–361 (esp. pp. 74f. (I, 44)): 'Il qual [i.e. il cortegiano] voglio che nelle lettere sia più che mediocremente erudito, almeno in questi studii che chiamano d'umanità; e non solamente della lingua latina, ma ancor della greca abbia cognizione per le molte e varie cose che in quella divinamente scritte sono. Sia versato nei poeti, [...] ed ancor esercitato nel scriver versi e prosa, massimamente in questa nostra lingua volgare [...]'.

elevate his spirit.[89] In Renaissance theory, these poets therefore rule the class of *vates*. Ficino, Cristoforo Landino and Angelo Poliziano read their texts as *theologia poetica*, i.e. as Christian theology enveloped in poetic fiction.[90]

Yet, looking back at the painting, the clear emphasis on Homer, almost literally marginalising the volume of Virgil, comes as a surprise. At the beginning of the sixteenth century, the poet of the *Aeneid* was considered as the sole and uncontested model for epic poetry;[91] as the golden, immortal singer, he stands at the centre of Marco Girolamo Vida's influential treatise on poetry of 1527. Virgil went far beyond the Greek poets, the humanist maintains, so his is the only model to be followed. Vida stresses above all Virgil's 'ars',[92] but also his exemplary handling of decorum, a quality in Vida's view lacking in Homer. The latter, since the times of Plato, had been reproached for being too laboured in his descriptions, and for having violated the rules of decorum when he told of the gods in his *Iliad*.[93] Homer had

---

[89]   *De institutione oratoria*, I, 8, 4f: 'cetera admonitione magna egent, in primis, ut tenerae mentes tracturaeque altius quidquid rudibus et omnium ignaris insederit, non modo quae diserta, sed magis quae honesta sunt, discant. Ideoque optime institutum est, ut ab Homero atque Virgilio lectio inciperet, quamquam ad intellegendas eorum virtutes firmiore iudicio opus est: sed huic rei superest tempus, neque enim semel legentur. Interim et sublimitate heroi carminis adsurgat et ex magnitudine rerum spiritum ducat et optimis inbuatur'.

[90]   See A. Levine Rubinstein, 'The Notes to Poliziano's Iliad', *Italia medioevale e umanistica*, 25, 1982, pp. 205–39 (esp. p. 211). In a letter to his pupils Varchi wrote in October 1539: '[...] et credete che Vergilio in latino, et Homero in greco seppero et insegnarono ogni cosa forse meglio ch'Aristotile [...].'; cited after M. Plaisance, 'Une première affirmation de la politique culturelle de Côme Ier: La transformation de l'Académie des "Humidi" en Académie Florentine (1540–1542)', in A. Rochon et al. (Eds), *Les Écrivains et le pouvoir en Italie à l'époque de la Renaissance* (Centre de recherche sur la Renaissance italienne, 3), 2 vols, Paris 1973–4, vol. 1, pp. 361–438 (esp. p. 373); already cited in Wildmoser 1989 (as in n. 61 above), p. 194.

[91]   See M. McLaughlin, *Literary Imitation in the Italian Renaissance. The Theory and Practice of Literary Imitation in Italy from Dante to Bembo*, Oxford 1995, p. 262.

[92]   See M. G. Vida, *The 'De Arte Poetica' of Marco Girolamo Vida. Translated with Commentary, & with the Text of c. 1517*, R. G. Williams (Ed.), New York 1976, p. 14 (I, 170): 'Unus hic ingenio praestanti, gentis Achivae | Divinos vates longe superavit, arte, | Aureus, immortale sonans.' Cf. also ibid., p. 16 (I, 208) and the exuberant eulogy of Virgil at the end of the text, ibid., p. 120 (III, 554): 'Virgilio ante omnius laeti hic | super astra feremus | carminibus patriis laudes'.

[93]   Vida's assessment of Homer and Virgil is summed up in A. Buck, *Italienische Dichtungslehren vom Mittelalter bis zum Ausgang der Renaissance*, Tübingen 1952, p. 145. Cf. the references to such views in Sperone Speroni's *Dialogo primo sopra Virgilio*, first naming Virgil a 'buon Platonico' and then stating about Homer: '[...] per vero troppo empiamente favoleggiava di quei suoi Dei, cui, quai che si fossero, doveva avere in più riverenza, che egli non ebbe ne' doi poemi, e nella Iliade specialmente.'; S. Speroni, *Opere*, Venice 1740, vol. 2, p. 184. This statement

shown them to be as capricious and subject to emotions as their mortal underlings and he was therefore accused of godlessness.

An increased attention to the writings of Aristotle in Padua and in particular in the Accademia degli Infiammati[94] changed some scholars' assessment of Homer. The philosopher often cites the poet of the *Iliad* and *Odyssey* as an unsurpassable example. A renewed respect for Homer can be felt, above all, in the works of Sperone Speroni, whom Ugolino must have known well in his Paduan days.

Speroni's apology of Homer is a specifically Christian one. He judges the bard's violations of decorum not as a failure but as proof of his profound understanding. Homer had come to realize, declares Speroni, that the Greek gods were nothing other than human beings or demons.[95] For this reason he concludes:

> [...] Homer is not godless when he attributes to vile men, called gods by the people, many vile actions: he rather in this way wants to intimate to those who believe too easily that they should pay more attention to the deeds than to the renown of persons. [...]. This is why Homer, as a lover of virtue, has deservedly been given to read by some learned and holy men to those who believe in Jesus Christ. [...][96]

---

by one of the dialogue's interlocutors does not reflect Speroni's own opinion; see below.

[94] On the reception of Aristotle in Bembo's circle, see Mendelsohn 1982 (as in n. 2 above), pp. 4–6. The first public lecture on Aristotle's *Poetics* was delivered at the Paduan academy in 1540/41; see Samuels 1976 (as in n. 68 above), p. 611. Ugolino himself remarks in a speech of 1544 that at Padova he had studied the 'sacra santa philosophia [...] salendo dietro i detti del grande Aristotile.'; cited after M. Plaisance, 'Culture et politique à Florence de 1542 à 1551', in Rochon et al. (Eds) 1974 (as in n. 90 above), pp. 149–240 (esp. p. 157).

[95] Speroni 1740 (as in n. 93 above), vol. 1, p. 408 ('Apologia dei Dialogi'): 'Sapeva Omero come Platone, che Giove e gli altri adorati, non eran Dei, ma nomi d'uomini o di dimoni: e degna cosa è da creder, che essendo savio e da bene, caro li fusse che tutto'l mondo il sapesse: ma non avendo ardimento solo o con pochi di farsi incontro liberamente a sì fatto errore, Dei chiamandoli, come il vulgo; fa lor far cose, che per ver dire non son da uomini ragionevoli, non che da Dei, ma o da bestie o da ubbriachi: e perchè il vulgo non abbia a schifo, come bestemmia, la novità; con altri esempli, conformi a quella, comunemente approvati, la fa parer verisimile.' Speroni here exploits an argument of Petrarch, *Invective contra medicum*, III, 470–7. Although it is a late writing (1574), the 'Apologia' can be considered as a summary of Speroni's earlier thoughts; see J. L. Fournel, *Les dialogues de Sperone Speroni: libertés de la parole et règles de l'écriture*, Marburg 1990, pp. 25f. He also emphasizes that Speroni's manuscripts can often be shown to have circulated long before their publication.

[96] Ibid., p. 409: 'Empio adunque non è Omero, attribuendo a malvagi uomini, volgarmente chiamati Dei, molte malvagie operazioni: anzi in tal modo vuole accennare chi troppo crede, che attenda ai fatti più che alla fama delle persone [...]. Però Omero, come amator di virtù, meritamente da alcuni dotti e santi uomini è

Homer's authority was also invoked in the quarrel about the language to be used by contemporary writers. In this *questione della lingua*, the Infiammati played an important part as advocates of Italian. In accordance with the theory of imitation that Bembo had expounded in his *Prose della volgar lingua*, aiming to assist a reform of the national language, the members of the Paduan academy initiated a series of translations into Italian. These included famous ancient texts, both poetic and theoretical, the content and technical refinement of which were to benefit the *volgare*.[97] Defenders of Latin, on the other hand, considered Italian as a degradation of Latin, as a disease.[98] As the importance of Latin in the formation of Italian could not be denied entirely, Benedetto Varchi, with Mendel-like logic, maintained that the Latin language was the daughter of Greek and the mother of Tuscan, but that in this case, as is often found, the last was more similar to her grandmother than to her mother.[99] This preference for Greek is directly related to the condemnation of Latin as means of expression. Pietro Bembo argued that the *volgare* 'is not only close, but also innate and pertinent to us, whereas Latin is

dato a leggere alli fedeli di Gesù Cristo. [...] Finalmente tutto il biasimo, che dà Platone ad Omero intorno ai fatti dei falsi Dei, è somma laude, se ben si nota, di chi è amico alla verità: la qual sempre sopra ogni cosa ed in ogni causa dee esser cara alli sapienti, e nella religion molto più.' Ibid., p. 408: 'Aristotile in questo loco con due parole difende Omero da tutto'l male, che se ne dice.' Homer followed the common use of the people. Because of his particular insight, Speroni calls the 'divine blind man' 'a second Argus in the sciences'; everyone had learnt from him, he is 'the father of all doctrine and goodness.'; ibid., vol. 1, p. 407: 'quel divin cieco, che fu un altro Argo nelle scienze [...] Il qual cieco pien di occhi [...].'; ibid., p. 408: 'Omero, da cui ognuno ha imparato'; ibid., vol. 3, p. 469 ('Al Duca d'Urbino in Morte di Virginia'): 'Omero padre d'ogni dottrina e bontà'.

[97] On Bembo's concept of imitation, see McLaughlin 1995 (as in n. 91 above), pp. 264-9, and F. Penzenstadler, 'Elegie und Petrarkismus. Alternativität der literarischen Referenzsysteme in Luigi Alamannis Lyrik', in K. W. Hempfer and G. Regn (Eds), *Der petrarkistische Diskurs. Spielräume und Grenzen*, Stuttgart 1993, pp. 77–114 (esp. pp. 83-6).

[98] See, for example, Rodolfo Amaseo's *De linguae Latinae usu retinendo* (two speeches of 1529). Francesco Florido in 1537 explicitly attacked the academies in his *Apologia* and called the Italian language a disease and barbaric; see A. L. de Gaetano, *Giambattista Gelli and the Florentine Academy. The Rebellion against Latin*, Florence 1976, pp. 78f. In a letter to M. Michiel of 1530 Francesco Bellafini referred to the *volgare* as 'latinae linguae fragmentum'; see M. Vitale (Ed.), *La questione della lingua*, Palermo 1960, p. 48.

[99] B. Varchi, *Discorso sopra le lingue* [ca. 1551], in *Collezione d'opuscoli scientifici e letterarj ed estratti d'opere interessanti*, vol. 12, Florence 1810, pp. 1-10 (esp. p. 6): '[...] le tre più belle lingue, che oggi fioriscono, [...] la latina, come quasi figliuola della greca, e madre della Toscana. Nel qual ragionamento si potrà, credo, apertamente conoscere che la nostra lingua [...] più all'avola, come assai volte suole avvenire, che alla madre si rassomiglia.' The following *ragionamento* supporting this thesis deals predominantly with grammatical structures.

alien'.[100] Naturalness and closeness to the proper tradition thus become central arguments and in this respect Speroni can again claim Homer's superiority over Virgil. He criticises Virgil's faulty *imitatio*, making him little more than an epigone; the *Aeneid* is but a 'portrait of Homer'. Virgil did not fully possess the faculty of judgement; he was, in Speroni's words, 'nothing by himself, like a shadow.'[101] He contrasts the undeniable 'ars' of Virgil with the immediacy found in Homer's work, his line of argument reminiscent of Bembo's defense of the *volgare*; the verses of Homer 'do not seem an adornment of his poem, [...] but naturally born and grown up with it'. [102]

Bearing in mind the concerns of the Accademia degli Infiammati, the connection between the 'unequalled poetry'[103] of Homer and the work of Bembo established by Ugolino's posture acquires a powerful meaning. Not only did Bembo's *Prose della volgar lingua* (1525), with Speroni's *Dialogo delle lingue*, constitute the foundation of the Infiammati's poetics of the *volgare*; the poetic production of the cardinal was itself regarded as perfect contemporary poetry.[104]

Ugolino's acquaintance with Bembo dates back to his boyhood days in Florence. Already in 1536 he had sent a sonnet to the Venetian, asking his teacher Benedetto Varchi to apologize for this 'daring' enterprise.[105] Later, among the Infiammati in Padua, he gave lectures on Bembo's poetry, earning him considerable respect. On 19 September 1540, for instance, he discussed the famous sonnet 'Piansi e cantai ...' which opens Bembo's *Rime*. Only a few weeks later, the learned engineer Luca Martini in Florence possessed a copy of the manuscript.[106]

[100]   '[...] a noi la volgar lingua, non solamente vicina si deve dire che ella sia, ma natìa et propria, et la Latina straniera.'; cited after Bembo 1997 (as in n. 11 above), p. 80.

[101]   Speroni 1740 (as in n. 93 above), vol. 4, p. 423, judges the *Aeneid* as being 'da Omero talmente tolta e tradotta, che altro non fosse che un ritratto di Omero.' Ibid., p. 424 he adds that Virgil had shown with his work, 'che egli fosse poeta non con la propria ragione, ma col giudicio d'altrui: ed in summa che fosse nulla da se, come l'ombra, ma ad Omero accostandosi paresse d'esser qualche cosa'.

[102]   Ibid., p. 578 ('Discorso ottavo sopra Virgilio'): '[...] Omero, li cui versi non pajono ornamento del suo poema, ma naturalmente nati e cresciuti con lui. Questo è cosa notabile'.

[103]   Ibid., vol. 1, p. 407, one reads about Homer: 'la poesia di quel vecchio, la qual ebbe mai pare'.

[104]   See Cerreta 1957 (as in n. 68 above), p. 250, and Samuels 1976 (as in n. 68 above), pp. 617, 619.

[105]   Varchi writes: 'M. Ugolino Martelli è tornato da Pescia, & dice haver mandate lettere costì, & con esse un sonetto a V.S. [...] Egli prega quella, che l'abbia per iscusato, se forse le paresse prosontoso o temerario [...].'; cited after *Lettere da diversi Re e Principi e Cardinali e altri uomini dotti a Mons. Pietro Bembo scritte*, [Venice 1560], repr. D. Perosso (Ed.), Bologna 1985, p. 66 (letter III, 52).

[106]   Luca Martini states in a letter dated 20 November 1540: 'Di Luigi Martelli hebbi la lettura di messer Ugolino sopra il primo sonetto del Bembo [...].'; cited after

In Ugolino's hometown, Bembo's fame was by no means undisputed. Notwithstanding the quality of his poetry, the theoretical works of a Venetian concerned with the reform of the Tuscan language were either regarded with suspicion or explicitly condemned by humanists such as Giambattista Gelli.[107] Ugolino's manuscript can be seen as an early instance of the promotional work performed by him and Benedetto Varchi and concluded in the 1540s when they, as members of the Accademia Fiorentina, finally achieved a general acceptance of Bembo as a model for both poetry *and* language in Florence. Ugolino, in 1545, just a year before the polemic against Bembo reached a last peak with Gelli's *Capriccio*,[108] gave a lecture on the former's sonnet 'Verdeggi all'Appennin la fronte e'l petto'.[109] Bembo, then in Rome, wrote a long letter to his advocate, expressing his gratitude for an interpretation 'so beautiful, so learned and so exhaustive'.[110]

Considering this context, the Berlin portrait may be seen as illustrating the literary theory of a young Florentine academician, which Bronzino, as a friend of Varchi and admirer of Bembo, must have shared.[111] The 'Venetian Petrarch', though still disputed, is here explicitly shown as a support to the Florentine poet,[112] and his authority is affirmed in proximity to the natural and 'Christian' poetry of Homer.

Plaisance 1973 (as in n. 90 above), p. 436. Already on 11 November Francesco del Garbo had shown his interest in the manuscript in a letter to Varchi: 'Io ho inteso che ci è una lezione di messer Ugolino la quale per esser stato molto occupato non ho veduto. Desidero vederla [...].'; ibid., p. 380, n. 78.

[107] Gelli writes in his *Ragionamento intorno alla lingua*: 'E sappi che chi non è nato ed allevato in Firenze non la [lingua Fiorentina] impara mai perfettamente [...].'; cited after de Gaetano 1976 (as in n. 98 above), pp. 142f.

[108] See C. Dionisotti, 'Pietro Bembo', in *Dizionario biografico degli Italiani*, vol. 8, Rom 1966, pp. 133–51 (esp. p. 147).

[109] See Salvini 1717 (as in n. 65 above), p. 31 and Plaisance 1974 (as in n. 94 above), p. 168.

[110] The letter dates from 20 February 1546: '[...] sì bella e sì dotta e sì piena isposizione avete voi fatta sopra quel mio picciol parto.'; P. Bembo, *Lettere*, E. Travi (Ed.), vol. 4, Bologna 1993, p. 554, no. 2515.

[111] When Bembo in October 1539 on his journey to Rome paid a short visit to Florence, Varchi wrote from Padua to Carlo Strozzi: '[...] e mi par di vedervi hora quando eravate con Luca [Martini], col Tribolo et col Bronzino a considerare gli occhi et gli atti del Reverendissimo Bembo, [...].'; cited after Plaisance 1973 (as in n. 90 above), p. 375. Cf. Cropper 1985 (as in n. 74 above), p. 157.

[112] Varchi calls Bembo the 'Petrarca Viniziano' in his famous lecture on a sonnet by Michelangelo; see Varchi 1834 (as in n. 71 above), p. 104. Ugolino is holding the Bembo volume like, on later portraits of artists, painters hold their sketchbooks, the token of their *disegno*. Cropper 1985 (as in n. 74 above), p. 157, also connects the choice of texts on the portrait with the Paduan academy. N. Schneider, *Hauptwerke europäischer Bildniskunst 1420–1670*, Cologne 1992, p. 78, judges the selection of authors as a 'Dokument für das in dieser Zeit aufkommende Nationalgefühl'.

Bearing in mind Varchi's and Ugolino's sophisticated modes of interpretation, we shall now take a close look at the portrait. [113]

Passion

We are not granted any access to Ugolino's thoughts: his eyes are turned away, he keeps his distance. His gesture is thus charged with all the more importance, and it refers to the 'small print' of the image. His right hand ostentatiously rests on Homer's text, which is not only opened up, but turned towards the beholder. We do not interrupt the young scholar's studies: he rather invites us to study and read ourselves (Pl. 18). We can easily decipher, at the top of the page, the title of the epic as well as the Greek symbol for '9', the letter *iota*, marking the beginning of the ninth book. We are asked to look at the *Iliad*, which sings, as stated in the famous first line of the entire work, of a strong emotion, namely 'the wrath [...] of Peleus's son, Achilles'.[114] Homer was regarded as a master of the representation of emotion, and Book IX of the *Iliad*, shown on the portrait, as exemplary of this art. [115] It

[113] Sixteenth-century interpretations cannot be measured by modern philological standards. They were always directed at a specific purpose. The commentator received most praise for 'imagining and adding' his own thoughts, as is documented in Bembo's reply to Ugolino's lecture on the Venetian's sonnet 'Piansi e cantai...': '[...] non solamente siete col vostro maestrevole ingegno entrato nel mio animo, e in lui avete scorti minutamente tutti que' pensieri, senza mancarne un solo, che io già ebbi nel comporlo, ma questo ancora, che voi ce ne avete cotante altri belli e lodevoli a maraviglia imaginati e aggiunti sopra i miei, che si può giustamente estimare che voi abbiate molto maggiormente meritato dichiarandolo, e quasi col vostro latte crescendolo, che io fatto non ho generandolo.'; Bembo 1993 (as in n. 110 above), vol. 4, p. 554.

[114] Homer, *Iliad*, I, 1. English translation cited after Homer, *The Iliad*, transl. A. T. Murray [1924], repr. Cambridge, Mass., London 1978. As the *Iliad* deals with the quarrel of the Greek allies before the walls of Troy, Elizabeth Cropper, Detlev Heikamp and S. W. Reed tried in different ways to interpret the painting as an allusion to discord among the Florentines. This led to an anti-Medicean reading of the image in which David is considered as a 'symbol of Florentine freedom' (Cropper 1985, as in n. 74 above, pp. 155f.). An anti-Medicean stance of Ugolino's cannot, however, as far as I know, be documented. In addition, Book IX of the *Iliad* is not concerned with battles, but contains a succession of speeches. Rudolf Wildmoser linked the prominence of speech in this chapter with Ugolino's rhetorical studies; the text reveals, in his opinion, 'die Überlegenheit rhetorischer Leistungen vor dem bloßen Waffengebrauch' (Wildmoser 1989, as in n. 61 above, p. 196). It must be said, though, that the content of the book shows just the contrary, as Achilles will not be moved to join the fighting by rhetorics, but by the unbridled wrath that overcomes him when seeing the dead body of his friend Patroclos. A. Pontani, 'Iscrizioni greche nell'arte occidentale: specimen di un catalogo', *Scrittura e civiltà*, 20, 1996, pp. 205–79, does not cite Bronzino's portrait.

[115] See Quintilian, *Institutio Oratoria*, X, 1, 47f. The title of the ninth book, also

describes Agamemnon's despair when the defeat of the Greeks seemed imminent, his awareness of having unrightfully taken the beautiful Briseis from Achilles, and Achilles's incessant wrath, his refusal to participate in the combat. Homer here portrays extreme emotional turmoil.

The fact that this text is so clearly emphasized by Ugolino's gesture has so far attracted little attention.[116] Ugolino's index finger rests on the right page of the book, at the beginning of verse 14 (Pl. 18). The line tells us about the beginning of Agamemnon's address to the council of the Greeks, suggesting they take refuge in flight. It says: '[Agamemnon] stood up weeping even as a fountain of dark water',[117] and the next verse adds 'that down over the face of a beetling cliff poureth its dusky stream'. These lines, not undisputed among the exegetes of antiquity, were commonly called the 'simile of the fountain of the rock'.[118] Aristarchos classifies it as rhetorical *auxesis*, or, in Latin, *amplificatio*, meaning augmentation, increase, amplification.[119] Cicero explains that *amplificatio* is used to reach a higher level of credibility, that it not only shows states of emotion such as compassion, lament or indignation, but also communicates them to the audience.[120] Rudolf Agricola, in his *De inventione dialectica* of 1505, recommends amplifying the topics of a speech 'so that we can say of the listener that he is shaken, swept away, inflamed'. Among the

---

legible on the portrait, is 'Εξεσίη Ἀχιλῆος 'απειθέος 'εστιν 'Ιῶτα'; see Wildmoser 1989 (as in n. 61 above), p. 195.

[116] Carlo del Bravo, the only author to date to have commented on this verse, reads it as a reference to the victory over worldly passion. Joanna Woods-Marsden merely encourages a closer look at the verse. C. del Bravo, 'Ritratti petrarcheschi', *Artista*, 1994, pp. 128-35 (esp. p. 130); J. Woods-Marsden, '"In la Persia e nella India il mio ritratto si pregia": Pietro Aretino e la costruzione visuale dell'intellettuale nel Rinascimento', in *Pietro Aretino nel cinquecentenario della nascita*, Rome 1995, vol. 2, pp. 1099-1125 (esp. p. 1107). Most scholars have overlooked the fact that the text is turned towards the spectator; the remark of McCorquodale 1981 (as in n. 74 above), p. 50, may be seen as typical: Ugolino 'has interrupted his reading for a moment, marks his place with a finger, and remains wrapped in thought.' Cf. Cecchi 1996 (as in n. 42 above), p. 20.

[117] 'ίστατο δάκρυ χέων 'ὡς τε κρήνη μελάνυδρος', *Iliad*, IX, 14. English translation after Homer 1978 (as in n. 114 above). Bronzino wrote 'ίσατο' instead of the now conventional 'ίστατο'; in doing so he follows a contemporary edition, *OMEPOY IΛIAΔE. Homeri Ilias*, Venice 1524, p. 93. When transcribing the participle, Bronzino, who did not know Greek, merged 'χέων' with the following word.

[118] It is found a second time in *Iliad*, XVI, 2-4 ; see H. Fränkel, *Die homerischen Gleichnisse*, [1921] repr. Göttingen 1977, p. 21.

[119] See G. S. Kirk (Ed.), *The Iliad: A commentary*, vol. 3 (B. Hainsworth Ed.), *Books 9-12*, Cambridge 1993, p. 60. On 'amplificatio' see B. Bauer, in G. Ueding (Ed.), *Historisches Wörterbuch der Rhetorik*, vol. 1, Tübingen 1992, cols 445-71.

[120] Cicero, *De partitione oratoria*, 4 f., 27, 52; see Bauer 1992 (as in n. 119 above), col. 446.

means to achieve this goal he places comparison first.[121]

Homer, a master of *auxesis*, here amplifies Agamemnon's emotion by means of a comparison and thus arouses the audience's compassion. Ugolino's gesture isolates the simile from its context. As the Greek phrase can be read without the subject, as '*He* stood up ....' ('Agamemnon' being the last word of the preceding line), it can be understood as referring to the sitter.[122] In the portrait, he is characterised by the legendary force[123] ascribed to Homer's verses, their visual power, consisting in the ability, as Quintilian states, 'to show the things we talk about clearly and in such a way that one seems to see them'.[124] Angelo Poliziano calls this extraordinary effect *enargeia* or *evidentia*.[125] Homer, 'the blind man with a thousand eyes',[126] is a painter with words, even 'the best painter',[127] if one believes Lucian. Aristotle, in his *Poetics*, characterises Homer as an ideal portraitist; all his inventions have a 'character of their own'.[128] Alberti was aware that Phidias had used Homer's

---

[121] Ibid., col. 453.

[122] Similarly, in Petrarch's dialogue *De segreto conflictu curarum mearum*, 'Augustinus's' description of 'Franciscus' (on whom the author bestowed autobiographical traits) draws on a simile borrowed from the *Iliad* that portrays him as grieving and weeping: '[...] ut de te non minus proprie quam de Bellerophonte illud homericum dici posset: "qui miser in campis merens errabat alienis | ipse suum cor edens, hominum vestigia vitans."'; see F. Petrarca, *Il mio segreto*, E. Fenzi (Ed.), Milan 1992, p. 226. Petrarch alludes to *Iliad*, VI, 201f. The 'universal' epics of Homer had since antiquity been considered as treasuries of literary inventions, as can be deduced from the words of Demetrius, cited in Politian's commentary to the *Iliad*: 'Omnibus enim (ut ipse ait) mortalibus libros suos quasi immensum quoddam atque infinitum pelagus proposuit, ut ex eo singuli quantum cuique usu esset, exhauriret [...]'; cited after Levine-Rubinstein 1982 (as in n. 90 above), p. 223.

[123] Quintilian, *Institutio Oratoria*, V, 11, 40, reports that Athens won the battle of Salamis only because of a verse from the *Iliad*.

[124] Ibid., VIII, 3, 62: 'magna virtus res, de quibus loquimur, clare atque, ut cerni videantur, enuntiare'. Politian gives 'representatio' as a further synonym for *auxesis* (Levine-Rubinstein 1982, as in n. 90 above, p. 210). Quintilian adds 'illustratio'; see S. Galland-Hallyn, *Les yeux de l'éloquence. Poétiques humanistes de l'évidence*, Orléans 1995, pp. 99f.

[125] See Levine-Rubinstein 1982 (as in n. 90 above), p. 210.

[126] Speroni 1740 (as in n. 93 above), vol. 1, p. 407: 'Il qual cieco pien di occhi'.

[127] Lucian, *Eikones*, 8; Petrarch calls him 'Primo pintor delle memorie antiche' (*Trionfo della fama*, III, 8), see Lee 1967 (as in n. 25 above), p. 4, n. 6. Petrarch's verses on Homer are also cited in Varchi 1960 (as in n. 3 above), p. 53, and in L. Dolce, *Dialogo della pittura intitolato l'Aretino*, in Barocchi (Ed.) 1960 (as in n. 3 above), vol. 1, p. 155.

[128] Aristotle, *Poetics*, 24, 14. English translation after Aristotle, *The Poetics*, transl. W. Hamilton Fyfe, Cambridge, Mass., London [1927] 1973. Benedetto Varchi sees tragedy, founded by Homer with his epics, as the essential description of a person, comparing it in this respect with sculpture; see Mendelsohn 1982 (as in n. 2

description as a model to arrive at a convincing depiction of Zeus. [129] It is in connection with the Greek poet's epic poems that the topos of poetry's immortality is invoked most often; Homer provides proof that nothing keeps the memory of heroes alive more effectively than literature. An epigram on Ulysses might be cited as a succinct example:

> Ever is the sea unkind to the son of Laertes; the flood has bathed the picture and washed off the figure from the wood. What did it gain thereby? For in Homer's verses the image of him is painted on immortal pages. [130]

Timanthes

The single verse of Homer's epic with its amplifying comparison and vivid force forms a picture within the picture, a literary image of sorrow bestowing an inner life on Ugolino's painted likeness. Such indirect depiction recalls the device of Timanthes, who relied on the intelligence of the beholder when painting his *Sacrifice of Iphigenia*. This work, as described by numerous ancient authors, showed the relatives of Iphigenia with faces and gestures charged with mourning. Only the face of her father, King Agamemnon, remained veiled, not because Timanthes was not able to paint his strong emotion, but rather 'because he could not depict it appropriately' ('digne'). [131] The painter on the one hand responded to the high social decorum of a king, on the other hand he implicitly showed the father's immeasurable grief by his very refusal to paint it, thus creating a deliberate gap which the initiated beholder can fill with his own imagination. This picture has consistently been praised in the tradition of rhetoric, cited as an example of decorum or propriety, as 'we call proper that, which is appropriate to time and person'. Some things therefore have to be left out, because 'for reasons of dignity they cannot be expressed'. [132]

---

[129] above), p. 133.

'Fidias [...] confessava avere imparato da Omero poeta dipingere Iove con molta divina maestà.'; Alberti 1973 (as in n. 17 above), p. 94, following Valerius Maximus, *Facta et dicta memorabilia*, III, 7, 4, with reference to *Iliad*, I, 528-30.

[130] *Anthologia Graeca*, XVI, 125; cited after Shearman [1988] 1992 (as in n. 2 above), p. 115, n. 20.

[131] The most exhaustive accounts of this anecdote are found in Valerius Maximus (see n. 146 below) and Pliny, *Naturalis historia*, 35, 73f: 'Nam Timanthi vel plurimum adfuit ingenii. eius enim est Iphigenia oratorum laudibus celebrata, qua stante ad aras peritura cum maestos pinxisset omnes praecipueque patruum et tristitiae omnem imaginem consumpsisset, patris ipsius voltum velavit, quem digne non poterat ostendere.' The story is told in a similar way by Quintilian (*Institutio Oratoria*, II, 13, 13): '[...] non reperiens quo digne modo patris vultum posset exprimere, velavit eius caput [...].' Alberti 1973 (as in n. 17 above), p. 74, comments on Timanthes's device: '[...] e così lassò si pensasse qual non si vedea suo acerbissimo merore.' Also Dolce 1960 (as in n. 127 above), p. 147, cites Timanthes as an exemplary painter.

[132] Cicero, *Orator*, 74: '[...] decere quasi aptum esse consentaneumque tempori et

The notion of a decorum appropriate to high social standing might account for a characteristic of Bronzino's portraiture that a number of scholars have criticised, judging his likenesses as rigid, insensitive, or distanced.[133] Contemporaries, on the other hand, never saw the sitters' lack of movement as a deficiency. Giorgio Vasari, for example, calls the Martelli portrait, along with some others, 'all very natural, executed with incredible diligence, and finished so well that nothing more could be desired'. A few lines below, he cites the portraits of Bartolomeo Panciatichi and his wife as being 'so natural that they seem truly alive, and nothing is wanting in them save breath'.[134] The masterful imitation of surfaces, their naturalness and *verosimile*,[135] are here construed as signs of liveliness.

Bronzino's precise, calm mode of representation may be seen as related to the discourse of the *paragone*. Bronzino's friend, Benedetto Varchi, in his *Due Lezzioni*, points out that painting can approach sculpture's truth to life only by use of colours and the depiction of details ('minutiae').[136] Through a sufficient accumulation of such 'accidentals' painting can approximate, Varchi continues, the 'universality' of sculpture which defines its subjects 'substantially'.[137] With Bronzino the accurate, documentary description of the outside appearance reaches a state of perfection as yet unknown in the Florentine Cinquecento, approximating his paintings to sculpture's 'universal' description.[138] In rhetorical terms, this manner of representation could be

---

personae [...].' Then he refers to the painting of Iphigenia's sacrifice. Quintilian, *Institutio Oratoria*, II, 13, 12: 'Quid? non in oratione operienda sunt quaedam, sive ostendi non debent, sive exprimi pro dignitate non possunt?' Before he had addressed Apelles's portrait of Antigonos, and he now turns to Timanthes.

[133] Schulze 1909 (as in n. 74 above), p. 7, describes Bronzino's sitters as 'verschlossen in ihrer Würde'. Similarly, A. Emiliani, *Il Bronzino*, Busto Arsizio 1960, p. 33, understands them as enclosed in their external dignity.

[134] '[...] tutti furono naturalissimi, fatti con incredibile diligenza, e di maniera finiti che più non si può desiderare.' '[...] i ritratti di lui e della moglie, tanto naturali che paiono vivi veramente e che non manchi loro se non lo spirito.'; Vasari (as in n. 11 above), vol. 6, 1987, p. 232. English translations cited after G. Vasari, *Lives of the Most Eminent Painters, Sculptors and Architects*, transl. G. Du C. De Vere [1912–15], repr. New York 1976, vol. 10, p. 5.

[135] Vasari calls the portrait of Francesco de' Medici 'pittura molto simile al vero'; Vasari (as in n. 11 above), vol. 6, 1987, p. 237. He probably refers to the portrait of c. 1551 in the Uffizi which is likely to depict Francesco (Baccheschi 1973, as in n. 74 above, cat. 88), as he cites it in connection with the portrait of Giovanni de' Medici of about the same period (1550–51; ibid., cat. 86).

[136] See Mendelsohn 1982 (as in n. 2 above), p. 121.

[137] See ibid., p. 122.

[138] The essential advantage of sculpture, as emphasized by Varchi, the substance of its three-dimensional material, is in Bronzino's opinion not a merit of the sculptor's art. In his fragmentary letter to Varchi, dealing with the *paragone*, he writes about sculptors: '[...] non imitano più la natura per far di rilievo che altrimenti, anzi

‘E NUOVI OMERI, E PLATI’

called 'evidence', or, in Italian, *chiarezza* – and 'chiaro' is indeed the term employed by Varchi to characterise Bronzino's art, writing, in several sonnets, about his friend's 'chiaro pennello' or 'chiaro stile'. [139]

The untroubled dignity of the sitters and their elegant, but unaffected poses correspond with the demand expressed in courtly literature that one's behaviour should be natural, measured and without affectation. [140] Varchi, on the other hand, following a long art theoretical tradition, sees the depiction of emotion as the essential strength and task of painting, indeed as its only possibility to visualize the inner life of a person, 'il di dentro'. [141] Thus each portrait embodies the challenging conflict between the depiction of emotion, of liveliness as the core of a person's presence, and quiet dignity as the conventional and obligatory attitude of the individual within society. A solution to this

---

tolgono la cosa che già era di rilievo fatta della natura, onde tutto quello che vi si truova di tondo o di largo o l'altro non è dell'arte, perché prima vi erano e larghezza et altezza e tutte le parti che si dànno a' corpi solidi, ma solo è dell'arte le linee che cercondano detto corpo, le quali sono in superficie; onde, com'è detto, non è dell'arte l'essere di rilievo, ma della natura [...].'; see Varchi 1960 (as in n. 3 above), pp. 66f. On Varchi's different view, see ibid., p. 43. The combination of a sculptural, yet exclusively artificial 'rilievo' of his figures through an accumulation of surface details might be seen as Bronzino's own, original way to create a universal art of painting. Bronzino's opinion parallels in many ways that of Leonardo; see Leonardo, Pedretti (Ed.) 1964 (as in n. 17 above), p. 39. Wildmoser 1989 (as in n. 61 above), p. 200, also refers to Bronzino's letter, without however pointing out its central argument. In the eyes of Mendelsohn 1982 (as in n. 2 above), p. 152 and n. 54, the statuettes on Bronzino's portraits show only a limited three-dimensionality, thereby emphasizing the three-dimensional appearance of the sitters and their *anima*. On Bronzino's 'sculptural' style, see Cox-Rearick 1993 (as in n. 77 above), pp. 118, 125f.

[139] See Appendix 1.1., v. 2; Appendix 10., v. 9. Cf. Gaston 1991 (as in n. 38 above), p. 268. Bronzino even wrote a 'Capitolo' entitled 'Dell' esser chiaro', see A. Bronzino, *Rime in burla*, F. Petrucci Nardelli (Ed.), Rome 1988, p. 379. Of course, 'chiaro' can also mean 'illustrious, famous'. In Quintilian's opinion, the detailed representation of an object belongs to the category of evidence; the object must not necessarily be represented in its true form, its 'probability' – 'verosimile' – is enough to generate a credible image in the minds of the audience and to arouse their passions; Quintilian, *Institutio Oratoria*, 4, 2, 123; 8, 3, 67-70. See H. Lausberg, *Handbuch der literarischen Rhetorik. Eine Grundlegung der Literaturwissenschaft*, Munich 1960, p. 402. For Quintilian, *Institutio Oratoria*, 8, 3, 61, evidence belongs to the 'ornatus' of speech, which recalls Varchi's expression of Bronzino's 'ornato stile' (see Appendix 1.10., v. 10). Cf. Mendelsohn 1982 (as in n. 2 above), p. 128, for Varchi's account of 'ornatus' in his *Due Lezzioni*.

[140] Castiglione 1960 (as in n. 88 above), p. 71 (1, 41) writes about the 'affettazione, la qual or potete comprender quanto sia contraria, e levi la grazia d'ogni operazion così del corpo come dell'animo'.

[141] See n. 6 above.

79

conflict demands a painterly intelligence like Timanthes's, exceeding mere technical refinement. Bronzino appears to have realized and in some cases taken up this challenge. A solution worthy of Timanthes is found in his *Portrait of a lute-player* (Pl. 19). Observing the musician's face, one will at first make out only its left side, brightly lit and of stoic tranquillity. On closer inspection, however, one perceives the right, the dark side of the sitter, where the eyebrow is raised in anger, setting the whole forehead in motion. Momentary impulse seems at first glance controlled in favour of a dignified appearance, but a second look charges the countenance with all the more impact. Bronzino thus found a way to express both aloof calm and lively passion.[142] In a similar way, though even more concealed, only the Greek poetry on the *Portrait of Ugolino Martelli* brings the sitter's emotions out into the open. Homer's verses give a description of Ugolino, grant insight into his soul, load the image with meaning. More clearly than in the *Lute-player*, the painter challenges an elite, learned audience, as he solves the problem of twofold propriety by relying on an external element: the intelligence of the beholder.[143]

What we are invited to read is a comparison, a figure of speech, used, as Cicero put it, to move the soul.[144] Ugolino's gesture pushes it into a strategic position right at the beginning of the visual 'reading' of the painting. There it assumes a function analogous to that of the human figure which Alberti suggests should be placed at the edge of a composition, inviting the beholder through an expression of emotional involvement to share the passions of the depicted figures, be they crying or laughing.[145] Similarly, in the rhetorical

[142] Already in antiquity the word 'supercilium' was used metonymically for 'superbia', 'gravitas' and 'severitas'. Dolce 1960 (as in n. 127 above), p. 152, mentions the raising of eyebrows as a means to depict emotion: 'Aretino' maintains: '[...] il pittore [...] dipinge non di meno i pensieri e gli affetti dell'animo'. 'Fabrini' replies: 'Ben dite signor Pietro, ma questi per certi atti esteriori si comprendono; e spesso per uno inarcar di ciglia, o increspar di fronte, o per altri segni appariscono i segreti interni, tal che molte volte non fa bisogno delle fenestre di Socrate.' Already L. Campbell, *Renaissance Portraits. European Portrait-Painting in the 14th, 15th and 16th Centuries*, New Haven, London 1990, p. 25, emphasizes the diverging treatments of the two halves of a face regarding Bronzino's *Portrait of a woman* in Turin (Baccheschi 1973, as in n. 74 above, cat. 92).
[143] Quintilian, *Institutio Oratoria*, II, 13, 13, concludes his version of the story of Timanthes with the words: '[...] velavit eius caput et suo cuique animo dedit aestimandum'.
[144] 'ad commovendum', here after Bauer 1992 (as in n. 119 above), col. 445.
[145] Alberti 1973 (as in n. 17 above), p. 72 (II, 42): 'E piacemi sia nella storia chi ammonisca e insegni a noi quello che ivi si facci, o chiami con la mano a vedere, o con viso cruccioso e con gli occhi turbati minacci che niuno verso loro vada, o dimostri qualche pericolo o cosa ivi maravigliosa, o te inviti a piagnere con loro insieme o a ridere.' Cf. ibid., p. 70 (II, 41): 'Poi moverà l'istoria l'animo quando gli

theory of 'evidence', emotions are defined as means to convey meaning effectively and to motivate cognition and insight. [146] 'Words pronounced with a certain strong emotion' will, remarks Marsilio Ficino, have the power to direct 'images' and their effects to the audience. [147]

Knowledge of Greek was restricted, even among those with humanist interests, to a small community. [148] Ugolino's choice is elitist, and the glance into his 'di dentro' is permitted only to a beholder with linguistic ambitions equal to his own. Such a limitation of the audience is appropriate to the poet, as Marco Girolamo Vida, following Horace, states: 'A gift of the gods are the Muses. Stay away, uninitiated crowd'. [149] The path leading to a deeper understanding of the poet's portrait is as narrow as that to poetry itself, open only to few. [150] They will be able to carry out the task set by the Greek text and every time they read, or rather, recite the ancient poet's words, they can make his young follower cry. [151]

---

uomini ivi dipinti molto porgeranno suo proprio movimento d'animo. Interviene da natura, quale nulla più che lei si truova rapace di cose a sé simile, che piagniamo con chi piange, e ridiamo con chi ride, e doglianci con chi si duole.' One might add that already Quintilian paralleled figures of speech to those of art. After discussing the *Diskobolos* of Myron, he points out: 'Quem quidem gratiam et delectationem adferunt figurae, quaeque in sensibus quaeque in verbis sunt.'; Quintilian, *Institutio Oratoria*, II, 13, 11.

[146] Cf. also the famous words of Horace (*Ars Poetica*, 101–103): 'ut ridentibus adrident, ita flentibus adflent | humani vultus: si vis me flere, dolendum est | primum ipsi tibi.' Similarly, Valerius Maximus – interestingly when treating Timanthes's painting of the sacrifice of Iphigenia – sees the excitation of passion in the beholder as the reason for his insight and understanding: 'Itaque pictura eius aruspicis et amici et fratris lacrimis madet, patris fletum spectantis adfectu aestimandum reliquit.'; Valerius Maximus, *Facta et dicta memorabilia*, VIII, 2, 6.

[147] Marsilio Ficino, *De vita libri tres*, II, XXI, 1–3: 'Verba praeterea quaedam acriore quodam affectu pronuntiata vim circa imagines magnam habere censent ad effectum earum illuc proprie dirigendum, quorum affectus intenduntur et verba'.

[148] See F. Bruni, 'Sperone Speroni e l'Accademia degli Infiammati', *Filologia e Letteratura*, 13, 1967, pp. 24–71 (esp. p. 33).

[149] Vida 1976 (as in n. 92 above), p. 36 (I, 515): 'Dona deûm Musae. vulgus, procul este, profanum', and ibid., p. 34 (I, 503): 'Parcite, mortales, sacros vexare poetas'.

[150] Cf. Vida 1976 (as in n. 92 above), p. 1 (III, 360f.): 'Ipse deûm genitor divinum noluit artem | Omnibus exposituram vulgo, immeritisque patere. | Atque ideo, turbam, quo longe arceret inertem, | Angustam esse viam voluit, paucisque licere'.

[151] The concept that the moving tongue of the reader or his breath re-animates the person described in a poem is an old one and gains increased importance during the sixteenth century; cf. W. Shakespeare, sonnet 81, V. 1–3: 'Your monument shall be my gentle verse, | Which eyes not yet created shall o'er-read; | And tongues to be your being shall rehearse'.

The Weeping Song

But why does Ugolino cry? Already the simile of the fountain leads us to his
principal occupation, to poetry. On the Parnassian mountain springs Castalia,
giver of poetic inspiration, where the laurel grows and the Muses gather. [152] As
a metaphor of eloquence, the fountain can stand for the poet himself, alluding
to the richness and usefulness of his speech. This is why Dante calls Virgil
'that fountain, | which issues such a large river of words'. [153] The verse
indicated by Ugolino describes a dark fountain of black waters, and the mere
sound of the word 'melánhydros' may recall melancholy as an aspect of the
poet's creative state. [154]

[152] See E. Meyer, 'Kastalia', in *Der kleine Pauly. Lexikon der Antike in fünf Bänden*, K.
Ziegler and W. Sontheimer (Eds), vol. 3, Munich 1979, col. 150. On the
sixteenth-century view cf. Vida's advice to the young poets: 'Jam tunc incipiat
riguos cedere fontes, | Et Phoebum, & dulces Musas assuescat amare.' Vida 1976
(as in n. 92 above), p. 8 (I, 87f.).

[153] Inferno, I, 79f.: 'O! sei tu Virgilio, e quella fonte, | che spande di parlar sì largo
fiume.' Cf. again Vida 1976 (as in n. 92 above), p. 30 (I, 409–11): 'Nulla dies tamen
interea, tibi nulla abeat nox, | Quin aliquid vatum sacrorum e fontibus almis |
Hauseris, ac dulcem labris admoveris amnem.' The image of the fountain is
already common in humanistic self-representation of the Quattrocento, the most
conspicuous example being the medal of Lodovico Carbone, where one reads a
version of Dante's verse; see Woods-Marsden 1995 (as in n. 116 above), pp. 1105f.,
pls 15, 16.

[154] The well-known concept of melancholy as a 'sacred disease' of poets had been
developed most explicitly in the ancient peripatetic text known as *Problem XXX*,
where it is stated that sibyls, prophets and those who are 'divinely inspired' are
melancholics, as well as 'most of the poets'; cited after R. Klibansky, E. Panofsky
and F. Saxl, *Saturn and Melancholy. Studies in the History of Natural Philosphy,
Religion and Art*, Cambridge 1964, pp. 19, 24. Several of the examples of
melancholy referred to in *Problem XXX* are taken from the *Iliad*. Marsilio Ficino
connected the concept of melancholy with the Platonic 'furor poeticus'. For a
'divinely inspired' Christian poet, melancholy is an appropriate mood. Ugolino
might have alluded to it, when, in his inauguration speech as consul of the
Florentine academy, he records the 'strana et horribile malattia' that had affected
him in 1541. Varchi wrote a sonnet to Ugolino describing his 'infino a qui gelata
mente' (Varchi 1834, as in n. 71 above, p. 567, 'S'amor che sempre più
velocemente', v. 5), recalling the concept of 'frigiditas', the primal cold state of
black bile; see Klibansky, Panofsky and Saxl 1964 (as above), p. 23. Homer himself
was presented as a melancholic in Agrippa von Nettesheim's *Occulta Philosophia*
of 1531; see ibid., p. 499, n. 271. Varchi seems to have known Agrippa's writings
reasonably well; see Mendelsohn 1982 (as in n. 2 above), pp. 23f., n. 60. In late
antiquity Agamemnon was considered a melancholic, at least by Aretaios in his
work on chronic deseases. His testimony is again the text of the *Iliad*, though not
the verse indicated by Ugolino, but I, 103f. See H. Flashar, *Melancholie und
Melancholiker in den medizinischen Theorien der Antike*, Berlin 1966, pp. 76f. The
Greek 'melánhydros' could be conceived of as a pun, as 'mélan' also means 'ink'.

In fashioning himself as a poet, Ugolino creates an image that had not always been a positive one. The precarious question of whether poetry was a useful occupation or idleness, *otium*, was much debated. The defenders of poetry were confronted with the authoritative weight of Plato's reproaches, who judged the poet unfit for any society founded on reason and religion. Nonetheless, a successful defence was possible, and one can be read in Bernardino Daniello's *Della Poetica* of 1536.[155] The author's point of view is most likely to have been known to Ugolino and to have conformed with his own opinion.[156] Daniello starts his tract with a conversation among learned men disputing the old question of whether philosophy or poetry should be given preference. 'Messer Domenico' acts as defender of philosophy. He exposes the poets' 'fables and lies'; their descriptions are, in his view, loaded with inappropriate 'affects of the soul', above all where the gods are concerned. Furthermore, they have 'burdened the minds of the others with useless fright through their horrible and terrifying inventions, sorrowful lamentations and weeping'.[157] Works of this kind excite 'a thousand incurable worries and a thousand improper desires in the chaste hearts of youths, and light a thousand scorching flames'. With this observation, he believes he has demonstrated that poets are of no use at all to society, that they 'choose for

The first melancholic cited in *Problem* XXX is Hercules, as proven by his suicide on Mount Oeta (see Klibansky, Panofsky and Saxl 1964, as above, p. 18). This very scene served as emblem for the Accademia degli Infiammati, accompanied by the words 'Arso il mortale al Ciel n'andrà l'eterno' (see Cerreta 1957, as in n. 68 above, p. 251). I should like to see the arm of the infant Hercules wrestling with a snake in the much-damaged relief in Ugolino's portrait that is so deliberately 'uncovered' by the tablecloth.

[155] Daniello 1970 (as in n. 38 above). On circumstances and interlocutors see ibid., pp. 231-3.

[156] Already since the 1530s Ugolino knew Daniello and his circle, which he himself belonged to by the time the portrait was painted. On Daniello, see B. Weinberg, *A History of Literary Criticism in the Italian Renaissance*, 2 vols, Chicago 1961, vol. 2, pp. 721-4, and M. R. De Grammatica, in *Dizionario biografico degli Italiani*, vol. 32, Rome 1986, pp. 608-10. Daniello, born in Lucca, resided in Padua from 1533 until his death in 1565. He first stayed with his teacher, Trifone Gabriele. The latter was known to Ugolino, as he salutes him in a sonnet of c. 1537 addressed to Varchi departing for Padua ('Voi ve n'andate senza me per l'onde'): 'Infinite per me grazie rendete | Umilmente al gran Bembo, e'l buon Trifone | Salutate a mio nome [...].' (v. 9-11), cited after Varchi 1834 (as in n. 71 above), p. 566. The proximity of Daniello's evaluation of poetry to Varchi's view is pointed out in Mendelsohn 1982 (as in n. 2 above), p. 9.

[157] Daniello 1970 (as in n. 38 above), p. 236: '[...] i quali con le lor favole e menzogne hanno molte cose false e bugiarde narrato degli idii loro, cose di loro non degne attribuendo sovente, sì come sono gli affetti dell'animo, i risi, i giuochi e mille altre lascive et inconvenienti cose; et oltre a ciò con orribili e spaventevoli fizioni e tristi lamenti e pianti l'altrui menti di vano terrore ingombrate'.

imitation what they should flee most'.[158]

'Messer Domenico' wields the weapons provided by Plato in his criticism of poetry in the *Republic*[159] where he suggests that poets and painters, with their art of imitation, cannot reach the ideal archetypes of reality. The poet is not tolerated in Plato's state because he 'sets up in each individual soul a vicious constitution by fashioning phantoms far removed from reality'.[160] Thus the poet cannot be a useful teacher to humankind, his art is 'a corruption of the mind of all listeners'.[161] Like 'Messer Domenico', Plato did not shy away from citing Homer as a bad example, though he is called the 'first teacher and beginner'[162] of tragedy. In Book 10 of the *Republic*, Socrates states:

> Listen and reflect. I think you know that the very best of us, when we hear Homer or some other of the makers of tragedy imitating one of the heroes who is in grief, and is delivering a long tirade in his lamentations or chanting and beating his breast, feel pleasure, and abandon ourselves and accompany the representation with sympathy and eagerness, and we praise as an excellent poet the one who most strongly affects us in this way.[163]

This is the very effect which for Plato generates the negative influence of poetry. When we share the tragic accidents of others, 'after feeding fat the emotions of pity there, it is not easy to restrain it in our own sufferings'.[164] As he esteems it manly and useful to rely on the restraining force of reason rather than on the vile, compulsive faculties of the soul, the poet is denied admission to his state.

Looking at the portrait again, we are now able to recognise that Ugolino's finger touches an old sore. The verse he points at contains exactly such a 'lamentation', a 'hero in grief'. With his gesture, Ugolino not only evokes the trick question of Plato-Socrates, the question of whether he was touched by the magic of Homer's poetry,[165] but also provides an answer to Plato's criticism with an equally Socratic 'yes, but...'. Turning back to Daniello's treatise, 'Messer Lampridio' helps us to understand why Homer's account of the emotional hero Agamemnon can be used to beat Plato with his own weapons. 'Lampridio' takes up Plato's arguments and reforges them one

---

[158]   Ibid., p. 273: 'Domenico' records the 'atti propriamente a destar ne' casti petti de' giovani mille insanabili cure, mille illeciti desii e mille cocenti fiamme accendervi.' He adds: 'quelle cose a imitare si pongono che più per loro fuggire si deveriano'.

[159]   He argues, as Daniello 1970 (as in n. 38 above), p. 236, points out 'col testimonio di Platone'.

[160]   Plato, *The Republic*, X, 605c; English translation here and below after Plato, *The Republic*, transl. P. Shorey [1935], repr. Cambridge, Mass., London 1980.

[161]   Ibid., 595b.

[162]   Ibid., 595c.

[163]   Ibid., 605c–d.

[164]   Ibid., 606b.

[165]   Ibid., X, 607c: 'Do not you yourself feel her [poetry's] magic and especially when Homer is her interpreter?'.

by one into a defence of poetry. Homer is restored as prime example of poetic usefulness:

> [...] that the poet teaches us to live well and in a civilised way and [furthermore] that he is for us a companion on our way to virtuous deeds, I could prove through the testimony of Horace and the latter with the authority of Homer.[166]

Plato himself had stated, 'Lampridio' continues, that the entirety of divine and human wisdom is encapsulated in one work of Homer. Furthermore, the philosophy of Plato is, just like Aristotle's, deeply indebted to the rhapsodist.[167] Ultimately, Plato himself was not only a philosopher, but also a poet. Every poet who deserves this title, on the other hand, has to be versed in philosophy and theology. Wisdom is the writer's source, and as the imitative art of the poet is directed by the 'divine' power of his intellect, his works are not necessarily, as Plato had claimed, inferior to nature and 'three removes from reality',[168] but have the capacity to correct nature by avoiding its errors.[169] Moreover, the poet's form of teaching is the most pleasant.[170] He can be a leader for those who went astray morally, a lawgiver for the savages, a founder of states. He surpasses the philosopher not only because he preceded him historically in fulfilling all these tasks, but above all because he will always perform these tasks better – the philosopher's speech lacks the overwhelming effect on the audience, it lacks the force of excitement, in short, the 'poetic stimulus'.[171]

It is conceded to the poet alone to portray passion, and thereby to arouse passion in the listener. Through passion, poetry aims at a 'persuasion' of the audience, the purpose of which is a deeper understanding of the essential truths concealed in the verses.[172] The model for this poetry of passion

[166]   Daniello 1970 (as in n. 38 above), p. 239: 'E che 'l poeta a bene e civilmente vivere n'ammaestri e ci sia scorta alla via delle virtuose operazioni, vi potrei io col testimonio d'Orazio e quegli con l'auttorità d'Omero far chiaro'.

[167]   'Gabriele Trifone' maintains that Plato had stated: 'l'arti e le scienze tutte, così divine come humane, in un poema d'Omero esser raccolte'; Daniello 1970 (as in n. 38 above), p. 241, and n. 6.

[168]   Plato, *The Republic*, X, 599 a.

[169]   Daniello 1970 (as in n. 38 above), p. 230.

[170]   Cf. Varchi's summary in a letter to a disciple, dated 8 November 1539: '[...] non merita il nome di scrittore non che di poeta chi non insegna i costumi buoni, ma, perché son più modi d'insegnare, quel dei poeti è più bello e più utile [...]'; cited in Plaisance 1973 (as in n. 90 above), p. 372.

[171]   Daniello 1970 (as in n. 38 above), p. 239: 'Laonde all'ncontro l'orazione et il parlare del filosofo (per lo più) suol esser secco senza niuna forza in sé, senz'alcun poetico stimolo [...]'.

[172]   Daniello 1970 (as in n. 38 above), p. 235: 'Solo il poeta co'suoi versi risveglia altrui dal sonno corporeo alle vigilie della mente; dalle oscure e folte tenebre della ignoranza scorge nel chiaro e bello splendore del vero; richiama dalla morte alla vita, dalla oblivione delle cose celesti e divine alla rimembranza e riconoscenza di

is first and foremost Homer, whose *Iliad* Aristotle called 'affective' ('pathetikós'),[173] and along with him Orpheus.[174] This 'sacred interpreter of the gods had', according to Daniello,

> with his eloquent chanting put an end to the murders and violence that the rough people, living without any laws, perpetrated each day against one another, and led them from the woods into the cities, to a civilised and proper life.[175]

Orpheus was regarded as a pagan predecessor of David, who in turn mirrors Ugolino's pose in the portrait. A year before Daniello's treatise appeared in Venice, an interpretative essay on the psalms had been published in the same city, written by Pietro Aretino and destined to have wide success.[176] It tells the story of David's sins and explains the writing of the psalms as the result of recognition, remorse and change, in short, of Aristotelian 'katharsis'. The king realizes his sins and burns with desire to 'purge [his] soul through the purifying power of penitence'.[177] In this process weeping has a decisive rôle. In Aretino's words, David says: 'with the tears that come from the veins of my heart I pray you, my Lord, to heal my body'.[178] In tears, the 'shepherd of the Jewish people'[179] begins to sing the psalms, that is, to compose his poetry:[180]

---

    quelle; preme, stimola, infiamma e commove; l'altrui belle et alte operazioni con grandissima copia e con bellissime figure descrive'.

[173] Aristotle, *Poetics*, 24, 3.

[174] Orphic poetry already gained considerable importance in the works of Ficino; see J. B. Allen, *The Platonism of Marsilio Ficino*, Berkeley, Los Angeles, London 1984, p. 43.

[175] Daniello 1970 (as in n. 38 above), p. 234: 'Né per altro essersi lasciato scritto nelle antiche carte il sacro interprete degli iddii, Orfeo, aver mitigato le crudelissimi tigri, fatto a' superbi e feroci leoni deporre la rabbia loro, se non perché esso con la sua eloquenza poetando tolse gli uomini, rozzi e senza alcuna legge viventi, dalle occisioni e violenti rapine che tutto dì fra essi medesimi commettevano, e dalle selve nelle città a civilmente e costumatamente vivere ridusse.' Daniello here refers to the most famous defense of poetry, to Horace, *De Arte poetica*, esp. 391–407.

[176] Ugolino's relative and friend, Niccolò Martelli, was moved to tears of contrition when reading Aretino's *Salmi*, proving the success of such 'passionate' poetry; see *Lettere scritte a Pietro Aretino* 1968 (as in n. 54 above), vol. 3, pp. 119f. (Letter of 10 April 1540): '[...] chi non è di sasso a leggere la bella esposizione delli sette Salmi che facesti del gran Cantore non verserà egli per gli occhi la contrizion del core?'.

[177] Cited after [Pietro Aretino], *I sette Salmi della penitentia di Davit. Composti per Pietro Aretino e ristampati nuovamente*, Venice 1539, fol. 3v: '[...] io bramo purificar l'anima mia, col purgo de la penitentia'. The importance of Aristotelian concepts for the (art) theory of Speroni and Aretino has been studied in von Rosen 2001 (as in n. 54, above), esp. pp. 182–7.

[178] Ibid., fol. 4r: '[...] & col pianto che pure esce de le vene del core; ti prego Signore che renda sane le mie membra'.

Now David, inflamed with the Holy Spirit that the Lord had bestowed on him for the virtue of his penitence, turned to reform his people, who, moved by the example of the good king, set all their actions on that one aim, to be perfect in the face of God.[181]

Like David, the members of the Paduan academy understood themselves as inflamed, 'infiammati'; the purpose of their compositions was the transmission of theological truth. Backed up by David, Ugolino can play his last trump card against Plato, with the book he holds under his left hand. Pietro Bembo had introduced his *Rime*, in imitation and self-confident emulation of Petrarch, with a sonnet explaining the genesis and aims of his compositions.[182] The poem, which Ugolino had discussed in one of his Paduan lectures, starts with the following words: 'I wept and sang of the anguish and the cruel struggle that I had to endure for many, many years'.[183] Bembo then invokes the help of the Muses to keep his writings alive even after his death. Those who read his verses will learn from his 'harsh example' to turn their backs on their 'vain desire' and to find the right path, leading to God.[184] This form of poetry, drawing its persuasive power from the same remorseful weeping that also moves Ugolino in his portrait, is thus proven to be a Christian and moral art, and the poet of such verses can no longer be denied admission to Plato's or any other society.[185]

---

[179] Ibid., fol. 6v: 'il Pastor de i popoli Hebrei'; ibid., fol. 33r: 'pallido per il digiuno, & oscuro per la penitentia [...]'.

[180] Ibid., fol. 33r, Aretino describes 'le salmi che egli aveva pianti col canto [...]'.

[181] Ibid., fol. 33r: 'Hora David infiammato da lo Spirito Santo, che in lui haveva infuso il Signore, per la vertù del pentimento, si ritornò a correggere i popoli suoi; i quali mossi da lo esempio del buon Re, tutte le operationi loro volsero al fine di farsi perfetti nel conspetto di Dio'.

[182] On Bembo's *Rime*, see A. Kablitz, 'Lyrische Rede als Kommentar. Anmerkungen zur Petrarca-Imitatio in Bembos "Rime"', in K. W. Hempfer and G. Regn (Eds) 1993 (as in n. 97 above), pp. 29–76.

[183] Bembo 1997 (as in n. 11 above), p. 507 (sonnet 1): 'Piansi e cantai lo strazio e l'aspra guerra | ch'i'ebbi a sostener molti e molti anni'.

[184] Ibid., v. 5–14: 'Dive, per cui s'apre Elicona e serra, | use far a la morte illustri inganni, | date allo stil, che naque de' miei danni, | viver, quand'io sarò spento e sotterra. | Chè potranno talor gli ammanti accorti, | queste mie rime leggendo, al van desio | ritoglier l'alme col mio duro exempio, | e quella strada, ch'a buon fine porti, | scorger da l'altre, e quanto adorar Dio | solo si dee nel mondo, ch'è suo tempio'.

[185] Repentance as a theme of sixteenth-century Italian portraiture is worth a special study; the same has recently been suggested for Dutch seventeenth-century art in S. Dickey, '"Met een wenende ziel ... doch droge ogen." Women Holding Handkerchiefs in Seventeenth-Century Dutch Portraits', *Nederlands kunsthistorisch Jaarboek* ('Image and Self-Image in Netherlandish Art, 1550–1750'), 46, 1995, pp. 332–67.

But Plato had also exiled the painter, maintaining, among other reproaches, that imitative art could easily represent an irrational and irritated disposition, whereas 'the intelligent and temperate disposition, always remaining approximately the same', was not easy to imitate. [186] In the likeness of Ugolino Martelli, however, the painter succeeded in shaping an image of a young, virtuous, Christian poet, foreshadowed in the statue of David. His socially appropriate appearance of calm and contemplation is shown by the verse of the *Iliad* to be the controlled surface of internal passion, a passion which lends overwhelming force to the sitter's literary compositions, signposts on the way to virtue.

Bronzino's portrait of Ugolino, together with the earlier Lorenzo Lenzi and the later, better-known likeness of Laura Battiferra form a group of their own. They all depict poets and are probably the first series of paintings in which poetry plays a not merely functional part but becomes the core of the aesthetics of visual representation. In numerous sonnets on Bronzino's portraiture[187] his contemporaries pointed out how in the person of this painter the competing arts of poetry and painting met. In Varchi's words, he is ' such a great Apelles and no smaller an Apollo', [188] drawing on a formula so far usually reserved for Michelangelo. He succinctly characterises his friend's areas of expertise: as a painter he can depict a 'precise likeness' of a person's external appearance, but, so Varchi states in another sonnet, only as a poet can he represent the 'beauty inside'. [189] As he masterfully handles both arts, however, his 'double style' ('doppio stile') [190] enables him to bring forth the perfect image of a person.

[186]   Plato, *The Republic*, X, 604d–e. Translation as in n. 160 above.

[187]   The *Portrait of Laura Battiferra* (Florence, Palazzo Vecchio) is in many respects a close relative of Ugolino's likeness; it was analysed by Carol Plazzotta (1998, as in n. 30 above, passim), and, referring to her results, von Flemming 1996 (as in n. 33 above), passim. Plazzotta emphasizes the relation to Simone Martini's portrait of Laura as described by Petrarch and the importance of the *paragone*-debate. See also G. Smith, 'Bronzino's "Portrait of Laura Battiferri"', *Source*, 15, 1996, pp. 30–8. The sonnets on the *Portrait of Laura Battiferra* are collected in the appendix of Plazzotta 1998 (as above), pp. 260–3; some sonnets on various other portraits by Bronzino are assembled in the Appendix following this article, which can be seen as a supplement to Deborah Parker's recent analysis *Bronzino. Renaissance Painter as Poet*, Cambridge 2000, published when this essay was already in press.

[188]   See Appendix 5., v. 10. Cf. Gaston 1991 (as in n. 38 above), p. 262. Cf. also Appendix 2., v. 9, where Varchi calls Bronzino a 'new Apelles and a new Apollo'. The same expression is used by Sellori in Appendix 7.1., v. 14. Francesco Berni. already in 1534 applied this concept to Michelangelo in his capitolo 'A Fra Bastian del Piombo', v. 28; see Segre and Ossola (Eds) 1998 (as in n. 33 above), p. 648.

[189]   See Appendix 10. Cf. Appendix 1., v. 1–8 and note.

[190]   See, for example, Varchi's sonnet in Appendix 2., v. 10. Cf. Gaston 1991 (as in n. 38 above), p. 268. Cf. Carol Plazzotta's interpretation (1998, as in n. 30 above, p. 260) of Bronzino's 'doppio stil': '[Bronzino's portraiture] borrows the idea of

We cannot be certain that Varchi alluded to the kind of portraiture Bronzino devised for the likeness of *Ugolino Martelli*. Even though we therefore do not know if the subtlety of Bronzino's painting was fully grasped by his contemporaries, I would like to suggest that it was a logical conclusion for the poet-painter Bronzino to bring together on the surface of a poet's portrait what had already been joined inside the artist's mind. The image-text relation in this work differs considerably from Andrea del Sarto's ' *Laura*', where the image gives the poems the rôle of description, and therefore accords them a subordinate position. Developing his experiment in the *Portrait of Lorenzo Lenzi* further, Bronzino in the *Portrait of Ugolino Martelli* left the *paragone* as a competition of genres behind. Poetry with its specific capacity of describing inner life is now intertwined with the visual strategy of the portrait. The superficiality of the brushwork is negated, as the text directs the 'reading' of the image and allows the beholder to discover in the painting the inner values of the sitter. Bronzino's 'double style' thus effectively counters the assessment of painting as a merely mimetic art, and his portrait reaches far beyond the likeness of his sitter.[191] The arts of poetry and painting are united as the complementary parts of the image, which comes to life every time these arts enter into a dialogue in the mind of the viewer.

---

non-representational expression from poetry, so that formal and textual elements become allusively charged, allowing the viewer to make leaps to meaning by association, in the manner of poetic tropes'. Cf. also Sanleolino's 'Angeli Lauri Cognominato Bronzino Pictoris ecellentissimi; necnon Poetae Hetrusci elegantis Tumulus', in S. Sanleolino, *Serenissimi Cosmi Medycis Primis Hetruriae Magniducis Actiones*, Florence 1578, p. 119: 'Divite Bronzinus longè preciosior auro | Naturam cuius vicerat arte manus, | Carmine cum Vates, Pictorq[ue]; coloribus atro | Eriperet letho tempus in omne Viros, | Indoluit Clotho: dixitq[ue]; Sororibus uno hoc | Occiso, innumeris ultima fata damus. | Quarè illum unanimes Parcae rapuere, Sepulchro | Ignarae vivum nunc superesse magis'.

[191] Cf. Varchi's poem, Appendix 2., v. 14.

APPENDIX

'You write and paint alike'
Sonnets on Bronzino's portraiture[192]

1.1.   Di M. Benedetto Varchi[193]

1   Voi, che nel fior della sua verde etate
    Coll'alto vostro, e si chiaro pennello,
    A nome mio, BRONZIN, formaste il bello
    Di fuor cui par non fu mortal beltate:

5   Se di me punto calvi, ò se curate
    Di Voi, coll'altro stile, e non men bello
    Formate il buon di dentro, che con ello
    Posta, vizio sarìa mortal bontate.

    Anzi scrivete, e dipignete insieme
10   Cercondato Avignon da quelle torme
    Empie, che di Giesù sprezzan le norme;
    E'l mio sacro Signor, che l'urta, e preme

---

[192]   The sonnets are, if not otherwise indicated, by Bronzino himself. Here they are cited either as in the manuscript in the Biblioteca Nazionale, Florence (MS Magliabecchiano II, IX, 10, 'Le Rime del Bronzino Pittore | Libro Primo'; cited below as Bronzino MS), or as in the rare edition of the nineteenth century (*Sonetti di Angiolo Allori detto il Bronzino ed altre rime inedite di più insigni poeti*, D. Moreni (Ed.), Florence 1823). On the manuscript and the date of 1566 as *terminus ante quem* for its compilation, see Plazzotta 1998 (as in n. 30 above), p. 263.

[193]   Bronzino MS (as in n. 192 above), fol. 76v. Varchi apparently refers to a painting commissioned by himself ('a nome mio') and praises the sublime and clear/famous ('chiaro') brush of Bronzino, who surpassed mortal beauty through his imitation of the outward appearance. The second quartet analogously addresses Bronzino the poet, who with his depiction of inner virtues exceeds mortal virtue to such an extent that it may seem like vice by comparison. Both modes of representation are then merged in v. 9: 'you write and paint alike'. Bronzino might have sent Varchi the painting together with another sonnet. The last five lines seem to refer to the subject of both, the struggle against the 'godless troops' of the Turks ('torme empie'). Perhaps Varchi had ordered one of the numerous copies or versions of Cosimo I de'Medici's portrait in armour. Plazzotta 1998 (as in n. 30 above), p. 255, n. 30, also cites parts of this poem and draws attention to the fact that the patron's reference to himself harks back to Petrarch's sonnet to Simone Martini (Petrarca 1996, as in n. 8 above, p. 404, no. 78, v. 2).

Con tal virtù, che nel suo sangue immerso
Fugge l'audace, e rio popolo perverso.

1.2.   Risposta[194]

1   Tali, e tante vid'io grazie adunate
        Nel vostro, o nuovo Apollo, Angel novello,
        Che non, che trarne a pieno esempio in quello,
        Di rimirar perdei le forze usate:

5   Angel, che di Michel l'armi onorate
        Oggi contra il diabolico, e rubello
        Stuolo a Gesù si veste, e'l sacro ostello
        Salva della cristiana potestate;

        Ben troppo ardito, e par, ch'ancor ne tremo,
10   Fui, ma chi voi potea negarlo? a porme
        Con l'un stile a ritrar sì rare forme:

        Or ch'io l'altro ancor muova? E chi non teme,
        Se non voi, gir tant'altro, e'n ira averso
        Il Ciel vedersi, e l'Arno in Po converso?

2   Di M. Benedetto Varchi[195]

1   BRONZINO, ove si dolce ombreggia, e suona
        Quel, che s'aguzza al Cielo, e quasi appunta
        Famoso monte, e di sua verde punta

---

[194] Bronzino 1823 (as in n. 192 above), p. 49. The response of Bronzino calls Varchi a new Apollo and the person described in the poems and in the painting a new angel, who defends the church with the weapons of the archangel Michael against the 'develish' pack (first and second quartet). Then Bronzino again refers to both kinds of portraits, the pictorial and the poetic.

[195] Bronzino MS (as in n. 192 above), fol. 116v; Bronzino 1823 (as in n. 192 above), p. 112. This sonnet is most explicit about Bronzino's double talent. Its subject is the laurel that crowns itself, that is, a person that both inspires and produces poetry. The branch of laurel, cut by Cupid, will be Varchi's crown that he will never lose. The second part praises Bronzino's 'double style', his 'double honour' as painter and poet, as 'new Apelles and new Apollo'. Varchi then begs the artist to give eternal fame to the 'sacred tree' with his poetry and in his painting to exceed mere similarity. The poem might be intended to refer to a namesake of the laurel-tree, 'Lauro', and thus perhaps to Bronzino's *Portrait of Lorenzo Lenzi*, who, as discussed above, 'inspired' Varchi in the late 1520s. Most of the poems in the MS with an identifiable subject date from the 1540s to the 1560s; if Lenzi was indeed the sitter, the present poem would be an unusually early example.

Se stesso intorno alto corona,

5   Quivi è'l Parnaso mio, quivi Elicona
Quivi di taglio Amor diemmi, e di punta
Per la Fronde, che mai da me disgiunta
Non sia, e mi sarà di se corona.

Hor voi, che nuovo Apelle, e nuovo Apollo
10   Con doppio honore hornate, e doppio stile
Hor di rime 'l bell'Arno, hor di colori

Date, prego, con l'uno eterni honori
All'Arbor sacro, ond'ebbe il sol tal crollo
L'altro'l renda qual'è non pur simile.

3.1.   Del Lasca sopra il Ritratto di M. Filippo Peruzzi [196]

1   BRONZIN, che col giudizio, è col Pennello
Benigne havendo si le Stelle, e l'Arte,
Questo vil secol nostro a parte, a parte
Rendete più d'ogni altro illustre, e bello:

5   Voi vivo, e vero l'Idol mio novello,
In cui tutt'ha sue grazie il Cielo sparte
Effigiato avete, e con tal arte,
Ch'ognun s'ammira, e s'inchina a vedello.
Quanto per voi si pregia la pittura,
10   Non inviduando i secoli passati,

---

[196]   Bronzino MS (as in n. 192 above), fol. 144v; Bronzino 1823 (as in n. 192 above), p. 28. Lasca's sonnet begins with a general praise of Bronzino, who is said to possess the intellectual quality of judgement ('giudizio') which is crucial to the individual implementation of imitation, and a corresponding artistic ability ('pennello'). The arts and the stars (destiny) are both on his side. This might be read as a reference to the creation of Laura through the arts of the stars and the elements, as told in Petrarch's sonnet 154 (see n. 15 above). More than all others, he has rendered his otherwise vile century famous and beautiful. The second stanza gives a description of the portrait that Bronzino had made for Lasca. Again alluding to Petrarch, Filippo Peruzzi is called Lasca's 'idol', endowed with all heavenly graces. This portrait is lifelike/alive and gives a true image of the sitter ('vivo, e vero'). This truthful naturalism is underlined by the rare verb 'effigiare', which derives from the Latin 'effigies' and connotes the imprint-like similarity of a death-mask. Through Bronzino, painting has gained such praise that past centuries need no longer be regarded with envy. Likewise, nature is proud of Peruzzi's beauty. Bronzino and his sitter will be famous as long as the portrait survives.

Di lui si gloria, e vanta la natura.

Felici dunque voi, anzi beati,
Che mentre si bell'opra al mondo dura,
Sarete sempre mai chiari, e lodati.

3.2.   Risposta[197]

1   Mentr'io, Lasca gentil, meco favello
        Per le vostre alte rime, e vive carte
        Ogni tema, ogni duol da me si parte
        Del secondo morir, che primo appello;

5   Che se mio nol potrà valor, nè quello
        Angel nuovo imitar, che'l cor vi parte,
        L'eterno di voi inchiostro in ogni parte
        Chiaro pur mi farà viver con ello.

        E se ben or m'assal doppia paura
10   Pochi merti veder troppo lodati,
        Ch'a me di gioia, a voi del dritto fura;

        Vivon gli scritti, e muoion l'opre, o fati
        Propizii, e di Simone alta ventura,
        Cui fur tai versi, o veri o no, cantati.

---

[197] Bronzino 1823 (as in n. 192 above), p. 28. Bronzino in his answer takes up the praise of Lasca, more clearly than Lasca referring to the painting's eventual decay and thus drawing attention to the immortality of literature. Because of Lasca's 'living sheets', he has now lost any fear of a 'second death', as the 'eternal ink' of Lasca will secure his fame. Still, he feels overcome by the two-fold fear that too few merits are praised too much, as the written words outlive the works. He then recalls Simone Martini's portrait of Laura, whose fame is preserved in Petrarch's verses, may they recount the truth or not; with this last observation, he demonstrates his awareness of the possibility of fictionality in literature. The last lines are also cited in Plazzotta 1998 (as in n. 30 above), p. 259. The 'second death' refers to the destruction of the image. On the topos of the immortal lyrical portrait, see Cropper 1986 (as in n. 2 above), p. 175; cf. also Plazzotta 1998 (as in n. 30 above), p. 259.

4.1.   [M. Bendetto Varchi] Al Bronzino Dipintore [198]

1   Nuova casta Ciprigna e nuovo Marte
         L'alta Isabella e'l buon PAULO GIORDANO
         Genero e Figlia del gran Rè Toscano
         A cui sue grazie il ciel, tutte comparte.

5   Questa del Mondo avventurosa parte
         A' piè di dolci Colli ameno Piano
         Rendon si lieta o, BRONZIN mio che'nvano
         Tento, e fatico altrui ritrarla in carte

         Voi sol, sol Voi, che già gran tempo havete
10   La dotta penna al pennel dotto pari
         Farne doppia potete eterna storia[;]

         I colori vostri soli omai non rari
         E i chiari inchiostri mai non vedran Lete,
         Ond'addoppio per Voi l'Arno si gloria.

4.2.   Risposta [199]

1   Quanto dal vero, Amor, sovente, parte
         Chi troppo il crede? hor non son'io, sovrano
         D'ogn'altro ingegno, da tentare invano
         Quand'io l'ardissi ben, l'una, è l'altr'arte!

5   Non è quest'opra da chiamarsi à parte
         Molto miglior di mè, da Voi che'nvano
         Lo scettro havete di Parnaso, e piano
         V'è pur qual servitù da lui mi parte:

---

[198]   Bronzino MS (as in n. 192 above), fol. 185v. Varchi first describes Isabella and
        Paolo Giordano Orsini, daughter and son-in-law of the Tuscan 'king', and then
        the beauties of the Arno valley that he is not able to portray in words. Only
        Bronzino knows how to employ both his learned pen and his learned brush so as
        to form a doubly eternal 'storia'. His colours and ink will never decay and the
        Arno will thus be doubly famous. Isabella and Paolo married in 1555 and the
        sonnet may have been written soon afterwards.

[199]   Bronzino MS (as in n. 192 above), fol. 186r. Bronzino's answer is an extreme
        gesture of modesty, denying his abilities in either art. He merely produces 'mortal
        memory' of the gods. Only Varchi's art equals the glory of its subjects.

Di questa al tutto indegno Arte, vorrete
10   Chiamarmi all'altra? ond'à mio danno impari
Che sia cercare à Dei mortal memoria?

Beltà divina, e vie più, che'l sol chiari
Gesti sol Voi ritrar, Voi sol potete
Lodare cantando, e parreggiar di gloria.

5.   [Benedetto Varchi] Al Bronzino, pittore[200]

1   D'ogni cosa rendiam grazie al Signore
Che le ci da', che così vuole Dio,
Caro e chiaro cortese Bronzin mio,
Cui ebbi ad aggio ed avrò sempre onore.

5   E se'l vostro Alessandro al primo fiore
La bell'opera ha fatto ove ancor io
sempre vivrò fuor del commune oblio,
Solo è stata di Dio grazia e favore.

Noi siam nulla Bronzin, e voi che sete
10   Sì grande Apelle e non minor Apollo;
Nulla che vostro sià non, nulla avete

E che Voi Bronzin mio, come dovete,
Ogni ben Vostro e suo da Dio tenete;
Il credo certo anzi per certo sollo.

6.1.   Il Prete dell Asino al Bronzino[201]

---

[200]   Bronzino MS (as in n. 192 above), fol. 186v, also in Varchi 1834 (as in n. 71 above), p. 612. Varchi draws attention to the fact that all talents are God-given. The same holds for Bronzino's disciple Allori, whose portrait of Varchi will protect him from oblivion. This sonnet must date from the late 1550s, as it refers to Alessandro Allori (1535-1607) as an already independent master, but still very young ('nell primo fiore'). His first known paintings date from 1552; see E. Pilliod, 'Bronzino's Household', *The Burlington Magazine*, 134, 1992, pp. 92–100 (esp. p. 93).

[201]   Bronzino MS (as in n. 192 above), fol. 187v, Bronzino 1823 (as in n. 192 above), p. 48. This sonnet plays with the topoi of the living image and mastery over nature. Nature, when regarding Bronzino's paintings, boasts that she is the source of the 'emotion' ('sentimento') displayed in them, but fears nonetheless to be outdone by the painter, as she cannot match the beauty of his works. Of all the works of nature endowed with intellect, there is none without any defect. The implication is that Bronzino's works are indeed faultless; the 'divine Bronzino' thus surpasses

1   S'il vivo senso, o ver qualche parola
        Havesse il bel lavor del tuo figmento
        Tu fai Pitture d'un tale hornamento,
        Ch'un Dio saresti in la terrestra scola.

5   Natura in contemplarle si consola
        E brama di prestarli il sentimento
        Ma teme de suo honor qual sarìa spento
        Che si bell'opra non sa far lei sola.

        Di tante forme sue, c'han l'intelletto
10   Far mai non puote si gentil Figura,
        Che non havesse in sè qualche difetto.

        Ma tien la tua virtù tanta misura,
        Ch'ognun stupisce, e grida con diletto:
        Dal divin Bronzo, è vinta la Natura.

6.2.   Risposta[202]

1   Non pur Natura il senso, e la parola
        Hà più dell'arte, ma col suo fimmento
        sempre l'avanza, e col vero hornamento
        Come ben sà, chi'mpara à la sua scola.

5   Ben l'arte sceglie, onde s'horna, e consola,
        Di lei'l più alto, e vivo sentimento
        Hor giugnendo, hor levando, e'l troppo, o'l spento
        Color temprando: in ch'ella hà potere sola.

        Ma non grazia, o vaghezza, occhio, o'ntelletto
10   Riceve, o porge d'essempio, o figura,

---

nature.

[202]   Bronzino MS (as in n. 192 above), fol. 188r, Bronzino 1823 (as in n. 192 above), p. 48. Bronzino's response reestablishes nature as the model for imitation, but stresses the artits's judgement as the cause of beauty in art: it is art's prerogative to choose among nature's most beautiful parts. The painter is paralleled to the bee, an old simile for the nobilitation of nature through human creation, derived from Seneca, which Bronzino might have known from contemporary poetic theory. Cf. G. C. Delminio, *Della Imitazione* (1530): '[...] qual fa l'ape, la qual, benché faccia il suo mèle della virtù de' fiori, che non è cosa sua, nondimeno essa la trasforma sì che noi non possiamo nella opera sua riconoscer qual fior in questa o in quella parte del mèle sua virtù mettesse [...]'; cited after B. Weinberg, *Trattati di Poetica e Retorica del Cinquecento*, vol. 1, Bari 1970, pp. 161–85 (esp. p. 164).

Di che manco Natura haggia, o difetto.

Senza la norma sua non è misura
Se ben, qual'Ape il mel, l'arte il diletto
Trae dalli sparsi fior d'essa Natura.

7.1.   Del Cav. Sellori[203]

1   Cinga le tempie a te, saggio Bronzino,
      La sacra Fronde di Parnaso onnore,
      Poichè sicuro, e fuor del cieco errore
      Per farsi eterno all'uom mostri il cammino.

5   Io, ch'oggi lieto e riverente inchino
      Con alta meraviglia il tuo splendore;
      Sento un dolce desìo pungermi il core
      D'essser mai sempre a te caro, e vicino.

      Intanto il nome tuo s'ode sonare
10   Ovunque io sia, che con l'erranti stelle
      Trapassa i monti, i piani, i fiumi, e'l mare;

      E le tue dotte rime altere, e belle,
      E le pitture tue pregiate, e care,
      Ti fanno un nuovo Apollo, un nuovo Apelle.

7.2.   Risposta[204]

1   Non mio valor, ma grazia di destino,
      E vostro natural cortese amore
      Uscir vi fa, nobil Sellori, fore
      Troppo del dritto, e debito confino:

5   Tant'alte lodi, e stile alto, e divino
      M'hanno ripien di gioja, e di dolore,
      Ma più di duol, ch'all'antico rossore
      Giunto fammi il cor mesto, e'l viso chino;

---

[203] Bronzino 1823 (as in n. 192 above), p. 18. Sellori's poem is a general eulogy which states that the poet Bronzino has revealed the path to immortal fame. The last three lines compare his abilities as a learned writer to those as a famous painter, employing the formula 'a new Apollo and new Apelles'.
[204] Bronzino 1823 (as in n. 192 above), p. 18. Bronzino's answer again is marked by understatement, he suggests that Sellori's praise exceeds his merits.

E mi stringe pietà veder sì chiare
10 Vostre note adombrar velando quelle
Di tal, che poco è certo, e nulla appare:

Ma chi giunger potrebbe ai merti d'elle?
Potess'io pur, ch'assai fora, mostrare
Quanto n'è l'alma accesa, e care tielle.

8.   Pien d'onesto...[205]

1   Pien d'onesto gentil giusto desìo
D'imitar fra i più belli il più bel viso
Per adornarne il Re del Paradiso
Lieto mirai nel vago aspetto pio,

5   Lasso, ma ben allor certo sepp'io
Quanto il celeste è dal terren diviso,
Che tosto infermo al gran lume, e conquiso
Venne l'occhio, e l'ingegno, e'l studio mio.

L'alma smarrita in sì leggiadro aspetto
10 Ammirando or la grazia, or la bellezza
Lasciava il corpo, e all'alte idee saliva;

Onde, che'l ver non so, forse il concetto
La parte aggiunse a sì divina altezza,
Ma l'arte nè la man non l'obbediva.

---

[205] Bronzino 1823 (as in n. 192 above), p. 108. This Platonising sonnet of Bronzino is among the most beautiful presented here; it describes a failed attempt at 'portraying' the Lord. He had planned to imitate the most beautiful of faces. He then understood the difference between earthly and heavenly beauty and the latter's 'great light' weakened his eye and intellect and hampered his studies. Through the contemplation of this beauty his soul departed from the body and ascended to the realm of ideas. There he glimpsed the 'concept' of this work, but his art did not suffice to put it into practice. The last part is a clear, but understated reference to the famous sonnet by Michelangelo, cited by Varchi in his lecture, where the 'concetto' marks the intellectual beginning of the creative act, and the obeying hand its practical end: 'Non ha l'ottimo Artista alcun concetto | Ch'un marmo solo in sè non circonscriva | Col suo soverchio, e solo a quello arriva | La mano ch'ubbidisce all'intelletto'; Varchi 1834 (as in n. 71 above), p. 100.

9.   Al Sig. Don Luigi di Toledo[206]

1   Signor alto, e gentil, ch'al vivo Sole,
     Che dal nuovo Oriente in sì liet'ora
     Surse a dar luce, e vita all'alma Flora,
     Sete degno fratel d'amore, e prole;

5   Deh con le vostre sagge alte parole
     Pregate lui, che benigno talora
     S'assida in parte, ove'l bel, che di fora
     Con sì chiaro splendor rilucer sole

     Ritrar si possa con disegno, ed arte,
10   Acciò che'l mondo ancor nell'altra etade
     Scorga, ed onore un sì gentil sembiante,

     E membrando il valor, che'n ogni parte
     Di lui risplende, le sue virtù tante
     Imitar cerchi, e sua vera bontade.

10.   [Benedetto Varchi an Bronzino][207]

1   Ben potete, Bronzin, col vago, altero
     Stil vostro, eletto a sì grande speranza,
     Formare coi color l'alta sembianza
     Della donna gentil d'Arno e d'Ibero:

5   Ma'l bel di dentro e quello invitto, intero
     Cortese cor, che sol tutti altri avanza,

---

[206] Bronzino 1823 (as in n. 192 above), p. 51. Bronzino here explains the moral usefulness of painting to Don Luigi di Toledo, brother-in-law of Cosimo I. The patron, characterised as a brother of Apollo, shall beg this god for help so that Luigi's beauty may be portrayed. The following centuries will then not only pay honour to such a 'noble countenance' but also try to imitate his virtues.

[207] Varchi 1834 (as in n. 71 above), p. 508. Cited partially in Wildmoser 1989 (as in n. 61 above), p. 185. Varchi exploits the theme of the artist's double talent: he first praises the painter, who can form the 'lofty resemblance' of a person with his beautiful and proud/sublime ('altero') style. The 'donna [...] d'Ibero' refers to the portrait of Eleonora of Toledo (Baccheschi 1973, as in n. 74 above, cat. 55). Inner beauty, the undefeated heart, cannot be portrayed by painting, but only by poetry. In the latter art Bronzino's style is no less famous/evident ('chiaro') than in painting, but poetry employs the 'more beautiful' colours given by Apollo. Thus Bronzino is able not only to give eternal life to the mortal veil, i.e. the body, but also to immortalise the sitter's exemplary character.

Chi ritrarrà dove non ha possanza
Vostra arte, e nulla val gran magistero?

Voi, ma con altro e non men chiaro stile,
10 Nè meno ornato che dal quarto cielo
Febo v'inspira e con più bei colori;

Raro ed esempio e pregio il mortal velo
Potete eterno e l'eterno a' migliori
Far dal mar d'India conto a quel di Tile.

The Brush in Poetry and Practice: Agnolo Bronzino's Capitolo del pennello *in Context*

FRANÇOIS QUIVIGER

In their efforts to dissociate painting from the crafts,[1] Renaissance artists and writers devoted numerous pages to its intellectual character, but almost none to its technique.[2] This context casts Agnolo Bronzino's burlesque praise of the painter's brush, the *Capitolo del pennello*, as a unique and surprising document. The text first appeared in Florence in 1538 and was reprinted in 1542 in an anthology of poetry by Giovanni della Casa and others.[3] Thus, written a decade before art literature became common in the late 1540s, the *Capitolo* stands out as an important witness of the ideas which circulated in artistic circles while Renaissance art theories were still largely part of an oral tradition.

In order to place Bronzino's verses in their context I will first examine evidence regarding the materials, manufacture and care of the brush and its representation in Renaissance self-portraiture. I will then discuss three issues highlighted by the *Capitolo*: the question of variety and abundance in painting, the status of the painted figure, and the role of the brush as a sensory intermediary between the painter and the painted figure.

We know very little about Renaissance brushes. The main literary source, the *Libro dell'arte* of Cennino Cennini (c. 1390), explains what hair to choose and how to prepare it. There were two main types of brushes: those made from squirrel tails and those made from bristle.[4] If we are to believe Cennini, squirrel tails hung in every respectable painter's workshop. Although no sixteenth-century source provides as much evidence as Cennini's *Libro,* scattered evidence suggests that Bronzino and his contemporaries used

[1]   I am grateful to Tristan Garcia Fons and Manuela Morgaine for advice and suggestions.

[2]   On the rising social status of the artist see M. Warnke, *The Court Artist. On the Ancestry of the Modern Artist,* transl. D. McLintock, Cambridge 1993.

[3]   *Le terze rime di messer Giovanni della Casa di messer Bino e d'altri,* s. l., 1542. I quote the *Capitolo* after A. Bronzino, *Rime in Burla,* F. Petrucci Nardelli (Ed.), Rome 1988.

[4]   See C. Cennini, *Il libro dell'arte o Trattato della pittura,* F. Tempesti (Ed.), Milan 1973, ch. LXIV–LXVI, pp. 66–5; see also A. Thomas, *The Painter's Practice in Renaissance Tuscany,* Cambridge 1995, pp. 152–3.

instruments similar to those described by Cennini.[5]

Cennini does not discuss the care of the brush, but some remarks of the late-sixteenth-century manual by the Bolognese painter Francesco Cavazzoni dwell on this issue. Brushes must be cleaned with nut oil immediately after use, pressed until the oil runs clear, and then washed. The artist must ensure that paint never dries on them.[6]

While brushes are common in Northern self-portraiture they rarely appear in Italian self-portraits or portraits of artists. None of Raphael's four presumed self-portraits includes a brush; Giorgione poses as David, Parmigianino hides his working hand in his self-portrait in a convex mirror.[7] Only one of Titian's five surviving self-portraits includes a brush.[8] In the dome of Florence Cathedral Federico Zuccari represented himself in fresco holding an oil palette, but no brush;[9] his other self-portraits, in his house in Rome, do not include any brushes.

Pinturicchio's self-portrait in S. Maria Maggiore in Spello is unusual in displaying three different brushes (one pointed and two flat), but they appear in the context of an allegory of painting, outside the frame surrounding the artist's countenance.[10] Unlike self-portraits, allegories of painting invariably include one or several brushes. Four can be seen in the hands of Vasari's personification of painting at the Casa Vasari in Arezzo,[11] and in Zuccari's *Apotheosis of the Artist* in the Casa Zuccari she holds two.[12] Brushes also appear in scenes featuring painters such as St Luke painting the Virgin and Apelles and Campaspe.

The brushes exceptionally shown in Italian self-portraits are thin and slender. In five cases the artist has concealed their hairy end loaded with

[5]   Ibid., p. 179. Bronzino 1988 (as in n. 3, above), p. 23, describes the brush as 'nato di pel di setola o di coda'. For his remarks on size and function see n. 55, below.

[6]   F. Cavazzoni, *Essemplario*, in R. Varese, *Francesco Cavazzoni critico e pittore*, Florence 1969, p. 195: 'Sarà bene doppo l'avere imparato di preparare colori, e quadri bisogna ancora il modo di conservare li penelli cosa molto importante per fare onore al pittore: il penello, subito adoperato si laverà con l'oglio di noce premendo col coltello senza taglio sopra il dito sino che viene l'oglio chiaro, e poi bagnarlo, ed aver al così che non si secchino, che non sarà più buono così quel divario come quello di vedere'.

[7]   On Raphael's self-portraits see J. Woods-Marsden, *Renaissance Self-Portraiture. The Visual Construction of Identity and the Social Status of the Artist*, New Haven, London 1998, pp. 120–32; on Giorgione, ibid., pp. 116–9. Giorgione's self-portrait survives in W. Hollar's engraving (see Holberton in this volume). On Parmigianino see Woods-Marsden, pp. 133–7.

[8]   H. E. Wethey, *The Paintings of Titian, Complete Edition*, 3 vols, London 1971, vol. 2, pp. 49–51.

[9]   Woods-Marsden (as in n. 6, above), p. 175.

[10]   Ibid., p. 109.

[11]   Ibid., pp. 206–7.

[12]   Ibid., p. 181.

colour from the viewer: Battista Paggi,[13] Alessandro Allori (Florence, Uffizi),[14] Titian (Madrid, Prado) and Annibale Carracci (Milan, Brera).[15] Titian is reported to have used brushes as big as brooms, but the only brush he represented, in the Prado self-portrait, is thin and oriented towards his lower body,[16] an orientation that, as we shall see, may have been intended to be meaningful.

Such concealing of the soiling and colourful part of the brush accentuated the association between the writer's quill ('penna') and the painter's brush ('pennello'), terms which in Italian share the same root. The intellectual aspirations of artists undoubtedly explain this reluctance to represent an instrument still closely associated with workshop practice.[17] Thus, according to Paolo Pino's *Dialogo di pittura* (1548), painters should appear in public clean and perfumed, as if they did not work with brushes and colours:

> And our painter should not be seen with his hands smeared with every colour, his cloths stained and shirts filthy as if he were washing dishes. He must on the contrary be delicate and clean and use perfumes as these things bring comfort to the brain.[18]

Towards the end of the sixteenth century the painter Giovan Battista Paggi expressed a similar dislike of soiled hands which he perceived as a compromising sign of clumsiness detrimental to the nobility of the art.[19]

---

[13] Martin von Wagner Museum, Würzburg, see ibid., p. 131.

[14] Ibid., p. 231.

[15] Ibid., pp. 241-51. Annibale's other two self-portraits do not include any brushes (Hermitage Museum, St Petersburg; Parma, Pinacoteca Nazionale).

[16] See D. Rosand, 'Tintoretto e gli spiriti nel pennello', in *Jacopo Tintoretto nel quarto centenario della morte* (Quaderni di Venezia arti, 3), Padua 1996, pp. 133-7 (esp. p. 137, n. 15).

[17] On the association of brushstroke and practice see P. Sohm, *Pittoresco. Marco Boschini, his Critics, and their Critiques of Painterly Brushwork in Seventeenth- and Eighteenth-Century Italy*, Cambridge 1991, p. 25.

[18] P. Pino, *Dialogo di pittura*, in *Trattati d'arte del Cinquecento fra Manierismo e Controriforma*, 3 vols, P. Barocchi (Ed.), Bari 1962, vol. 1, p. 74: 'Ne apparisca il nostro maestro con le mani empiastrate di tutti i colori, con i drappi lerci e camise succide [sudicie], come guataro [sguattero]; ma sia delicato e netto usando cose odorose come confortatrice del cerebro'.

[19] In G. Bottari and S. Ticozzi, *Raccolta di lettere sulla pittura, scultura ed architettura ...*, 8 vols, Milan 1822-1825, vol. 6, p. 74: 'E cominciando dall'imbrattarsi le mani dico che non è necessario toccare i colori con le mani, ma che quando vengano tocchi, più per disgrazia che per bisogno, pregiudica tanto alla nobiltà delle leggi, se, mentre un dottore scrivegli vien tocco, o sia per caso, o per volontà; come pregiudica alla nobiltà del cavaliere, se il cavallo, nel maneggiarsi, o con ispuma o con sudore, o con saltare il fango addosso al padrone, in qualche modo le imbratti'.

Thus, contrary to Northern painters who customarily depicted themselves in the act of painting, Italians seldom did. When they did they hid the end of their brush and adopted poses suggesting that their art requires as little physical effort as writing.

In the context of these conventions Palma Giovane's self-portrait showing the artist whilst painting a Resurrection (c. 1580) seems highly unusual (Pl. 20).[20] Some scholars have associated this picture with the Counter Reformation ideal of the Christian painter.[21] The subject chosen, however, is also an ideal means of expressing the topical ability of painting to make the dead come alive.[22] It is also a subject in which, according to Giovan Andrea Gilio, painters can freely display their skill in representing figures.[23]

The picture is as much a self-portrait as it is a set of five variations on the movements of a single figure – including that of the painter – displayed in a counter-clockwise sequence. This exercise in virtuosity is reminiscent of a contention attributed to Giorgione by Vasari, according to which a good painting shows all the aspects that one man can produce with the variety of his gestures.[24] More broadly, Palma's Resurrection reflects the sixteenth-century appreciation of painting as variation on the human figure.[25]

Palma's left hand thrusts a palette towards the viewer. This soiling part of the image contrasts with his prominent fur-lined coat. Highly unpractical in the context of workshop practice, Palma's coat is nevertheless fitting in terms of artistic aspirations wide-spread during the sixteenth century. Titian wears a similar coat in two of his self-portraits,[26] while Vasari represented himself as Saint Luke with an ermine collar.[27] Fur lining frequently features in

[20] *Palma il Giovane 1548–1628. Disegni e dipinti*, S. Mason Rinaldi (Ed.), Milan 1990, p. 188.

[21] See especially Woods-Mardsen 1998 (as in n. 7, above), pp. 238–40.

[22] See L. B. Alberti *Della Pittura*, in *Opere volgari*, 3 vols, C. Grayson (Ed.), Bari 1973, vol. 3, p. 44: 'E così certo il viso di chi già sia morto, per la pittura vive lunga vita.' Bronzino's burlesque (Bronzino 1988, as in n. 3, above, p. 25) includes an allusion to the Resurrection: 'O cosa benedetta e singolare, tu ci fai, come Dio, tornare al mondo altre volte e ogni dì rifare!'.

[23] See G. A. Gilio, *Dialogo degli errori e degli abusi de' pittori circa l'istorie*, in *Trattati d'arte del Cinquecento fra Manierismo e Controriforma*, 3 vols, P. Barocchi (Ed.), Bari 1962, vol. 2, p. 40.

[24] G. Vasari, *Le vite de' più eccellenti pittori, scultori e architettori nelle redazioni del 1550 e 1568*, R. Bettarini and P. Barocchi (Eds), Florence 1966–, vol. 4, p. 46: '... Giorgione – che era d'oppinione che in una storia di pittura si mostrasse, senza avere a caminare a torno, ma in una sola occhiata tutte le sorti delle vedute che può fare in più gesti un uomo ...'.

[25] See C. Hope, '"Composition" from Cennini and Alberti to Vasari', in *Pictorial Composition from Medieval to Modern Art* (Warburg Institute Colloquia, 6), F. Quiviger and P. Taylor (Eds), London, Turin 2000, pp. 27–44.

[26] Madrid, Prado; Berlin, Staatliche Museen, Gemäldegalerie.

[27] Florence, SS. Annunziata, Cappella di S. Luca.

portraits of noblemen and rulers such as Vasari's *Cosimo I* or Lotto's *Andrea Odoni*; its high value and prestige have been confirmed by research into economic history. [28]

It would seem logical to interpret brushes and fur as evocative of the contrast between manual work and gentlemanly status. However, Renaissance brushes and luxury furs came from the same animal, the minever ('vayrus', Italian 'vaio'), a squirrel prized for the whiteness of its abdominal fur, grey polychrome back and bushy tail which, according to Cennini, provided the only suitable hair for brushes. [29] In his Munich self-portrait Dürer appears to point to the common source by pinching a piece of his fur-collar into the shape of a brush. Palma perhaps takes this notion further as the resurrecting Christ literally emerges from his fur collar.

Palma presents the palette to the viewer with his left hand of which he shows only the thumb. Four brushes seem to have replaced the four hidden fingers. If the brushes stand for the fingers, then their coloured ends stand for the fingertips. These are the most sensitive part of the hand where modern physiology has located one of the highest concentrations of tactile receptors. [30] The painter's brush is thus associated with a zone of high sensitivity, mediating perceptions of shape, texture and temperature. The tip of the brush is the place where the three-dimensional imagination of the artist encounters and overcomes the flatness of the pictorial surface in order to create figures expressive of depth and relief. Palma is likely to have thought in such terms since he worked with Titian who sometimes painted with his fingertips. [31] As we shall see the theme of the brush as a sensory extension of the painter is central to Bronzino's *Capitolo del pennello*, which pre-dates Palma's self-portrait by forty years.

The *Capitolo del pennello* belongs to a vernacular genre of burlesque encomia of objects popularised by Francesco Berni in the 1520s and successful not least due to their obscene double-entendres. [32] In Bronzino's *Capitolo* the

[28] A. Nada Patrone, 'Le pellicce nel traffico commerciale pedemontano del tardo medioevo', *Cultura e società nell'Italia medievale. Studi per Paolo Brezzi* (Studi Storici, fasc. 188–192), Rome 1988, pp. 561–84 (esp. p. 582) and R. Delort, *Le Commerce des fourrures en Occident à la fin du Moyen Age (vers 1300 – vers 1450)*, Rome 1978, pp. 141–55.

[29] Cennini 1973 (as in n. 4, above), p. 66: 'Togli códole di vaio (ché di nessun altro son buone) ...'; Nada Patrone 1988 (as in n. 28, above), p. 578.

[30] See R. F. Schmidt (Ed.), *Fundamentals of Sensory Physiology*, Berlin 1986, pp. 44–5.

[31] Palma entered Titian's workshop in 1570. For Titian's use of his fingers see M. Boschini, 'Breve instruzione premessa a le ricche minere della pittura veneziana', in *La carta del navegar pitoresco*, A. Pallucchini (Ed.), Venice 1966, p. 712 and Sohm 1991 (as in n. 17, above), pp. 26, 119, 146, 152.

[32] S. Lunghi, *Il capitolo burlesco nel Cinquecento*, Padova 1983, pp. 33ff. The introduction and notes of the edition of Petrucci Nardelli 1988 (as in n. 3, above) highlight the obscene content of Bronzino verses. See also D. Parker, 'Towards a

painter's tool is the male organ of generation, colour is semen and the exploits of the burlesque brush also include anal prowess. In other words, Bronzino parallels artistic creation with sexuality as a means of generating life and of pursuing forbidden pleasures.[33] As a result, the *Capitolo* sets the commonplaces of humanistic art theory outside the context and restraints of the art treatise and provides a remarkable vision of pictorial practice.

The poem begins with an imaginary picture, the double portrait of a nude couple which Bronzino sees and acquires at a high price:

> These last few days I saw a good portrait
> of a man and a woman: they were naked
> painted together in a pleasing act.
>
> I got it expensive – a couple of scudi
> For one could see that there was inside
> Everything nature or long studies can give.[34]

He sets the picture in motion while contemplating it attentively:

> I looked at it attentively for a while
> For it seemed to me that I saw it move about
> Like someone experiencing contentment.
>
> For this reason I was forced to judge
> The brush which produced it, worthy of praise
> And if I can praise it I want to.

Instead of describing a single picture Bronzino uses the two figures as the elements of a potentially large number of variations which he allows the reader to imagine and to multiply. This unstable image suggests that painting and sexuality are facets of the same art:

> One is depicted on a bed or adopts
> a tiring position, erect or seated;
> one holds something in his hand the other has it hidden;

Reading of Bronzino's Burlesque Poetry', *Renaissance Quarterly*, 50, 1997, pp. 1011–44 and idem, *Bronzino. Renaissance Painter as Poet*, Cambridge 2000, which came to my notice while the present article was in press. I concur with Parker's remarks on the *Capitolo del pennello* (pp. 24–6, 105–7). The artist's brush, however, falls outside the scope of her book.

33   On sodomy in Florence see M. Rocke, *Forbidden Friendships*, New York 1996.

34   Bronzino 1988 (as in n. 3, above), p. 23: 'Io vidi a questi giorni un buon ritratto | d'un uomo e d'una donna: erano ignudi | dipinti insieme in un piacevol atto. | Ebbilo Caro – una coppia di scudi | Ché si vedea che v'era tutto dentro | Ciò che può dar natura o i lunghi studi. | Io gli stetti a guardar un pezzo attento, | Ché mi parea vedergli dimenare | Come colui che n'avea contento. | Per quest'io fui forzato a giudicare | Il pennel, che gli fe', degno di loda | E s'io potrò lodarlo, io lo vò fare'.

one wants to be seen behind someone else;
another wants to be depicted in front;
one holds on tight, another seems to be falling.

I myself would not know how to recount one of the thousand
different extravagant gestures and modes;
you should know that variety pleases everyone.

Suffice to say that to do it from the front or the back,
sideways, in foreshortening or in perspective,
the brush can be used for every purpose.[35]

Bronzino's literary sources are two anonymous Florentine carnival songs, [36] but he also relies on visual sources. The best-known are *I Modi*, sixteen engravings by Marcantonio Raimondi after drawings by Giulio Romano, representing various positions of love-making and accompanied by sonnets of Pietro Aretino.[37] *I modi* took inspiration from Ovid's *Ars amatoria*, which Bronzino may have known. Ovid, who in turn followed a lost tradition of ancient sex manuals, lists several positions for love. He emphasises that their number is unlimited and adds that there are one thousand possibilities ('mille modi veneris').[38]

Bronzino's evocation of a thousand diverse acts and extravagant modes are not only reminiscent of Ovid, but also of Antonio Vignali's *Cazzaria*, a priapic dialogue written around 1526 in the ambience of the Sienese Accademia degli Intronati.

The dialogue begins with a defence of scholars against commoners and vile artisans. Vignali asserts that scholars are far better lovers than commoners: from their books and studies they know a *thousand* ways of providing pleasure to their partners.[39] They know a *thousand* stories to

---

[35] Ibid., pp. 23-4: 'Chi si ritrae sul letto o faticose | attitudine fa, ritto o a sedere; | chi tien qualcosa in mano, chi l'ha nascose; | chi si vuol dietro ad un altro vedere; | chi vuol essere dipinto innanzi ad uno; | chi s'attien; chi fa vista di cadere. | Io non saprei contare de'mille uno | de'diversi atti e modi stravaganti; | sapete che il variar piace ad ognuno. | Basta che a fargli o dirietro o davanti, | a traverso, in iscorcio o in prospettiva | s'adopera il pennello a tutti quanti'.

[36] See *Canti carnascialeschi del Rinascimento*, C. S. Singleton (Ed.), Bari 1936, pp. 184–5, 193–4. Bronzino may have known of these compositions through his friend Anton Francesco Grazzini, known as Il Lasca, who collected, and produced one of the first editions of Renaissance carnival songs (Florence 1559).

[37] See R. Gaston, 'Love's Sweet Poison: a New Reading of Bronzino's London Allegory', *I Tatti Studies*, 4, 1991, pp. 247–88 (esp. p. 271). For *I modi* see P. Aretino, *I modi*, L. Lawner (Ed.), Milan 1984, and B. Talvacchia, *Taking Positions. On the Erotic in Renaissance Culture*, Princeton 1999.

[38] Ibid., pp. 52–3; Ovid, *Ars amatoria*, 3, 787.

[39] A. Vignali, *La cazzaria*, P. Stopelli (Ed.), Rome 1984, p. 45: '... imperochè essi, che studiano, sanno mille colpi buoni e mille tratte dolci sopra quel fatto, li quali trovano scritti nei libri; e come quei che sanno come la potta sta dentro, sanno

entertain them between intercourse, a *thousand* ways of avenging their honour, as well as a *thousand* modes of praising their beloved in writing, and they can compose perfumes, eau de toilette and a *thousand* similar things.[40]

The reoccurrence of the number thousand, both in Bronzino's account of the imaginary picture and in Vignali's evocation of scholarly potency, is indicative of broad categories used to appreciate artistic and literary accomplishment as well as natural generative powers: variety and abundance. Alberti applied these same categories to painting in his *Della Pittura* of 1436:

> That which gives pleasure in the *istoria* comes from copiousness and variety of things. In food and in music variety and abundance please ... so the soul is delighted by all copiousness and variety. For this reason copiousness and variety please in painting.[41]

These categories remained stable throughout the fifteenth and sixteenth centuries and beyond, as is confirmed by a passage of Federico Zuccari's *Idea* of 1607:

> And since nature is varied and abundant, so are the arts; in the same way a good painter should be varied and abundant ...[42]

Variety and abundance are essential in the art of inventing new positions. To quote Alberti again:

> In every istoria variety is always pleasant. A painting in which there are bodies in many dissimilar poses is always especially pleasing.[43]

The variety Bronzino praises applies both to the painter's mind and to the inventive lover. His assertion that the picture he saw contains everything that can be acquired by nature and long studies ('natura o i lunghi studi') disrespectfully blends allusions to sodomy and other sexual practices with Renaissance ideas on artistic education. Both threads coincide in the image which Bronzino's contemplative gaze sets in motion.

By 'lunghi studi' Bronzino refers to the art of drawing and painting figures. While not all renaissance artists attended dissections and studied proportions they all cultivated the ability to draw anatomically credible human figures in order to depict a story without recourse to live models. A passage of Vasari's introduction to the *Vite* describes the acquisition of this skill as a discipline of memory and imagination:

---

ritrovare tutte le vie piacevoli e secreti'.

[40]   Ibid., pp. 45-6.

[41]   Alberti 1973 (as in n. 22, above), p. 75. On variety and abundance see T. Cave, *The Cornucopian Text*, Oxford 1979, pp. 3-34.

[42]   F. Zuccaro, *Idea de' pittori, scultori e architetti,* Turin 1607, in *Scritti d'arte,* D. Heikamp (Ed.), Florence 1961, p. 239: 'E si come la natura è copiosa e varia, e varie sono l'arti; così il buon pittore deve esser vario e copioso ...'.

[43]   Alberti 1973 (as in n. 22, above), p. 76. On *copia* in Alberti see M. Baxandall, *Giotto and the Orators*, Oxford 1971, pp. 136-7.

... the best thing is to draw men and women from the nude and thus fix in the memory by constant exercise the muscles of the torso, back, legs, arms and knees, and the bone underneath. Then one may be sure that through much study attitudes in any position can be drawn by help of the imagination without a live model. Again, having seen bodies dissected one knows how the bones lie, and the muscles and sinews, and all the order and conditions of anatomy, so that it is possible with greater security and more correctness to place the limbs and arrange the muscles of the body in the figures we draw.[44]

Since the male artist of the sixteenth century could draw on his own anatomy, the art of painting figures tended to involve some degree of self-observation and self-projection. In his *Della Pittura* Alberti highlights the former. He himself seems to have studied the range and limits which anatomy imposes on movement in order to decide which movement is natural and which is not.[45] His condemnation of excessively contorted figures, which anticipates Counter Reformation criticisms, implies that a good figure is one in a position in which any viewer can imagine himself.[46]

That painters project themselves into their works is further confirmed by the Italian proverb 'ogni pittore dipinge se stesso', which Leonardo quoted to account for the tendency of his contemporaries to reproduce their facial and anatomical features in all their figures.[47]

[44] Vasari 1966– (as in n. 24, above), vol. 1, p. 115: 'Ma sopra tutto, il meglio è gl'ignudi degli uomini vivi e femine, e da quelli avere preso in memoria per lo continovo uso i muscoli del torso, delle schiene, delle gambe, delle braccia, delle ginocchia e l'ossa di sotto, e poi avere sicurtà per lo molto studio che senza avere i naturali inanzi si possa formare di fantasia da sé attitudini per ogni verso ...'. English translation from *Vasari on Technique* ..., transl. L. S. Maclehose, London 1907, p. 210. On figure and movement in Renaissance art see D. Summers, *Michelangelo and the Language of Art*, Princeton 1981, pp. 71–96, 406–17.

[45] Alberti 1973 (as in n. 22, above), p. 76: 'E veggiamo che chi sul braccio disteso sostiene uno peso fermando il piè quasi come ago di bilancia, tutta l'altra parte del corpo si contraponga a contrapesare il peso. Parmi ancora che, alzando il capo, niuno più porga la faccia in alto se non quanto vegga in mezzo il cielo, né in lato più si volge il viso se non quanto il mento tocchi la spalla; in quella parte del corpo ove ti cigni, quasi mai tanto ti torci che la punta della spalla sia perpendiculare sopra il bellico. ... E veggo dalla natura quasi mai le mani levarsi sopra il capo, né le gomita sopra la spalla, né sopra il ginocchio il piede, né tra uno piè ad un altro essere più spazio che d'n solo piede. E posi mente distendendo in alto una mano, che persino al piede tutta quella parte del corpo la sussegua tale che il calcagno medesimo del piè si leva dal pavimento'.

[46] Ibid., p. 78.

[47] F. Zöllner, '"*Ogni pittore dipinge sé*." Leonardo da Vinci and *Automimesis*', in *Der Künstler über sich in seinem Werk*, M. Winner (Ed.), Weinheim 1992, pp.137–60 (esp. p. 141).

This intimate knowledge of the human figure acquired by the artist through an awareness of his own body may be explained in terms of a sense for which sixteenth-century art theorists had no word but which they undoubtedly experienced: proprioception. Identified by modern physiology, proprioception enables the transition from stillness to movement. Proprioceptive receptors are located in the muscles and the articulations. From there they provide an inner spatial image of the positions of every limb at every moment of consciousness. In this respect the art of imagining and articulating figures in various positions depends as much on the study of anatomy as on postural awareness and postural imagination. [48]

More importantly, proprioception links together all the sensory receptors of the body – those providing information on the inner organs and those transmitting data from the outside world. The term has played an important role in the formation of the twentieth-century notion of the body image, an umbrella concept in which the scientific knowledge of the human body established by physiology and neurology enters into a dialogue with phenomenology and psychoanalysis. [49] In the latter discipline sensitive and erogenous zones become significant points at which the unconscious principally operates. [50]

These aspects of a non-visual self-image of the body may help to comprehend the *Capitolo del pennello* as an erotic fantasy as much as an encomium of a discipline prizing the ability of imagining and depicting sentient bodies in various positions. In the text the brush stands as the sensory intermediary between two bodies: the painter and the painted figure. This character of the brush may have been emphasised by the use of oil paint in the sixteenth century.

From the late fifteenth century onwards the diffusion of oil painting in Italy changed not only the appearance and methods of painting but also the role played by the brush. [51] Artists could remodel and retouch their work indefinitely and even modify the positions and limbs of their figures, thus

[48] On proprioception see P. Schilder, *The Image and Appearance of the Human Body: Studies in the Constructive Energies of the Psyche*, New York 1950, pp. 17–118: 'The physiological basis of the body-image'. See also Schmidt (Ed.) 1986 (as in n. 30, above), pp. 47–9.

[49] G. Weiss, *Body Images: Embodiment as Incorporeality*, London, New York 1999, pp. 7–38.

[50] See R. Le Goffey, *Le Lasso spéculaire. Une étude traversière de l'unité imaginaire*, Paris 1997, p. 28. On the body image in psychoanalysis see F. Dolto, *L'Image inconsciente du corps*, Paris 1984.

[51] On the introduction of oil painting in Italy see J. Dunkerton, 'Nord e Sud: tecniche pittoriche nella Venezia Rinascimentale', in *Il Rinascimento a Venezia e la pittura del Nord ai tempi di Bellini, Dürer, Tiziano*, B. Aikema and B. L. Brown (Eds), Venice 1999, pp. 93–103. On the impact of this technique on style see Sohm 1991 (as in n. 17, above), pp. 4–9.

prolonging the process of articulating the figures, a process extending from the stage of sketching to that of painting, from charcoal to brush. [52] The new medium was also endowed with sensuous qualities, as Vasari points out:

> This manner of painting kindles the pigment and nothing else is needed save diligence and love, because the oil in itself softens and sweetens the colours, and renders them more delicate and more easily blended than do the other media. While the work is wet the colours readily mix and unite one with the other; in short, by this method the artists impart wonderful grace and vivacity and vigour to their figures, so much so that these often seem to us in relief and ready to issue forth from the panel, especially when they are carried out in good drawing with invention and a beautiful style. [53]

The tactile qualities of the unprocessed oil medium – 'morbido, più dolce e dilicato' – produces figures which Vasari described in terms of liveliness and relief. In all likelihood the oil medium also enhanced the importance of the brush as a sensory intermediary between painter and figure. A case in point is Bronzino's technique in works dating from the same years as the *Capitolo*, such as the Florentine portraits of the 1530s (Pl. 19). Bronzino's tendency to hide brush strokes must have emphasised the magic character of the brush. Its skilful handling turned the raw qualities of the scented paste into a range of eminently tactile organic or artificial materials – flesh, hair, fabrics, ink, gems, wood and stone. But the role of the brush as a sensor, dipped in colour rather than ink in the portrait of a young man with a lute (Florence, Uffizi), applies also to the painterly style introduced by Tintoretto in 1548 and usually associated with the Venetian school. Here brushwork follows the contour and volumes of the figure instead of drawing attention to the flatness of the painted support. [54]

The importance of the brush led Bronzino to associate its three main types with the three styles of classical eloquence:

> And since I, myself, am also a painter
> I want to make you see what
> the big, the medium size and the small brush are good for. [55]

---

[52]   For examples of Bronzino's revisions of his compositions see C. Plazzotta and L. Keith, 'Bronzino's "Allegory": New Evidence of the Artist's Revisions', *The Burlington Magazine*, 141, 1999, pp. 89–99.

[53]   Vasari 1966– (as in n. 24, above), vol. 1, p. 133: 'Questa maniera di colorire accende più i colori né altro bisogna che diligenza et amore, perché l'olio in sé si reca il colorito più morbido, più dolce e dilicato e di unione e sfumata maniera più facile che li altri, e mentre che fresco si lavora, i colori si mescolano e si uniscono l'uno con l'altro più facilmente; et insomma li artefici dànno in questo modo bellissima grazia e vivacità e gagliardezza alle figure loro, talmente che spesso ci fanno parere di rilievo le loro figure e che ell'eschino della tavola, e massimamente quando elle sono continovate di buono disegno con invenzione e bella maniera'; transl. Maclehose 1907 (as in n. 44, above), p. 230.

[54]   Rosand 1996 (as in n. 16, above), p. 134.

The biggest brushes, which should correspond to the orator's elevated style are in reality fat and short ('corti e grossi') and used only in grisaille painting. [56] Bronzino does not link any specific style or genre with the medium-size and small brush. He merely emphasises the importance of robustness, especially when the brush is long and its end so fine and subtle that it may bend. Thus the correspondence between three types of brush and the three styles of rhetoric is deliberately very loose and tends to highlight dissimilarities rather than correspondences.

Bronzino's *Capitolo*, with its praise of practice, 'brushwork' and erotic indulgence could not be further removed from the ideal of love and beauty expounded in art theory in the tradition of Neoplatonic aesthetics. Bronzino's approach does, however, converge with the definition of *disegno* in the 1568 edition of Vasari's *Vite*:

> Disegno is a visual expression and declaration of the concetto that is held in the mind and of that which one has imagined in the intellect and fabricated in the idea.[57]

This definition, as well as Bronzino literary brushwork, in turn converge with the Aristotelian conception of the soul as it was commonplace in the sixteenth century. According to perceptual theory in the tradition of Aristotle, we acquire knowledge through the external sense data which are collected in the common sense, synthesised into images by the imagination, examined by the intellect and kept in the memory. [58] The empirical basis of

---

[55] Bronzino 1988 (as in n. 3, above), p. 26: 'E perch'è io sono anch'io pur dipintore, | io vi vo' fare vedere a quel ch'è buono | il pennel grosso, il mezzano, il minor'. On the three styles of rhetoric see *Rhetorica ad Herennium*, 4. 8. 11; see also B. Vickers, *In Defence of Rhetoric*, Oxford 1988, pp. 80-4.

[56] See Vasari 1966- (as in n. 24, above), vol. 1, p. 139: 'Del dipingere nelle mura di chiaro e scuro di varie terrette, e come si contrafanno le cose di bronzo; e delle storie di terretta per archi o per feste a colla, che è chiamato a guazzo, et a tempera. Vogliono i pittori che il chiaroscuro sia una forma di pittura che tragga più al disegno che al colorito, perché ciò è stato cavato da le statue di marmo, contrafacendole, e da le figure di bronzo et altre varie pietre'.

[57] Ibid., p. 111: '... esso disegno altro non sia che una apparente espressione e dichiarazione del concetto che si ha nell'animo, e di quello che altri si è nella mente imaginato e fabricato nell'idea'.

[58] See for example G. B. Gelli, *I capricci del bottaio*, I. Sanesi (Ed.), Florence 1952, p. 147: 'Ma perchè in quell'instante medesimo ch'ella è creata l'anima nostra si ritrova rinchiusa in questo nostro corpo sensibile non può già mai acquistare cognizione alcuna per altro modo che per quello de le cose sensibili, aiutata non di manco da i sensi esteriori, conoscitivi di quelle, per i quali passando, le loro forme si imprimono ne i sensi esteriori, o, per meglio dire, si scrivono sì nella fantasia e sì nella memoria, come in un libro, dove leggendo poi l'intelletto perviene a la cognizione delle cose intelligibili'. For a broad view of Renaissance faculty psychology see K. Park, 'The Organic Soul', in *The Cambridge History of Renaissance Philosophy*, Cambridge 1988, pp. 464-84.

Aristotelianism implies that mental images shaped in the imagination and articulated by the intellect are made up of sensory impressions. Such inner images are what artists aimed to compose and to represent. In Aristotelian philosophy they are referred to as common sensibles.

According to Aristotle each sense has its own object: '... colour is the special object of sight, sound of hearing, flavour of taste.'[59] Common sensibles, on the other hand, are simultaneously perceived by several senses. They are the categories set in motion by Bronzino's brush:

> *Common sensibles* are movement, rest, number, figure, magnitude; these are not peculiar to any one sense, but are common to all.[60]

The *Capitolo del pennello* as much as Palma's self-portrait are rare witnesses of poetry of practice, usually concealed by the intellectual ambitions of sixteenth-century art theory. Composed at a time when brushes had almost become *parti vergognose* ('shameful parts'), they connect the concrete practice of painting with the mental discipline of imagining and depicting sentient figures which, by means of postures and gestures, express the artist's experience of reality.

---

[59]   Aristotle, *De Anima*, 418a.
[60]   Ibid.

Courtesan and Connoisseur: Veronica Franco on the Villa della Torre at Fumane

MARY ROGERS

The subject of this essay is a chapter taken from the 1575 *Terze rime* by the Venetian courtesan and writer Veronica Franco.[1] This 565 line descriptive poem, the last in a cycle of 25, is declared by the author to be a word painting: 'artlessly I draw and paint what I know'[2] and was based on her recollection, back in Venice, of a 'sweet and tranquil nest' which had given her refuge and solace.[3] This was the della Torre villa at Fumane, in the province of Verona, whose setting, gardens and contents she extolled. To my knowledge, this is the longest and most sustained passage of writing on an ensemble of art works by a woman writer of the Renaissance, whether or not the building and grounds, or only some of its contents, can be counted as such. It therefore deserves more examination than it has so far received from art historians, either those concerned with critical writing on art, or those who share the current interest in women as spectators and users of artefacts. Franco presents the landscape around Fumane as a *locus amoenus* of preternatural beauty and fertility, favoured by the heavens and pervaded by the presences of mythological beings such as Apollo, Flora and Pomona, satyrs and nymphs of the forests and of the streams. The descriptions fall into three main sections. The first, lines 64–129, evokes the countryside around Lake Garda, where the villa is situated, and the wooded meadows irrigated by the mountain streams which provide water for the ponds, fountains and rare plants of the garden. Nature and art are seen as working in harmony.[4] The next section (from line 133) deals with the villa 'worthy of the palace of the

[1] XXV, pp. 152–67 in the edition *Veronica Franco: Rime*, S. Bianchi (Ed.), Milan 1995, from which I will be quoting. An older edition of Franco's poems is: A. Salza, *Gaspara Stampa, Veronica Franco: Rime*, Bari 1913; and the most recent *Poems and Selected Letters*, A. R. Jones and M. F. Rosenthal (Eds and Trans.), Chicago, London 1998.

[2] 'senz'arte quel ch'io so disegno e pingo'; XXV, 39. References given by line only will henceforward be to this poem/chapter, XXV.

[3] 'vago nido ... a la tranquillità soave e grato'; 11–2.

[4] ' ... l'acque in vario corso | declinan verso 'l pian soavi e quete; | ... | e da natural arte a far instrutte | bello quel sito a maraviglia ...'; 110–6.

Sun the poet described'[5] (that is, in Ovid's *Metamorphoses* II, 1–18) but extols its architectural features only in vague, general terms:

> ... [the palace] is well worth a priceless treasure
> for the building itself, and for its ornaments,
> which in richness and in beauty are unequalled.
> The fine marbles and the shining porphyry,
> cornices, arches, columns, carvings and friezes,
> figures, perspectives, gold and silver,
> are found here of a kind and value
> unequalled by the palaces
> of ancient emperors and kings.[6]

Franco doubtless lacked the competence to analyse the architectural features in any detail: what detain her most are some of the contents of the building, textiles figured with images of the loves of the gods (148–183) and paintings of popes and prelates (187–222). Lastly, in a third section (226–453), ascending to a balcony on an upper storey, she absorbs the sounds and scents of the garden and feasts her eyes on its delights (263–7) and on those of the surrounding pastoral landscape with its shepherds and shepherdesses, hunters, fishers and snarers of birds (349–417), and seems to sense its presiding deities (424–441). The poem ends with an encomium to the wisdom, eloquence and courtesy of the owner of the villa, Count Marcantonio della Torre (1531–1591), canon of the cathedral at Verona and apostolic protonotary (457–565).[7]

Most recent critical studies have seen the Fumane poem as an appropriate and ambitious finale to the cycle, tying together some of the themes, and resolving some of the conflicts, found in earlier chapters within the cycle, such as those between the city and the country, man and woman, art and nature. This paper will build on such scholarship, but also call attention to sources of inspiration more familiar to art historians than to literary critics and additional to the classical and Trecento literature usually emphasised by the latter;[8] it will also attempt to show how Franco used descriptive poetry, and in particular the descriptions of the textiles and portraits, in one sense to draw attention to herself, to her subjectivity and to her position in the world, but in another to extend her literary persona and expand the scope of the cycle beyond the purely personal. Although it will

---

[5]   131–2; see Appendix.

[6]   133–41; see Appendix.

[7]   See G. Benzoni, in *Dizionario biografico degli Italiani*, vol. 37, Rome 1989, pp. 613–5 for entry on Marcantonio della Torre.

[8]   The most recent long study on Veronica Franco is M. Rosenthal, *The Honest Courtesan*, Chicago, London 1992, with pp. 240–55 on the Fumane poem; others are A. Zorzi, *Cortigiana veneziana: Veronica Franco e i suoi poeti*, Milan 1986 and M. Diberti Leigh, *Veronica Franco: Donna, poetessa e cortigiana del Rinascimento*, Ivrea 1988.

not mainly be concerned with relating the poem to the actualities of the
real-life villa, it is worthwhile at the outset briefly to outline what we know
of the building, in order to illuminate Franco's selection of material.

The building, in the territory of Verona near Lake Garda, is still extant
today, currently being restored from its previous neglected condition (Pl. 21). [9]
Its plan is most convincingly attributed to Giulio Romano, though it seems to
have been executed posthumously, and certain scholars favour the notion of
some degree of intervention by Michele Sanmicheli. Its striking architectural
features include many of the rich and fanciful effects one would expect from
Giulio, including a heavily rusticated courtyard (Pl. 22) and an entrance via a
walkway over a fishpond (Pl. 23). [10] It is unclear to what extent Franco's lines
on 'fine marbles and shining porphyry, cornices, arches, columns, carvings
and friezes' describe actual stonework as opposed to painted architectural
detail found in the interiors of Veneto villas, best exemplified by Veronese's
work at Maser. Only a little survives of interior sculpted detail, such as the
fireplaces in the form of giants' mouths (Pl. 24). The 'figures and perspectives'
could well have been done by Veronese's associate, Paolo Farinati, who is said
by Ridolfi to have painted frescoes in della Torre residences, though nothing
of them remains at Fumane today. [11] Though the interior is now bereft of its
furnishings, the textiles described by Franco have been linked to tapestries
mentioned in an inventory of the contents of the villa, although we do not
know if their subject-matter corresponded to the Ovidian stories mentioned
in the poem, or indeed if they included figurative material at all. [12] Taken
together, all these indications make credible the claim by Onofrio Panvinio, a
seventeenth-century antiquarian, that Fumane was the most splendid villa in
the territory of Verona, and one of the richest in Italy, for its gardens,
orchards, fountains and other ornaments. [13]

[9] For the villa, see G. F. Viviani, *La Villa nel Veronese*, Verona 1975, pp. 432–41, on
its garden, pp. 191–2, and on Franco's poem on it, pp. 238–9; L. Franzoni,
'Raccolte d'arte e di antichità', in *Palladio e Verona*, P. Marini (Ed.), Verona 1980,
pp. 124–30, with full bibliographies.

[10] The case for Giulio is made most effectively in P. Carpeggiani, 'Giulio Romano
architetto di villa', *Arte Lombarda*, 7, 1972, pp. 1–13, with a review of other
scholars' opinion p. 11, n. 46.

[11] C. Ridolfi, *Le Maraviglie dell'arte*, Rome 1965, vol. 2, p. 130: Farinati painted
'altre opere a fresco nelle case de' Conti dalla Torre'. L. Crosato, *Gli affreschi nelle
ville venete del Cinquecento*, Treviso 1962, p. 119, gives an assortment of references
to Farinati's frescoes for the della Torre and for other villas in the territory of
Verona.

[12] An inventory of the furnishings of Fumane was made in November–December
1573, only a summary of which, from a later era, is now preserved, which merely
lists five pieces of tapestry from one bedroom and seven from another; see
Franzoni 1980 (as in n. 9, above), pp. 127–8.

[13] Quoted in Viviani 1975 (as in n. 9, above), p. 192; O. Panvinio, *Antiquitatum
veronensium libri VIII*, Padua 1648, vol. 1, ch. XX, p. 26.

From this material, Franco selected for emphasis only those elements which could serve in her project of self-fashioning in words. Her main theme of the cycle as a whole is the discovery and presentation of a multi-faceted self, an 'honest courtesan' (*cortegiana onesta*), who does not deny that she is such, but who seeks both to place her profession within an ethical framework and to carve out other roles for herself. Some of these are suffering lover, candid friend, Venetian patriot, vengeful warrior, social critic and writer on art. Incorporating as it does chapters written by male authors, the *Terze rime* starts off as a dialogue initiated by a would-be lover, Marco Venier, but half-way through the cycle is transformed into a monologue conducted by Franco alone. This structure dramatises the emergence of Franco's increasingly versatile and vigorous voices, as she first counters, then vehemently silences the males and comes to range in theme far beyond the confines of the conventional poetic love-cycle. In thus constructing a complex and distinctive literary persona, Franco was determined to demonstrate her rhetorical skill and to rework current literary *topoi* so that they engaged with her own concerns, in writing and in life, as recent critics have emphasised.[14] What has not been fully examined is her use of descriptions of scenes, persons or artefacts as part of this process. A series of what can loosely be called word-paintings occur throughout the cycle, evoking Venice or the *terraferma*, bedrooms or battlegrounds, in which Franco's transformation from object into subject is seen, and her shifting moods and allegiances are registered. They associate her with alternative personae, which could be brusquely dismissed by the author or adopted as guises. Those which frame the whole work show the most dramatic change in her stature. The opening chapter, written by Marco Venier, after praising Franco in conventionally Petrarchan terms for her chaste beauty and virtuous behaviour, becomes a word-painting of an imagined nude Veronica of a very different kind:

> Oh how sweet to admire your naked limbs
> and sweeter still to languish in their midst
> ... I would take in my hands the polished gold
> of your tresses, drawing towards my prey
> little by little, the ultimate treasure in my revenge.
> When you lie stretched out on the feathery mattress,

---

[14] Apart from Rosenthal 1992 (as in n. 8, above), critical studies of particular help on these points are A. R. Jones, 'Surprising Fame: Renaissance Gender Ideologies and Women's Lyric', in *The Poetics of Gender*, N. K. Miller (Ed.), New York 1986, pp. 74–95, and idem, 'City Women and their Audiences: Louise Labé and Veronica Franco', in *Rewriting the Renaissance*, M. W. Ferguson et al. (Eds), Chicago, London 1986, pp. 299–316; M. F. Rosenthal, 'Veronica Franco's "Terze Rime": the Venetian Courtesan's Defense', *Renaissance Quarterly*, 42, 2, 1989, pp. 227–57; idem, 'A Courtesan's Voice: Epistolary Self-Portraiture in Veronica Franco's *Terze Rime*', in *Writing the Female Voice: Essays on Epistolary Literature*, E. C. Goldsmith (Ed.), Boston 1989, pp. 3–24.

how sweet to assail you, and in that aspect
to take from you all refuge, all defense.
Venus recognises you by your enticing ways in bed,
and by the delights she so fully discovers in you ....[15]

Here Franco is pictured as the silent object of male desire, a Venus reclining on a bed calling to mind any number of examples from sixteenth-century Venetian painting, starting with Titian's famous *Venus of Urbino* in the Uffizi, Florence. However, by the last chapter, when she writes her long poem on Fumane, a major shift in viewing position has taken place: she has transformed herself from an erotic spectacle into an assured and articulate spectator, aware, as we shall see, of the language and concepts of current art criticism. The Fumane chapter, however, does not display only a desire to show herself as objective, rational, and well-informed: it also deliberately makes explicit the subjective and sensual nature of her responses, the limitations of her viewing and her understanding, and the constructed character of her transmission of her remembered impressions.

The opening passage of the landscape description dramatises the contrast between the intense emotional pull of the memory of Fumane, using words such as 'exceeding pleasure', 'delights' and 'joy' (27–33), and the role of the writer's reflecting mind in recounting it and disciplining her emotions into a long passage of objective and systematic description:

Here I take in ready hand my pen,
and to indulge my feeling, I counterfeit
this place as true to life as I can. (34–36)[16]

The two separate passages on the landscape setting demonstrate different ways of doing this. In the first, in an ordered sequence, she maps out a movement from the heavens to the surrounding circle of hills and down to the meadows surrounded by woods. A similar descent is seen as the water nymphs pour their liquid from mountain torrents down to more gently flowing streams, which then become canalised so that they can irrigate the rare evergreen trees and plants of the garden of the villa:

instructed by natural art
to make this site marvellously beautiful.[17]

---

[15] 'Oh che dolce mirar le membre ignude, | e più dolce languir in grembo a loro, | ch'or a torto mi son sí scarse e crude! | Prenderei con le mani il forbito oro | de le trecce, tirando de l'offesa, | pian piano, in mia vendetta il fin tesoro. | Quando giacete ne le piume stesa, | che soave assalarvi! e in quella guisa | levarvi ogni riparo, ogni difesa! | Venere in letto ai vezzi vi ravvisa, | a le delizie che 'n voi tante scopre'; I, 118–28.

[16] 'In questo piglio in man pronta lo stile; | e per gradir al sentimento, fingo | quel loco quanto possi al ver simíle'; 34–6.

[17] 'da natural arte a far instrutte | bello quel sito a maraviglia ....'; 115–6.

In contrast with this ordered, topographical approach, the second passage tends much more towards the stream of consciousness, and emphasises her embodied presence. The author ascends to the upper balcony of the villa and responds to the almost superabundant delights first of the garden and then of the open landscape beyond, to sounds (birdsong and murmuring fountains: 232–37) and to scents (the 'Arabian perfumes' of air and flowering earth: 254–58), as well as to the manifold sights which pull her gaze in all directions:

Oh what a pleasing and most lovely dwelling,
where, the more you admire its beauty,
the more remains for you to see.
Wherever one turns the gaze to look,
one finds something in the beauty one has beheld,
which the eyes are drawn to look at more intently;[18]

And the subsequent lines envisage a competition between nature and art in attracting the eye by means of the landscape and of the palace interior respectively (262–276), giving a 'prodigal banquet' (278) for the spectator. In recalling this experience of viewing, with a gaze that now seems darting, random and uncontrolled, Franco in this section allows herself to seem more spontaneous, even overwhelmed, as she would state later on in relation to her memory:

my mind remains defeated and conquered ...
thus in the task of imagining you,
the understanding [l'ingegno] is left useless and confused;
and if still, rambling, I come to praise you,
being confused inside, I mistake
the order and the parts of your praise.[19]

The limitations of rational control are made evident.

The different treatment of the two landscape passages allows Franco, who in an earlier chapter had offered a calumniator generally thought to be Maffio Venier a choice of literary styles and languages in which to debate, to demonstrate alternative ways of dealing with her memories and sense-impressions, alternative sorts of viewing.[20] In analysing particular features of

18 'Oh che grata e dolcissima dimora, | dove quanto di vago ognor più miri, | tanto più da veder ti resta ancora! | Dovunque altri la vista a mirar giri, | ne la beltà veduta oggetto trova, | che più intente a guardar le luci tiri'; 259–64.
19 'resta la mente mia vinta e conquisa ... | così ne l'opra de l'imaginarti | riman l'ingegno inutile e confuso; | e se vaga pur vengo di lodarti, | come confusa son dentro, confondo | de le tue lodi l'ordine e le parti.'; 445, 449–53.
20 See XVI, 112–17: 'La spada, che 'n man vostra rade e fóra, | de la lingua volgar venezïana, | s'a voi piace d'usar, piace a me ancora; | e se volete entrar ne la toscana, | scegliete voi la seria o la burlesca, | ché l'una e l'altra è a me facile e piana.' Franco's deliberate use of different sorts of language and literary voices has been best discussed in Rosenthal 1989 (both studies as in n. 14, above).

her descriptions of scenery, recent criticism has concentrated on Trecento or classical precedents, and particularly the Petrarchan sources underlying some of the phrases and the basic combination of memories of landscape and intense, overwhelming emotion, though it has also been noted how in other respects Franco subverted Petrarch's themes and motifs.[21] But other writers nearer in time to Franco shaped both the elements and imagery of the landscape and garden passages, and their underlying aesthetic. Sannazaro's *Arcadia* opens with descriptions of a *locus amoenus*, a mixed forest beside grassy, flower-studded meadows and clear fountains underneath a mountain; these are more elaborate versions of those found around line 80 in the Fumane poem. Sannazaro's section alludes to Apollo and Daphne, as does Franco in the first of her passages on the landscape, and Sannazaro's countryside with its amorous herdsmen and sensed presences of nymphs and classical deities is analogous to that seen by Franco from the balcony window in the second half.[22] And of course his descriptions of paintings and other precious objects form some of the many precedents for Franco's, especially his account of the tapestry depicting the death of Eurydice in chapter XII.[23]

Sannazaro, however, was dealing with pastoral countryside, lauding the untamed beauties of wild terrain distant from civilised living. In the Fumane poem, by contrast, the landscape is used for producing fruit and grain as well as for hunting and grazing sheep. It is given still further beauty when adapted for the use and the delight of humans, a co-ordination that forms part of the wider theme of the reconciliation of potentially antagonistic elements that makes the poem an appropriate termination of the cycle. Nature, in the form of water and of vegetation, is tamed and endowed with superior harmony by the art of the gardener (115-129).[24] Franco is not fleeing the civilities of the town, as Sannazaro/Sincero fled Naples, for they exist in the setting of the countryside: the comforts of the interior are exceptional (142-44), Marcantonio della Torre is 'courteous and wise' (523), his servants well instructed and well dressed (545-549). Relationships are established between

[21] Both Bianchi (Ed.) 1995 and Rosenthal 1992 (as in n. 1 and n. 8, above) point to the Petrarchan references; Franco's 'deconstruction and reconstruction' of Petrarchism is discussed in S. M. Adler, 'Veronica Franco's Petrarchan "Terze Rime": Subverting the Master's Plan', *Italica*, 65, 3, 1988, pp. 213-33.

[22] *Arcadia*, I, in Jacopo Sannazaro, *Opere volgari*, A. Mauro (Ed.), Bari 1961, pp. 5-6. Franco invokes the story of Daphne in 88-93.

[23] *Arcadia*, XII, 16-18: Mauro (Ed.) 1961 (as n. 22, above), pp. 113-4. Other objects described are the paintings in the temple in III, the cup in IV and the vase in XI. N. Land, *The Viewer as Poet*, University Park, Pa. 1994, though not mentioning Franco's poem, provides a useful account of classical *ekphrasis* as it influenced Renaissance literature and criticism.

[24] The waters from the streams 'da natural arte a far instrutte | bello quel sito a maraviglia, vanno | per canali angustissimi ridutte' (115-8) and (127-129), see Appendix. The rivalry between nature and art is again treated in 271-6.

the surroundings and the interior of the villa by means of Ovidian references
in both. The lives of the country people viewed from the balcony (357–369)
are idealised, not seen as ugly or threatening to the idyllic way of life of their
lord. These are themes that had been developed in many of the writings on
villas and agriculture in the three decades or so before the publication of the
Terze rime, some of which Veronica Franco is likely to have read. A tradition
of descriptive writing on villas, many of them around Verona, had developed
in the fifteenth and sixteenth centuries, emphasising both the beauties of their
sites and the gentlemanly way of life they accommodated. Part of this
tradition are humanist letters, meant to be published. [25] One such easily
accessible example was a letter by Pietro Aretino of around 1542 on the villa
of Agostino Brenzone, which, like Fumane, was situated in the fertile
landscape around Lake Garda and was rich in its gardens and in its
Sanmichelian architecture. [26] This earthly paradise, Aretino alleged, had the
power to cure melancholy, just as Fumane could calm Veronica Franco's
emotional turmoils. Its ground, like the della Torre dwelling, had
preternatural fecundity with its sweet-scented flowers and fountains and
abundantly productive fruit and olive trees. [27]

   This aesthetic of abundance, influenced both by classical writings on the
locus amoenus and by the actual character of the countryside around Verona,
also pervades the other literary genre: treatises on country life like Agostino
Gallo's *Le dieci giornate della vera agricoltura* of 1566, which also extols the
landscape around Lake Garda, this time on the Brescian side. [28] The features of
the villas he describes are comparable to those at Fumane, such as gardens
with sweet scents and the sound of birds, fishponds and fountains watered

[25] A useful survey of Renaissance writing on villas, including letters, such as those
by Guarino da Verona and Ermolao Barbaro, is in Viviani 1975 (as in n. 9, above),
pp. 231–51. See also D. Thornton, *The Scholar in his Study*, New Haven, London
1997, pp. 115–6, for letters describing visits to villas, though more for their art
collections than their landscape settings.

[26] Pietro Aretino, *Lettere sull'arte*, E. Camesasca (Ed.), 3 vols, Milan 1957–6, vol. 1,
CLXIX, pp. 249–52. Viviani 1975 (as in n. 9, above), pp. 231–51 or p. 237 for the
Villa Brenzone.

[27] The landscape is in the first sentence, and repeatedly, lauded for its 'fertilità', the
letter citing 'la varia sorte dei fiori diversi, la inusitata condizione degli alberi cari
e la bella moltitudine dei frutti cordiali', mentioning oranges, lemons, olives,
cherries, figs and pears. Their scents, and the harmonious birdsong, provide
additional sensuous delights, as does the 'palazzo eccelso', so that 'non è
maraviglia a stimare che gli umori maninconici diventano gioviali, e che le donne
sterili ... diventino di prole dividiziose'. The mention of the hunting of hares and
snaring of game birds also resembles the poem on Fumane, where the garden
likewise has 'fiere, augei, pesci, rivi, arbori e foglie, fior sempre novi, e d'ogni
stagion frutte' (335–6) and is 'pien d'aranci e di cedri' (443) as well as grapes and
grain (436–7). Fumane is referred to as 'un terren paradiso' in 422.

[28] A. Gallo, *Le dieci giornate della vera agricoltura*, Venice 1566.

from nearby rivers, and groves of olive and fruit trees in the surrounding hills. Many of Gallo's practical, manual-like passages – on the art of pruning, for instance – are presented in terms similar to those used by Franco in relation to the orchard and the garden at Fumane: nature is tamed by art, the savage made temperate.[29] His more lyrical passages, praising the delights of fine prospects over hills and sky, the pure air, and the wholesome country pastimes of peasants and huntsmen are also reminiscent of Franco, as is the ambivalent attitude to town life. While both writers sometimes presented city life as corrupt – as with the chapters immediately preceding the Fumane poem, which deal with the slander and threats of physical attack of an enemy – elsewhere they extolled it, as with Franco's paean to Venice in chapter XXII, or Gallo's praise for the fine buildings in the nearby cities of Verona, Bergamo and Mantua.[30] Certainly the interdependence of town and country is taken for granted in both texts. And many other villa treatises – Bartolomeo Taegio's *La Villa* published in Milan in 1559 is one example – present similarities to Franco's chapter XXV, either in the constituent parts of the estates referred to, or in their underlying aesthetic, or in their use of classical metaphor (gardens are the abode of Flora and Pomona, the countryside of Apollo and the Muses, woods of Diana and her nymphs).[31] The parallels are compelling enough to suggest that Franco did derive ideas from some examples of this genre of villa writings. One of her goals would seem to have been to win favour with della Torre, just as the villa authors often sought to ingratiate themselves with the other landowners whose estates they fawningly extolled. In presenting a portrait of Marcantonio della Torre via his property, she shared the strategies of these and other sixteenth-century writers who used multiple dedication, or name-dropping within their works, as a means of gaining approval and patronage.

Yet the differences are crucial. Unlike the authors of the villa treatises, Franco was not writing a guide for a proprietor or aspiring to own a country property herself: her declared goal was emotional, not economic, equilibrium. This leads one back to the Petrarchan sources of the *Terze rime*, while also showing how Franco has transformed them. In her earlier chapters dealing with landscape, XXI and XXII, the Petrarchan references had been very much more direct, with the beauties of nature contrasting with the melancholy of the lover-author. In the final poem, both the recollection of the beauties of Fumane and the task of recreating them on paper provide a solace for the

[29] Ibid., 5th day, fols 77v–97r, especially passages like: 'Veramente che l'arte dell'incalmare è una delle piu belle cose, che siano nell'agricoltura; poiche si trasmutano gli arbori selvatichi ne i domestichi, gli sterili ne i fruttiferi, gl'insipidi ne i delicati, i tardi ne i temporiti, & i temporiti ne i tardi.' (fol. 84v).

[30] Ibid., fols 3r ff. The countryside is seen as providing not only food and water for the towns, but metals for its industries and marbles for its buildings.

[31] B. Taegio, *La Villa*, Milan 1559; see especially pp. 54–69 and 100–2 for the most dense mythological references.

writer, as they did not for Petrarch. Phrases and themes from Petrarch, descriptive elements from Arcadian or villa literature, and allusions from classical mythology, are balanced and tailored to accord with Franco's own subjective concerns. The treatment of erotic themes, much more evident in Franco's writing than in Gallo's or Taegio's, is a case in point. Petrarchan sexual frustration is only occasionally alluded to, for instance by mentioning Daphne transformed into a laurel to escape Apollo's grasp (88–93), and a natural eroticism is the dominant note. The mountain streams 'offer themselves' (120) to the gardener, the birds sing their 'amorous passion' (240), a fecund earth and air conjoin to produce fruits (487–88), the surrounding hills draw the palace into their laps (343–48), the shepherd gazes at his beloved shepherdess with intense desire.[32] Highly pictorial passages like the latter, so reminiscent for the art historian of sixteenth-century Venetian paintings such as Titian's *Three Ages of Man* in the National Gallery of Scotland, Edinburgh, form appropriate frames for the descriptions of the objects in the interior of the villa. Here again one finds the combination of sensuous response controlled by the intellect and informed by reading that is found in the landscape passages.

The first of these object-based descriptions has to do with the luxurious furnishings of the villa, and above all the 'white beds' with 'gilded feet' that stand upon the shining, inlaid pavements.[33] Their textile adornments are given a thirty-three line description:

> Girding each one from on top
> are purple hangings, of varied silks and gold,
> which embrace and maintain the dignity of the beds;
> each one is adorned and covered with embroidered quilts
> or other spreads of rich fabric
> so that nothing more remains to furnish them.
> With diverse designs and diverse techniques
> on the covers and curtains on every side
> varied and painstaking craftsmanship [artificio] is revealed.[34]

Various mythological erotic episodes are described: Jove with Danae, with Europa, with Ganymede, and with Callisto (163–177).

It is easy to smile at a courtesan-author who, entering the sumptuous palace, neglects the more public reception rooms, goes straight to the bedroom, and focuses on lascivious scenes depicted on its hangings. Certainly the choice both of bed-hangings and of erotic mythologies does serve as a way of re-inserting Franco within the text, reminding the reader of her profession and of the erotic pleasure on which it was based, pleasure which she explicitly celebrated elsewhere in the cycle. In particular, the choice of the episode of

---

[32] 'in modo che di lui cresce la brama: | fisse le luci avidamente ei tiene | ne le braccia e nel sen nudi, e nel viso, | e d'abbracciarla a pena si ritiene.'; 366–9.

[33] 147–56; see Appendix.

[34] 148–56; see Appendix.

Danae 'rejoicing in her heart to see Jupiter rain down in a cloud of gold' (166-7) recalls Franco's earlier identification with this mythological figure in one of the pair of sonnets, also published in the *Terze rime*, which had been written for Henry III of France after he had spent an evening at her house in 1574.[35] There, she had used it to convey her abasement before the French king, as well as to exploit its contemporary associations with courtesans, though she was careful to neutralise the mercenary overtones by accompanying the two sonnets by a gift.[36] The citation of the mythologies, apart from demonstrating the author's classical erudition, allowed the artefacts to be linked with the classical personages pervading the landscape outside, some of which, like the subjects shown in the textiles, were Ovidian: Flora and Pomona (66), Apollo and Daphne (88-93), and particularly Procne and Philomela (232-3). Though these sisters transformed into birds are mentioned only for their sweetly lamenting song, a knowledgeable reader might have picked up the reference to tapestry, woven by the tongueless Philomela to narrate her rape and mutilation.[37] Ovid's description of another tapestry woven by a woman, Arachne's showing the rape of Europa in *Metamorphoses* VI, 1-152, though not alluded to by Franco, is the most obvious source for her descriptions of textiles in the Fumane poem, together with the tapestry described in the *Arcadia*.

The literary ambition of Franco's section on textiles is also evident in the aspiration to master the language and concepts of art criticism, as it had developed in Venice from the late 1530s onwards. Franco would certainly have known the poems and letters of Pietro Aretino, the latter of which include, as we have seen, one on a villa, and would have formed an obvious precedent for her own volume of letters, the *Lettere familiari*, which she would publish five years after the *Terze rime*.[38] She seems also to have read some of the main theoretical works on painting produced in Venice, possibly

35   166-7; see Appendix. The sonnet for Henry III begins: 'Come talor dal ciel sotto umil tetto | Giove tra noi qua giú benigno scende, | e perché occhio terren dall'alt'oggetto | non resti vinto, umana forma prende; | cosí venne al mio povero ricetto'; Bianchi (Ed.) 1995 (as in n. 1, above), p. 171, I, 1-5.

36   For which see M. M. Kahr, 'Danae: Virtuous, Voluptuous, Venal Woman', *Art Bulletin*, 58, 1978, pp. 43-55; C. Santore, 'Danae: the Renaissance Courtesan's alter ego', *Zeitschrift für Kunstgeschichte*, 54, 3, 1991, pp. 412-27.

37   The story of Procne and Philomela is in *Metamorphoses* VI, 425-675. Other Ovidian stories mentioned in Franco's XXV are the birth of Minerva (427-9), or Jupiter, Semele and Bacchus (430-6). Most helpful on the use of mythological material in the *Terze rime* are Jones 1986 (as in n. 14, above), p. 93 and E. Favretti, 'Rime e lettere di Veronica Franco', *Giornale storico della letteratura italiana*, 163, 1986, pp. 355-82, as well as Bianchi (Ed.) 1995 (as in n. 1, above) and Rosenthal 1992 (as in n. 8, above); for the passages on the furnishings, see ibid., pp. 246-9.

38   The most modern edition is Veronica Franco, *Lettere familiari*, B. Croce (Ed.), Naples 1949.

Paolo Pino's 1548 *Dialogo di Pittura* and almost certainly Lodovico Dolce's *Dialogo della Pittura* of 1557.[39] An echo of both their terminology and their aesthetic is found after the enumeration of the mythological episodes on the textiles, where she exclaims:

> How powerful is our human intelligence [ingegno],
> which makes fictitious things appear alive
> by force of colours and design!
> With silk and gold and various tinted wools,
> in the tapestries which adorn these rooms,
> real things are surpassed by imitation.[40]

The words she uses, 'ingegno', 'colori', and 'disegno', are reminiscent of the triad of qualities essential to excellence in painting according to both Pino and Dolce: 'invenzione', 'colorire' or 'colorito', and 'disegno'. Dolce had used the word 'ingegno' and its cognates repeatedly in relation to the creative faculty, the 'invenzione' of painters. It is painters' superior 'ingegno' that causes them to be deservedly esteemed among men, and enables them to endow their figures with varied and lively poses and gestures.[41] Titian is twice commended for his 'ingegno', and Michelangelo's 'invenzione' is said to be 'ingegniosissima', a superlative form also given to a poet, Ariosto, for his 'word-painting' of Alcina.[42] It may be that Franco's adoption of the word 'ingegno' rather than 'invenzione' was encouraged by its use in Dolce's and in other texts in relation to literary as well as artistic creativity.

Franco also follows Dolce in commending the mimetic and the affective in pictorial art, highlighting the variety of figures and emotional states depicted as gods descend from heaven driven by sexual passions, and like their human lovers are transformed into bulls, bears, eagles and clouds of gold:

> Here one sees the enamoured gods
> descend from heaven upon the nymphs
> transformed into different shapes;
> and, faces flushed with amorous passion,
> restlessly they pursue their desire,
> when driven by the hot fire.[43]

But, unlike Dolce, Franco first selects textiles, rather than any of the other images that were found within the villa, as the medium in which this expressiveness is perceived, together with the desired qualities of high art, 'ingegno', 'colore' and 'disegno'. This choice might well have carried a complex polemical charge. In one sense, it may have been intended to counter

[39] Published in P. Barocchi (Ed.), *Trattati d'arte del Cinquecento*, Bari 1960, vol. 1, pp. 93–136 and 141–206.
[40] 178–83; see Appendix.
[41] Barocchi (Ed.) 1960 (as in n. 39, above), pp. 161, 171.
[42] Ibid., pp. 201, 206 (on Titian), p. 191 (on Michelangelo), p. 172 (Ariosto is called 'ingegniosissimo' in 'painting' Alcina).
[43] 157–62; see Appendix.

Renaissance aestheticians' frequent denigration of tapestries and other luxurious textiles in comparison with painting, which Dolce had displayed when he wrote:

> and even if the interior walls of buildings, public or private, are draped with the finest tapestries, and the chests and the tables covered with the most beautiful carpets, lacking the adornment of some painting they greatly lose beauty and grace.[44]

Even though Dolce believes that the 'disegno' proper to painting can also inform the art of the embroiderer, as he stated earlier in his treatise,[45] the present passage suggests a hierarchy in which luxury fabrics clearly rank beneath painting.[46] Franco's passage may be intended to counter such assumptions by stressing how figured textiles could possess all the praiseworthy qualities of good painting.

Another aspect of Franco's discussion of textiles could have been the complex connections between textiles and women. In the antique literary tradition, which had been continued in Sannazaro, weaving was a woman's art, the art of Minerva, a goddess with whom Franco had earlier in the cycle been compared.[47] In some of the more famous tapestry-weaving episodes in literature of which she would have been aware (those of Penelope or Philomela), women make figured cloths for self-protection or self-expression. The textiles actually at Fumane, whether the tapestries in the inventory, or the various forms of needlework adorning the bedrooms evoked in 148–83, might not literally have been produced by women let alone by Franco.[48] However, a female author might have considered these literary associations of textile-making with the craft (in all senses of the word) of women to be highly appropriate for her purposes. By evoking the creativity of women in the plastic arts, the creativity of the female writer could be validated, just as by

---

[44] Barocchi (Ed.) 1960 (as in n. 39, above), p. 163: 'e i publici edifici et i privati, benché siano i muri di dentro vestiti di finissimi arazzi, e le casse e le tavole coperte di bellissimi tapeti, senza l'ornamento di qualche pittura assai di bellezza e di grazia perdono'.

[45] Ibid., p. 162.

[46] For discussion of the Renaissance humanists' dislike of excessive opulence as derived from antique suspicion of ornament in rhetoric, see P. Sohm, 'Gendered Style', *Renaissance Quarterly*, 48, 1995, pp. 759–808 (esp. pp. 780ff.).

[47] In VII, 38, written by an anonymous male author.

[48] In the critical literature on XXV, it tends to be assumed that the Loves of the Gods were portrayed on tapestries: for example, the 'tapeti' which imitate 'le cose vere' (182–3) are understood by Bianchi (Ed.) 1995 (as in n. 1, above), p. 233, as such. However, a variety of needlework techniques seem to be suggested by phrases such as 'gli agi ... molli' (142–3) or 'coltre ricamata' (151) or 'diverse opre su coverte e cortine' (154–5), and the use of embroidery or appliqué work perhaps seems more likely for the various hangings and spreads that would have dressed a sixteenth-century bed.

showing the erotic passions of the gods the sexual activity of the courtesan could be celebrated.

However, another aspect of Franco's obvious fascination with elaborate fabrics was less positive. A taste for luxurious dress or furnishing fabrics was associated with courtesans, real or fictitious, in many literary sources from the sixteenth century. Where the tone is of admiration, tapestries, gilded leather and cloth-of-gold wall hangings are understood as entirely appropriate linings for the luxurious dwellings of these women, 'showcasing' their beauty and registering their social success. Matteo Bandello's description of the palace of the Roman courtesan Imperia, in whose chambers 'there was nothing to be seen but velvets and brocades, and the finest carpets on the floor' would be one example.[49] Pietro Fortini's fictitional Venetian courtesan, with her 'rich and lordly chamber, all decked out in silk draperies, where there was a bed with the most superb curtains and a truly royal coverlet' another.[50] In these cases, the mention of expensive fabrics conveys the aristocratic style of life these women had achieved, but where the tone is more hostile, their taste for luxurious textiles seems to serve as one indicator of the courtesans' stereotypical vices: avarice, deceit, presumption and extravagance. This is the case in a satirical poem directed against the Venetian courtesan Angela Zaffetta, perhaps by Lorenzo Venier.[51] Venier attacked Angela as a robber whore, whose rotten flesh was decked in lavish velvets and brocades, its stench masked by perfumes and cosmetics. She was ruining both patrician and plebeian alike with her extravagant tastes, which included a taste for inappropriately rich fabrics. On the fateful outing to Malamocco which culminated in her multiple rape, the fact that she wanted to embark on a shopping spree for textiles and tapestries, for six beds draped in silk and gold, suggested her disordered appetites as much as did her gorging on partridges, oysters, and wine. The association of expensive materials with the folly of courtesans is found again in Aretino: in his *Sei giornate* the naive would-be courtesan, Pippa, dreaming of her future success, is made to say: 'This morning at dawn I imagined I was in a high, large, beautiful room, whose walls were adorned with green and yellow satin....' and which contained 'a bed covered in brocade with gold-weft loops'.[52] But her mother and mentor,

[49]   M. Bandello, novella XLIII, 3rd part, in *Tutte le opere di Matteo Bandello*, F. Flora (Ed.), Verona 1942, p. 462: 'una sala e una camera e un camerino si posposamente adornati, che altro non v'era che velluti e broccati e per terra finissimi tapeti. Nel camerino ... erano i paramenti, che le mura coprivano, tutti di drappi d'oro riccio sovra riccio, con molti belli e vaghi lavori'.
[50]   Pietro Fortini, novella XI, in *Raccolta di novellieri italiani*, Florence 1834, p. 1180: 'una signorile e ricca camera, tutta apparata di vari drappi di seta, dove era un letto con superbissime cortine e regal cuperta'.
[51]   L. Venier, *Le Trente et un de la Zaffetta*, Paris 1883, pp. 22–8 for the most pertinent passages.
[52]   P. Aretino, *Sei giornate*, 2nd day, 2; in G. Aquilecchia (Ed.), Bari 1969, p. 217:

Nanna, is more cautious about succumbing to the temptation of fancy fabrics which might not have much resale value: 'leave embroideries to those who want to throw away their gold'.[53]

At times, it seems as though Franco herself endorsed this association of expensive materials and foolish extravagance. In the poem just before *capitolo* XXV, she wrote of the tyranny of men, to which women all too feebly submit. Men pretend to do women honour, showering them with compliments and expensive presents:

... silks, embroideries, silver and gold,
jewels, purple fabrics, and whatever is most costly
they place as ornaments on their esteemed treasure ....[54]

but they are really women's enemies. Lavish expenditure on the textiles used in women's clothes is here relocated and redefined as a male vice: on the one hand being pride in displaying men's sumptuously dressed female trophies, and on the other being a ruse to placate women and maintain masculine domination.

Although, judging from her wills, Veronica Franco in her heyday, the 1570's, enjoyed a good standard of living, occupying premises of reasonable size, employing servants, owning a silver candelabrum and silver dishes, as well as a fair, though not large, number of expensive clothes, winning prestige through the acquisition of material goods never seems to have been one of her goals.[55] Her *Lettere familiari*, through which she presented a picture of herself, her social contacts and her everyday doings, have little to say about her material environment or her buying forays. Both these and the *Terze rime* show an intermittent desire to distance herself from the negative stereotypes of the courtesan, which included accusations of avarice.[56] Rather, she sought both to practise and to advertise her generosity. The pair of sonnets she had written to Henry III after he had spent an evening at her house, and published with the *Terze rime*, had accompanied the gift of an enamelled portrait of herself, presumably some sort of luxurious medallion. Thus she employed finely-wrought artefacts both to demonstrate and publicise her generosity and her visual taste, and to serve as a subject for her literary talents. Her

'Stamane in su l'alba mi pareva essere in una camera alta, larga e bella, la quale era parata di raso verde e giallo'; 'un letto di brocato riccio'.

[53] Ibid., p. 202, 1st day, 2; 'ricami per chi vuole gittar via l'oro'.

[54] 'Quinci sete, ricami, argento ed oro, | gemme, porpora, e qual è di più pregio | si pon in adornarne alto tesoro'; XXIV, 97-9.

[55] Franco's wills of 1564 and 1570 are reproduced in Rosenthal 1992 (as in n. 8, above), pp. 111-5, as well as in G. Tassini, *Veronica Franco: celebre poetessa e cortigiana*, Venice 1888, pp. 66-81; further information about her material way of life can also be gained from the reports of her inquisition trial, printed in A. Zorzi, *Cortigiana veneziana: Veronica Franco e i suoi poeti*, Milan 1986, pp. 143-53.

[56] For example, *Terze rime*, II, 94-9; letter XVIII, in Croce (Ed.) 1949 (as in n. 38, above), pp. 29-31.

admiration for the embroideries, tapestries and bed-hangings at Fumane is another comparable attempt to convert material goods into moral and intellectual capital. Rather than exemplifying a courtesan's appetite for luxurious items, the poem, in celebrating fabrics associated both with women creators and women consumers, allowed Franco to display her mental agility by showing that artefacts little admired by critical theorists could meet Dolce's criteria for pictorial excellence. Her description, as well as highlighting 'ingegno', 'colore' and 'disegno', also acknowledges the inherent expense of their raw materials, silk and gold (181). Yet it places more stress on the artistic skills and the fine craftsmanship their creation had involved:

> With different designs and different techniques,
> on the covers and the curtains and on every side
> one discovers varied and painstaking craftsmanship [artificio].[57]

And, not least, it gave due weight to the sensuous appeal of the textiles: they are numbered among the 'soft' comforts of the furnishings (142–3), and the curtains are said to 'embrace' the bed (150), implying tactile pleasures for its inhabitant as well as hinting at the erotic pleasures they could enclose.[58] Franco in this passage could reconcile thinking about art with enjoying art, being a connoisseur without ceasing to be a courtesan.

However, in case the mythological subjects of the textiles were regarded as too unabashedly hedonistic for a poem praising a prelate in the age of the Catholic Reformation, Franco's next description shrewdly provides balance. Immediately after the description of the fabrics, she launches into an account of a collection of portraits of popes, cardinals, and other ecclesiastics (184–222) apparently displayed in another room (197), providing a much-needed note of moral elevation:

> These men, though dead, can give instruction to the living,
> indeed in heaven they live thus, that their name
> may reach earth ever glorious.
> And although I cannot make out or name each one,
> I recognise that they were innocent,
> and subdued the powers of the devil.
> Admiring their faces, thus painted,
> makes us reverent, and arouses in us
> thoughts of the highest things.[59]

This is comparable to Aretino's recurrent stressing that faces can communicate and instil spiritual qualities, not only in his letters and poems on portraits, but also in his remarks on devotional pictures such as the *Ecce Homo* painted by Titian:

> the sorrow that grips the figure of Christ moves to penitence anyone

---

[57] 154–6; see Appendix.
[58] 142–3; see Appendix.
[59] 211–9; see Appendix.

who as a Christian views his arms, cut by the rope that binds his hands.....
he who perceives the peaceful grace that his face shows forth has not
the boldness to hold in himself a speck of hate and rancour[60]

But the prime stimulus might again have been Dolce's treatise on art, in the section on the excellence of painting where he praises the inspirational power of religious paintings:

there is no doubt that seeing painted the image of Our Lord, of the Virgin and of various male and female saints is of great benefit to men ... images may lead their beholders to devotion ... Thus the images of the good and the virtuous enflame men ... to virtue and to good works.[61]

Dolce's declared aim was for these passages on religious images to form part of a justification of painting in terms of its utilitarian, pleasurable and ornamental qualities.[62] Franco's two contrasting descriptions provide 'practical criticism' through demonstration.

Thus in the passages on the landscapes, the gardens, the building, and the contents of the villa, Franco demonstrates her awareness of current critical terminology and ideas, and her ability to extend them into novel areas, integrating them with the wider purposes of her poetic cycle. By drawing attention to their utilisation of 'ingegno', 'colore' and 'disegno', she implicitly defends the textile arts – the arts of Minerva – suggesting that they can be appraised in the same way as can high art. She can succumb to the enjoyment of the vividly mimetic mythological scenes, while also responding to the inspirational power of the images of the clerics, thus showing herself as the moral being she declared herself to be in some of the other poems. As with the descriptions of landscape, her descriptions of artefacts blend sensuality, emotion and intellect.

A final point emerges through a return to the key passage where she muses on the artist's creative fictions:

How powerful is our human intelligence [ingegno],
which makes fictitious things appear alive
by force of colour and design!
With silk and gold and various tinted wools,
in the tapestries which adorn these rooms,
real things are surpassed by imitation.[63]

The praise may primarily be for the 'ingegno' of the embroiderer or weaver, and perhaps also of the artist who might have supplied their designs. Yet the introduction of 'our', 'nostro', includes Franco in this capacity to lend credibility to these counterfeits. Does this only mean that she as a human

---

[60] The translation is that in Land 1994 (as in n. 23, above), p. 139.

[61] Barocchi (Ed.) 1960 (as in n. 39, above), pp. 161–2.

[62] Ibid., p. 161: 'Veggiamo ora quanto ella [la pittura] sia utile, dilettevole e di ornamento'.

[63] 178–83; see Appendix.

spectator is willing to be deceived? Or does it bring to the reader's mind the fact that, as a writer, Franco like the weaver is a sharer in creative 'ingegno' and a skilled counterfeiter of realities? She would, after all, use the word 'ingegno' in relation to her task of fashioning an image of Fumane:

> ... in the task of imagining you
> my mind is left useless and confused;[64]

We may then also reflect that description of artefacts has the capacity, by focusing on a visual artist's fictions, to call attention to the wider literary fiction in which accounts of these crafted objects are embedded, and might recall Franco's words at the beginning of her passages of evocation:

> ... I take in ready hand my pen,
> and, to indulge my feeling, I counterfeit ['fingo']
> this place as true to life as I can.[65]

Perhaps her comments on the fictions worked in the textiles also incorporate oblique comments on the fictionality on her vision of Fumane as a Utopian world where conflict between man and woman, nature and art, sexuality and morality, the city and the country has been abolished, and suggest the disingenuousness of her claims in her writing to ramble confusedly and spontaneously, to 'artlessly draw and paint what I know'.[66]

[64] 449–50; see n. 19, above.
[65] 34–6; see n. 16, above.
[66] 39; see n. 2, above.

APPENDIX

Veronica Franco: Rime,
S. Bianchi (Ed.), Milan 1995, pp. 155-8 (XXV, 127-222)

    Non cede l'arte a la natura il vanto
ne l'artificio del giardin, ornato
d'alberi cólti e di sempre verde manto;
      sovra 'l qual porge, alquanto rilevato,   130
d'architettura un bel palagio tale,
qual fu di quel del Sol già poetato:
      infinito tesor ben questo vale
per l'edificio proprio, e gli ornamenti,
che 'n ricchezza e in beltà non hanno eguale.   135
    I fini marmi e i porfidi lucenti,
cornici, archi, colonne, intagli e fregi,
figure, prospettive, ori ed argenti,
      quivi son di tal sorte e di tai pregi,
ch'a tal grado non giungono i palagi   140
che fêr gli antichi imperadori e regi.
    Ma le commodità di dentro e gli agi
son cosí molli, che gli altrui diletti
al par di questi sembrano disagi.
      Per li celati d'òr vaghi ricetti,   145
sul pavimento, che qual gemma splende,
stan sopra aurati piè candidi letti.
    Di sopra da ciascun d'intorno pende
di varia seta e d'òr porpora intesta,
che 'l contegno de' letti abbraccia e prende;   150
      di coltre ricamata o d'altra vesta
di ricca tela ognun s'adorna e copre,
sí ch'a fornirlo ben nulla gli resta.
    Di diversi disegni e diverse opre
su coverte e cortine in tutti i lati   155
vario e lungo artificio si discopre.
    I dèi scender dal cielo innamorati
dietro le ninfe qui si veggon finti,
in diverse figure trasformati;
      e d'amoroso affetto in vista tinti,   160
seguitar ansïosi il lor desio
dove dal caldo incendio son sospinti.
    Qui trasformata in vacca si vede Io,

e cent'occhi serrar il suo custode,
al suon di quel, che poi l'uccise, dio.   165
   Da l'altra parte Danae in sen si gode
vedersi piover Giove in nembo d'oro,
dov'altri piú la chiude e la custode;
   il quale altrove, trasformato in toro,
porta Europa; ed altrove, aquila, piglia   170
Ganimede e 'l rapisce al sommo coro.
   Di Licaon fatta orsa ancor la figlia,
mentre ucciderla il figlio ignota tenta,
assunta in cielo ad orsa s'assomiglia:
   né pur orsa celeste ella diventa,   175
figurata di stelle in cotal segno,
ma 'l figlio in ciel l'altr'orsa rappresenta.
   Quanto è possente il nostro umano ingegno,
che vive fa parer le cose finte
per forza di colori e di disegno!   180
   Di seta e d'oro e varie lane tinte,
nei tapeti ch'adornan quelle stanze,
da l'imitar le cose vere èn vinte.
   E perché nulla a desïar avanze,
ch'orni di Giove un'alta regia degna,   185
dove, lasciato 'l ciel, qua giuso ei stanze,
   qualunque ebbe tra noi la sacra insegna,
ch'a quei con le sue man Dio stesso porge,
che d'esser suoi vicari in terra ei degna,
   qualunque di pastor al grado sorge   190
de la chiesa divina, in espresso atto
nobilmente dipinto ivi si scorge:
   quivi ciascun pontefice ritratto
piú che dal natural vivo si vede,
di tela, di colori e d'ombre fatto;   195
   e com'a tanta maestà richiede,
da l'altre in parte eccelsa e separata
sí reverende imagini han lor sede.
   Similmente, in maniera accomodata,
di quei l'effigie ancor son quivi, i quali   200
del ciel sostengon la felice entrata:
   quanti mai fûr nel mondo cardinali
quivi entro stan co' papi in compagnia,
e vescovi, e prelati altri assai tali.
   Perché conforme al paradiso sia   205
quell'albergo divino, in sé ritiene

133

di gente i volti cosí santa e pia.
    Di quel ch'al sacerdozio si conviene,
da l'essempio di molti espressi quivi,
in perfetta notizia si perviene: 210
    questi, ancor morti, insegnar pònno ai vivi,
anzi in ciel vivon sí, che 'l loro nome
in terra sempre glorïoso arrivi.
    E perch'alcun io non distingua o nome,
di quelli intendo che fûro innocenti,   215
e del demonio fêr le forze dome.
    Le costor fronti a mirar riverenti,
cosí pinte, ne fanno, e in noi pensieri
destano de le cose piú eccellenti:
    seguendo l'orme lor, fan ch'altri speri,   220
che tien lo scettro de la casa vaga,
d'alzarsi al ciel per quei gradi primieri.

Prose, Poetry and Biography

CHARLES FORD

This paper discusses *Het Schilderboeck*, written by the poet, painter and historian Karel van Mander (1548–1606), and published in two seventeenth-century editions in 1604 and 1618. The discussion concerns two aspects of the book: its visual appearance, and the combination of poetry and prose in its organisation.

Het Schilderboeck has been treated as a compendium, a thing of parts. It has rarely been treated as a whole of itself. This is hardly surprising, given its size and the complexity and the range of materials it contains. It has been mined for information and attitudes. It is best known as a source of information on pre-1600 painting and *Het Schilderboeck* makes its largest appearance in the footnotes of histories of Netherlandish painting. [1] Its two editions were produced over a period of time, printed by different masters in different places. This bittiness is not concealed, it is manifest in the errata supplement and the two frontispieces (Pl. 25). And we know that, as well as the two principal editions of 1604 and 1618, there were a number of editions of one part of the whole, the commentary on Ovid (the first Dutch emblem book). [2] Historians of art and literature have read it both as a fulfillment of and terminus to the sixteenth-century 'mannerist' phenomenon, and as a body of scattered prophetic leaves incoherently foretelling the 'realism' of the 'Golden Age'.

---

[1] The best general introduction to Karel van Mander's work remains Hessel Miedema's introductions and notes to his modern Dutch edition of *Den grondt der edel vry schilder-const*, Utrecht 1973, and the English edition of *The Lives of the Illustrious Netherlandish and German Painters*, 6 vols, Doornspijk 1994–. See also n. 3 below.

[2] For the publishing history of the Ovidian commentary see *Bibliotheca Belgica* M94–99. In his edition of *Den Grondt* (as in n. 1, above), Miedema lists all the extant copies seen by him of the 1604 and 1618 editions. He states his own preference for the 1604 edition as being nearer to the author and freer of errors, using it as the core for his own research. I refer to the 1618 edition (hereafter: *Grondt* 1618 and *Leven* 1618) in this paper, a copy being convenient in the Warburg Institute, London. My thanks to the librarian and staff.

So for several reasons *Het Schilderboeck* does appear to a modern reader to be a thing of parts held together by no more than a binding and a title. This essay begins with a description of the whole book. Description cannot be a neutral activity. Explicit in the description is an argument for re-textualising the book as a whole. It is necessary for the argument that *Het Schilderboeck* should become more difficult and alien than it has been when employed to other purposes. From some important points of view, this has already been done.[3] Then we shall address one suture in the text between a passage of poetry and a passage of prose to emphasise further the argument for a synthetic reading of the text.

Secondly, some comment will be made about the appearance of the book. *Het Schilderboeck* is without a doubt one of the most complex and ambitious books on the visual arts ever to have appeared and this is immediately visually apparent. It is made up of images, verse, prose, marginalia and footnotes woven together into a brilliant fabric. At first glance, we see this variety and note how it is signalled in the font, lineation, juxtapositions and contrasts of the text. Though this is no more than typical of any book produced at that time and place (or any time and place), the particular historical contexts must be considered. It will be argued that the appearance is a manifestation of an essential contingency of its creation – the didactic function of the work, and the inevitable traces of the performance of mannerist rhetoric. In rhetorical terms, this rendering of the text submits the *logos* to the conventions of *ethos*, but with (we must assume) some consideration of a desired *pathos*,[4] in other words, there is a relation of the content and the appearance of the text to its imagined readership.

Thirdly, we shall recover some of the direct statements of intention made by Van Mander, especially in the prefaces which punctuate his text. What did he mean by choosing to write here in verse and there in prose? How does that signify, or how does it inflect the significance of the content?

Fourthly, we shall note the employment of one particular group of borrowed poems in the *leven* (lives, biographies) of the northern artists. These poems were written by Dominicus Lampsonius, secretary to the Bishop of Liège, and were published by Hieronymus Cock at Antwerp in 1572 under the title *Pictorum aliquot celebrium Germaniae Inferioris effigies*.

3   For example, H. Miedema, 'Karel van Mander's Grondt den edel vry schilder-const', *Journal of the History of Ideas*, 34, 1973, pp. 653–668, attacks the 'realist' tradition of reading Van Mander, dominant since the mid-nineteenth century, and argues the rhetorical and emblematic reading of *Het Schilderboeck*. W. S. Melion, *Shaping the Netherlandish Canon: Karel van Mander's Schilder-Boeck*, Chicago 1992 reads the work in the context of discourses on national identity.
4   For the employment of these terms, see W. J. Kennedy, *Rhetorical Norms in Renaissance Literature*, Princeton 1978, esp. pp. 6–16: 'Introduction: Rhetorical criticism and literary theory'.

Fifthly, and finally, we shall return to the role of Van Mander – poet, painter and historian – as the author of the book by referring to a fable drawn from Ariosto's *Orlando Furioso* (another of Van Mander's borrowings). The story is recounted at length in the first chapter of *Den Grondt der edel vry schilder-const* (The Foundations of the noble and free art of painting), the first and versified section of *Het Schilderboeck*. We shall then consider the significance of the difference between poetry and history, and in particular the different but necessarily equivalent roles of both in securing fame and ensuring eternal life through commemorating names.

A Description of Het Schilderboeck

Het Schilderboeck consists of three distinct and very different parts; I shall describe it as a triptych. First, on the left, there is what Van Mander refers to as the 'leerdicht' (teaching poem), the *Grondt*, 14 verse chapters directed ostensibly at the young painter. The second, central, section is the *leven*, themselves divided into three sets – Ancient, Italian and Northern. The Ancient *leven* are principally, though not directly, from Pliny (through a French translation), the Italian from Vasari (Van Mander is Vasari's best editor – he cuts the *Vite* right down, losing very little, as well as augmenting Vasari's account by bringing it up to date through his own research) and the Northern he assembled himself. The third, distaff panel of this triptych is that first Dutch emblem book in two parts, the *Wtlegghinghe op den Metamorphosen Pub. Ovidij Nasonis* (Interpretation of the Metamorphoses of Ovid) and the *Wtbeeldinghe der Figueren* (Depiction of figures) which together form a deconstructive gloss on Ovid directed as much to the amateurs of painting as to painters.

In all three parts, poetry and prose work together to represent (or to manifest) to the reader the essential business of *Het Schilderboeck* as represented (or manifested) in the first frontispiece of the book: the equality of painting with the other liberal and intellectual arts; the equivalence of painting to the other liberal and intellectual arts; and the mutuality of painting (and the other visual arts) with literature in establishing the fame of the painters of the past and present. The redemption role of this last process will be returned to at the end of this paper. Verse and prose sit side by side throughout the book, or rather are woven together to make the book. The introductions to the parts are given over to celebratory poems by the most distinguished men of the time and place. (A roll call of the contributors of these poems is the single most compelling testament to the importance of *Het Schilderboeck* and its author and a more or less complete introduction to the literary luminaries of Holland at the turn of the seventeenth century.) [5]

---

[5] Furthermore, Van Mander was one of only two men in his generation to earn a celebratory posthumous anthology of verses: *Epitaphien ofte Graf-Schrijften Ghemaeckt op het Afsterven van Carel van Mander ...*, Leiden 1606. This includes a

Whatever they say, as verse these verses testify to the importance of *Het Schilderboeck* more powerfully than any conventional list of subscribers or ambitious dedication.

The *Grondt* is in verse. It is a broad introduction to the themes of the book and the numerous marginalia in the poem frequently cross-reference sections of the *leven*. The relation of the poem to the *leven* is that of theory to practice or experience.

The *leven*, although frequently prefaced by elaborate rhetorical introductions, are very definitely prose. Van Mander was a strict historian.[6] He frequently parenthesises on the difficulties of getting exact documentary evidence – for example in the life of Holbein.[7] He happily includes apocryphal information as illustrative fable if it points a moral,[8] even though he is usually scrupulous in citing his sources. His information on Antwerp artists ubiquitously refers to the archival sources of the Antwerp guild books.

The Ovidian commentary is a prose deconstruction of a poet's work. We learn how to weave poetry into pictures and to read pictures from poetry. It is in itself evidence of the mutuality of painting and poetry. It is a resolution of the *paragone* between the visual and the literary arts.

Everything works together. The prefatory poems celebrate the enterprise in a manner analogous to the lives celebrating the painters. The *Grondt* lays out the general principles which are amplified in the examples set forth in the artists' biographies. The general principles of artistic competence and value are grounded in the analogy of the arts asserted by the Ovidian emblem book.

You cannot simply pick a piece from this synthetic fabric without removing it from a context which provides meaning or violating the integrity

---

description of the elaborate pomp of his funeral.

[6] See Melion 1992 (as in n. 3, above).

[7] At *Leven* 1618, fol. 142v, Van Mander tells us that he has had dealings with a Dr. Isley in Switzerland who obstinately refused to supply information concerning the life of Holbein and crossly states '... die eenighe meenen of hy most heeten Doctor Esely; dan ick docht | den Man is gelijck zijn Landt | onbeweeghlijck als de Switsersche rootsen.' ('... some might wonder if he should be called Dr. Donkey; and I considered that he is like his homeland, as unmoving as the Swiss rocks.').

[8] For example in his life of Jan and Hubert van Eyck where he relates a fanciful account of the accident which brought about the invention of oil paint (*Leven* 1618, fol. 123v) and describes the wonderment of contemporaries upon first viewing the Ghent altarpiece (*Leven* 1618, fol. 124v). Neither incident is offered with any documentary evidence, even though both sit alongside elaborately documented information, such as a transcription (modified and transformed into alexandrines, no less) of an ode by Lucas de Heere (*Leven* 1618, fols 124v–125v) and the carefully copied Latin verse of Jan van Eyck's grave inscription (*Leven* 1618, fol. 126r).

of the whole, the whole which is woven of quotation and allusion from the pre-text which is the whole domain of history, literature, art and civilisation.

Take one page opening, which sets on opposite pages prose and verse. [9] It is the *Opdracht*, or dedication, of the Ancient lives (Pl. 26). Each part of *Het Schilderboeck* is dedicated to a different person; the Ancient lives are dedicated to Jaques Razet, public notary and secretary of the city of Amsterdam. Jaques Razet is complimented as an accomplished captain, experienced in knightly combat. And, we are told, Razet is compiling a book on military topics.

A *topos* frequently encountered in Van Mander's prefaces emerges here – the unjust preference given by historians to the history of warfare which has done nothing but harm to the world, whereas art has done nothing but good for the world and has gone unsung. [10] The contrast is often articulated as one of a preference for Mars over Minerva or Venus.

But in the case of Razet, we are told, the balance is weighed evenly. As well as being a military man, Razet is a man of culture. He had been a judge at a literary competition (the term Van Mander uses to describe the competition is 'veder-strydt', battle of the pens/feathers). Furthermore, he was a supporter of young painters and a collector of art.

On the opposite page is a poetic dialogue between Karel van Mander and his brother, Adam van Mander, written (or as if written) by Adam. Tell me, says Adam, what is the origin of the word 'schilder' (painter). The word, says Karel 'comt van den Schilden voort' – the word comes from shields. Repeating an explanation given elsewhere in the book, [11] van Mander points out that some of our earliest evidence regarding the excellence of the painter's art is to be found in the descriptions of finely-decorated shields in Homeric epic. Furthermore, he explains, Pliny tells us that the Romans displayed the shields of their ancestors in public buildings. The Latin word 'clypeus', he adds, means precisely a decorated shield. He adds, as an aside, that 'schilder' might also come from an old Flemish word 'schillede', meaning pied or dappled. 'Schillede' at that time was probably only used by Flemish countryfolk to describe cattle. Van Mander himself uses the word in this sense in the eighth chapter of the *Grondt* to add a suitably rustic tone to his chapter on landscape.

Yes, adds Adam, now go and exhibit your 'schilder helden cloeck', a pun meaning both 'the shields of your brave heroes' and 'your brave painting heroes'. Remember that being a prefatory poem to the dedication of the Ancient lives, this was also a prefatory poem to the *leven* as a whole.

The two sides of the opening amplify each other, they play upon linked themes. In the prose, we see the relative merits of military prowess and the culture of art finding an appropriate balance in the person of the dedicatee of

---

[9]   *Leven* 1618, fols *1v-*2r.
[10]   For example, in the *Voor-rede* (preface) to the Dutch *leven*, *Leven* 1618, fol. 122r.
[11]   In the *Voor-rede* to both the *Grondt* and the Ancient *leven*.

the Ancient lives. In the poem we see an elegant play of words asserting a strange equality of another kind between Mars and Venus, a traditional tension deflated by a clever pun. A more elaborate, three-sided *disputa* of Olympians is developed in the preface to the Ancient lives which immediately follows the dedication to Razet: between Mars, Venus and Vulcan. It gets much more interesting but not, unfortunately, interesting in ways relevant to the topic of this paper.

The Visual Appearance of Het Schilderboeck

The way that the book looks, specifically the mingling or variation of typefaces in the book, signifies in an important way. So used are we to variety of font in book design and textual layout (think of the front page of any newspaper) that it can seem trivial and obvious to insist on it being meaningful in itself, such things are the domain of convention. Every element of the page is capable of being faithfully recorded in the traditional bibliographic sign-system, it is not invisible to modern knowledge. But how are these features to be read? The bibliographical sign-system was born of connoisseurial anxieties over identification in later Enlightenment culture; in our period, it has retreated to the domain of a highly-specialised discipline and discourse, perhaps because it has nothing to say to soothe the hermeneutic anxieties of post-war readerships.[12] Thus, in new editions of older works original typography is rarely represented. Unless, that is, the features are so striking that they cannot be ignored, as with the games played on the reader by Laurence Sterne in *Tristram Shandy*. Along with Julian calendar dates, multiple-variant spellings and decorative capitals, typographic variety is tidied up to allow the text to 'speak for itself'. This represents a modernist theory of meaning posited upon principles which are, if not anti-rhetorical, then post-rhetorical (although the apparent absence of rhetoric is probably a rhetorical mode of its own). These absences are a manifestation of a confidence in the 'textual' meaning, where the text is imagined as autonomous and somewhere remote from the actuality of the printed page. The look of older books is allowed to be a decorative feature of some historical significance which otherwise hardly signifies for us. But as the (admittedly extreme) example of Sterne insists, the visuality of the book must surely be of historical significance, with at least connotational associations for an imagined ideal historical reader, and certainly also for us.

[12] See, for example, W. Waterschoot, 'Karel van Mander's *Schilder-Boeck* (1604): a Description of the Book and its Setting', *Quaerendo*, 13, 1983, pp. 260–86. Waterschoot abstracts the typographic appearance of the book into the scientific formulae of bibliography in order both to describe and to collate the book in relation to its two editions, and 11 other productions of Jacob de Meester's printed production in Alkmaar at the time. For him, description is entirely a neutral activity and produces very little insight with regard to the book.

I have hardly enough space to do more than assert that the typeface almost certainly plays a role in the registering of some of the effects of rhetoric. It helps us as we leaf through to note the *dispositio* of the elements, and we might consider that it plays a role in helping us to read, playing a part in the *elocutio* and *pronunciatio* of the text. Rhetorical expression was Van Mander's only medium. He could not step outside his own means of expression any more than he could avoid the codified and formalised discursive *topoi* of his time, elements of the text most obviously significant in our modernist tradition of reading.

If we went no further than noting the most striking contrast between the roman type of the verse and proper names, and the gothic type of the bulk of the rest, we would be touching upon a key element in the representational complexity of the fonts. Even the punctuation used in the verse in gothic font signifies. Van Mander employs the Germanic comma, a forward slash, derived from the music-like notation of devotional manuals and marking the breathing, indicating that the text is imagined within a tradition of reading out loud. Roman fonts (*romeyn* in a seventeenth-century source)[13] derive from, among other places, carved classical inscriptions and Carolingian manuscripts. It was not 'rediscovered' during the Renaissance, it was invented. Gothic fonts (*duyts*) were developed in imitation of late medieval handwriting and, we must imagine, succeeded by being mistaken for handwriting, at least for the first generations of *incunabula*.

Unlike the occasional verse in the book the *Grondt* is set entirely in gothic – excepting the marginalia, some proper names, loan-words and quoted poems. In *Het Schilderboeck*, as a whole, some of the occasional poems are in an italic version (*cursijf*) of the roman type, although most are in roman. This kind of mingling is so widespread in books of the period that it scarcely registers with a modern reader and is suppressed in modern editions, as noted above. Martin and Febvre discuss the very specific associations which might lie behind the choice of either gothic or roman fonts: gothic, they say, was the preferred typeface of legal, theological and medical texts; roman the preferred typeface (from the manuscript era on) for humanistic and classical texts. [14] The favouring of one font over another probably had to do with the field of discourse, which is also to say with the imagined readership.

To the modern eye, the roman is more legible. This was by no means the case in the late-sixteenth century. At that time, the lower end of the printing market was still dominated by gothic script, the higher end by

---

13 For the three terms 'romeyn', 'duyts' and 'cursijf' see the reproduction of Christoffel van Dyck's sale specimen in D. B. Updike, *Printing Types: Their History, Forms and Use. A Study in Survival*, vol. 2, Cambridge, Mass., London 1962, pp. 20–1.

14 L. Febvre and H.-J. Martin, *The Coming of the Book: The Impact of Printing, 1450–1800* (1958), London 1976, pp. 77ff.

roman. Might the difference of typeface indicate not only a difference of content or kind in the text, but also a difference within the readership? Between those whose education and taste set them at a higher level and who would be comfortable with both typefaces, preferring perhaps the associations of intellectual status registered by roman script, and those who would read the book at the 'lower level' of the gothic?

In *Het Schilderboeck*, the immediate opposition of difference (represented by roman versus gothic fonts) seems to lie between verse and prose – with the exception that the *Grondt* is, like the bulk of the prose, in gothic. There is a further oddity. The introduction to the Italian *leven* is also in roman script.

We now turn briefly to the third consideration, Van Mander's stated intention in and for *Het Schilderboeck*.

Statements of Intent

Van Mander makes a number of statements in relation to verse and poetry. The most developed is in the *voor-rede* to the *Grondt*. It begins with a relation of how the ancients valued painting – how much they paid for it, how celebrated artists were in former societies; a shameless *argumentum ad crumenam* in favour of the distinction of painting. He adds that the purpose of the *Grondt* is specifically to address the younger reader. There follows an explanation of why the *Grondt* is written in verse, and what considerations went into the choice of particular verse format. It is in verse, we are told, because the young are often drawn to poetry, and the author will succeed the better by appealing to the tastes of his readership; secondly, because poetry is easier to learn by heart and remember, so that the lessons learned will stay fixed in the memory.

The *Grondt*, he explains, is written not in the traditional Flemish metre, but one adapted by himself from his reading of French and Italian poetry (while retaining a certain number of features necessitated by writing in the Dutch language). He employs an Italian *ottava rima* with a Dutch alternate rhyming scheme. He eschews masculine for feminine rhymes and has sought to avoid repeating rhymes in any hundred lines. He apologises for introducing loan-words, but explains that this is often necessary in the painting profession where such words are widely used. He continues:

> I may perhaps have better pleased those who have an understanding of poetry had I let my verse run on French feet, but I might have found that more difficult and the young may have found it more obscure. I appreciate that the Alexandrine used in the French manner could produce something very good, but great attention and much time would be necessary to fill it with elevated matter and yet sustain the flow.[15]

---

[15]   *Grondt* 1618, fol. *4v. Van Mander's text reads as follows: 'Thadde misschien den Dicht-verstandighen beter behaeght | dat ick dit mijn ghedicht met Fransche Voeten hadde laeten voort-treden: Dan 't hadde my swaerder | en de Jeught

The *Grondt* was not set in roman type, as is the rest of the poetry in *Het Schilderboeck*. In the *voor-rede*, Van Mander stated that he intended the poem to be read specifically by the young, perhaps habituated to and more comfortable with a schoolbook gothic. Thus the font and the verse format were specifically for the benefit of the intended reader.

The discussion of technical matters quotes two lines Van Mander translated from Ronsard's commentary on poetry,[16] one quotation from a published poem of his own, and an example of bad poetry the source of which has not been traced. He argues that the verse must be rational, the *caesura* adding to the sense, the line ending occurring after a proper closure of sense.

On a more general level, he asserts the familiar decorum argument for purity of language – avoiding common, everyday speech. He also makes a general plea for a more regular treatment of assimilation between words (common in Dutch: e.g. 'de elfde' which might stay two words or assimilate into 'delfte') and a more regular employment of what might seem like arbitrary use of accidence by pragmatic poets (e.g. 'Heere' rather than 'Heer' where it might suit them) when trying to get the right number of syllables in lines of verse. All of this literary good taste analogically informs the discussions of purity, decorum, combination of figures and composition in the discussion of painting in the *Grondt* itself.

The attractive power and rememberability of verse make it the appropriate medium for the 14 chapters of the *Grondt* (which for his own part he usually refers to as the 'leerdicht' – didactic poem). Why was the rest of *Het Schilderboeck* not versified? Surely, attractiveness and mnemonic accessibility would be as useful for the representation of the lives of great men as for the general theoretical principles of art? And further to that, the writing of an entire book in verse would have exemplified Van Mander's virtue even more.

Van Mander certainly articulates what the difference is between verse and prose and to a great extent this is all that I have written about. But his distinction between verse and poetry is not apparent, it is not clear whether the two are exchangeable terms. To some extent, given the looseness of his employment of the words 'gedicht' and 'dichter' (poem and poet), it is likely that they are. For another account we might turn to a Dutch contemporary, Theodoor Rodenburgh, who wrote a defence of poetry in 1615.[17] Or, rather

---

      duysterder moghen vallen. Ick bekenne wel | datmen Gallischer wyse | op
      Alexandrijnsche mate wel wat goets soude doen: Dan daer hoeft groot opmerck |
      en langhen tijdt toe | om vol schoon stoffe | en vloeyende te wesen: ...'.
[16] Pierre Ronsard, *Abbregé de l'art poétique francois*, Paris 1565. This text is an immensely helpful starting point for understanding not only the basic codification of forms and their appropriate prosody, but also how Van Mander and his generation might have understood the role of vernacular, contemporary poetry.
[17] See W. Abrahamse, *Het toneel van Theodore Rodenburgh (1574–1644)*, Amsterdam

than turning to Rodenburgh, we might turn to Philip Sidney, whose *Apologie for Poetrie* of 1580 was comprehensively plagiarised by Rodenburgh. There we find an example of a contemporary view of the domain of poetry. For Sidney, as for Rodenburgh and for a great many of their contemporaries, Van Mander included, it would seem, poetry may or may not involve the employment of specific verse forms – although obviously, to a large degree, it certainly does. What makes poetry distinct is not a contrast with prose, so much as a contrast with history. Poetry is imaginative literature, history is the literature of fact. Either can appear in verse form.

If we turn again to *Het Schilderboeck*, we see a much more meaningful contrastive pair formed by the opposition of history and poetry, than prose and poetry. Given the reiterated assertion by Van Mander of the sisterhood of the arts and the analogy between literature and painting, we might further see how an equivalent difference is manifest in Van Mander's own visual art categories of 'nae 't leven' and 'uit den gheest'. 'Nae 't leven' is the direct mimetic act, it means 'after life'; the term is employed by Van Mander to describe copying both from the model and from nature generally. 'Uit den gheest' is altogether more approved of. While by no means abusing the example of the model or nature, 'uit den gheest' is the composing and developing of a picture from the imagination. The imagination, previously stocked by 'nae 't leven' study, all held in a good memory alongside many good examples, is given full expressive range and the image produced addresses the intellect of the spectator more directly than a mere copy after life. Ironically, or perhaps paradoxically, we, like Van Mander, use the term 'history' to describe that kind of narrative painting which most demands the 'uit den gheest' skills. So the *Grondt* might be printed in gothic script because, unlike the other verse in the book, it is more properly to be read as a kind of improved prose, where the 'leer' (teaching) element is more significant than the 'dicht' (versifying) element, which only plays a role in making the 'leer' easier for less sophisticated readers.

Fishing in Other Men's Ponds[18]
Dominicus Lampsonius's *Pictorum aliquot celebrium Germaniae Inferioris effigies* of 1572 is the source of twenty-three poems contained in Van Mander's Lives of the Northern painters. In fact, Van Mander copied every single one of Lampsonius's poems, translating them from the Latin. They are set in roman type within the gothic text of the biographies, as are all the poems

---

1997.
[18] In the last lines of chapter 1 of the *Grondt* (Grondt 1618, fol. 4r), Van Mander writes: 'Dat oock selve wel treffelijcke Schrijvers | Hebben moeten visschen in ander Vijvers.' ('... even the most excellent writers have had to fish in other ponds.').

within the biographical section. Van Mander's translations are rhymed and metered.

Lampsonius's poems are very brief, in fact they are little more than mottoes, exercises of poetic wit to set below Hieronymus Cock's engraved portraits. Lampsonius was a celebrated humanist, a correspondent of Vasari's, though these poems hardly constitute a significant body of work in themselves. Nor do they tell us anything much about the painters. Take the poem in praise of Jan den Hollander. Lampsonius writes:

> Netherlanders always win praise with landscape painting,
> The Italians by painting people or gods well.
> This is no great wonder and may well be believed,
> For the Italian has brains in his head.
> But it is not unfair to say that the Netherlander
> Has intelligence in his hand. So this Brabanter
> Would rather paint landscapes than, without enough insight
> Painting heads, human figures or gods wrongly.[19]

This particular poem connects with a great variety of issues in *Het Schilderboeck*, in the biographies as well as the *Grondt*, but, like any of the others I might have chosen, it hardly constitutes conventional evidence for the biography. The information given in Van Mander's biographies of those few painters picked out by Lampsonius and Cock (and it is likely that Cock played the greater part in the choosing) is not amplified by the content of Lampsonius's poems, rather, Lampsonius's poems constitute evidence of the fame of the painters. It is not the business of a poem to tell, but rather to

---

[19]   The text beneath plate 11 in Lampsonius (in engraved cursive script) reads: 'Propria Belgarum laus est bene pingere rura; | Ausoniorum, homines pingere, siue deos. | Nec mirum in capite Ausonius, sed Belga cerebrum | Non temere in graua fertur habere manu. | Maluit ergo manus fani bene pingere rura, | Quam caput, aut homines, aut male scire deos.' Van Mander's text (*Leven* 1618, fol. 137r–v) runs as follows: 'Neerlanders altijt lof met Landtschap maken halen, | D'Italiaen met Mensch en Goden wel te malen, | Dit is geen wonder groot, en can wel zijn ghelooft: | Want den Italiaen heeft d'hersens in sijn hooft. | Maer niet vergeefs men seght, hoe dat de Nederlander, | Heeft in zijn handt vernuft, soo wouw desen Brabander | Landtschappen maecken eer, dan qualijck te verstaen | Hooft, Godt, oft menscher beeldt, oft hem daer in misgaen.' Melion 1992 (as in n. 3, above), esp. pp. 1–12, 95–142, discusses at length the particular ways in which Van Mander deals with the Italian critical tradition regarding northern painting; this activity by Van Mander defines what Melion believes to be the articulation of a 'Netherlandish Canon'. The general negative assessment of northern painting by Italians was a recent phenomenon in *c*. 1600; it can be traced back to reports of Michelangelo's sayings written during the mid-sixteenth century – at much the same time that Vasari was composing his *Vite* and shortly before Van Mander travelled to Rome. Lampsonius, a correspondent of Vasari, is here used as a mediator, expressing the *equivalence* of difference between the Italian and northern traditions.

mark historical significance in celebratory display. Together with the prose history, and the versified 'prose' of the *Grondt* (which exploits the attractive and mnemonic power of poetry while remaining a *leerdicht* rather than a pure poem), the true poetry in *Het Schilderboeck* works towards celebrating the everlasting life, through fame, of the Netherlandish painters, just as the occasional poems prefacing the volume celebrate Van Mander's eternal fame. The relationship is, to our eyes, one of decoration to structure, or sweetness to usefulness to use Horace's pairing, but our understanding of such a distinction would have seemed obtuse to contemporaries raised within the world-view of rhetorical discourse.

Font, Form and Genre

In the first chapter of the *Grondt*, Van Mander gives over several verses to relating an allegorical fable from cantos 34 and 35 of Ariosto's *Orlando Furioso*.[20] We are shown the three Fates busily weaving life's tapestry, continually clipping off bits of thread, which Van Mander calls 'namen', names. The 'namen' flutter to the ground, but are swept up by an old greybeard (Time) who, gathering them together, takes them down to a nearby river and casts them in. The river is Lethe. Time condemns all to oblivion.

Out of the sky crows sweep down and pick these 'namen' out, cawing the while, but soon drop them back into the water and grab another. These are the superficial dictators of fashion. But as well as the crows, there is a swan who picks out certain 'namen' and carries them to the far bank of the river where on a small elevation there stands a temple. This is the Temple of Fame, where the 'namen' are carved onto the pillars, thereby ensuring eternal life for the worthy. The swan is the poet or the historian, two distinct tasks combined in the person of the author, Karel van Mander.

History and poetry, although they lie towards opposite ends of a significant polarity of difference, work together in *Het Schilderboeck* to ensure the redemption from oblivion of the great artists of history. Indeed, the idea of anonymous art is a paradox to Van Mander, he does not deal with unattributed works unless to attribute them. The idea of anonymous history would seem equally absurd to him; how could anything happen without agency? Van Mander could no more comfortably write a 'history from below' than we could embrace the synergy of decoration and structure as manifest in Van Mander's expressive medium of rhetoric. Poetry and history work together in the person of the author, Karel Van Mander, whose family arms, it is worth remarking, employed a swan with a coronet about its neck (Pl. 27). As well as being a compendium, *Het Schilderboeck* is a Temple of Fame, a glorious mausoleum, a mausoleum built of history and formed by poetry.

[20] *Leven* 1618, fol. 2r–v, v. 37–42.

'Sentences, pressées aux pieds nombreux de la poësie'?
Pierre Le Moyne's Poussin Sonnet of 1643 and its Context

HENRY KEAZOR

In 1643 a slim folio-booklet of 35 pages was published in Paris, bearing the title *Basilica in honorem S. Francisci Xaverii a fundamentis extructa, Munificentia illustrissimi viri Domini D. Francisci Sublet de Noyers, Baronis de Dangu, Regi ab intimis consiliis, et secretis, &c. A collegii claromontani alumnis, Societatis Iesu, laudata & descripta*.[1] As indicated in this title, the volume praises Saint François Xavier, the church of the Jesuit novitiate in the Faubourg Saint-Germain in Paris (Pl. 28), founded in 1630 by the Surintendant des bâtiments, François Sublet de Noyers, in honour of his patron saint François Xavier and inaugurated in 1642.

The thirteen poems, with one exception in Latin, were written by the Pères (not, as claimed in the title, by alumni) of the Collège de Clermont in Paris.[2] The poems describe the building in the rue du Pot-de-Fer/Saint-Sulpice (today rue Bonaparte),[3] famous among the historians of architecture as one of

[1] I am indebted to Martin Kaufhold (Historisches Institut, Heidelberg), who kindly helped me with the translation of the Latin poems. The booklet was first referred to in A. de Montaiglon, 'Nicolas Poussin – Lettres de Louis Fouquet à son frère Nicolas Fouquet (1655-1656)', *Archives de l'art français*, 12, 2nd ser., 2, 1862, pp. 267–309. Afterwards, it was mentioned by L. Charvet, *Etienne Martellange: 1569-1641*, Lyons 1874, p. 102; finally, the publication found its way into the bibliographies of works on Pierre Le Moyne and Nicolas Poussin such as H. Chérot, *Étude sur la vie et les oeuvres du P. Le Moyne (1602-1671)*, Paris 1887 (reprint Geneva 1971), p. 20, and É. Magne, *Nicolas Poussin. Premier peintre du Roi*, Brussels, Paris 1914, p. 127, n. 2 (both erroneously indicating Montaiglon's article as located in the *Nouvelles archives de l'art français*). In 1664, the booklet was re-edited under the same title, this time printed duodecimo, with some changes in the poems on Vouet and Stella on pp. 28–31.

[2] According to Chérot 1887/1971 (as in n. 1, above), pp. 13–25 and R. G. Maber, *The Poetry of Pierre Le Moyne (1602-1671)* (University of Durham Publications), Berne, Frankfurt/Main 1982, p. 28, Le Moyne was resident at the Collège de Clermont in Paris from 1638 until 1650.

[3] See R. Gobillot, 'Le noviciat des Jésuites de la rue du Pot-de-fer', *Bulletin de la Société Historique du VIe arrondissement de Paris*, 36, 1930, pp. 88–106 (esp. p. 88). According to Gobillot, p. 105, the church was situated at the present rue Bonaparte 80–86.

Etienne Martellange's finest creations,[4] in considerable detail. Not only the architecture of the church, destroyed in 1806/07,[5] but also its ornaments are celebrated, among them the chalice, the paten, the lamps,[6] and not least the three altarpieces by Nicolas Poussin, Simon Vouet and Jacques Stella.

The paintings are the subject of four poems: the three pictures are treated together in the poem 'Princeps laudator (Templi)' (poem No. IV, attributed on the grounds of the initials 'G.L.' to Guillaume Léonard);[7]

[4]   See Charvet 1874 (as in n. 1, above), pp. 93–102; Gobillot 1930 (as in n. 3, above), p. 93 and (for a detailed description of the whole decoration from 1643 until 1722) pp. 95ff.; for the architecture see P. Moisy, 'Martellange, Derand et le conflit du baroque', *Bulletin monumental*, 110, 1952, pp. 237–61; idem, *Les Églises des Jésuites de l'ancienne assistance de France* (Bibliotheca Instituti Historici S.I., 12), Rome 1958, pp. 251–3, no. 112; J. Vallery-Radot, *Le Recueil des plans d'édifices de la compagnie de Jésus conservé à la Bibliothèque Nationale de Paris* (Bibliotheca Instituti Historici S.I., 15), Rome 1960, pp. 166–8, nos 564–73.

[5]   Gobillot 1930 (as in n. 3, above), p. 105.

[6]   See *Basilica in honorem S. Francisci Xaverii a fundamentis extructa, Munificentia illustrissimi viri Domini D. Francisci Sublet de Noyers, Baronis de Dangu, Regi ab intimis consiliis, et secretis, &c. A collegii claromontani alumnis, Societatis Iesu, laudata et descripta*, Paris 1643 (hereafter: *Basilica extructa* 1643), pp. 23f. ('Calix'), pp. 24–7 ('Patina'), pp. 27–9 ('Lampas'). The latter two poems were attributed by C. Sommervogel, S.J., *Bibliothèque de la Compagnie de Jésus*, Paris 1960, vol. 2, col. 156 (under 'Briet, Philippe') on the grounds of their signatures ('G.L.', 'S.D.') to Guillaume Léonard and Etienne Dechamps. The author of the other poem (signed 'F.D.') has remained anonymous – he could perhaps be identified with a certain 'Fr. De Langle', also mentioned in the list published by Chérot 1887/1971 (as in n. 1, above), and he might be identical with a certain P. de Langle, named by the R.P. Rigoleux, S.J. in his *Traité de l'homme d'oraison*, p. 43 (cited by Sommervogel 1960, vol. 4, col. 1484). For Léonard see likewise Sommervogel 1960, vol. 4, cols 1697ff. These monograms are nevertheless a complicated matter since it has so far escaped notice that only some of them were actually printed in the 1643 edition: only the initials for the 'Lampas', 'F.D.' (pp. 23f.), for the poem on Vouet's painting, 'M.G.' (pp. 31ff.), for the poem 'Fundamenta', 'P.B.' (pp. 38f.) and for the poem 'Conditoris Templi Elogium', 'S.D.' are printed whilst the others were written by hand into the copy in the Bibliothèque Nationale, Paris (Yc 226). Even the word 'Templi' in the title of the section 'Princeps laudator Templi' was inserted manually in the synopsis. It remains difficult to decide whether these parts were included immediately after the publication of the booklet or whether they were copied from the 1664 re-edition of the booklet where initials are printed. The hand which wrote Le Moyne's monogram into the 1643 edition made a mistake, giving the initials as 'P.L.', in this form also cited by J. Thuillier, 'Pour un "Corpus Pussinianum"', in *Nicolas Poussin, Actes du colloque 1958*, A. Chastel (Ed.), Paris 1960, vol. 2, pp. 49–238 (esp. p. 71), and corrected in idem, *Nicolas Poussin*, Paris 1994, p. 210, n. 5, whereas they – correctly – figure as 'P.L.M.' in the later re-edition, p. 26 (for Le Moyne's initials see also notes 8 and 16).

[7]   *Basilica extructa* 1643, pp. 19–21; for the attribution see Sommervogel 1960 (as in

individually entitled sections of this poem are devoted to each of the paintings in turn. In addition, each painting is discussed in an independent poem. Poussin's painting on the high altar depicting *The miracle of Saint Francis Xavier resuscitating a dead girl at Kagoshima* (Paris, Louvre; Pl. 29) is the subject of poem No. VIII: 'Le tableau du Grand Autel, fait par le Poußin', signed with the initials 'P.L.(M.)', i.e. Pierre Le Moyne. [8] The painting for the right chapel,[9] Jacques Stella's *The child Jesus found in the Temple* (today in the church of Notre Dame des Andelys; Pl. 30) [10] is treated in poem No. IX: 'Minoris alterius aræ tabula quam pinxit Stella', attributed on the grounds of the initials 'G.C.' to Gabriel Cossart. [11] Finally, Vouet's painting for the left chapel, *The Madonna of the Jesuits* (destroyed in 1944 and therefore here shown in an engraving of 1643 by Michel Dorigny; Pl. 31) [12] was addressed in the verses of poem No. X: 'Minoris unius aræ tabula quam pinxit Vouet', [13] whose author has so far remained anonymous, since the initials 'M.G.' could not be identified; however, in a list from the *Catalogus Provinciae Franciae*, enumerating those persons present at the 'Collegium Parisiense' in 1640, we not only meet again almost all the authors of the other poems, but we also find a certain Michel Guillonnet, with whose name the initials M.G. correspond.[14]

The two poems dedicated to Poussin's altarpiece (one in Latin, the other surprisingly in French and in the form of a sonnet) rank among the earliest poetry on the French artist we know today: already published in 1643, they antedate the other eight poems known to have been printed before Poussin's death in 1665.[15] Furthermore, the one French poem in the booklet is

---

[8]   n. 6, above), vol. 2, col. 156 and vol. 4, cols 1697ff.

    Basilica extructa 1643, p. 30; concerning these initials and the attribution see below, n. 16.

[9]   For the location of the paintings in the two side-chapels, see A. N. Dezallier d'Argenville, *Voyage pittoresque de Paris*, Paris 1757, p. 374, and *Saint-Paul – Saint-Louis. Les Jésuites à Paris*, exh. cat. Musée Carnavalet, Paris 1985, p. 71.

[10]   For the painting see *Saint-Paul – Saint-Louis* 1985 (as in n. 9, above), pp. 71f., no. 67.

[11]   *Basilica extructa* 1643, pp. 31–3; for the attribution and Cossart, see Sommervogel 1960 (as in n. 6, above), vol. 2, cols 1495ff. and col. 156.

[12]   For the painting, see *Saint-Paul – Saint-Louis* 1985 (as in n. 9, above), p. 71, no. 66.

[13]   *Basilica extructa* 1643, pp. 33–5; for the attribution see Sommervogel 1960 (as in n. 6, above), vol. 2, col. 156. Both these poems on Vouet's – and especially Stella's – paintings are the subject of an article by E. Hénin, '"L'enfant Jésus au milieu des docteurs": une image de la parole au XVIIème siècle. A propos d'une ekphrasis jésuite d'un tableau de Stella', *Gazette des Beaux-Arts*, 136, 2000, pp. 31–48.

[14]   This list is also published in Chérot 1887/1971 (as in n. 1, above), pp. 463f., 'pièce justificative' no. VI.

[15]   For the other poems on Poussin, published by Georges de Scudéry (1646), Tristan l'Hermite (1648), Berthod (1652), Desmarets de Saint-Sorlin, Saint-Amant, Hilaire Pader (all 1653) and Cornelis de Bie (1662), see Thuillier 1960 (as in n. 6, above),

interesting to us as it is signed with the initials 'P.L.(M.)', a signature which enabled scholars to attribute the verses to the distinguished pen of Pierre Le Moyne (Pl. 32).[16] Poussin scholarship has so far ignored the fact that the poet himself 'confirmed' this attribution by including a slightly revised version of the sonnet in his two books of collected poems (his *Poésies* of 1650 and his *Oeuvres poétiques* of 1671).[17]

Le Moyne was the first Jesuit to have become famous as a poet;[18] however, his considerable reputation during his life was followed after his death by obscurity and neglect.[19] He was born in 1602 and entered the Jesuit order in 1619;[20] before his participation in the *Basilica extructa*,[21] he had already distinguished himself with royalist poetry: titles such as 'Le Portrait du Roy passant les Alpes',[22] published in 1629, 'Hymne de la Maiesté au

---

pp. 75–115 and idem 1994 (as in n. 6, above), pp. 160–73; the subjects of Scudéry's poems, two paintings by Poussin, have so far not been identified in a satisfactory way – but, given the judgement by C. Biet, '*Ut poesis pictura*, ou le tableau à l'épreuve du poéme, dans Le Cabinet de Monsieur de Scudéry, 1646', *Littératures classiques*, 11, 1989, pp. 121–49 (esp. p. 124) ('on peut en effet soupçonner Scudéry de prêter à certains peintres des tableaux qu'ils n'ont probablement pas réalisés'), they could even be Scudéry's inventions; L'Hermite's and Saint-Sorlin's verses merely contain descriptions of Poussin's *Tancred and Erminia* and his Richelieu-triumphs, the latter interesting for a reconstruction of the Cabinet du Roi at Château Richelieu; Poussin is only mentioned in Berthod's and Saint-Amant's poems while Pader's verses, describing and judging some pictorial themes dear to Poussin, are of somewhat greater interest; finally, de Bie's verses are epigrammatic in character.

16 On the use of Le Moyne's signature 'P.L.M.' in his *Cabinet des devises* (1666), see Maber 1982 (as in n. 2, above), p. 76. For the poem, see Chérot 1887/1971 (as in n. 1, above), p. 542, no. 3 and Sommervogel 1960 (as in n. 6, above), vol. 5, col. 1361, no. 12. The attribution has never been doubted since it is confirmed by the fact that Le Moyne himself included the poem in his *Poésies*, Paris 1650, p. 510 (under 'Poésies diverses | Cabinet des peintures') and, again, in his *Oeuvres poétiques*, Paris 1671, p. 432 (under 'Tapisseries, et peintures poetiques | Cabinet des peintures'). For the *Oeuvres poétiques* (from where the engraving by Poilly after a portrait by Philippe de Champaigne shown in Pl. 32 has been taken), see also Chérot 1887/1971 (as in n. 1, above), pp. 540f., no. XL; for the changed title of the poem in these later re-editions see n. 46, below.

17 See, for example, J. Thuillier, 'Poétes et peintres au XVIIe siècle: l'exemple de Tristan', *Cahiers Tristan l'Hermite*, 6, 1984, pp. 5–23 (esp. p. 21, n. 16): '... le sonnet, *probablement* dû au Père Le Moyne ....' (emphasis mine).

18 See S. Bradley (Ed.), *Archives biographiques françaises*, London 1988, vol. 'Lemoine des Forges – Lemp', fiche 643, no. 401 and Maber 1982 (as in n. 2, above), p. 29.

19 See Maber 1982 (as in n. 2, above), p. 15.

20 For the life of Le Moyne, see Chérot 1887/1971 (as in n. 1, above), pp. 1–29 and Maber 1982 (as in n. 2, above), pp. 28–52.

21 Maber 1982 (as in n. 2, above), pp. 186ff. dates the beginning of the poet's maturity to Le Moyne's arrival in Paris in 1638.

Roy'[23] of 1630 or 'Sonnets sur la naissance de Monseigneur le Dauphin' [24] of 1638 preceded his later and more ambitious undertakings which finally should render him famous. His most popular works were the *Peintures morales* of 1640/43,[25] the *Gallerie des femmes fortes* published in 1647[26] and illustrated with engravings designed by Pietro da Cortona and Claude Vignon, [27] and the epic poem *Saint Louis ou le heros chrétien* of 1653.[28]

'Peintures', 'Galleries' – titles already chosen by Le Moyne for some of his early works point to the poet's affinity with the realm of art. [29] Indeed, Poussin's painting was not to remain the only work of art commemorated in Le Moyne's verses: in his *Oeuvres poétiques*, published in Paris the year of his death 1671,[30] we find a sonnet on Guido Reni's *Magdalen* which is stylistically very close to the sonnet on Poussin. [31]

Le Moyne aspired to create a connection between poetry and art: in the 'Advertissement' of his *Peintures morales* of 1642, he proudly claimed: 'I'ay

---

[22] See Chérot 1887/1971 (as in n. 1, above), pp. 57ff. and p. 506, no. III, Sommervogel 1960 (as in n. 6, above), vol. 5, cols 1357f., no. 3 and Maber 1982 (as in n. 2, above), pp. 31f.

[23] See Chérot 1887/1971 (as in n. 1, above), p. 507, no. IV, Sommervogel 1960 (as in n. 6, above), vol. 5, col. 1358, no. 4 and Maber 1982 (as in n. 2, above), p. 33.

[24] See Chérot 1887/1971 (as in n. 1, above), p. 508, no. VIII, Sommervogel 1960 (as in n. 6, above), vol. 5, col. 1359, no. 8 and Maber 1982 (as in n. 2, above), p. 35.

[25] 1640 (part I), 1643 (part II), re-edited in a revised version in 1645. See Chérot 1887/1971 (as in n. 1, above), pp. 80ff. and pp. 509ff., no. X, Sommervogel 1960 (as in n. 6, above), vol. 5, cols 1359f., no. 10 and Maber 1982 (as in n. 2, above), pp. 37, 40.

[26] See Chérot 1887/1971 (as in n. 1, above), pp. 152ff. and pp. 517ff., no. XV, Sommervogel 1960 (as in n. 6, above), vol. 5, cols 1362f., no. 16 and Maber 1982 (as in n. 2, above), pp. 40ff., esp. p. 42.

[27] For the Vignon-illustrations (engraved by Abraham Bosse) and the frontispiece, engraved by Charles Audran after Pietro da Cortona, see Maber 1982 (as in n. 2, above), p. 41. Concerning Claude Vignon, see also P. Ramade, 'Une source d'inspiration du XVIIe siècle: la galerie des femmes fortes, de Claude Vignon', *Bulletin des Amis du Musée de Rennes*, 4, 1980, pp. 19–26; B. Baumgärtel and S. Neysters (Eds), *Die Galerie der starken Frauen*, exh. cat., Düsseldorf 1995, pp. 170–4, nos 54–6.

[28] Newly edited in a completed version in 1658; see Sommervogel 1960 (as in n. 6, above), vol. 5, col. 1366, no. 23, Chérot 1887/1971 (as in n. 1, above), pp. 527ff., no. XXI and Maber 1982 (as in n. 2, above), pp. 8, 45ff.

[29] See also Maber 1982 (as in n. 2, above), p. 208: 'The relationship between poetry and the visual arts is often very close in Le Moyne's work, but he is never in any doubt as to the great superiority of the former'.

[30] See Sommervogel 1960 (as in n. 6, above), col. 1370, no. 44 and Maber 1982 (as in n. 2, above), pp. 50f. The poem is already inserted into the *Poésies*, Paris 1650, p. 510 (under 'Poésies diverses: Cabinet des peintures'); concerning the *Poésies*, see Chérot 1887/1971 (as in n. 1, above), pp. 524f., no. XIX.

[31] On the poem on Reni, see Maber 1982 (as in n. 2, above), pp. 197f.

ajousté la Poésie à la Peinture; ce que personne n'a auoit entrepris auant moy: elles sont alliées, & se ressemblent en beaucoup de choses; & i'ay crû que si elles sont treuuées si agreables, & si elles donnent tant de plaisir à l'esprit & à la veuë, quand elles sont separées, elles recreuroient vn nouueau lustre, & s'embelliroient mutuellement, & comme par contagion, quand elles seroient mises l'vne auprez de l'autre ....'[32] Since Le Moyne knew the poems by Giambattista Marino,[33] he probably did not mean to say that he was the first to devote verses to paintings[34] – Le Moyne rather claimed to have developed a new kind of poetic description, inspired by the example of painting and aiming – in a very Aristotelian way[35] – at arousing and purifying the public's

[32] 'I have added poetry to painting, something that nobody has done before me: they are connected and resemble each other in many respects; and I have thought that if they are perceived as pleasant to such a degree and if they are giving so much delight to the mind and to the eye when they are separated, they will yield a new splendour and will embellish each other, as by contagion, when they are put together ...'; Pierre Le Moyne, *Les Peintures morales*, Paris 1645 (second edition), 'Advertissement necessaire à l'instruction du Lecteur', n.p. [p. 9].

[33] In his *Traité du poème héroique* (reprinted under the title 'Dissertation du poéme héroique' in the *Oeuvres poétiques*, Paris 1671), a poetological text prefacing his *Saint Lovys ov la Sainte Couronne Reconqvise*, Le Moyne (cited here after the unpaginated edition of 1658 [pp. 71f.]) shows himself informed about 'les Imitateurs du Marin'. Concerning this topic, see also Maber 1982 (as in n. 2, above), p. 44 and esp. pp. 114f.; concerning the *Traité* in general see Chérot 1887/1971 (as in n. 1, above), pp. 250ff.; for the *Saint Lovys* see ibid., pp. 527ff., no. XX and Sommervogel 1960 (as in n. 6, above), col. 1366, no. 23.

[34] See the interpretation in M. Albrecht-Bott, *Die bildende Kunst in der italienischen Lyrik der Renaissance und des Barock*, Wiesbaden 1976, p. 22. Nevertheless, Marino conspicuously remains absent in the list of conceptual predecessors (prudently restricted to ancient authors such as Philostratus, Tacitus, Lucian and Callistratus) which Le Moyne compiles in the 'Advertissement' to emphasize his own merits: 'Mais les Tableaux & les Statuës de ces Autheurs estans en prose, ie pense auoir fait pour le contentement du Lecteur, plus que n'ont fait tous ceux qui m'ont precedé. I'ay ajousté la Poésie à la Peinture ...'.

[35] For the influence of Aristotle on Le Moyne, see G. Bosco, *Il 'meraviglioso' barocco come segno della trasgressione: il Saint Louys di Pierre LeMoyne* (Collana di critica linguistica e poetica, 1), Turin 1985, p. 13 (concerning the *Poetica di Aristotele vulgarizzata e sposta per Ludovico Castelvetro*, Vienna 1570, pp. 147ff. and p. 167 and the *Discorsi del Signor Torquato Tasso dell'arte poetica; et in particolare del Poema Heroico*, Venice 1587) and Maber 1982 (as in n. 2, above), p. 65 (Castelvetro), pp. 113ff. (Tasso) and p. 67, p. 94, n. 50 (Aristotle). Le Moyne, in his *Traité du poéme héroique* (as in n. 33, above, cited here after the unpaginated edition of 1658 [pp. 9, 44f., 47 and 105]) names Aristotle, Ludovico Castelvetro and Tasso. For the influence of the last see esp. J. Cottaz, *L'influence des théories du Tasse sur l'épopée en France*, Paris 1942, pp. 45–50 and passim. For Le Moyne's view of the passions, see A. Levi, S.J., *French Moralists. The Theory of the Passions: 1585 to 1649*, Oxford 1964, esp. pp. 170–6 and pp. 240f.

emotions and at directing them towards higher and more noble goals. Or, as Le Moyne writes in his *Traité du Poeme Héroique*: 'La perfection des Grands est la fin de la grande Poesie ....'[36] 'Ce n'est donc pas assez qu'il (le poete) purifie les Passions des Grands; il faut encore qu'il forme, il faut qu'il acheue en eux les Vertus. ... d'exciter en l'Ame des Grands, l'admiration des grandes Vertus & de l'Honneste Heroique.'[37] To achieve all this, to 'instruire en diuvertissant',[38] poetry, as the highest form of expression,[39] seems more suited than prose, since – as also Montaigne wrote in his *Essais*: 'tout ainsi que la voix, contrainte dans l'étroit canal d'une trompette, sort plus aigue et plus forte, ainsi me semble il que la sentence, pressée aux pieds nombreux de la poésie, s'eslance bien plus brusquement et me fiert d'une plus vive secousse'.[40]

So much for theory – what about practice?

Let us take a look at the French sonnet Le Moyne wrote in order to celebrate Poussin's altarpiece, showing *The Miracle of St Francis Xavier resuscitating the daughter of an inhabitant of Kagoshima in Japan*. Since the poem has so far not been studied in-depth and has been transcribed only in a very unreliable way, its original 1643 version[41] is here given in full:

[36] 'The perfection of noble men is the goal of grand poetry ...'; Le Moyne 1658 (as in n. 33, above), p. [97].
[37] 'It is therefore not enough that the poet purifies the passions of noble men, but he should also form and perfect the virtues within them ... inspiring in the souls of noble men admiration of great virtues and heroic uprightness.' Ibid., p. [99]. See also Maber 1982 (as in n. 2, above), p. 68 and esp. p. 69: 'Almost all of his poetry is moved by the same spirit of impressing, dazzling, or overwhelming the reader ...'.
[38] Le Moyne 1645 (as in n. 32, above), p. 15; on pp. 11ff. he lists the passions he is dealing with in order to achieve this goal.
[39] Maber 1982 (as in n. 2, above), p. 58 and p. 209: 'Poetry differs ... not in the depiction of scenes and events, but in the bold and extraordinary images with which it conveys them, and especially the emotions which they arouse ...'.
[40] 'Just as the voice of the trumpet sings out clearer and stronger for being forced through a narrow tube, so too thoughts, pressed into the metres of versification, leap forth more vigorously, striking me with a livelier shock.' Michel de Montaigne, *Essais*, A. Micha (Ed.), Paris 1969, Book I, chapter 26: 'De l'institution des enfans', pp. 193f. Indeed, Maber 1982 (as in n. 2, above), p. 128, n. 27 has discovered many reminiscences of Montaigne in Le Moyne's prose text of the *Peintures*, vol. 1, pp. 697f.
[41] Montaiglon, who re-published the sonnet for the first time in 1862 (as in n. 1, above), p. 307, consulted the 1643 *folio*-edition (even though caring little for the punctuation of this edition), while Chérot 1887/1971 (as in n. 1, above), pp. 19f. obviously cites the In-12 *editio altera* of 1664.

HENRY KEAZOR

PEINTVRE DE SAINCT FRANÇOIS XAVIER RESVSCITANT VN MORT: OV TABLEAV DV GRAND AVTEL. SONNET.

Est-ce du grand XAVIER la personne,[42] ou l'image,
Qui force icy du Ciel les rigoureuses loix?
Oüy, c'est luy qui reuit, & qui tout à la fois
De sa foy sur vn mort fait vn illustre ouurage.

Tout est miracle en luy, tout parle en sõ[43] visage,
Ses yeux ont de l'ardeur, son geste a de la voix,
La merueille qu'il fait rauit ces Iaponnois,
Et le rauissement leur oste le langage.

Certes, qu'en ce Tableau par vn diuin effort
La priere d'vn Sainct fasse reuiure vn mort,
C'est bien vne merueille estrange à la Nature:

Mais l'effet qui rẽplit tout nostre estõnement,[44]
C'est qu'vn Sainct, sãs quitter encor la sepulture,
Y ressuscite en gloire auant le Iugement.

PAINTING OF ST. FRANCIS XAVIER, RAISING A DEAD [GIRL] OR MAIN ALTARPIECE. SONNET

Is it the person or the image of the great XAVIER,
who forces here heaven's rigorous laws?
Yes, it is he who resuscitates, and at the same time with his faith is doing a famous deed upon someone dead.

Everything in him is a miracle, all his face is telling,
His eyes have ardour, his gesture has voice,
The miracle he is performing enraptures the Japanese,
And the rapture makes them speechless.

Sure, that in this painting by a divine effort, the prayer of a saint is raising someone from the dead –
This is a miracle, alien to nature:

But what is astonishing us completely
Is the fact that a saint, without yet leaving his tomb,
Is here gloriously resuscitated before Judgement Day.

---

[42] The version quoted by Thuillier 1960 (as in n. 6, above), p. 71 and idem 1994 (as in n. 6, above), p. 159 is unreliable: Thuillier here omits the comma whilst introducing a comma in the first line of the first tercet; in the second line of the second tercet, he again omits it. In the last line of the second quartet, he renders 'le rauissement' as 'ce rauissement'. Moreover, his orthographical modernizations are not always consistent (sometimes he substitutes 'I' for 'J' ['Iaponnois'/ 'Japonnois'], sometimes he does not ['Iugement']).

[43] In the 1664 edition the abbreviations have been expanded; see also n. 44.

[44] See n. 43, above.

When Le Moyne inserted these alexandrines[45] in the editions of his *Poésies* in 1650 and in his *Oeuvres poétiques* in 1671, he not only changed the orthography and the punctuation in some lines (separating for example in the first stanza the third and the fourth line by a colon[46] and structuring some lines anew with the help of commas),[47] he also made major changes in lines three and four of the first stanza. Whilst line three in the original version immediately answers the question asked in the first line ('Est-ce du grand Xavier la personne ou l'image') with a 'oui, c'est luy qui reuit', line three in the later version gives an answer by saying 'C'est luy-mesme, il reuit'; more in line with the ideal dramaturgy of a sonnet,[48] the full impact of the answer is

[45] See Maber 1982 (as in n. 2, above), p. 242 and W. Mönch, *Das Sonett. Gestalt und Geschichte*, Heidelberg 1955, pp. 16, 21 and idem, 'Das Sonett. Seine sprachlichen Aufbauformen und stilistischen Eigentümlichkeiten', in *Syntactica und Stilistica. Festschrift für Ernst Gamillscheg zum 70. Geburtstag*, G. Reichenkron, M. Wandruszka and J. Wilhelm (Eds), Tübingen 1957, pp. 387–409 (esp. p. 397). Mönch underlines the fact that this metre is to be considered as typical of French sonnets, as is the rhyme pattern of the present sonnet abba/abba/ccd/ede.

[46] In the *Poésies* 1650 (as in n. 16, above), p. 510 (under 'Poésies diverses | Cabinet des peintures'), the same happens in stanza two at the end of the second line (after 'voix') and in the *Oeuvres poétiques* 1671 (as in n. 16, above), p. 432 (under 'Tapisseries, et peintures poetiques | Cabinet des peintures') in stanza two at the end of the first line (after 'visage'). In both re-editions, the poem carries the title 'S. Xavier ressucitant vn mort. De Poussin.'; this heading is in accord with the poem itself where the Saint is called by his second name whilst the original titles in both editions of the *Basilica extructa* in 1643 and 1664 give his full name: 'SAINCT FRANÇOIS XAVIER RESVSCITANT VN MORT.' Since the editio altera of 1664 does not reflect these changes at all (whilst alterations were made in the other poems – see n. 1, above), it is likely that no one from Le Moyne's circle was involved in this re-edition.

[47] See the version in the *Poésies* 1650 (as in n. 16, above), p. 510 (under 'Poésies diverses | Cabinet des peintures'): I. 'Est-ce que du grand Xavier la personne ou l'image ....' II. 'La merueille qu'il fait ravit ces Iaponnois;' III. 'Certes, qu'en ce tableau par vn divin effort, | La priere d'vn Saint fasse reuiure vn mort, | C'est bien vne merueille estrange à la Nature;' IV. 'C'est qu'vn Saint sans quitter encor la sepulture ....' Le Moyne, who (following the preface of the 'Imprimeur' in the *Poésies* had 'reueu aux heures de son loisir, toutes les Poësies' changed again some lines for the 1671 edition. Thus, the differing passages (containing also a small misprint) in the *Oeuvres poetiques* 1671 (as in n. 16, above), p. 432 are: I. 'Est-ce que du grand Xavier la personne ou l'image ... De sa foy, sur un mort, vn glorieux ouvrage.' II. '... son geste a de la voix; | La merveille qu'il fait, ravit ces Japonnois; | Et le ravissmenr [sic] leur oste le langage.' III. 'Certes, qu'en ce tableau, par vn divin effort, | La priere d'vn Saint, fasse revivre vn mort ...'.

[48] See Mönch 1955 (as in n. 45, above), p. 33 and Mönch 1957 (as in n. 45, above), p. 402, who describes the relation between the octave and the sextet verses in terms such as 'tension' and 'easing' or 'premise' and 'conclusion'.

transferred to the last two lines of the sonnet where the hyperbolic claims of
the described picture are fully played out:

> vn Sainct, sans quitter encor la sepulture,
> Y ressuscite en gloire auant le Iugement.

But since these changes also had repercussions on the rythm of the
surrounding verses, Le Moyne had to alter the sequence of their elements.
Thus,

> Ouy, c'est luy qui reuit, & qui tout à la fois
> De sa foy sur vn mort fait vn illustre ouurage.[49]

had to become

> C'est luy-mesme, il reuit, & fait tout à la fois,
> De sa foy sur un mort vn glorieux ouurage.

The alliterative and almost anaphoric repetition of the verbs 'fait', 'fois' and
'foy' is given greater emphasis, and the whole poem finally turns out to be
not just a composition enlivened by contrasts and antitheses such as the
'gesticulating voice' of the Saint opposed to the Japanese, deprived of speech
by astonishment, but a 'poetic fugue'[50] (as Théophile Gautier put it when
characterizing the sonnet form in general) on the crucial words
'miracle-merveille', 'revivre', 'ravir' and 'ravissement'. Some of these words
are furthermore employed to bind together the quartets and the tercets (see
the 'revit' in line three, returning in the second line of the first tercet under
the form 'revivre' as does 'merveille' in lines seven and eleven).

But of what kind are the 'sentences', put into this fugue and thus
'pressées aux pieds nombreux de la poésie'?

Whoever is acquainted with the poetry of Pietro Aretino or
Giambattista Marino will immediately recognize the topos expressed in the
tercets: the notion of a dead person resuscitated by the painter and thus given
a higher state of existence had already been explored by Aretino – and I just
quote two lines from his sonnet on Titian's (now lost) portrait of Francesco
Vargas:

> In carne io l'ho partorito mortale,
> Tu procreato divino in pittura ....[51]

---

49 Perhaps in order to reduce the excessive use of the beginning 'C'est' in the first,
the third and the fourth stanza, Le Moyne in both the editions of 1650 and 1671
eliminated the 'C'est' in stanza IV, line 2 and replaced it with the simpler 'Est'.
50 In his study on Baudelaire's *Fleurs du mal*, cited here after Mönch 1957 (as in n. 45,
above), p. 408.
51 See *Lettere sull'arte di Pietro Aretino*, E. Camesasca (Ed.), Milan 1957, vol. 2, pp.
433f., no. DCLX; Albrecht-Bott 1976 (as in n. 34, above), p. 75 erroneously
renders the second line as beginning with 'Fu' instead of the correct 'Tu'. For the
(apparently now lost) portrait, see H. E. Wethey, *The Paintings of Titian*, vol. 2,
'The Portraits', London 1971, p. 206, no. L 34.

> In the flesh I have given birth to him as a mortal being,
> You made him divine in painting ....

as well as by Marino,[52] who even supplies the model for verses on a painting depicting a resuscitation. In his madrigal 'Il figlio della Vedova di Naino di Paolo Veronese', Marino expresses the awe and amazement felt at the might of the painter who equals the powers of Christ when calling back to life the dead son:

> Sorgi, sorgi a la luce,
> (PAOLO il comanda) o Giovinetto morto.
> Eccoti già risorto, e senso e moto
> a dispetto di Cloto
> un color spiritoso in te produce.
> Certo l'alta virtù de la parola,
> ch'a Morte empia t'invola,
> è stata per miracolo novello
> partecipata a quel divin pennello.[53]

> Come, come into the light,
> (Paul is giving the order), oh dead youth.
> There you are, already resuscitated, and sense and motion, defying Clotho,
> are producing a vivid colour in you.
> Sure, the great power of the word
> which saves you from impious death
> has by unheard-of miracle been
> bestowed upon this divine brush.

In his analysis of Le Moyne's poems, Richard Maber has noticed that his originality frequently consists 'in taking a conventional concept to extremes';[54] here, too, in an attempt to top a common concept, the poet emphasizes the fact that Poussin in his painting not only resuscitates the dead daughter but also the miracle-working Saint Francis Xavier himself[55] – a poetic strategy as typical of Le Moyne's style as is the contraction of his two favourite expressions 'merveille'/'chose étrange'[56] into 'merveille étrange' in

---

[52] See e.g. Marino's madrigals 'In morte d'Annibale Carracci', p. 191, no. 8b and 'Monsignor Melchior Crescenzio, Cherico [sic] di Camera', p. 193, no. 1 in Giovanni Battista Marino, *La Galeria*, M. Pieri (Ed.), Padua 1979, vol. 1, 'Ritratti', XIV ('Pittori, e Scultori'), XV ('Ritratti di diversi Signori, e Letterati amici dell'Autore').

[53] Marino 1979 (as in n. 52, above), vol. 1, p. 56, no. 15. See in this respect also Marino's 'Lazaro risuscitato di Luca Cangiasi', vol. 1, p. 64, no. 28. The topos of the 'Immortal pennello' as 'l'uccisor di morte' became very frequent concerning Guido Reni – see for example J. L. Colomer, 'Un tableau "littéraire" et académique au 17e siècle: *L'Enlévement d'Hélène* de Guido Reni', *Revue de l'art*, 90, 1990, pp. 74–87, for this quotation see there p. 82 and n. 58.

[54] Maber 1982 (as in n. 2, above), p. 221.

[55] Idem, p. 197 sees this idea as inspired by Le Moyne's effort to close with a neat antithesis.

line three of the second tercet. The originality of the Marinesque contention of the Saint's resuscitation[57] is further drawn into question by the fact that it is also referred to by Père Guillaume Léonard, the author of the Latin poem on all three altarpieces, in his praise of Poussin's picture.[58]

Much of the Latin poem seems today to be of limited interest since it focuses on puns on the names of the artists: concerning Jacques Stella, for example, the obvious association of the words 'star' ('Stella') and 'sun' is used to establish a hierarchy of day and night, bright and dark; Poussin is claimed to be the 'Sol pictorum', but concerning Stella's painting we learn that

> ... non tamen est huius Solis lux tanta, propinquum obscuret ut Stellae iubar
> ...[59]

The section of the Latin poem devoted to Poussin's painting uses similiar, obvious puns: the French painter is introduced as 'le Poussin, Gallus pictor', and in the sequel this interplay between the name 'Poussin', meaning 'little chicken' in French, and the 'Cock', the symbolic animal of France, is developed further:

> ... patrij retinere velis si nominis umbram,
> Pullum latiné nuncupes.
> ... Galli soboles, ait, inclyta patris[60]

Since Poussin had the honour to paint the main altarpiece he is addressed directly in the Latin verses, whereas Stella and Vouet are referred to in the third person singular. The Latin verses on Poussin furthermore go beyond mere puns by dealing with the represented subject. In this respect, already the

[56] See the examples listed by Maber 1982 (as in n. 2, above), p. 190.
[57] On novelty and originality as fundamental principles of Marino's aesthetics, see W. T. Elwert, 'Zur Charakteristik der italienischen Barocklyrik', *Romanistisches Jahrbuch*, 3, 1950, pp. 421–98 (esp. pp. 436f).
[58] Nevertheless it seems very likely that Le Moyne was the creator of this *pointe*; see also n. 54.
[59] '... the light of this sun is not bright enough to obscure Stella's splendour nearby.' The last verses from Cossart's Latin poem ('Minoris alterius Arae Tabula quam pinxit Stella') employs similar arguments. It is also worth noting that Le Moyne's as well as Léonard's poems are original inasmuch as they both refrain from using the hackneyed acclamation of the respective painter as a new Apelles, amply utilized by Cossart and Michel Guillonnet in their – comparatively talkative – poems on Stella and Vouet. Perhaps not accidentally Guillonnet (*Basilica extructa* 1643, p. 33) closes his poem on Vouet with the thought: 'Sed tacuisse iuvat (neque enim quod muta poësis | Eloquitur pictura; loquax pictura poësis | Enarrare valet) superant miracula vatem'.
[60] '... if you want to preserve a shadow of his paternal name, you might call him "Pullum" [little chicken] in Latin. ... Famous offspring of a French Father ....' In Vouet's case, the equivalent of these puns on the names Stella and Poussin is the use of an anagram (the letters 'S-i-m-o-n-V-o-e-t-i-u-s' are rearranged as 'sine vitio sum').

title of the section differs from those of the other two: 'Tabula quam pinxit *Stella*' and 'Tabula quam pinxit *Voëtius*' are the laconic titles of these poems whilst the verses on Poussin's painting are entitled 'Principis Altaris tabulam, cuius argumentu(m) est reddita puellæ à Xauerio vita, fecit *Le Poussin*, Gallus pictor'. The poem closes with the topos also found in the French poem:

Prodigium quamvis Xaverius edat in Illâ,
Animamque reddat Virgini,
Tu tamen hunc superas; dat enim vitam iste Puellae,
Sed ipse das Xaverio.[61]

In order to better understand and appreciate the two poems on Poussin's work, we need to consider the painting in question since its commission, its making and its iconography were highly problematic. Nicolas Poussin was less than enthusiastic about the project when he received the order for the painting in June 1641: having been urged to come to Paris in October 1640, he felt himself overburdened with far too many projects of far too little ambition. Furthermore, when he received the measurements for the projected altarpiece (the greatest of the few public commissions he executed), he immediately lamented not only the great pressure exerted upon him by the short time granted for the execution (he was already involved in other projects and he should have delivered the work within four months);[62] he also complained that his studio was too small to shelter the huge canvas of 4.44 x 2.34 metres[63] (indeed, when the picture in 1778 – after the suppression of the Jesuit order in France in 1763 and the sale of its possessions on 14 March 1764[64] – was to be transported to the Apartement du Roy au Louvre it was

---

[61] 'Xavier here might have worked miracles, giving back the spirit of life to a virgin, but you have exceeded him; because he has resuscitated the girl but you have resuscitated Xavier himself'.

[62] See C. Jouanny, 'Correspondance de Nicolas Poussin', in *Archives de l'art français*, N.P., vol. 5, Paris 1911: letters from 3 August 1641 (Jouanny, p. 87), 20 September 1641 (Jouanny, p. 97) and 21 November 1641 (Jouanny, p. 106): 'quadrone', 'troppo fretta'. See also p. 107, n. 1, the quotation from Roland de Chambray's *Traité*: 'peint avec une grande précipitation et pendant l'hyver'. Given this pressure, it seems rather unlikely that Poussin first had to execute a modello, as sold in the Dufourny sale: M. H. Delaroche, *Catalogue des tableaux, dessins et estampes composant l'une des collections de feu M. Léon Dufourny* ..., Paris 1819, 2nd edn, p. 54, lot 87, where a picture (canvas, 58 x 36 pouces = ca. 147 x 91 cm) is listed, believed to be 'l'étude de celui que le Poussin a peint pour le maître-autel du noviciat des jésuites'; the price for this piece – following the copy in the British Library (786.1.46) where the selling prices are noted by hand – was 71 – 95 (no currency specified).

[63] Letter from 2 July 1641: Jouanny (as in n. 62, above), p. 83.

[64] See Gobillot 1930 (as in n. 3, above), p. 89 and pp. 98f. G. Wildenstein, *Les graveurs de Poussin au XVIIe siècle*, Paris 1957, p. 218, no. 87 nevertheless indicates the selling date as 1763 (reporting also that the painting was sold to Louis XV). He is seconded by A. Blunt, *The Paintings of Nicolas Poussin. A Critical Catalogue*,

suggested to cut it down 'par le haut et par le bas, et corriger par ce moyen sa forme désagréable'[65] – a plan which fortunately was immediately abandoned because judged impracticable).[66] But when Poussin finally delivered the painting at the beginning of the year 1642, polemics started: infuriated by the King who had greeted the newly-arrived Poussin in 1640 – 'Voilà Vouet bien attrapé' (Here we have Vouet being nicely outwitte) – the envious Vouet started a campaign against the painting. He had obviously learnt from the diatribe he himself had suffered only one year before when his painting of the *Apotheosis of St Louis* (today Musée des Beaux-Arts at Rouen)[67] for the church Saint-Louis-des-Jésuites was accused of copying so shamelessly an *Assumption of the Virgin* by Annibale Carracci that Vouet's saint still showed female features. Henri Sauval remarked: 'Ce n'est pas assés dans une figure d'y remarquer une tête & un habit d'homme, il faut que le reste soit d'homme aussi ...'[68]

London 1966, p. 70, no. 101 and J. Thuillier, *L'opera completa di Poussin*, Milan 1974, p. 101, no. 128 and idem, *Nicolas Poussin*, Paris 1994, p. 257, no. 151; however, in the catalogue of the *Exposition Nicolas Poussin*, Paris 1960, p. 96, Blunt indicates 1764 as the date.

[65] Letter from Jean-Baptiste-Marie Pierre to the Directeur général des Batiments du Roi, Comte M. D'Angiviller of 13 April 1778, published by M. Furcy-Raynaud in *Nouvelles Archives de l'art français*, 3rd ser., vol. 21, 1905, p. 195, no. 202. Already H. Sauval in his *Histoire et recherches des antiquités de la ville de Paris*, Paris 1724, vol. 1, p. 462 reports the fact that the painting was judged to be 'trop long & trop peu large'. O. Grautoff, *Nicolas Poussin – Sein Werk und sein Leben*, Munich, Leipzig 1914, vol. 1, pp. 212, 449, n. 207 states that Sauval's text was already written in 1654, but printed only in 1722; Thuillier 1960 (as in n. 6, above), p. 147 and idem 1994 (as in n. 64, above), p. 181 presumes the text to have been written between 1652 and 1655.

[66] Furcy-Raynaud 1905 (as in n. 65, above): '... la diminution n'est pas practicable, la page est trop bien remplie pour le permettre le moindre retranchement.' The plan to cut down the painting is discussed in F. G. Pariset, 'Les "natures mortes" chez Poussin', in *Actes* 1960 (as in n. 6, above), pp. 213–22 (esp. p. 220), Blunt 1966 (as in n. 64, above), p. 70, no. 101 and M. Davies and A. Blunt, 'Some corrections and additions to M. Wildenstein's "Graveurs de Poussin au XVIIe siècle"', *Gazette des Beaux-Arts*, 104, 1962, pp. 205–22 (esp. p. 212, n. 87), D. Wild, *Nicolas Poussin. Leben, Werk, Exkurse*, Zurich 1980, vol. 2, p. 99, no. 102 and Thuillier 1994 (as in n. 64, above), p. 213, n. 24.

[67] For this painting, see *Saint-Paul – Saint-Louis* (as in n. 9, above), p. 38, no. 30 and J. Thuillier (Ed.), *Vouet*, exh. cat., Rome 1991, p. 191 (under no. 36).

[68] 'It is not enough to see in a figure the head and dress of a man, the rest should likewise be fitting for a man.' Sauval 1724 (as in n. 65, above), p. 464. In spite of the fact that the iconography of the apotheosis of St. Louis tends to lack characteristics that clearly distinguish it from the apotheoses of other saints, Chérot 1887/1971 (as in n. 1, above), p. 26 sees Le Moyne inspired by Vouet's painting when describing the same episode in his *Saint Louis ou le heros chrétien*.

Vouet now levelled the same kind of criticism at Poussin: he accused him of having copied his Christ from the antique and critized him severely for not having depicted a merciful God but a 'thundering Jupiter' [69] (a depiction which, by the way, would have pleased the marinesque poet Giuseppe Battista who - in his poem 'Lo studio delle lettere' - likewise called the Christian God by the name of 'Giove'). [70] That all this was just a subterfuge for a slanderous polemic can easily be demonstrated with two sets of observations:

When conceiving the figure of Christ, Poussin indeed had taken the thundering Jupiter from the Column of Trajan (Pl. 33) [71] as his starting-point, [72] but he had blended this motive with elements taken from Raphael's *Transfiguration* (Vatican, Pinacoteca; Pl. 34) [73] - as he had already done before

---

[69] See Jouanny 1911 (as in n. 62, above), p. 147 where Poussin's famous answer is reported: 'qu'il ne peut, dis-je, et ne doit jamais s'imaginer un Christ en quelque action que ce soit, avec un visage de tortico lis ou d'un père doûillet, veû qu'estant sur la terre parmi les hommes, il estoit mesme difficile de le considérer en face.' See for this also André Félibien, *Entretiens sur les vies et sur les ouvrages des plus excellens peintres anciens et modernes*, Trevoux 1725, vol. 4, VIII. Entretien, pp. 40, 49.

[70] See the poem by Giuseppe Battista (1610-1675) in the anthology edited by B. Croce, *Lirici marinisti*, Bari 1910, p. 431, no. XLV. Interesting in this context, R. Buscaroli, 'Lettere artistiche inedite del generale Marsili', in *Atti e memorie della R. Accademia Clementina di Bologna*, vol. 2, Bologna 1837, pp. 29-61 (esp pp. 55ff.) publishes a letter by Luigi F. Marsili of 17 November 1714 with a report about the discovery of the chest of an antique statue of Jupiter in Rome which is then commented upon: 'son sicuro che ogni Maestro la baciarà, e lo designarà una ventina di volte, e massime, quando vogliono dipingere Crocifissi.' (I owe this reference to Frank Martin, Berlin).

[71] See also Pietro Sante Bartoli, *Colonna Traiana eretta dal senato e popolo romano all'Imperatore Traiano Augusto nel suo foro in Roma*, s.d. (1667), pl. 18, no. 133.

[72] Only Sauval 1724 (as in n. 65, above), p. 462 suggests that Poussin was suspected of having copied from the Column of Trajan: '... les soupçonneux la croyent prise de la Colonne Trajanne ....' For the 'Jupiter tonnant' see Jouanny 1911 (as in n. 62, above), p. 147; for the Column of Trajan see C. Cichorius, *Die Reliefs der Traianssäule*, Berlin 1836, vols. 2 - 3 (text), pp. 116f. and S. Settis, *La Colonna Traiana*, Turin 1988, p. 288. For the French *fortuna critica* of the reliefs see P. Morel, *La Colonna Traiana e gli artisti francesi da Luigi XIV a Napoleone I*, Rome 1988, pp. 81-3, nos 28-9 where drawings by Edmé Bouchardon and an anonymous artist after the 'Jupiter Tonans' are published (Paris, Musée du Louvre; inv. F. 20.24080/RF 38.618).

[73] Sauval 1724 (as in n. 65, above), p. 462: 'Les envieux & les intelligens disent que Poussin, Raphaël & l'Antique ont fait la même figure, ou que Raphaël n'en pourroit pas faire une meilleure; les soupçonneux la croyent prise de la Colonne Trajanne, mais les désintéressés & tous les intelligens tiennent qu'il n'est redevable de la beauté des attitudes toutes divines qu'à son grand genie.' ('The envious and the judicious say that Poussin, Raphael and the antique have produced the same figure, or that Raphael could not make a better one; the suspicious think that it

when executing two other Parisian commissions, the *Moses and the burning bush* (Copenhagen, Statens Museum for Kunst), commissioned in 1641 by Richelieu, and the title-page for the *édition de luxe* of the bible, designed in August 1641 and printed by the Imprimerie Royale (Pl. 35).[74] Although this repeated recourse to the appearance of the pagan god did not remain unnoticed (see the passage in Perrault's *Les Hommes illustres*: 'Quelques-uns le blâmèrent aussi d'avoir donné à l'air de teste du Christ de S. Germain en Laye & de plusieurs autres Tableux quelque chose qui tenont plus d'un Jupiter tonnant que du Sauveur du monde...'),[75] Poussin was severely criticized only

has been copied from the Column of Trajan, but the impartial and all the judicious [observers] hold the view that the beauty of its most divine posture is due only to his great genius.') Sauval does not explicitly mention Raphael's *Transfiguration*, but since the features of the God in Trajan's Column, in the *Transfiguration* and Poussin's painting are very similar, it is likely that Sauval specifically had the *Transfiguration* in mind when making this comment. For Raphael's painting, see H. von Einem, 'Die "Verklärung Christi" und die "Heilung des Besessenen" von Raffael', *Akademie der Wissenschaften und der Literatur (Mainz). Abhandlungen der geistes- und sozialwissenschaftlichen Klasse*, 5, 1966, pp. 3–50 and K. Oberhuber, *Raphaels Transfiguration. Stil und Bedeutung*, Urachhaus 1982. For reports on Poussin's great admiration for the *Transfiguration* see A. Blunt (Ed.), *Nicolas Poussin. Lettres et propos sur l'art*, Paris 1989, p. 193 (Bellori: 'Nicolas Poussin ... le citait avec la *Transfiguration* de Raphaël ... comme les deux tableaux les plus célèbres pour la gloire du pinceau.') and p. 196 (Félibien: '... Poussin comptait la *Transfiguration* de Raphaël, la *Descente de croix* de Daniel de Volterre, et le *Saint Jérôme* du Dominiquin, pour les plus beaux tableaux qui fussent à Rome.'). For a recent re-evaluation of the importance of this combination of Raphaelism and the antique as ingredients of Poussin's style in Paris between 1641 and 1642 see G. S. Davidson, 'Nicolas Poussin, Jacques Stella, and the Classical Style in 1640: The Altar Paintings for the Chapel of Saint Louis at Saint-Germain-en-Laye', in J. Hargrove (Ed.), *The French Academy. Classicism and its Antagonists*, London, Toronto 1990, pp. 37–67.

[74] Poussin sent the (now lost) drawing to Chantelou on 3 August 1641, see Jouanny 1911 (as in n. 62, above), p. 87. The engraving was executed by Claude Mellan. In a copy of a lost drawing for the altarpiece the similiarities between the two figures of Christ are even more evident; for this copy, today in the Hermitage at St. Petersburg see P. Rosenberg and L. A. Prat, *Nicolas Poussin 1594–1665. Catalogue raisonné des dessins*, Milan 1994, vol. 2, pp. 1072f., no. R 1119. For a comparison between the depiction of God in the *Moses and the burning bush* and an engraving by Marcantonio Raimondi representing *Noah* see M. Stein, 'Notes on the Italian Sources of Nicolas Poussin', *Kunsthistorisk Tidskrift*, 21, 1952, pp. 9ff.; for the painting in Stockholm see Blunt 1966 (as in n. 64, above), p. 16, no. 18.

[75] 'Some blamed him for having given the head of Christ at S. Germain en Laye and in some other paintings something which is more in keeping with a thundering Jupiter than with the Saviour of the world.' Charles Perrault, *Les Hommes illustres qui ont paru en France pendant ce siècle*, Paris 1696, p. 90. Poussin re-used the appearance of the thundering Jupiter once more for his painting *The Institution of the Eucharist* (Paris, Louvre; commissioned in December 1640 by Louis XIII for

when he – obviously working in a great hurry – re-used the image of the God for his *Francis Xavier*. Moreover, the critics, so eager in search of weak points, failed to notice that the girl in the left foreground was likewise derived from the antique: the source for the figure gently propping up the resuscitated girl's head can be detected in the relief of a Meleager-sarcophagus (Paris, Louvre; Pl. 36)[76] which Poussin had already consulted when painting his *Germanicus* thirteen years earlier as well as his first version of the *Extreme Unction* about nine years earlier. He returned once more to this source in the second version of the Extreme Unction of 1644.[77]

The slanderous nature of the polemic is further confirmed by the fact that the critics overlooked a detail in Poussin's painting which – had the critics really been motivated by religious ardour – could have served as a possible point of attack: while the orthodox iconography of St Francis Xavier, established on the grounds of an early posthumous portrait of 1583, held to be faithful and true (Rome, Cappellette di S. Ignazio; Pl. 37),[78] shows

---

the chapel at the Château de Saint-Germain-en-Laye). In all four compositions (*Moses, Institution*, title page, *Francis Xavier*) the figures of God or Jesus are not only showing similar gestures (the *Eucharist* here being excluded), but they also display the same type of hair-do and beard. For the painting in Paris, see Blunt 1966 (as in n. 64, above), pp. 54f., no. 78.

[76] For this sarcophagus, see F. Baratte and C. Metzger, *Catalogue des sarcophages en pierre d'époques romaine et paléochrétienne*, Paris 1985, pp. 97ff., no. 37.

[77] He re-used the posture of this woman a second time in 1647 for the figure of the penitent Magdalen in the second version of the *Penance* (Edinburgh, National Gallery of Scotland). Furthermore, the Meleager-sarcophagus provided him with motives when painting the second version of the *Extreme Unction* in 1644. For the Meleager-sarcophagus as a source for the *Germanicus*, see already Grautoff 1914 (as in n. 65, above), p. 75 and W. Friedländer, *Nicolas Poussin. Die Entwicklung seiner Kunst*, Munich 1914, p. 34. For the two versions of the *Extreme Unction*, see S. C. Emmerling, *Antikenverwendung und Antikenstudium bei Nicolas Poussin*, Würzburg 1939, pp. 3–7; already Michel-François Dandré-Bardon, *Costume des anciens peuples*, Paris 1772, vol. 1, cahier V, planche I refers to this source when showing the first version of the *Extreme Unction* together with an engraving of the sarcophagus. Finally, M. Praz, 'Milton e Poussin alla scuola dell'Italia', *Romana*, 2, 1938, pp. 30–53 (esp. p. 49) has shown that the jamb of the bed in the *Saint Francis Xavier* – praised by François-Georges Pariset, 'Les "natures mortes" chez Poussin', in *Actes* 1960 (as in n. 6, above), vol. 1, pp. 215–24 (esp. p. 220), as 'd'un classicisme robuste' – is likewise taken from the antique, citing a detail of the *Aldobrandini Wedding* (Vatican, Pinacoteca).

[78] The posthumous portrait of 1583, today in the Cappellette di S. Ignazio in Rome, was characterized by those who knew the Saint as providing a close likeness; for this painting, see W. Schamoni, *Das wahre Gesicht der Heiligen*, Leipzig 1938, p. 113. Francisco Zurbarán when painting his *Legado vega Inclán* (today: Museo Romántico, Madrid) obviously took the Roman portrait as a model; Zurbarán's picture is shown as fig. 7 in D. C. P. Bustamante and D. F. J. Sanchez Canton, *Cuarto centenario de la muerte de San Francisco Javier*, Madrid 1952 (comment on

the Saint with a full beard, Poussin – in his own words 'unaccustomed to portraiture'[79] – departed from this iconographic tradition: although likewise depicting the saint in slight profile with eyes turned upwards, other than e.g. Van Dyck[80] or Rubens (Pl. 38)[81] he gave his Francis Xavier only a very thin

p. 50). The frontispiece of this booklet shows a drawing by D. V. Carderera (Madrid, Biblioteca Nacional) with the inscription: 'Retrato verdadero de San Francisco Xavier que estuvo en Gandiá y debió pertenecer a San Francisco de Borja'. The Saint is here likewise portrayed with a thick beard; for a comment on this drawing see the text by Canton, p. 46. Concerning Zurbarán's work, see P. Guinard, *Zurbarán et les peintres espagnols de la vie monastique*, Paris 1960, p. 274, no. 543, where the painting is dated to about 1640 and the saint's face is characterized: 'les yeux au ciel, tel que l'a peint le P. Teixeira'.

[79] See Poussin's letter to Chantelou from 13 March 1650; Jouanny 1911 (as in n. 62, above), p. 412: 'Je confesse ingénument que je suis paresseux à faire cet ouvrage auquel je n'ai pas grand plaisir et peu d'habitude, car il y a vingt-huit ans que je n'ai fait aucuns portrait ....' ('I admit without embarrassment that I am listless in executing this work which does not please me greatly and in which I have little experience since I have not made a portrait for twenty-eight years.').

[80] See E. Larsen, *The Paintings by Anthony van Dyck*, Freren 1988, vol. 2, p. 174, no. 429 (Pinacoteca Vaticana) and no. 430 (Schloß Weissenstein, Pommersfelden). Many of the prominent pictures of Saint Francis Xavier that were painted later, such as the three paintings of Baciccio in S. Andrea al Quirinale (*S. Francis Xavier preaching in the Indies, Saint Francis Xavier baptising an Eastern Princess, Death of Saint Francis Xavier*), confirm this physiognomy. The only exception so far discovered, a print by Giovanni Giuseppe Dal Sole (1654 – 1719) depicting the dispute of the saint with heathen scholars, does not show him with a heavy beard, but nevertheless gives him the faint indication of a sprouting full beard. It is perhaps this engraving which is described by G. Gori, *Notizie istoriche degl'intagliatori*, Siena 1771, p. 248 as done after a painting by Lorenzo Pasinelli, showing 'un S. Francesco Xaverio, che con sante dottrine confonde i Satrapi del Giappone'; for Baciccio's paintings see R. Enggass, *The Painting of Baciccio*, University Park 1964, p. 141. Concerning Saint Francis Xavier as a poet, a writer, as well as the subject of poems, sculptures and paintings see Canton 1952 (as in n. 78, above), pp. 23–55: 'San Francisco Javier en las letras y en las artes españolas'.

[81] Cf. his lost painting of St. Francis Xavier (formerly London, Asscher and Welker, destroyed by fire in 1940) which perhaps was commissioned for Il Gesù in Rome, but was later transferred to the Jesuit church in Brussels; see H. Vlieghe, *Corpus Rubenianum Ludwig Burchard*, part VIII, 'Saints', vol. 2, Brussels 1973, pp. 71f., no. 114, missing among the copies listed there is the painting in the second chapel on the left in the church of S. Francesco Saverio at Palermo, traditionally attributed to Pietro Novelli (1603-1647). For the other portraits of the saint, all showing him with a beard, see S. Kimura, 'Catalogue des portraits de Saint François Xavier au début du 17e siècle', *Bulletin de la Faculté des Arts, Université de Nihon*, 26, 1996, pp. 87–99 (in Japanese); for later depictions of the bearded saint see the images listed by P. G. Lechner OSB, *Heiligenporträts. Eine Auswahl aus der Göttweiger Sammlung*, exh. cat., Stift Göttweig 1988, pp. 69–79, nos 65 (Gaulli), 66 (Seghers/Bolsward), 67 (Sangiorgi), 68 (Lublinski/Waldreich), 69

beard. Whilst this detail was overlooked, the critics focused on one ear of the depicted Francis Xavier which they judged as being too big.[82] The engraver Etienne Gantrel, when making a print after the painting (Pl. 39), which he dedicated to Père François de la Chaise (1624–1709), corrected the Saint's appearance by showing him with a thick full beard whilst his companion Jean Fernandez[83] (in the painting even more bearded than Saint Francis Xavier) is depicted in contrast as clean-shaven.[84] The poems in the *Basilica extructa* do not reflect the polemics of April 1642, preceding the publication of the booklet by only one year.

Some further points still need to be addressed: the miracle performed by Francis Xavier is called an 'illustre ouvrage' in the 1643 version of the poem, and 'glorieux' in the 1650 version. However one may read 'illustre' and 'glorieux', be it in the sense of 'famous' or of 'outstanding', neither meaning is ultimately appropriate since the miracle depicted in Poussin's painting is in fact highly unusual in the iconography of the missionary. As Saburo Kimura demonstrated in 1988, the resuscitation of the dead Japanese girl was invented only in 1594 by the Jesuit Orazio Torsellino. When writing a biography of Francis Xavier, Torsellino adopted elements from the *Historia de Japan* by the Jesuit historian Luis Frois, published ten years earlier in 1584. Frois's report about the Jesuit physician, Luis de Armeida, who had introduced western medicine to Japan and at Kagoshima saved a Japanese girl from a serious illness, was integrated by Torsellino into the story of Francis Xavier: he miraculously calls back from death the daughter of a rich and honoured citizen of Kagoshima.[85]

(Hainzelmann), 70 (Wolfgang), 71 (Küsell?), 72 (Küsell?), 73 (Amling), 74 (Amling), 75 (Anonymous), 76 (Anonymous), 77 (Pfeffel), 78 (Anonymous), 79 (Luyken) and 80 (Küsell). For the painting by Jean Le Clerc of a *Saint Francis Xavier preaching to the Indians* (Nancy, Musée Historique Lorrain de Nancy) where the Saint likewise appears bearded, see S. Kimura, 'Saint François-Xavier prêchant aux Indiens de Jean Le Clerc', in A. Reinbold (Ed.), *Georges de la Tour ou la nuit traversée, Actes du colloque*, Metz 1994, pp. 133–43.

[82] Germain Brice, *Description nouvelle de la ville de Paris, ou Recherche curieuse*, Paris 1698, vol. 2, pp. 236f.: 'quelques critiques trop & peut-être jaloux du mérite extraordinaire du Peintre ... ont soûtenu qu'il avoit fait une oreille trop grande à Saint François Xavier'.

[83] For the identification of Jean Fernandez, see S. Kimura, 'La source écrite du *Miracle de saint François-Xavier* de Poussin', *Revue du Louvre*, 5–6, 1988, pp. 394-8 (esp. p. 394).

[84] See also early descriptions of the Saint, always mentioning his beard (P. Manuel Teixeira: 'el cabello y barba, negros' (1694); P. Simón Bayard: 'la bocca rubiconda e la folta barba'), cited by Canton 1952 (as in n. 78, above), p. 44.

[85] Kimura 1988 (as in n. 83, above), pp. 394ff. It should nevertheless be noted that Poussin did not follow Torsellino's report too faithfully, perhaps in order to better emphasize the emotions depicted in and aroused by his painting; he gave the mother of the resuscitated girl rather than her father a prominent role (see n.

Given these origins, it is no wonder that this event does not form part of the canonical iconography of the taumaturgous Saint.[86] It is indeed very telling that Louis Réau in 1958, when publishing his *Iconographie de l'art chrétien*, erroneously listed Poussin's painting as representing a miracle done in India[87] since the Indian episodes – together with the disputation between the Saint and heathen scholars – were the most frequently represented scenes from his life (see, for example, Rubens's painting of 1620 in the Kunsthistorisches Museum in Vienna depicting the episode of a dead Indian child resuscitated by the Saint,[88] or two engravings, one by Johann Georg Wolfgang from after 1662 showing Francis Xavier resuscitating a dead Indian,[89] the other by Martin Anton Lublinski and Johann Georg Waldreich from 1675, depicting the disputation).[90]

97, below).

[86] See e.g. the cycle of 20 paintings by the Portuguese painter André Reinoso (1610–1641) in the Sacristy of the Jesuit church of Sâo Roque in Lisbon, where the scene of the resuscitation of the Kagoshima girl is suspiciously absent; the only Japanese miracle depicted there concerns the healing of a sick woman; for this painting, as well as for the whole cycle see: V. Serrão, *A lenda de Sâo Francisco Xavier. Pelo pintor André Reinoso*, Lisbon 1993, pp. 90f., no. XVII (*Sâo Francisco Xavier curando um enferma, no Japâo*), for Reinoso in general see Serrão's entry in *The Dictionary of Art*, J. Turner (Ed.), vol. 26, London 1996, pp. 129f. where the cycle in Lisbon is dated to about 1619. Likewise the scene of the resuscitation of a dead man, illustrated by Serrão on p. 52, does not show the Kagoshima miracle but an event that happened in Ceylon. The picture forms part of a pictorial cycle by Padre Manuel Henriques (1593 - 1654), executed in 1640/50, Sacristia de Sé Nova de Coimbra (once Colégio da Companhia de Jesus); see Serrão, pp. 50-2. Finally, a fresco cycle in the Cloisters of the Convent of La Merced in Quito (Ecuador; datable on the grounds of stylistic evidence to the 18th century) likewise does not include this event – the only miraculous resuscitation shown there is a posthumous miracle, a relic of the Saint reviving a dying child (Warburg photo: V.7.4311).

[87] L. Réau, *Iconographie de l'art chrétien*, vol. 3, 1, 'Iconographie des Saints', A–F, Paris 1958, p. 540. Kimura 1988 (as in n. 83, above), p. 396 erroneously charges Bellori with having confused the episode depicted by Poussin with a scene in India: however, Bellori (*Le vite de' pittori, scultori e architetti moderni*, Rome 1672, p. 429) clearly names the miracle as 'San Francesco Xaverio, quando risuscita la donna morta nel Giappone'. If Bellori then (p. 430) speaks of 'altre teste naturalissime d'indiani', he perhaps does so because Japan was then still considered as part of the Eastern Indies (as opposed to the Western Indies, i.e. America).

[88] For Rubens's painting with the miracles of St. Francis Xavier for the church in Antwerp (Vienna, Kunsthistorisches Museum), see Vlieghe 1973 (as in n. 81, above), pp. 26-9, no. 104 and, recently, S. Kimura, 'A propos des Miracles de Saint François de P. P. Rubens: aspects iconographiques', *Bulletin de la Faculté des Arts, Université de Nihon*, 28 1998, pp. 55–60 (in Japanese).

[89] See Lechner 1988 (as in n. 81, above), p. 72, no. 70.

[90] Ibid., p. 71, no. 68.

Why did the Jesuits – normally so eager to devise clearly defined iconographic schemes[91] – choose such an uncanonical subject for the high altar of the new church? We know from Poussin's correspondence that this subject was not the only one to have been considered. In a letter of July 1641 the painter reports that he is reading the Lives of St Ignatius and St Francis Xavier in order to find an appropriate subject for the painting, hoping nevertheless that De Noyers's suggestion to depict the miracle in Japan could be accepted.[92] Thus, De Noyers's proposal does not seem to have been the first choice. Both his suggestion and the final choice might have to do with a tendency observable in the hagiography of St Francis Xavier during these years. In several Jesuit theatre plays, written and performed in the late sixteenth and early seventeenth centuries, the deeds of the Saint performed in Japan are emphasized, since they were the last acts he accomplished before his death and his entry into Heaven.[93] Already Torsellino's account of the miracle worked in Japan might reflect a desire to provide the last stage of the Saint's

[91] See e.g. Serrâo 1993 (as in n. 86, above), p. 105 in his English summary on the Reinoso paintings: 'The "absolute modernity" of the series is evidenced in the clear iconographic programme for the paintings laid down in the specific guidelines of the Society of Jesus, in order to record through imagery the miraculous life of the [sic] fiftteenth-century saintly missionary, who died in 1552, in order to further the process of his canonization. It was, therefore, important to establish a clear iconography, attractive, strictly accurate, based on known biographical texts ....' Serrâo on p. 105 (perhaps due to a typographical error?) incorrectly states that Saint Francis Xavier was canonized in 1662 (instead of 1622).

[92] In a letter of 16 June 1641 Poussin asks if De Noyers could submit an idea for the subject of the painting: Jouanny 1911 (as in n. 62, above), p. 77; 29 June 1641 he still has not received any suggestions concerning this point (ibid., p. 80). Thus, the interpretation of the events given by Thuillier 1974 (as in n. 64, above), p. 101, no. 128 and idem 1994 (as in n. 64, above), p. 257, no. 151, who thinks that the subject was Poussin's own decision is not correct, whilst Wild 1980 (as in n. 66, above), vol. 1, p. 101 rightly states that the suggestion was due to De Noyers. Interestingly, in the *editio altera* of 1664 Cossart clearly stresses De Noyers' possible influence upon the depicted subjects by expanding the hints (p. 35, v. 4f.) given in the 1643 edition ('... neque linea ducta est | Te sine: pingenti dictabas omnia dextrae.') to the hyperbolical claim (v. 35ff.): '... Sublete: hoc ore docentem | His jussisti oculis hoc pingi simplice cultu. | Et potuit merito tabulae subscribere pictor | Auctorem Subletum: operis nam linea ducta | Te sine nulla fuit: dictabas uncius auctor | Singula, et ingenium artificis radiumque regebas'.

[93] See for example the 'Comoedia de SS: patribus Ignatio et Xaverio' (Vienna, Handschriften- und Musiksammlung der Österreichischen Nationalbibliothek, Cod. 9881), written at the end of the sixteenth century; in act IV the deeds of S. Ignatius in Rome are parallelized with those of S. Francis Xavier in Japan; both plays then narrate the deaths of the saints and the welcome prepared for them in Heaven. For these plays, see also K. Adel, *Das Wiener Jesuitentheater und die europäische Barockdramatik*, Wien 1960, pp. 6, 51.

life with appropriate deeds – deeds which gained a special importance as they were so close to the Saint's afterlife in Paradise.

Returning to Le Moyne's poem, we observe that the iconographic pecularities mattered to the author as little as the polemics surrounding the work. But if so: what did matter to him? Of what kind are his 'sentences, pressées aux pieds nombreux de la poësie'? And are there any original thoughts, not already expressed or hinted at by other poets?

In fact, there are: perhaps guided by the inherent dramatic form of the sonnet[94] and sensitized by his own poetic concept of arousing and purifying the public's emotions and of directing them towards higher and more noble goals, Le Moyne shows himself capable of perceiving an aspect of the painting which succeeding authors were likewise to address: the emotions expressed and provoked by Poussin's painting.

> Tout est miracle en luy, tout parle en son visage,
> Ses yeux ont de l'ardeur, son geste a de la voix,
> La merveille qu'il fait ravit les Japonnois,
> Et ce ravissement leur oste le langage

the second stanza runs.

Even though the topos expressed in the tercets of the sonnet is not – as has been shown – an original one, Le Moyne becomes a precursor within the context of French poetry. The importance of the portrayal of emotions was crucial to him, due to his familiarity both with the Aristotelian concept of poetry and with a specifically Jesuit[95] aesthetics of effect. Like his colleague, Père Menestrier, who in a sonnet of 1681 praised Le Brun as a painter who 'peint les Passions' and who 'rend l'ame visible',[96] Le Moyne already in 1643

---

94 T. de Banville, *Petit traité de poésie française*, Paris 1872, here cited after the edition of 1884, p. 202: 'Enfin, un Sonnet doit ressembler à une comédie bien faite, en ceci que chaque mot des quatrains doit faire deviner – dans une certaine mesure – le trait final, et que cependant ce trait final *doit surprendre* le lecteur .... C'est ainsi qu'au théâtre un beau dénouement emporte le succès ..., parce que le poëte a revêtu ce dénouement d'une forme plus étrange et plus saisissante que ce qu'on pouvait imaginer d'avance.' ('Finally, a sonnet has to resemble a good comedy inasmuch as every word of the quartets has to make us guess – to a certain extent – the final feature, and as, on the other hand, this final feature must surprise the reader ... In this manner a good solution is successful in the theatre ... because the poet has given a stranger and more striking form to this solution than expected.') On the sonnet, appreciated as a dramatic form and even seen in an intimate relationship with drama, see also Mönch 1955 (as in n. 45, above), p. 37 and Mönch 1957 (as in n. 45, above), p. 405.

95 Maber 1982 (as in n. 2, above), p. 187: 'One can only speculate as to the influence that long connection with Jesuit education might have had on him, with its strong emphasis on rhetorical technique ... and dramatic effectiveness.' Maber, pp. 118f. – obviously without counting the poems on the *Magdalen* (see, above, n. 31) and the *Francis Xavier* – states that Le Moyne wrote only a small amount of religious verse.

valued an aspect which later authors likewise were to appreciate. Henri Sauval in 1654 wrote an enthusiastic description of the painting, centered upon the passions and the feelings of the Japanese; he closed his text with the exclamation: 'Il n'y a que Poussin au monde capable d'exprimer ce combat de passions si opposées dans une même personne, & sur un même visage.' [97] While Sauval focussed his attention especially upon the young woman supporting the dead girl, Bellori in his description was more interested in the mother, thrusting herself towards her daughter: 'Qui si rende vivissima l'espressione della madre a' piedi, che in quel motivo di vita apre le mani per

[96]   Claude-François Menestrier, *Des Representations en musique. Anciennes et modernes*, Paris 1681, p. 72.

[97]   Sauval 1724 (as in n. 65, above), vol. 1, p. 462; the whole passage runs: 'Il a disposé ses figures en sorte qu'elles voyent toutes le miracle, & a remué leurs passions avec un jugement & une adresse qui lui est toute particuliere: il a conduit & manié leur douleur & leur joie par degré à proportion des degrés du sang & de l'interêt, ce qui paroit visiblement sur leurs visages, & par leurs attitudes toutes differentes. L'un s'étonne du miracle, l'autre en doute; l'un par sa gaieté temoigne son contentement, l'autre par la continuation de sa tristesse montre qu'il ne s'en rapporte ni au recit d'autrui, ni à sa vû. Une femme au chevet du lit soutient la tête de la personne ressuscitée fort navement; elle est plantée & courbée avec une science & une force toute spirituelle & toute à fait merveilleuse. On remarque dans les yeux, la bouche, le mouvement des bras, les plis du visage, & toutes les actions d'une autre qui est au pied du lit, que la douleur qui s'étoit emparée de son ame, ne cede qu'à grande force à la joie; & cette joie encore ne se fait voir que comme le Soleil dans un tems fort chargé, qui simplement par quelque foible rayon, sans pouvoir percer la nue, à peine donne à connoître qu'il a envie de se montrer. Il n'y a que Poussin au monde capable d'exprimer ce combat de passions si opposées dans une même personne, & sur un même visage.' ('He has arranged his figures in such a manner that they all can see the miracle, and he has stirred their passions with a judgement and a skill which are particular to him: he has directed and handled their grief and their joy according to their different temper and the different degrees of involvement which can be seen on their faces and in their gestures, all completely different. One is astonished at the miracle, the other is doubting it; one is attesting his satisfaction by his cheerfulness, the other, continuing in his sadness, shows that he is caring neither for what he is being told nor for what he is seeing. A woman, standing at the head of the bed, is supporting the head of the resuscitated person with an unaffected manner; she is posed and bending forward with knowledge and with entirely spiritual and absolutely wonderful force. In the eyes, the mouth, the movements of the arms, the wrinkles of the face and all the actions of another woman at the foot of the bed, one can comprehend that grief has seized her soul and is giving way to joy only with difficulty, and yet this joy is showing itself just like the sun in an overcast sky, just making clear with some feeble rays that it wants to show itself, without penetrating the clouds. In the whole world only Poussin is capable of expressing the fight of such contrary passions in one and the same person and on one and the same face.').

abbracciare la filiuola ... altri, che appariscono con la testa, e con le braccia in senso di doglia e di maraviglia...'. [98]

From Félibien who rhetorically asks 'Trouve-t-on d'ailleurs des expressions de douleur, de tristesse, de joie & d'admiration plus belles, plus fortes & plus naturelles que celles qui se voyent dans ce merveilleux Tableau ...? Il n'y a point de figure qui ne semble parler, ou faire connoître ce qu'elle pense, ou ce qu'elle sent' [99] to Passeri who praises the 'mirabile espressione', [100] and from Passeri to Jacques Thuillier, who in our days honoured the painting by claiming it to be 'l'école de plusieurs générations' [101] because of its 'expression des passions,' the emotions, affections and sentiments shown in Poussin's painting have consistently commanded admiration. [102]

[98] 'Here, the expression of the mother, standing at the foot of the bed, is rendered most vividly who, in this motive of life, opens her arms in order to embrace her daughter [...] others appear with heads and arms signalling grief and astonishment.'; Bellori 1672 (as in n. 87, above), p. 429. Unlike R. P. Ciardi, 'Tra Francia e Italia: tracce della maniera in Poussin', in *Napoli, l'Europa – Ricerche di Storia dell'Arte in onore di Ferdinando Bologna*, F. Abbate and F. Sricchia Santoro (Eds), Catanzaro 1995, pp. 215–18, esp. p. 216, I fail to see any stylistic affinities between Poussin's depiction of the mother and Bronzino's figures in his *Deposition*. For the Bronzino painting see J. Cox-Rearick, *Bronzino's Chapel of Eleonora in the Palazzo Vecchio*, Berkeley, Los Angeles, Oxford 1983, pp. 149–78.

[99] Félibien 1725 (as in n. 69, above), vol. 4, VIII. Entretien, p. 91. See already there p. 39: '... celui du Poussin, qui est d'une beauté surprenante, & dont les expressions sont si belles & si naturelles, que les ignorans n'en sont pas moins touchez que les sçavans.' ('... the [painting] by Poussin which is of surprising beauty and where the expressions are beautiful and natural to such a degree that the uneducated are touched as much as the educated.') See finally also Félibien, vol. 3, VI. Entretien, p. 161: 'On ne peut rien voir de plus beau que les expressions de joie et d'admiration qui s'y rencontrent. ... Il y a des hommes & des femmes, qui ... passent tout d'un coup de la tristesse à la joie, & du désespoir à l'admiration.' ('One cannot see anything more beautiful than the expressions of joy and of admiration which one encounters here .... There are men and women who suddenly pass from sadness to joy and from despair to admiration.').

[100] J. Hess (Ed.), *Die Künstlerbiographien von Giovanni Battista Passeri*, Leipzig, Vienna 1934, p. 330.

[101] J. Thuillier, 'Premiers compagnons français à Rome', in *Actes* 1960 (as in n. 6, above), vol. 1, p. 106.

[102] See also the judgement by Lépicié in the preface to his *Vies des premiers peintres du Roi*, Paris 1752, p. lxix: '... celui de Poussin dont on admirera toujours la composition, les caractères et la vivacité variée des expressions.' Nevertheless, the painting was not unanimously acclaimed: voices praising it have always been contrasted by others. Thus, while Bernini obviously liked this work – see Paul Fréart de Chantelou, *Journal du voyage du Cavalier Bernin en France*, Clamecy 1981, p. 36 (13 June): 'le tableau du grand autel, et a dit qu'il lui semblait qu'il était du Poussin. Il l'a trouvé fort beau ....' – the painter Philippe Vleughles is said to have been left cold by it: 'ce tableau ne le toucha pas beaucoup' (cited after Guillet

The author of the Latin poem seemingly remained uninterested in such accomplishments, preferring to play with puns instead; and while the other – comparatively formulaic – Latin poems on the paintings by Vouet and Stella amply use the standard acclamation of the painter as a new Apelles, [103] Le Moyne refrains from such stereotypic phrases and concentrates instead on the emotions shown in the painting:

La merueille qu'il fait rauit ces Iaponnois,
Et le rauissement leur oste le langage.

and the emotions aroused in the spectator:

l'effet qui remplit tout nostre estonement

Le Moyne certainly did not just want to describe these emotions of awe and amazement, he also tried to emulate and to intensify them in his poem by introducing the final climax of the resuscitation of the Saint by the painter.

His sonnet numbers – as any sonnet should – fourteen lines; the poems on Vouet and Stella count 68 and 63 lines respectively. Even though Le Moyne's sonnet may not be entirely original, one might nonetheless take it as confirmation of what Nicolas Boileau-Despréaux wrote in his *Art poétique* of 1674: 'Un sonnet sans défaut vaut seul un long poème.' [104]

de Saint-Georges's report as rendered by Magne 1914, as in n. 1, above, p. 127, n. 2). Today, too, opinions are not unanimous – see e.g. the judgements by Thuillier 1960 (as in n. 101, above), as opposed to A. Blunt, in *Exposition Poussin* 1960 (as in n. 64, above), p. 96, no. 62 or R. Verdi, in *Nicolas Poussin*, exh. cat., London 1995, p. 192.

[103] On the history of this acclamation in general and its special application to Titian see R. Wedgwood Kennedy, 'Apelles Redivivus', in L. Freeman Sandler (Ed.), *Essays in Honor of Karl Lehmann* (Marsyas Supplement), New York 1964, pp. 160–70.

[104] 'One faultless sonnet alone equals a long poem.' Nicolas Boileau-Despréaux, *Art poétique*, Paris 1674, here cited after G. H. F. De Castres (Ed.), Leipzig 1856, chant second, p. 27, line 94.

APPENDIX

From *Basilica in honorem S. Francisci Xaverii a fundamentis extructa, Munificentia illustrissimi viri Domini D. Francisci Sublet de Noyers, Baronis de Dangu, Regi ab intimis consiliis, et secretis, &c. A collegii claromontani alumnis, Societatis Iesu, laudata & descripta,* Paris 1643 (Paris, Bibliothèque Nationale, Yc 226)

From
IV. PRINCEPS LAUDATOR (TEMPLI), pp. 19–22.

III: Principis Altaris tabulam, cuius argumentu(m) est reddita puellæ à Xauerio vita, fecit *Le Poussin,* Gallus pictor.

Tum perrexit, & ecce labor se maximus offert
Maioris.* Angelo viri,
Quem, patrij retinere velis si nominis vmbram,
Pullum Latinè nuncupes.
Vt vidit; Galli soboles, ait, inclyta patris
Te nullus extinguat dies!
Nullus & hanc tabulam violet, qua pulchrius ætas
Nil nostra, nil vetus tulit!
Prodigium quamuis Xauerius edat in Illâ,
Animámque reddat Virgini,
Tu tamen hunc superas; dat enim vitam este Puellæ,
Sed ipse das Xauerio.

(* Michel Ange)

(pp. 20–1)

IV.   Tabula quam pinxit *Stella.*

Vix ea finierat, deflexit lumina, Stellæ
Qua prostat excellens opus:
At Sol pictorum, dixit, Prior ille vocatur,
Nec habere creditur parem:
Non tamen est huius Solis lux tanta, propinquum
Obscuret vt Stellæ iubar,
Insignis Stellæ, media de nocte latentis,
Solóque lucentis die.

(p. 21)

V. Tabula quam pinxit *Voëtius*.

Hinc cernit Triadem, aduersâ quam parte Sacelli
Refert imago nobilis;
Fecerat hanc, tenero Princeps quem norat ab æuo,
Docta Voëtius manu;
Et placuit, dignúsque opifex, ait, ille laboris
Videre Prototypum fui:
In tabula Vitium non est reperire, suóque
Respondit auctor Nomini.*

(* Ex anagrammate, *Simon Voëtius, Sine vitio sum*.)

G.L. (= Guillaume Léonard)
(p. 21)

IX.
MINORIS VNIVS ARÆ TABULA
QUAM PINXIT VOVET.

Aspice quanta noui se industria prodit Apellis,
Angustâ in tabulâ gemini commercia mundi
Terrarum cælìque facit. suprema tabellæ
In superas abiêre domos, tenet infima tellus:
Nobile opus secat hinc atque hinc intersita nubes.
Cernis vt ante oculos se numinis explicet ingens
Regia? mentitum vt pictis laquearibus aurum
Fulguret? vt reliquos vincat lux sacra colores,
Eripiátque oculis? vt læuâ parte perennis
Æquæua cum prole parens stet desuper altâ
Nube sedens? genitor dextrâ, sobolésque sinistrâ
Pendentem in medio discrimine sustinet orbem.
Inter vtrumque vtriusq(ue) catena, & nexus amantis
Incumbit diuinus Amor. latè vndique totam
Maiestate domum præsentia Numinis implet,
Spectantúmque oculos insuetâ luce retundit.
Quid de te referam vacuâ quæ ludis in æthrâ
Aligerum manus? in duplicem partita cateruam est.
Hæc, perculsa nouâ surgentis imagine terræ,
Obstupet, attonitìsque oculis miracula spectat.
Illa, suis medium librata per aëra pennis
Præcipitat, mollèsque rosas, & lilia spargit,
Lilia diuini in Gallos monimenta fauoris.
Continuo lucis tractu demissa tabellæ

173

In dextrum latus, & paudis contermina terris
Apparet nubes. recto stat corpore suprà
Virgo parens, gaudere sub vectore patares:
Augusto titubare tamen sub pondere credas,
Impositæ tanta est nubi reuerentia matris!
At quam te memorem Virgo? quâ voce decorem,
Virtutúmque impressa tuis vestigia membris
Eloquar? immensis fateor vox laudibus impar.
Blanda serenatos animat clementia vultus:
Maiestate gràui frons eminet ardua: nutus
Imperium genitricis habet, sed amabile vocis
Imperium prohibet maior reuerentia nati.
Qualis in ore decor! pietas se quante benignis
Fert oculis! nihil vsque pedes à vertice ad imos,
Quod quâ voce potest, & quâ valet arte, sequacem
Virtutis quamuis tacite non prodat honorem.
Sed quid inhæremus paruis? quid tamdiu amoris
Virginei in famulos monimentum illustre moramur?
Ecce tibi pallâ distentâ vtrimque clientes
Virgo regit, pauidisque, Dei, patrona fauorem
Conciliat; viden' vt soboli, sua signa sequentem,
Móxque seruituram cælestia castra cohortem
Offerat? vt Natus dux annuat æthere ab alto,
Porrectáque manu superas inuitet ad arces?
Scilicet affusis iuuenum lectissima turba
Corporibus tellure iacet: pars veste profanâ
Depositâ dedit optatæ iam nomina Christi
Militiæ; sua differri pars altera luget
Gaudia, sacratóque priùs corpus amictu
Induat, ignotos sub Virgine iudice mores,
Ambiguámque probat mentem; sua quisque latentis
Sensa animi gerit in vultu, nutúve recludit.
Huius in ore legas patriæ cælestis amorem,
Exil(ii)q(ue) dolet ille moras; exæstuat alter,
Et desideriis exosam ad sidera vitam
Exhalat: superos hic mente perambulat axes:
Humanas gemit ille vices: languentibus alter
Arte laboratâ emittit suspiria labris:
Hic amat, ille timet, simul hic amat & timet: omnes
Suspiciunt & amant, omnes mirantur & ardent.
Vsque adeo potuit varios ars indere sensus!
Sed tacuisse iuuat (necque enim quod muta poësis
Eloquitur pictura; loquax pictura poësis

Enarrare valet) superant miracula vatem.

M.G. (i.e. Michel Guillonnet)
(pp. 31–3)

X.
MINORIS ALTERIUS ARÆ TABULA,
quam pinxit STELLA:
SIVE
PUER IESUS IN MEDIO DOCTORUM.

Ore fauete omnes, fatur Deus. Ecce perorat
Doctorum in pluteis æterni copia veri,
Diunus per; & sapentia pectoris hospes
Mollibus è labris aurato flumine currit.
Augusto sedet ore lepos, & blanda superbo
Vertice maiestas. mutus color edere voces
Cernitur ingenuas: aures si fallere posset,
Fallere vox oculos, intentáque lumina posset.
Vox certè, vox illa Dei est. en ore loquentis
Pendet hians, pronáque bibit sacer aure senatus,
Admirans puerúmque senem,fabrúmque; prophetam:
Et voces amat, & cæli responsa fatetur.
Nec me vana fides, aut mendax ludit imago.
Agnosco sedèsque patrum, Pharisæáque septa:
En vbi consilium sacris de rebus agebant:
En magni Salomonis opus, domus alta Tonantis,
Cara Deo sedes; quâ non augustior vlla
Aut priscis fuit, aut surget venientibus annis.
Hanc & ab integro faber est molitus Apelles;
Nec clamor fabricantum, aut ferræ stridor acutæ
Tympanáque, trochleæque, aut crebro malleus ictu [105]
Insonuit. Stetit, vt quondam, sacra Regia pacis, [106]
Pulsibus & nullis, & nullo structa tumultu.
Artificis tantum valuêre imitamina dextræ.
En etiam, en sæuum tridui solata dolorem, [107]
Errorsque viæ varios, audire docentem
Ardet amans genitrix, iuxtáque fabrilia Ioseph
Arma gerens: & se (quanquam est audire potestas
Paupere sub tecto) turbis mirantibus addunt:

[105] Et malleus & securis, & omne ferramentum non sunt audita in domo quum
ædificaretur. *3. Reg.6.*
[106] Post triduum inuenerunt illum in Templo. *Luc.2.*
[107] Dolentes quærebamus te. *ibid.*

Defixísque inhiant oculis ad cuncta, stupéntque,
Et dantem responsa, & legum arcana mouentem.
Parte aliâ exultant, & lene frementibus alis
Siderei applaudunt proceres: mirantur & ipsi
Fulgura missa oculis, & paruæ fulmina linguæ
Sic oculos hominum rapit vnicus, oráque Diuûm,
Diuûm hominúmq(ue); sator Diuus puer. Hæc tibi forma
Ante alias placuit, SVBLETE: hant Dædala fecit
Pictoris manus? an tua mens expressit? Apelli
Scilicet auctor eras operis, neque linea ducta est
Te sine: pingenti dictabas omnia dextræ.
Vnus agebat Amor templis efferre superbis
Doctorem puerum, talique efferre figurâ,
Qualis adesse tibi solitus, quum sacra volutas
Interiore domo, curisque excedere iussis
Grandibus, in IESV mens vno fixa quiescit,
Voce vnum votísque vocans: namque ocyus ille
Aduolat, ambrosiísque premens amplexibus hæret,
Et docet irradians, cælìque arcana recludit.
Te duce talem oculis IESUM mortalibus offert
Ingeniosa manus. nec opus mirabile pinxit
Vulgaris color; at solers hunc pingere solem
Stella suis potuit radiis. tum lumina soli
Stella dedit; sua sol non parcior, ipse vicissim
Reddet, & æternos Stellæ clarabit honores.
Æternùm radians Stellæ pictura micabit.
Nec radians tantùm, sed erit vocalis, & Echo
Inclyta: diuinæ vocis spectabilis Echo.
Quódque sibi æterno semel est Pater ore loquutus
Ante dies primos, & prima crepuscula Verbum,
Sæpius hæc oculis referens iterabit imago.
SVBLETVM CANET VNA, DEVMQUE LOQVETVR IMAGO.

G.C. (i.e. Gabriel Cossart)
(pp. 33–5)

A Contemporary Reading of Bernini's 'Maraviglioso Composto': Unpublished Poems on the Four River Fountain and the Cornaro Chapel

TOMASO MONTANARI

The inauguration of the Four River Fountain (Pl. 40) on 12 June 1651 increased the fame of Gian Lorenzo Bernini beyond measure: in Rome, diaries and other texts witness a reaction in terms of hyperbolic enthusiasm, whilst letters sent all across Europe aimed to give an idea of the monument to those who could not see it for themselves.[1]

In a letter to Paolo Giordano Orsini of 22 May 1652, the young Christina of Sweden, isolated in her ultima Thule, asked 'if Cavalier Bernini is resting after having completed this beautiful fountain, and if he is pondering something new';[2] her burning desire for information on Italian art, be it historical or contemporary, was clearly being met with great diligence by her many correspondents. In a very different frame of mind, and with no little

[1] For help and advice given I am grateful to my parents, Elio and Roberta Montanari, to Paola Barocchi, Francesco Caglioti, Marco Collareta, and to William Barcham. I thank Thomas Frangenberg for translating my text. On the contemporary *fortuna* of the fountain in word and image, see *Il mercato, il lago dell'Acqua Vergine ed il Palazzo Panfiliano nel Circo Agonale detto volgarmente Piazza Navona descritti da F. Cancellieri*, Rome 1811, pp. 40–6; S. Fraschetti, *Il Bernini*, Milan 1900, pp. 198–201; *Piazza Navona*, exh. cat., E. Gerini (Ed.), Rome 1943, pp. 106–9; N. Huse, 'La Fontaine des Fleuves du Bernini', *Revue de l'Art*, 7, 1970, pp. 7–17; R. Preimesberger, 'Obeliscus Pamphilius. Beiträge zu Vorgeschichte und Ikonographie des Vierströmebrunnens auf Piazza Navona', *Münchner Jahrbuch der bildenden Kunst*, 25, 1974, pp. 77–162; C. D'Onofrio, *Le fontane di Roma*, 2nd ed., Rome 1986, pp. 395–439; P. Romano and P. Partini, *Piazza Navona nella storia e nell'arte*, Rome 1987, pp. 118–36; O. Ferrari, 'Poeti e scultori nella Roma seicentesca: i difficili rapporti tra due culture', *Storia dell'arte*, 90, 1997, pp. 151–61; T. Montanari, 'Sulla fortuna poetica di Bernini. Frammenti del tempo di Alessandro VII e di Sforza Pallavicino', *Studi Secenteschi*, 39, 1998, pp. 127–64.
[2] 'se il cavalier Bernini riposa dopo haver finito cotesta bella fontana, e se vada meditando qualcosa di nuovo'; see C. de Bildt, 'Cristina di Svezia e Paolo Giordano II', *Archivio della Società Romana di Storia patria*, 29, 1906, pp. 5–32 (esp. p. 26).

nostalgia, Fabio Chigi, then still nuncio in Germany, must have read the beautiful letter sent to him by his friend Francesco degl'Albizi on 10 June 1651:

> Here we enjoy the peace of Octavian, and one does nothing other than adorn the city. In a few days, the superb fountain on Piazza Navona will be unveiled. It is truly a wonder of the world. Above a pierced rock rises the Pamphili obelisk, and on the corners of the rock are sculpted four superb colossi of marble that represent the principal rivers of the four parts of the world. The artist, Cavalier Bernini, adorned them so well with fruit, plants, metals and animals produced by the lands bathed by them that one cannot hope for more. The eye loses itself there in wonder, and one has to return several times to gaze at it with admiration. He will have created two works worthy to be remembered: one sacred, one secular. And the former is truly memorable, the columns supporting the Baldacchino that rises above the Confessio of St Peter. The secular work is this fountain which outdoes the most beautiful buildings of antiquity.[3]

The answer was laconic but of the greatest interest to us: 'Could Your Most Illustrious Lordship send us at least the print of the superb obelisk, so that we, from afar, may gaze with admiration at its appearance'.[4] A few days later, another experienced connoisseur of the Roman art scene, Francesco Albani, received in Bologna more concrete information regarding Bernini's fountain; he wrote back:

> Against my wishes I have been delayed in replying to your letter which was extremely welcome to me also because the promise was fulfilled to send me the design of the new obelisk, and in addition the attached poem on the eviction [of the merchants] from the square. With amazement I have admired the work of the sculptor, more whilst reading than [when beholding] the drawing, because if it is the obelisk that lay broken into several pieces in the

---

3   'Qui godiamo la pace d'Ottaviano, e non s'attende ad altro che all'abbellimento della città. Fra pochi dì scoprirassi la superba fontana di Piazza Navona. Veramente ella è un miracolo del mondo. Sopra uno scoglio spezzato s'erge l'Obelisco Pamphilio e sugli angoli dello scoglio vi sono scolpiti quattro superbi colossi di marmo che rappresentano i fiumi principali delle quattro parti del mondo. Dall'artista, che è il cavalier Bernino, sono stati così bene adornati dei frutti, delle piante, dei metalli e degli animali che producono questi terreni che da essi sono bagnati, che non si può bramare d'avantaggio. L'occhio vi si perde per maraviglia, e bisogna ritornare più volte a vagheggiarla. Due opere memorande havrà egli fatto: l'una sacra e l'altra profana. E veramente tale è la prima delle colonne che sostengono il Baldacchino che recuopre la Confessione di San Pietro. La profana è questa fonte, che supera i più begli edifici dell'antichità'; D'Onofrio 1986 (as in n. 1 above), p. 432. The changes with regard to the text published by D'Onofrio accord with the original in the Biblioteca Apostolica Vaticana, Chig. A III 55, fols 810v–811r.

4   'Vostra Signoria illustrissima ci mandi almeno la stampa del superbo obelisco, perché da lontano ne vagheggiamo la figura'; D'Onofrio 1986 (as in n. 1 above), p. 432, n. 44.

circus near San Sebastiano, it appears to me like the column of a canopied bed, and perhaps it was larger because of the dove placed on top which according to me (given the memory I have of it) is going to be a dove large like a cow. I conclude that the draughtsman was equal to or little more able than poetry. However, as I write, I receive another new drawing with ottave rime which I shall read when I have greater leisure; as night has fallen and somebody waits who wants to talk to me, I take leave of you asking for your forgiveness and thanking you on my own and on the behalf of Giovanni Maria Galli called Bibbiena, and we both send you cordial greetings.[5]

In September of the same year Cesare Bracci, capitular vicar in Montepulciano and known to art history as the author of large numbers of verses on the projects of Urban VIII and Bernini in the Vatican, wrote to Cardinal Camillo Astalli Pamphili: 'Some poems on the Fountain on Piazza Navona that I received induced me to write a poem, even though I am 70 years old, which I enclose so that you may present it to His Holiness'. [6]

This short survey may lead us to provide a characterization, albeit in approximate terms, of the phenomenology of such articulate responses from a distance. In the first instance it is evident that fast and precise communication had by the second half of the seventeenth century become essential for the devolopment of a 'public opinion' in the strata of society concerned with art.

[5] 'Contra mia volontà mi son ridotto al tardi a dar risposta alla lettera sua, che mi è stata gratissima per essersi di più da me conseguita la promessa del mandarmi il disegno della nuova guglia, e di più la giunta composizione sopra lo sfratto dalla piazza. Con stupore ho ammirato l'opera dello scultore più in leggere che in disegno, perché se è quella guglia che giaceva in più pezzi nel circolo vicono a San Sebastiano, mi si rappresenta come una colonna da lettiera, et era più grande forse per causa della colomba postavi in cima, che secondo me (per la memoria che ne riservo) viene a riuscire colomba grande come una bufala. Concludo che è stato il disegnatore equale o poco più della poesia. Mentre tuttavia scrivo, ecco che mi arriva altro novo disegno con ottave, le quali leggerò con più comodità, perché, essendo fatto notte, e sendo anco aspettato da chi mi vuole parlare, mi piglierò da lei licenza pregandola a scusarmi e ringraziandola per me e per il signor Gio. Maria Galli detto Bibbiena, che caramente la salutiamo.'; G. Bottari and S. Ticozzi (Eds), *Raccolta di lettere sulla pittura, scultura ed architettura scritte da' più celebri personaggi dei secoli XV, XVI e XVII*, vol. 1, Milan 1822, pp. 294-5, where the letter is dated, presumably because of a printing error, 8 July 1611 rather than 1651. Cancellieri 1811 (as in n. 1 above), p. 57 misunderstood the letter, thinking that Albani's criticism was directed at the work itself, not at the poor reproductions he had received.

[6] 'Alcune composizioni venutemi alle mani sopra la Fontana di Piazza Navona, sebbene nell'età di 70 anni, mi hanno fatto scrivere una poesia, che le accludo per presentare a Sua Santità.'; Fraschetti 1900 (as in n. 1 above), p. 198. On Bracci's Bernini poems, see S. Schütze, '"Urbano inalza Pietro e Pietro Urbano". Beobachtungen zu Idee und Gestalt der Ausstattung non Neu – St. Peter unter Urban VIII.', *Römisches Jahrbuch der Bibliotheca Hertziana*, 29, 1994, pp. 213-87 (esp. pp. 235, 269-73).

The efficient and reliable channels of diplomatic correspondence were employed ever more frequently, one of the reasons for the unprecedented development of the descriptive genre both in literature and in graphic reproduction. In fact, apart from inventories and travel diaries, exchanges of letters provided one of the most popular outlets for the habit of writing and reading descriptions of art works; the consequences of this phenomenon are yet to be assessed and to be put in relation with what happens at a more elevated level of art literature, which reached its apex in Bellori's *Lives*. As is well known, in the same context, graphic accounts of art works abound as well. Drawings and above all prints fill libraries and cabinets and are esteemed also because they can be enclosed in letters, and stored in envelopes and folders. The impatient request from Fabio Chigi ('send us at least the print') was thus entirely justified. In fact, an extraordinarily large number of graphic reproductions of the Four River Fountain were in circulation instantly. [7]

Albani's letter touches upon a point that is of particular interest in the present context. In addition to descriptions in letters, more or less high-quality drawings, and prints, poetic compositions played a significant part in the continuous exchange of information regarding the visual arts. Bracci's letter from the remote Montepulciano may serve to remind us of the important role played by topical poetry, often written without even having seen the celebrated work. Likewise, popular rhymes that were not always taken as serious and the more highly appreciated ottave rime, such as those received by Albani together with the design of the fountain, further document the degree to which contemporaries, be they men of letters, collectors, connoisseurs or artists, understood poetry as a suitable medium for lively art criticism or for the divulging of information about art works.

A payment already published by Fraschetti reveals that, after the completion of the fountain, Bernini requested that a painter portrayed it in 'seven drawings [portraying] seven views',[8] and we also are well aware of the attention with which he supervised the execution of prints and medals (for which he not rarely provided the designs) that spread, in particular during the papacy of Alexander VII, information about his architectural and urbanistic projects all across Europe. Even though we never find analogous payments to poets, it is certain that Gian Lorenzo did not ascribe less importance to their activity. A network of contacts, friendships and gifts linked the artist and his family with the world of letters and the Roman academies, and the historiography promoted by Bernini himself amply took account of the important and (at least in its intentions) long-lasting celebration in poetry of the artist's achievements.[9] It will, therefore, not seem surprising that the

[7]   See the bibliography given in n. 1 above.
[8]   'sette disegni in sette vedute'; Fraschetti 1900 (as in n. 1 above), p. 186.
[9]   For a survey of the problems regarding the poetic *fortuna* of Bernini, see Montanari 1998 (as in n. 1 above), and idem, 'Gian Lorenzo Bernini e Sforza

exceptional impact of the Four River Fountain instantly led to so imposing a literary output that it forms the apex of the artist's literary *fortuna* and sculpture replaced painting as the privileged interlocutor of poetry. [10] A contemporary sonnet could rightfully conclude that the monument 'has taken the brush out of the hand of the painter; | likewise, the poet trembles and flies into a rage | that today it is a chisel to astonish Rome' [11] and even ten years after the inauguration Giovanni Andrea Borboni's *Delle statue* managed to avoid describing the monument with a reference to the great quantity of poems already written or still to be written:

> Nobody should expect that I wish to describe the rock of the Agonale Circus where one sees the wonders dreamt up by necromancers who made copious springs of water rise high-up on solitary rocks. I do so because I do not wish to jeopardize the rightful desire that may take hold of anyone, to see a wonder of our times, rather I would invite the poets above all others to see it, as I think that the true spring of Helicon taught them to immerse their minds in it. [12]

The biography written by Domenico Bernini did not fail to address Gian Lorenzo's fame among men of letters: 'It is incredible ... to what extent the Cavaliere was for a long time the subject of all encomia in the academies of Rome, and how confused were his adversaries'. [13] Baldinucci's account to a large measure confirms this observation: 'it is impossible to say ... to what extent he received praise in public and in private, now having become the sole subject of eulogies of all the academies of Rome'. [14] An examination of one of these very numerous academies, the Accademia degli Intrecciati, confirms not only the importance of the fountain, the topic of encomia until the 1670s, but

---

Pallavicino', *Prospettiva*, 87–88, 1997, pp. 42–68.

[10] See n. 1 above.

[11] 'Ha 'l penelo di man tolto al pittore; | Il poeta ancor lui freme e s'adira | Ch'oggi muova un scarpel Roma a stupore'; the unpublished sonnet, dedicated to Prince Maffeo Barberini by a certain Giacomo Veneziano from Genoa, is quoted in full in Appendix B.

[12] 'Nissun si aspetti ch'io voglia descrivere lo scoglio del Circo Agonale, dove vedonsi le maraviglie sognate de' negromanti, che facevano sorgere sopra ermi monti copiose fonti di acque. Io non voglio altrimenti pregiudicare a un giusto desiderio che possa venire a chi che sia di vedere una maraviglia de' nostri tempi, anzi v'invitarei i poeti, più di tutti gl'altri, perché crederei d'havere loro insegnato, per attuffarvi la mente, il vero fonte d'Elicona.'; G. A. Borboni, *Delle statue*, Rome 1661, pp. 82–3.

[13] 'non è credibile ... come il Cavaliere fosse per molto tempo il soggetto di tutti gli encomii nelle accademie di Roma, e quanto confusi rimanessero i suoi avversari'; D. Bernini, *Vita del cavalier Gio. Lorenzo Bernino ...*, Rome 1713, p. 91.

[14] 'non è possibile dire ... quanto egli ne venisse applaudito in pubblico ed in privato, essendo egli da quel punto diventato oggetto unico degli elogi di tutte le accademie di Roma'; F. Baldinucci, *Vita del cavaliere Gio. Lorenzo Bernino*, (1st ed. 1682), S. Samek Ludovici (Ed.), Milan 1948, p. 105.

also the absolute predomincance acquired by Bernini amongst the artists active in Rome in terms of his celebration in poetry. [15]

I am not able to say if Fabio Chigi obtained the print he had asked for in 1651, but it is very probable that he received at least (and who knows, perhaps even from Monsignor degli Albizi) some poetic description of the work. His exchange of letters of his German period is richly interspersed with poems, mostly in Latin – sent and received, his own and others' – pertaining to events in Rome, to art works, to political developments and to personal circumstances.[16] One should also bear in mind that during the Pontificate of Alexander VII poetry in Latin became one of the foremost means of international propaganda of modern Rome, as is witnessed by a vast literary output in print and by hundreds of as yet unpublished poems that are found in the Chigi manuscripts in the Biblioteca Apostolica Vaticana. [17]

In one of these manuscripts (shelfmark D.III.41) one finds seven poems in Latin devoted to the fountain. The codex dates from the late seventeenth century and bears on its spine the indication 'Anonymorum carmina'; it contains verses of various argument that can be dated between 1649 and 1675. Regarding Bernini, there are also a poem on the church of San Tommaso di Villanova at Castelgandolfo (fol. 83r) and one on the statues of the Cappella del Voto in Siena Cathedral, entitled 'Patres quatuor Societatis Jesu dum equitis Bernini statuas Sanctæ Mariæ Magdalenæ ac Sancti Hyeronimi simul admirantur immoti stupent et elingues' (fol. 56r). [18] The seven poems on the Four River Fountain (fols 48r–53v) are followed by seven others dedicated to the Cornaro Chapel (fols 51r–53v; Pl. 41), transcribed by the same hand and laid out on the pages in an analogous way; style and content suggest that these fourteen unpublished texts are by the same author.

Whilst the verses on the Four River Fountain represent only one of the very numerous episodes of its enthusiastic reception in writing, the works on the Chapel of St Theresa are of unique interest because they are among the very few known attempts by contemporaries at describing this work. The link between the two groups of poems which present themselves almost as one single text subdivided into two halves helps to explain the author's decision to devote his attention to the second monument: there can be little doubt that it was the substantial literary *fortuna* of the fountain, a public work par excellence and a papal commission, that led the author to focus on the contemporary, but less obvious ecclesiastic project of Gian Lorenzo, an

---

[15] See Montanari 1998 (as in n. 1 above), pp. 157–64.

[16] See, for example, the letters addressed to Fabio by Gian Vittorio Rossi: I. N. Erytræi *Epistolæ ad Tyrrhenum*, Cologne 1645.

[17] See Montanari 1998 (as in n. 1 above). I am working on an edition of these very numerous poems, in Latin and Italian, devoted to the architectural, and more generally artistic projects of Pope Alexander VII.

[18] Following the indications of the author, this poem was published in A. Angelini, *Gian Lorenzo Bernini e i Chigi tra Roma e Siena*, Milan 1998, p. 172.

illustrious, but nonetheless private, commission. An indirect confirmation of this assumption may be found in the dedications of the poems. Three poems on the Pamphili commission are addressed to Innocence X, two to Bernini and one to the spectator. Among the dedications of the poems on the Cornaro Chapel, none addresses Cardinal Cornaro, five are directed to Bernini, one to the spectator, and the last is without addressee. In terms of the date, one may well think of 1651, the year in which both the fountain and the chapel were inaugurated; however, the description of the *Ecstasy of St Theresa* suggests a date after July 1652 when the sculpture was unveiled [19] (in this case the poems could not have been sent to Chigi in Germany, given that he finally returned to Rome on 30 November 1651). Regarding the identify of the author I have no more information than the bookbinder of the seventeenth century who considered the author anonymous. The poems are correct from a linguistic and metric point of view (seven are in hexameters, seven in elegiac couplets); they appear somewhat formal and are certainly not at the level of the best achievements to be found among the Latin poetry produced in Rome during the seventeenth century. Nonetheless, they are extremely useful in an analysis of the contemporary reception of Bernini's work.

The interpretation of the fountain is not devoid of interesting aspects, even though it is to a large measure conventional. In the first instance, one is struck by the dedications which make explicit the three true protagonists of the work: the patron, the artist and the beholder. The last is in fact at the core of the first three poems (Appendix A, I, II, III), in my opinion the most significant. They display a strong emphasis on aspects of the perception of the fountain as it could have been experienced by a sensible, but not necessarily erudite, viewer. The various languages of the elaborate structure are underlined: the inherent ones, such as the mysterious system of the hieroglyphs on the obelisk, juxtaposed with the overt celebratory rhetoric of the four Latin epigraphs placed beneath it, and the more accidental, but no less necessary ones – the various modulations of the roaring of the water, the reflections of the different parts in the basin, and the moving shadow that animates the square. The author describes the interaction, the super-imposition, and indeed the difficulty of comprehension of these expressive riches put into service for the Pope's glory. The play on words, acumen and preciousness may on occasion seem tiring, but ultimately succeed in translating the great perceptual complexity of the fountain, to reconstitute the sense of variety of expression which the work communicated in the seventeenth century and which it continues to communicate today. One cannot call banal the attempt to avoid description and accounts of the iconography or the overall invention, obviously the most frequently adopted

[19]   I. Lavin, *Bernini and the Unity of the Visual Arts*, New York, London 1980, pp. 205–6.

strategies in poems on art; instead, the texts present a varied metaphorical reading of Bernini's subtly differentiated artistic language.

Poems IV and VII employ iconographic conceits that one may find pedestrian: the entire world with its four parts forced into the area of one square in Rome; the river Nile struggling in the interpretation of its hieroglyphs. Poem VI indulges in a conventionally hyperbolic praise of the artist. Poem V, on the other hand, is more original. Addressing Bernini directly, the author decides to focus on one figure in particular, and he chooses the horse, a detail that was perceived as entirely autograph ('he carved the horse with his own hand', states a report of the Congregazione della Fabbrica di San Pietro of 1657 which documents the attempt to establish Bernini's recompense for the Colonnade on the grounds of what he had received for earlier papal commissions[20]). On the one hand, the author, unsurprisingly, refers to Ovid's *Metamorphoses* in comparing this elder brother of the war-horse ridden by Bernini's *Emperor Constantine* with the four horses pulling the chariot of the sun; on the other hand, he praises the features that are most characteristic of Bernini's style, such as the fierceness of movement, the 'hyperrealist' rendering of the mane, and the appearance of a 'petrification' of the horse's neighing.

The series of poetic texts dedicated to the Cornaro Chapel should in my opinion be counted among the most important contemporary readings of this monument. The anonymous author in fact felt the need not only to focus on the carved altarpiece, but also to interpret, as was within his powers, the complexity of Bernini's 'maraviglioso composto'. In a manner that is only apparently contradictory, his poems dissolve the unity of the chapel into several constituent elements, and it is the far from obvious choice of some of these elements that attests the author's intelligent engagement with the work. After three poems which contain a good interpretation of the subject, or rather of the subject of the principal marble group, the poet concentrates on the gallery of portraits of members of the Cornaro family, then on the polychrome marble incrustation of the chapel's walls, and lastly, the most penetrating insight, he turns his attention to the system of controlled illumination of the niche into which one glances above the altar.

Very few further poems were written on this work during the seventeenth century; apart from the brief madrigal by Pier Filippo Bernini preserved in the biographies of the artist,[21] I know only the late and very generic verses of Giuseppe Silos and Gabriele Baba.[22] All of these refer only to

[20] 'lavorò di sua mano il cavallo'; see D. Del Pesco, *Colonnato di San Pietro. "Dei Portici antichi e loro diversità". Con un'ipotesi di cronologia*, Rome 1988, pp. 48–9.

[21] For the madrigal, see Montanari 1998 (as in n. 1 above), p. 134.

[22] G. M. Silos, *Pinacotheca sive Romana pictura et sculptura*, Rome 1673, pp. 188–9; G. Baba, *La statua equestre di Luigi XIV re di Francia, di Navarra etc l'adeodato, il conquistatore, scoltura del cav. Gio Lorenzo Bernino, panegirico a Sua Maestà Cristianissima*, Bologna 1679, p. 18; see Ferrari 1997 (as in n. 1 above), p. 157. See

the group of St Theresa, hardly mentioning where it is found. Likewise, the few prose texts written on Bernini's masterpiece by contemporaries deal only with the statues, either to celebrate their supreme quality,[23] or to utter violent criticism of the iconography.[24] Likewise, the two biographies appear singularly reticent: Baldinucci does name the chapel among the 'works of architecture and mixed works' ('opere d'architettura e miste'), but the very few lines devoted to the chapel in the text all concern the 'wonderful group of St Theresa with the angel';[25] Domenico Bernini shows little more interest, stating no more than that his father 'provided a beautiful and noble design, outdoing all the many others he had so far produced'.[26] One needs to look to Passeri to find at least an awareness of the extraordinary nature of this monument:

> The last cardinal of the Cornaro family decided to found his chapel in the church called Madonna della Vittoria near the Baths of Diocletian, and it is that of St Theresa near the high altar on the left, where there is the marble figure of the Saint, her heart wounded with an arrow by an angel, a work of consummate beauty by the hand of Cavalier Bernini, and the entire chapel is his architecture, with inventions and curious fancies of which this is not the time or the place to speak. On the vault, where there are some gilt stuccos and some low reliefs of events [in the life] of the same saint, likewise gilt, Abbatini depicted a glory in the centre of which there is the Holy Spirit in the usual form of a dove, in the midst of a deep expanse of bright splendour, so luminous that it almost confuses and blinds the sight of the beholders. He represented descending clouds spread over the vault in an arrangement that is artful but seems casual; as they do not fill the sides evenly, they to a greater or lesser extent occlude the scenes in gilt stucco which are beneath them.

also Frangenberg in this volume, n. 31.

[23] E.g. L. Scaramuccia, *Le finezze de' pennelli italiani ammirate e studiate da Girupeno sotto la scorta e disciplina del genio di Raffaello*, Pavia 1674, p. 18.

[24] E.g. the booklet partially published in G. Previtali, 'Il Costantino messo alla berlina, o bernina, su la porta di San Pietro', *Paragone*, 13, 145, 1962, pp. 55–8 (esp. p. 58); or the insinuations in O. Boselli, *Osservazioni sulla scoltura antica*, P. Dent Weil (Ed.), Florence 1978, fol. 43v.

[25] 'il mirabile gruppo della Santa Teresa con l'angelo'; Baldinucci 1948 (as in n. 14 above), p. 101. In the catalogue that closes the biography he names, among the marble sculptures, only 'the last Cornaro Cardinal'. The curious omission of the principal group is due to the rushed preparation of the edition, as the group is mentioned in the manuscript versions of the catalogue: 'Gruppo di Santa Teresa e l'angelo. Alla Madonna della Vittoria'; Paris, Bibliothèque Nationale, Ms. Ital. 2084, fols 117r, 124r, another version in C. D'Onofrio, *Roma vista da Roma*, Rome 1967, p. 436. On the nature and chronology of these old catalogues of Bernini's works, see T. Montanari, 'Bernini e Cristina di Svezia. Alle origini della storiografia berniniana', in Angelini 1998 (as in n. 18 above), pp. 330–477 (esp. pp. 403–4).

[26] 'fece un vago e nobile disegno, sopra quanti fin'allora dati fuori ne havesse'; Bernini 1713 (as in n. 13 above), p. 83.

Angels in various movements are placed on them, all ravished by the sweetness of the glory; they are shown performing a concert with their voices and musical instruments. Within the window light he continued with his fanciful idea of employing an area in relief in conjunction with three painted putti on clouds scattering flowers, and everywhere he employed this illusionistic device of his, beautifully uniting the feigned and the real.[27]

The biographer considers the incrustation of coloured marbles, the arrangement of the portraits and the particular illumination amongst the 'inventions and curious fancies' which he did not wish to examine, and he must also have known that the invention of pictorial and stucco decoration of the vault (blatantly neglected in seventeenth-century sources, and yet essential) was not due to Abbatini for whom he held the greatest esteem.

The first poem on the chapel (Appendix A, VIII)[28] is dedicated to Bernini, with whom it establishes a dialogue about the 'image of St Theresa' in 'the ecstatic swoon of sacred love'. The *topos* of the duel between the life infused by the artist and the mortal inertia of the marble is ably intertwined with the iconographic problem of the passing of St Theresa from life to death. The fact that the saint died during an ecstasy had been accepted and divulged by the acts of her canonization and the liturgy devoted to her, and the poems of Silos and Baba likewise demonstrate a full comprehension of this crucial

---

[27] 'L'ultimo cardinale de' Cornari si risolse di stabilire la sua cappella nella chiesa chiamata la Madonna della Vittoria alle Terme di Diocleziano, et è quella di Santa Teresa vicino all'altar maggiore nella parte dell'Evangelo, dove è quella figura di marmo della Santa ferita nel cuore da uno strale per mano d'un angelo, opera di tutta bellezza, di mano del cavaliere Bernini, e tutta la Cappella è sua architettura, con invenzioni e capricci curiosi, della qual cosa non è questo il tempo né il luoco da parlarne. Nella volta di questa, ove sono alcuni stucchi dorati et alcuni bassi rilievi d'avenimenti della medesima santa, pure di stucchi messi a oro, vi ha l'Abatini finta una gloria, nel mezzo della quale è lo Spirito Santo in forma, come è solito, di colomba nel mezzo d'un abisso di splendore vivo, e così luminoso che quasi introduce la confusione e l'abbagliamento della vista ai riguardanti. Ha rappresentato una calata di nuvole sparse per quella volta con un ordine artificioso, ma finto a caso, che senza ripartirsi con uguaglianza nei lati, mostra occupare più o meno quelle storie di dorati stucchi, che a quelle rimangono al di sotto. Sopra di quelle sono angioli in vari moti, tutti rapiti dalla suavità della gloria, e mostrano formare tra di loro un musico concerto di voci e di istromenti. Nel vano della finestra ha continuato il suo capriccio di riportare qualche parte di rilievo unito col dipinto di tre puttini sopra nuvole che spargono fiori, e da per tutto si è valuto di quel suo arteficio d'ingannare con l'unire insieme vagamente il finto col vero.'; G. B. Passeri, *Die Künstlerbiographien, nach den Handschriften des Autors herausgegeben und mit Anmerkungen versehen*, J. Hess (Ed.), Leipzig, Vienna 1934, p. 238.

[28] This poem evidently functions as an index for the entire group; it contains Bernini's full name and his title, Cavaliere, and the exact name of the church. The fact that it appears only in fourth place is due to a reversal of sheets during binding. In the Appendix, the apparent original sequence of the poems is restored.

component of Bernini's representation; on the other hand, as Rudolf Preimesberger has noted, the simultaneous representation of life and death was a time-honoured rhetorical *topos* regarding the difficulty and success of figurative art, and the present poem demonstrates that learned contemporaries were fully aware of both of these aspects.[29] These poems do not, on the other hand, grasp two other aspects which Irving Lavin has pointed out, that is, the levitation above the altar (with its potential eucharistic connotations), and the mystic marriage between Theresa and Christ; the second poem of the anonymous author (Appendix A, IX) focuses on this last subject. Without any reticence, and in a tone that would be appropriate for an account of a Dionysiac possession, he describes the union of Creator and created: 'The beloved God, the loving God infuses life into the lifeless limbs, already full of God. Oh, how well are the loves of God and of the soul made visible in the stone!' The last line makes explicit that this is the essential subject of the altarpiece, the subject that is crucial also to the faithful, to the 'spectator': 'the spectator will drink Divine and wondrous love which offers itself as sweet drink'. It is tempting to perceive this use of metaphor and wording as a hardly veiled allusion to the eucharistic meaning of the ensemble.

The following poem (Appendix A, X) addresses the transverberation explicitly ('He represents the ecstasy of the saint and the angel who wounds her breast'), but it does so with a lightness of touch that permits the author to couple the pierced inner body of St Theresa with the 'depth of the stone' from which the image is carved, or to play with the hypothesis of an ironic dialogue between saint and artist who, as *alter deus*, can replicate the painful miracle of the golden arrow. To conclude, the first three texts analyse precisely, but without iconographic pedantry, the subject of the group in three of its fundamental aspects: Theresa dies during an ecstasy, Theresa enters into a mystic union with God, and Theresa's heart is wounded by an angel.

Then the poet examines the context, the 'theatre' (Appendix A, XI, XII) which is 'ennobled' by the portraits of the Cornaro Cardinals (they were aptly described as 'breathing depictions of their countenances' in the original inscription of the chapel).[30] The presence of the Doge does not attract the author's attention, which is generally not directed at the dynastic or commemorative content of the portraits. Nor does he wish to pay homage to the family of the patron: with a frankness and far-sightedness not common among his contemporaries, the author declares that the statues appear to him proud of their maker (to whom the first of these two poems is dedicated) rather than of their patron. The emphasis of the twelfth poem is in the first instance placed on aspects of content, focusing on the nobility and piety of

---

[29] See R. Preimesberger, 'Berninis Cappella Cornaro. Eine Bild-Wort-Synthese des siebzehnten Jahrhunderts? Zu Irving Lavins Buch', *Zeitschrift für Kunstgeschichte*, 49, 1986, pp. 190–219 (esp. pp. 202–7).

[30] See Lavin 1980 (as in n. 19 above), p. 199.

this large group of ecclesiastics. The attention then turns to the Cardinals' mozzettas, that is, to dress, perhaps the least significant feature on a qualitative level but obviously most highly appreciated by a large section of the audience. Nonetheless, the argument immediately takes an unforeseen turn, and the elegance of the pun that juxtaposes the candour of the marble and the Cardinals' purple provides a transition to the last two lines, a kind of concise and most acute epitaph: 'But why do you marvel at the fact that an artist has sculpted colours when the souls of so many heroes are sculpted here?' This conclusion displays a notable capacity to comprehend and give clear expression to the fundamental characteristics of Bernini's portraiture: the unmatched imitation of surfaces, imbued with colour, and the unprecedented power of the speaking likenesses, individual so as to suggest portraits of the soul.

The swift move from the St Theresa to the members of the Cornaro family documents that the author was able to grasp the innovatory dynamics in the unification of space (which Bernini himself emphasised in his discussions with Chantelou[31]); the author did not separate the sculptural masterpiece from its context, from the 'maraviglioso composto' that is as evident here as it is hard to translate into words. The following poem (Appendix A, XIII) moves in this direction even more clearly. Again addressing Bernini, it speaks of the 'stones, and in particular the spotted ones, which are wonderfully arranged in the same chapel of St Theresa'. Already this emphasis on an argument not concerned with images and therefore not easily accessible to descriptive literature is surprising; even more so is the focus on the principal innovation of the incrustation, the choice of an incredibly large number of different kinds of marble, unified above all by their very marked, bizarre and extravagant spots.[32] The poem's text dwells on the various kinds ('nomina varia') of stone which will constitute the fame of the chapel ('theatrum'), thanks to the ability with which they are arranged by Gian Lorenzo. He then continues with an - all things considered, successful - conceit which refers to the 'beautiful lues' of the walls that contrast with, and form background and frame of the 'sacred lucidity' of the virginal Theresa (but also of the pure Carrara marble from which she is carved).

The last poem, entitled 'The sun, via paths accurately arranged, is made to illuminate the altarpiece in a given way' is the most impressive text; its thirteen hexameters aim obsessively, and at the price of a notable loss of

[31] See *Journal de voyage du Cavalier Bernin en France par M. de Chantelou*, L. de Lalanne (Ed.), Paris 1885, pp. 170, 186. On the portraits, see Lavin 1980 (as in n. 19 above), pp. 98–103.

[32] On the incrustation, see Lavin 1980 (as in n. 19 above), pp. 88, 202–3; C. Napoleone, 'La transverberazione di Teresa. La Cappella Cornaro del Bernini', *FMR*, 119, 1996, pp. 17–44 (esp. pp. 38–44); eadem, 'Bernini e il cantiere della Cappella Cornaro', *Antologia di Belle Arti*, 55–58, 1998, pp. 172–86 (esp. pp. 180–1).

literary and stylistic quality, to ascertain and describe the most recondite details of Bernini's invention that regulate the system of controlled lighting of the niche within which St Theresa is levitating. The rays of the sun (which he addresses) enter the space by means of 'wonderfully constructed recesses', and embrace the marble group, they 'illuminate' according to 'a given project', 'as Bernini wished', 'to fulfil its splendid function': a three-fold and thus redundant emphasis on the control over light, on the ability to restrain and regulate it and to determine its quantity. The author does not stop here; he also points to the novelty of a sculptural representation of sun rays near the source of real light: 'Where could the brilliant kisses of the sun be materialised in more splendid a manner?' The author, furthermore, appears to grasp that this invention is not isolated in Bernini's work and he foresees that, thanks to Gian Lorenzo ('That light performs these extraordinary services to you, you owe to Bernini', he reminds the planet), light will play an important part in the rhetoric of the visual arts: 'Because of this artist you will be more famous than you once were because of the talking statue of Memnon'. The same sensibility for visual appearance, which had permitted the author to understand the profound relation Bernini established between the Four River Fountain and water, shadow, and flashing reflection, now allows him to grasp the calculated and indissoluble link that infuses a soul of light into the unified body formed by architecture, coloured marbles, sculptures and paintings.

It is not excessive to state that only in the studies of the second half of the twentieth century we may find a similarly lucid comprehension of the importance of the use of light in Bernini's work.[33] The author's effort to resist the conventions of the poetic genre is entirely successful and displays an independent critical mind rare among contemporaries. It seems impossible that this, regrettably anonymous, poet achieved so much without direct clarification in discussions with Bernini, in particular when one considers that the two biographies of Bernini do not even recognize the deployment of light as an issue. Perhaps the only other indication of contemporary awareness may be found in the fact that Francesco Borromini told Carlo Cartari that he wished to install 'some mirrors or steel reflectors' on the altar of Sant'Ivo alla Sapienza in order to create 'splendour in the manner of the chapel of St Theresa'.[34] But Borromini's was a profound and arduous empathy, hardly to be compared with the – albeit lively – intelligence of the maker of the Latin verses discussed in this paper.

---

[33] See Lavin 1980 (as in n. 19 above), pp. 104–6.

[34] See the memoirs of Carlo Cartari partially published in *Ragguagli borrominiani. Mostra documentaria*, exh. cat, M. Del Piazzo (Ed.), Rome 1968, pp. 227–8; see also Napoleone 1998 (as in n. 32 above), p. 182 (where Virgilio Spada, rather than Cartari, is erroneously cited as Borromini's interlocutor).

APPENDIX A

I

Innocentio X pontifici optimo maximo.
De fonte eiusque pyramidis hyeroglificis inscripta
in Foro Agonali mirifice excitata.

Ecce, peregrinis liquidisque effusa tributis,
Coniurata tibi, princeps, hic flumina Mundi
Se plaususque suos uno in cratere propinant.
Omnia iure tuæ exundantia murmura laudi
Se impendunt, totus præclaro enigmate fluctus
Te semper narrat, sensusque oblita vetustos
Te superimpositæ tollunt emblemata molis,
Et se sponte silet pudibundo in carmine Memphis.
En titulos fluitare tuos taciturna loquacis
Umbra iubet saxi, quæ cum te scribit in undis
Nomina prisca negat, felici naufraga voto
Quando natant in fonte tuæ miracula famæ.[35]

(To Pope Innocence X. On the fountain and its obelisk inscribed with
hieroglyphs wondrously erected in the Piazza Agonale.
Behold the rivers of the world who have come together here for you, oh
Prince; after pouring forth as uncommon and liquid tributes they and their
homage flow into the one basin. Rightfully, all their gushing murmurs
contribute to your praise, every flow always refers to you through a splendid
enigma, and the emblems of the massive stone placed above you, forgetful of
their ancient meanings, exalt you; and of its own accord Memphis no longer
speaks of itself in bashful song. And see, the quiet shadow of the eloquent
stone commands your inscriptions to float; as it writes you in the waters, it
negates the ancient names, shipwrecked in an auspicious sacrifice, as the
wonders of your fame float in the fountain.)

II

Eidem.
De eodem fonte

Ut variis celebrent te maxima flumina linguis
Murmure te vario cogitur unda loqui.
Noscit spectator facundo e gurgite plausus
Auribus attonitis dulce bibisse tuos:
Sed nescit queis grata colat te laudibus unda,

---

[35]   Roma, Biblioteca Apostolica Vaticana, Chig. D III 41, fol. 48r; hexameters.

Cum multo crepitant naufraga verba sono.
Fusilis elogii tibi plaudere iure tumultum
    Quis negat? A fluctu quis mage clara cupit
Quam tam multa tuæ tribui præconia famæ?
    Sic fons effundit carmina digna magis
Quam bene Niliaci voluerunt æmula saxi
    Arcanos plausus flumina ferre tibi!
Sic lapis et fluctus gaudent se posse fateri
    Hic sua te paribus vota carere notis. [36]

(To the same. On the same fountain.
So that the greatest rivers may praise you in different languages, the wave is
forced to speak of you with various murmur. The spectator knows to have
sweetly drunk your praises, with ravished ears, from the eloquent whirl: but
he does not know with what praises the grateful wave reveres you, when
with great noise the shipwrecked words resound. Who denies that the uproar
of the liquid eulogy applauds you rightfully? Who desires anything more
illustrious of the water than that it offers so much praise to your fame? Thus
the fountain spreads songs much more worthy than the arcane praises that
the rivers, following the example of the stone from the Nile [i.e., the
Egyptian obelisk], wished to offer you. Thus stone and water delight to be
able to admit that they cannot pay you tribute equal to you.)

III
Eidem.

Sole fabro geminata vides miracula molis,
Dum scopulosa natat vitreis in fluctibus umbra,
Naufragioque tumens cum se rescribit in undis
Niliaci lapidis duplicat Memphitica murmur:
Hæc quoque iure tibi gratanti ab imagine, princeps,
Per dociles undas plaudens inscribitur echo. [37]

(To the same.
Through the sun, you see the wonders of the stony mass doubled, when the
shadow of the rock floats in the glass-like waters, and when it duplicates the
murmur of Memphis borne by the stone from the Nile, as it re-writes itself
in the waters, agitated in its shipwreck. This echo, paying homage, is
rightfully inscribed among docile waves by the image that joyfully thanks
you, oh Prince.)

---

[36]   Ibid., fol. 48v; elegiac couplets.
[37]   Ibid., fol. 49r; hexameters.

IV

Ut moles surgat dignis fabrefacta tributis,
Cogitur ornandus mira in compendia mundus
Spectaturque datum sic totus inire theatrum
Fluminibusque suis iussum componere fontem. [38]

(So that the stony mass may rise worthy, made from tributes, the world is
condensed into a wonderful compendium, and one sees it enter the theatre
devoted to it in its entirety, making up the commissioned fountain with its
rivers.)

V
Equiti Joanni Laurentio Bernino.
De eodem fonte, et præcipue de equo inibi exculpto.

Quando triumphati vocalia saxa Canopi,
Et fontem, Bernine, tuum Sol spectat et ornat
Sede theatrali populis plaudentibus umbram
Molis prosternit, summoque in vertice coeli
Sistere se cuperet, tenebras ut pendula cunctas
Lux semper pellat. Pyrois tunc sponte maneret,
Et tui equi indomitam fremebundo corde sitiret
Mox libertatem; voti decerneret Æton
Tunc simulacra sui; hinnitum quem sculpis habere
Vellet in ore Phlegon; crines Eous amaret
Sic fluitare sibi. Debebunt ergo minori
Astra fabro quidquid Phoebi insignire iugales
Iactet, eosque diem circumvectare per orbem
Dignos efficiat! Sortem hanc non invidet illis
Exculptus sonipes: satius nam mole superbit
Quam curru Solis calcata per astra tumeret. [39]

(To the Cavaliere Gian Lorenzo Bernini.
On the same fountain, and in particular on the horse that is carved there.
When the sun beholds and adorns the speaking stones of conquered Canopus
and your fountain, oh Bernini, it casts the shadow of the stone mass in its
theatre setting to the applause of the people and it would wish to stand still
in the highest apex of heaven so that the light cast down might dispel all
shadows for ever. Then Pyrois would come to a halt of his own accord, and
would soon, with palpitating heart, desire the unbridled liberty of your
horse; Aethon then would choose it as his own portrait; Phlegon would wish
to issue from his mouth the neighing that you carve; Eous would love his

---

[38] Ibid., hexameters.
[39] Ibid., fol. 50r; hexameters.

mane to flow in the same manner. Thus the stars will owe gratitude to a lesser maker, whatever it may be that proudly adorns the horses of Phoebus and makes them worthy to carry day aroung the world. The carved horse does not envy them this fate: it is prouder of this stony load than it would be of the chariot of the sun on it starry path.)

VI
Eidem.
De eodem fonte.

Dum molem lustrare tuam Sol æmulus audet,
    Maiorem umbra cadens iactat habere fabrum:
At quidquid pangit si tecum certat Apollo,
    Spectrum iure iacens umbraue vilis erit. [40]

(To the same. On the same fountain.
When the jealous sun dares to illuminate your work in stone, the cast shadow prides itself of having a greater maker: but whatever Apollo ascertains when he competes with you, it will by right be a vain spectre, a vile shadow.)

VII
Spectatori eiusdem fontis Ægyptias notas intelligere cupienti.

Ægypti si scire cupis quid saxa loquantur
    ex oculis Nili tollere vela potes.
Inde leges doctam, opportuno interprete, molem,
    Fontesque, hic cernet, te tribuente, suos. [41]

(To the spectator who wishes to comprehend the Egyptian letters of the fountain.
If you wish to know what the stones of Egypt are saying, you can take the veils away from the eyes of the Nile. Then read the learned mass of stone and the springs with an appropriate interpreter. With your help, he will come to know his.)

VIII
Equiti Joanni Laurentio Bernino.
De simulacro Divæ Teresiæ in templo Beatæ Mariæ de Victoria [quæ] estaticum amoris sacri deliquium patitur.

Quicquid tu vitæ saxo, Bernine, negasti
    Deficit, atque patet te renuisse dare.
Ut vitæ et mortis simulacra expromeret idem,

---

[40]   Ibid., fol. 50v; elegiac couplets.
[41]   Ibid., elegiac couplets.

Te cogente lapis vivit et emoritur.
At nimium fallor! Vita meliore beasti
   Hac quicquid vita vivere rite vetas. [42]

(To Cavaliere Gian Lorenzo Bernini. On the image of St Theresa suffering
the ecstatic swoon of sacred love in the church of S. Maria della Vittoria.
What life you denied to the stone, Bernini, is now lacking, and it is clear that
you did not want to give it. Forced by you, the stone lives and dies, so that
the same stone may present images of life and death. But I err too greatly!
You blessed with a better life all that what in this life you rightfully did not
permit to live.)

IX

Exanimes artus animat, iam numine plenos:
Numen amatum, Numen amans. Oh, quam bene saxo
Numinis atque animæ spectandi dantur amores!
Sculpsit utrumque faber, quam das Bernine perennem
Vivet uterque tibi moribundo in marmore vitam.
Inde tibi multisque dabit, te auctore, beatam
E saxo mentem, cum qui se dulce propinat
Divinum mirumque bibet spectator amorem. [43]

(The beloved God, the loving God, infuses life into the lifeless limbs, already
full of God. Oh, how well are the loves of God and of the soul made visible
in the stone! An artist sculpted them both, and in the dead marble both live
the eternal life that you, Bernini, acquire for yourself. Thus due to your
workmanship, the stone will inspire a blessed state of mind in you and in
many others, when the spectator will drink Divine and wondrous love which
offers itself as sweet drink.)

X

Estasim Divæ representat angelumque præcordia ipsius vulnerantem.

Effingi Teresa sui per viscera saxi
   Verum deliquium vidit et obstupuit,
Et gratata sibi vulnus iam dulce paratum
   Cordi quod lapidi iussit inesse faber,
"Ignara me ergo" dixit "sub marmore possum,
   Si Bernine velis, vulnera vera pati"? [44]

---

[42] Ibid., fol. 52r; elegiac couplets. For the order in which the poems are here printed,
      see n. 28 above.
[43] Ibid., hexameters.
[44] Ibid., fol. 52v; elegiac couplets.

(He represents the ecstasy of the Saint and the angel who wounds her breast. Theresa saw, and was astounded, that in the entrails of a stone her true swoon was depicted, and rejoicing in the sweet wound already inflicted on her heart, created by the artist in the stone, she spoke: "So I, without my knowing it, if you want it, Bernini, can suffer real wounds in the marble?")

XI
Eidem Bernino.
De simulacris cardinalium Corneliorum.

Ut domus in Sacro numeret Cornelia Circo
    Purpureos promunt hic simulacra patres.
Sed mage de fabro cerno, Bernine, superba
    Quæ sub tam multo principe saxa tument. [45]

(To the same Bernini. On the portraits of the Cornaro Cardinals.
Here the images represent the fathers so that the Cornaro family may count how many [of their kin] were purple-clad members of the sacred College [of Cardinals]. But I see that the stones are more proud of their maker, Bernini, even though they pride themselves under so great a prince.)

XII
Spectatori.
De vestibus eorundem cardinalium affabre exculptis.

Cerne ut nobilitant Tyria sub veste theatrum
    Ingentes animæ votaque magna patrum.
En rubet arcano spectatus murice candor,
    Cum lapide in Pario purpura sacra patent.
Sed quid miraris fabrum sculpsisse colores
    Quando tot heroum sculpitur hic anima? [46]

(To the spectator. On the garments of the same cardinals, wonderfully sculpted.
See how, in their purple garments, the great souls and the abundant prayers of the fathers ennoble the theatre. And behold, as one looks, the whiteness turns red through an arcane purple, as the sacred purple is represented in the Parian stone. But why do you marvel at the fact that an artist sculpted colours when the souls of so many heroes are sculpted here?)

---

[45]   Ibid., fol. 51r; elegiac couplets.
[46]   Ibid., elegiac couplets.

XIII

Eidem Bernino.

De lapidibus et præcipue de maculosis in eodem Sacello Divæ Teresiæ
mirifice dispositis.

Nominibus variis insignitura theatrum
Exhylarant sese votis tua saxa superbis,
Nec maculosa pudet nitidæ molimina molis,
Si formosa lues pretiosis emicet umbris
Quando iubes sacro maculas servire nitori. [47]

(To the same Bernini. On the stones, and in particular the spotted ones,
which are wonderfully arranged in the same Chapel of St Theresa.
Your stones will ennoble the theatre with their various names, and they
delight in the superb project. And it is not shameful that the materials of a
pure construction are spotted, the beautiful lues glistening with precious
shadows, when you command that the spots serve sacred lucidity.)

XIV

Sol per aditus rite machinatos cogitur ex voto simulacrum illustrare.

Quonam vota tuæ lucis meliore beari,
O Sol, sorte vides quam, cum penetrata recessus
Mire molitos, præscripto munere divam,
Bernino statuente, colunt, ut splendida præstent
Officia, atque data famulentur lumina lege?
Quo præclara magis potuerunt fulgida Solis
Oscula defigi? Quanam de fronte recussi
Plus digna radii maiori foenore vultum,
Phoebe, tuum repetunt? Debes hæc maxima lucis
Munia Bernino. Hoc fabro tu illustrior ibis
Quam olim facundo simulacro Memnonis esses.
Diva loqueretur radiis animata disertis,
Si vox deliquiis non arceretur amoris. [48]

(The sun, via paths accurately arranged, is made to illuminate the altarpiece
in a given way.
What happier fate could the light issuing from you, oh Sun, enjoy than when
it enters by these wonderfully constructed recesses and venerates the Saint
with this pre-ordained gift, as Bernini wished, to fulfil its splendid function
and to do its task according to a given project. Where could the brilliant
kisses of the sun be materialized in a more splendid manner? From what
more worthy forehead could the rays be reflected back to your countenance

---

[47] Ibid., elegiac couplets.
[48] Ibid., fol. 53r; hexameters.

more fruitfully, oh Phoebus? That light performs these extraordinary services to you, you owe to Bernini. Because of this artist, you will be more famous than you once were because of the talking statue of Memnon. The Saint would speak, animated by eloquent rays, if her voice were not silenced by the swoons of love.)

APPENDIX B

All'illustrissimo et eccellentissimo signore, il signor don Maffeo Barberini. [49]
Sopra il Fonte Panfilio. Sonetto

Chi le stelle ha propitie al suo natale,
Che d'alte idee ne' peregrini ingegni
Stampan l'impronte, fa apparire li segni
Ne l'opre di virtù ch'in lui prevale.

Quindi hoggi ammira in te, Foro Agonale,
Roma il bel Fonte, e d'Innocentio i pegni,
Qual vuol ch'in lei magnificentia regni
E lasciar d'opre sue gloria immortale.

Immortala ancor sé l'opra, che spira
Energia nel scolpir, sì che d'honore
Dispera chiunque alla vittoria aspira:

Ha 'l penelo di man tolto al pittore,
Il poeta ancor lui freme e s'adira
Ch'oggi muova un scarpel Roma a stupore.

Giacomo Venetiano, genovese. [50]

(To the most illustrious and excellent Don Maffeo Barberini.
On the Pamphili fountain. Sonnet
He who at his birth has propitious stars which leave impressions of lofty ideas in unusual intellects, displays the signs in works of virtue which prevail in him.
Thus today Rome admires in you, Agonale Square, the beautiful fountain, and the tokens of Innocence, who wants magnificence to reign on it and who wishes to leave behind immortal glory of his works.
The work immortalizes itself as well; it breathes such energy in its carving that whoever wants to outdo it will not gain honours:

---

[49] Roma, Biblioteca Apostolica Vaticana, Barberiniano Latino 3880, fol. 158v.
[50] Ibid., fol. 157r.

It has taken the brush out of the hand of the painter; likewise the poet trembles and flies into a rage that today it is a chisel to astonish Rome. Giacomo Veneziano, Genoese.)

Innocentius X Pont. Max.

Emendato stagnantis Euripi vitro, aquam ex agro Os Leonis abductam, facto cum Trivii fonte divortio, in Agonis umbilicum transtulit. Quatergemino fonti novi Phidiæ signis additis, Obeliscum magnificentiæ renascentis ostentum, patriæ Urbis oculis speculum suæ magnanimitatis obiecit.

Epigramma.
Hic, ubi prisca ferum lusit monomachia Martem
    Pyramis attritum fert rediviva caput.
Ast Innocenti superat mens ardua molem
    Æmula Cæsareum dum reparavit opus.
Ars animat lapides, vivunt in marmore Nilus
    Ister et Euphrates, Martis in Urbe, Padus.
Æternum sonat unda decus Pamphilia fontis,
    Digna triumphali principe gesta probans.

Iacobus Venetianus, Genuensis.[51]

(Pope Innocence X drained the swamps of the Euripo, brought water from the Campo Boccadileone, separated it from the Trevi fountain and conducted it to the centre of the Agone. Images by the new Phidias were added to the four sides of the fountain, and an obelisk, a miracle of reborn magnificence, was placed before the eyes of the city of his residence, Rome, a mirror of his magnanimity.
Epigram.
Here, where the ancient duels were enacted as fierce battles, the re-born obelisk raises its worn head. But the daring mind of Innocence, entering into competition, outdid the imperial mass of stone in restoring it. Art animates the stones, and the Nile, Danube, Euphrates and Po live in the marble in the city of Mars. The water of the Pamphili fountain proclaims eternal glory, praising deeds worthy of a triumphant prince.
Giacomo Veneziano, Genoese.)

---

[51] Ibid., fol. 157v; elegiac couplets. The erroneous identification of the four rivers is surprisingly common in publications of the seventeenth century (for these, see n. 1 above).

Praise Beyond Reason.
Poems on Cerrini's Dome in S. Maria della Vittoria

THOMAS FRANGENBERG

Art theoretical literature intended to meet the specific intellectual requirements of non-artists developed in Venice and Florence between the 1540s and the late sixteenth century.[1] In both cities, publishers appear to have perceived sufficiently widespread interest in art to conclude that publication of art theoretical texts was financially viable. In particular, in Florence, a city where critical debates about contemporary art seem to have been common,[2] books of ambitious scale were published for the use of laymen.

Neither in the sixteenth nor during the first half of the seventeenth century did Roman publishers share their Florentine contemporaries' confidence in the interest in art theory among non-artist clienteles. Works concerned with art history and theory and art description, written by Giulio Mancini,[3] Giovanni Battista Agucchi[4] and Ferrante Carlo,[5] had some circulation in manuscript, and could thus exercise some influence on later art literature, but were not printed – and I see no evidence in support of the recent suggestion that the respective authors objected to publication out of

---

[1] Useful introductions to the development of art literature are found in J. Schlosser Magnino, *La letteratura artistica. Manuale delle fonti della storia dell'arte moderna*, Florence, Vienna 1956, and M. Barasch, *Theories of Art. From Plato to Winckelmann*, New York, London 1985. Florentine art literature specifically written for laymen is discussed in T. Frangenberg, *Der Betrachter. Studien zur florentinischen Kunstliteratur des 16. Jahrhunderts*, Berlin 1990.

[2] Vincenzo Borghini attests to the Florentines' good eye and biting tongue ('Noi siamo in una città che ha buon occhio e cattiva lingua'); G. Bottari and S. Ticozzi (Eds), *Raccolta di lettere sulla pittura, scultura ed architettura ...*, 8 vols, Milan 1822-25, vol. 1, p. 243.

[3] Mancini's most ambitious art theoretical work, his *Considerazioni sulla pittura*, written between 1617 and 1621, was first published only in 1956: G. Mancini, *Considerazioni sulla pittura*, vol. 1 A. Marucchi (Ed.), vol. 2 L. Salerno, Rome 1956-7; for the date of writing, see vol. 1, p. XV.

[4] Only a fragment of Agucchi's treatise was published in 1646; see D. Mahon, *Studies in Seicento Art and Theory*, London 1947, pp. 111-54, 241-58.

[5] See N. Turner, 'Ferrante Carlo's "Descrittione della Cupola di S. Andrea della Valle depinta dal Cavalier Gio: Lanfranchi"; a Source for Bellori's Descriptive Method', *Storia dell'arte*, 12, 1971, pp. 297-325.

contempt for the literary genre of art theory. [6]

These observations do not imply that no art literature written for or by laymen was published in Rome during the first half of the seventeenth century. Guide books to Rome, catering, among a variety of other concerns, to interest in the visual arts, continued to be published in large numbers. [7] Furthermore, pamphlets devoted to recently completed art works, ensembles of art works, or to ephemeral decorations, as they had become popular in the sixteenth century, were produced throughout the Seicento. Such pamphlets may contain prose descriptions. A significant percentage of the booklets published in the early and mid-seventeenth century, however, reflect a preference, widespread in polished social intercourse, for verse. Again, one may point to sixteenth-century precedents, both in Rome and Florence: published collections of poems were devoted to two prominent sculptures, Andrea Sansovino's *Anna Metterza* in S. Agostino in Rome[8] and Giambologna's *Rape of the Sabine woman* in Florence.[9]

Celebratory poetry on art may, to varying extents, be written in honour of the patron and his judicious patronage; in honour of the saint celebrated in a particular religious commission; or in honour of the artist and his art. Even though poetry on art does not rival either the scale or the art theoretical ambition of at least some of the late-sixteenth-century works, it deserves our attention as the form of literary engagement with art works employed by more seventeenth-century viewers than any other. In this paper, I shall look at the first collection of poems on a ceiling painting to have appeared in Rome, a book celebrating the dome decorated by Gian Domenico Cerrini [10]

[6]   This suggestion is found in M. Fumaroli, 'Rome 1630: entrée en scène du spectateur', in *Roma 1630. Il trionfo del pennello*, Milan 1994, pp. 53–82 (esp. p. 62).

[7]   For a full discussion of these texts, see L. Schudt, *Le guide di Roma. Materialien zu einer Geschichte der römischen Topographie*, Vienna, Augsburg 1930.

[8]   Blosio Palladio (Ed.), *Coryciana*, Rome 1524.

[9]   M. Sermartelli (Ed.), *Alcune composizioni di diversi autori in lode del ritratto della Sabina. Scolpito in marmo dall'eccellentissimo M. Giovanni Bologna, posto nella piazza del Serenissimo Gran Duca di Toscana*, Florence 1583.

[10]   For Cerrini's life, see L. Pascoli, *Vite de' pittori, scultori, ed architetti moderni*, V. Martinelli and A. Marabottini (Eds), Perugia 1992, pp. 119–25 (this section edited by F. F. Mancini); [A. F. Rau and M. Rastrelli], *Serie degli uomini i più illustri nella pittura, scultura, e architettura con i loro elogi, e ritratti incisi in rame*, 13 vols, Florence 1769–76, vol. 13, 1 ('Supplemento alla Serie dei trecento elogi e ritratti degli uomini i più illustri in pittura, scultura e architettura o sia abecedario pittorico dall'origine delle belle arti a tutto l'anno MDCCLXXV'), cols 674–5; E. Borea, 'Gian Domenico Cerrini. Opere e documenti', *Prospettiva*, 12, 1978, pp. 4–25; F. F. Mancini, 'Cerrini, Gian Domenico, detto il Cavalier Perugino', in *Dizionario biografico degli Italiani*, vol. 24, Rome 1980, pp. 16–20; A. Anselmi, 'Cerrini, Giovanni [Gian] Domenico', in *The Dictionary of Art*, vol. 6, London 1996, pp. 347–8; J. Schepers, 'Cerrini (Cerini), Giovanni Domenico (Gian

(1609–1681) in S. Maria della Vittoria (Pl. 42). The collection of poems was published in 1656 and bears the title *Poesie sopra il Ratto di S. Paolo nella cupola della Madonna della Vittoria. Pittura del signor Gio. Domenco Cerrini Perugino*.[11]

The church of S. Maria della Vittoria in Rome was originally dedicated to S. Paolo rapito al terzo cielo (St Paul ravished to the third heaven). The building was constructed from 1608 for the Discalced Carmelites. An

Domenico; gen. Cavalier Perugino), in *Saur Allgemeines Künstlerlexikon*, vol. 17, Munich, Leipzig 1997, pp. 608–9. See also R. Longhi, *Saggi e ricerche 1925–1928*, Florence 1967, vol. 1, pp. 19–23; D. Silvestri, 'I pittori perugini del Seicento che lavorarono in Roma. Gian Domenico Cerrini detto il "Cavalier Perugino"', *Perusia*, 5, 1, 1933, pp. 16–25; idem, 'La Cupola del "Cavalier Perugino" in Santa Maria della Vittoria in Roma', ibid., 5, 2, 1933, pp. 48–54; G. Matthiae, *S. Maria della Vittoria*, Rome 1965, pp. 44, 49; U. Vichi, 'Cappelle dedicate nelle chiese romane a Sant'Antonio di Padova', *Il Santo*, 12, 1972, pp. 391-7 (esp. pp. 391-3); M. Chiarini, 'Aggiunte al Cerrini', *Antologia di Belle Arti*, 2, 1978, pp. 279–82; idem, 'Postilla al Cerrini', ibid., 4, 1980, p. 253; A. Tantillo, 'Gian Domenico Cerrini', in *Un'antologia di restauri. 50 opere d'arte restaurate dal 1974 al 1981*, Rome 1982, pp. 75-7; B. Toscano, 'La pittura in Umbria nel Seicento', in *La pittura in Italia. Il Seicento*, M. Gregori and E. Schleier (Eds), 2 vols, Milan 1989, vol. 1, pp. 361-81 (esp. pp. 374-5); G. Sapori, 'Cerrini, Gian Domenico detto il Cavalier Perugino', ibid., vol. 2, pp. 688-9; A. Mignosi Tantillo, 'I dipinti dell'Eremo Carmelitano di S. Silvestro a Montecompatri', in *L'arte per i papi e per i principi nella campagna romana. Grande pittura del '600 e del '700*, 2 vols, Rome 1990, vol. 2, pp. 55-67 (esp. pp. 59-61); N. Righi, 'Cerrini, Gian Domenico detto Cavalier Perugino', in *Pittura italiana antica. Artisti e opere del Seicento e del Settecento*, A. Morandotti (Ed.), Milan 1995, p. 113; E. Schleier, 'Gian Domenico Cerrini e una rara iconografia', *Nuovi Studi*, 1, 1996, pp. 67-71. Mancini points out (Pascoli 1992, as above, p. 124, n. 18) that the title of Cavaliere must have been granted to Cerrini after the publication of the collection of poems, as he appears on the frontispiece as 'Signor'. The painter is, however, referred to as 'Eques' in a Latin epigram written by Capitano Bernardo Evangelisti (*Poesie* 1656, see n. 11 below, p. 72).

[11] *Poesie sopra il Ratto di S. Paolo nella cupola della Madonna della Vittoria. Pittura del signor Gio. Domenico Cerrini Perugino dedicate all'Illustriss. e Reverendiss. Sig. Monsig. Rospigliosi Arcivescovo di Tarso, e Segretario di Stato di N.[ostro] S.[ignore]*, F. Moneta (Ed.), Rome 1656 (this work will be referred to as *Poesie* 1656 in the remainder of the notes). As a manuscript note reveals, the richly gold-embossed presentation copy of the *Poesie* in the Vatican Library (Racc. I. IV. 1987) was given to the library in the year of publication by a high-ranking church official, Ranuzzo Scotti. Scotti was *maggiordomo* of the Apostolic Palace from 1653 until the early years of the reign of Alexander VII (the manuscript note does not yet contain a reference to Scotti's dismissal from his office). On Scotti, see G. Moroni, *Dizionario di erudizione storico-ecclesiastica*, vol. 41, Venice 1846, p. 267 (see also vol. 23, Venice 1843, p. 84). The gift to the library suggests that Scotti may have funded the publication; there are, however, no indications that he was also involved in commissioning Cerrini's fresco.

altarpiece painted by Gerhard van Honthorst in 1617, showing the rarely depicted subject of St Paul's ecstasy, was placed on the high altar (Pl. 43). In 1622 an image of the Virgin adoring the Christ Child, believed to have been the cause of the Catholic victory in the Battle at the White Mountain near Prague in 1620, was transferred to the church. The patronage was changed to S. Maria della Vittoria (St Mary of the Victory), and a shrine for the miraculous image, which would be lost in a fire in 1833, was installed in the apse. Honthorst's altarpiece was moved to the altar of the left transept. From there it was removed presumably very soon after 22 January 1647 when the transept was ceded to the Cornaro family, for whom Bernini designed his famous chapel. Honthorst's altarpiece survives in the retro-choir. [12] The importance of the subject of the ecstasy of St Paul to the Descalced Carmelites, however, is documented by the fact that only a few years after the removal of the altarpiece from the transept this theme was transferred to the dome. As collections of poems and other pamphlets commemorating important art works were almost universally published soon after the completion of the respective work, it is likely that Cerrini's fresco was executed in 1655. [13]

Paul's ecstasy is recounted in 2 Corinthians 12.2–4:

> I know a Christian man who fourteen years ago (whether in the body or out of the body, I do not know – God knows) was caught up as far as the third heaven. And I know that this same man (whether in the body or apart from the body, I do not know – God knows) was caught up into paradise, and heard words so secret that human lips may not repeat them. [14]

The parallelism of the two phrases is taken in Biblical scholarship to imply that St Paul talks about the same event in both instances; this is to say that he places Paradise in the third heaven. [15] Moreover, it is commonly

---

12   Matthiae 1965 (as in n. 10, above), pp. 15–16; W. Buchowiecki, *Handbuch der Kirchen Roms*, 4 vols (vol. 4 by B. Kuhn-Forte), Vienna 1967–97, vol. 3, pp. 280–2; for Honthorst's work, see G. J. Hoogewerff, 'De werken van Gerard Honthorst te Rome', *Onze Kunst*, 16, 31, 1917, pp. 37–50, 81–92, ('Honthorst in Italië. Een Naschrift') 141–4 (esp. pp. 45–7); idem, *Gerrit van Honthorst*, The Hague 1924, pp. 6–7; [E. Fusciardi], *Cenni storici sui conventi dei PP. Carmelitani Scalzi della provincia romana*, Rome 1929, pp. 107–26 (esp. pp. 115, 125); J. R. Judson, *Gerrit van Honthorst: A Discussion of His Position in Dutch Art*, The Hague 1959, pp. 34–8, 172–3; *Johann Liss*, Augsburg 1975, pp. 125–8, 175; I. Lavin, *Bernini and the Unity of the Visual Arts*, 2 vols, New York, London 1980, text vol., pp. 197–8; J. R. Judson and R. E. O. Ekkart, *Gerrit van Honthorst 1592–1656*, Ghent 1999, pp. 11–12, 92–3; *Giovanni Lanfranco. Un pittore barocco tra Parma, Roma e Napoli*, E. Schleier (Ed.), Milan 2001, pp. 338–9, with further literature.

13   For an author who died in 1656, see n. 33 below.

14   Quoted after *The Revised English Bible with the Apocrypha*, Oxford, Cambridge 1989.

15   H. Bietenhard, *Die himmlische Welt im Urchristentum und Spätjudentum*, Tübingen 1951, p. 164; see also M. Lechner, 'Paulus', in *Lexikon der christlichen*

accepted that the unnamed man is St Paul himself. The notion of the plurality of heavens is found in Jewish theology, including, on occasion, the Old Testament. In the New Testament, however, Paul's testimony of three heavens is entirely isolated.[16] The *Testament Levi* appears to be the oldest Jewish text to speak of more than one heaven.[17] Among the sources nearest in time to St Paul that assume three heavens, we find II Enoch 8.1–8, a text that may have been utilized by St Paul or was at least written in a literary tradition shared by him.[18]

In the seventeenth century, the implications of St Paul's statement were no longer fully understood. The writer of several of the poems interpreted the third heaven in terms of planetary spheres,[19] another playfully criticizes Cerrini for having conflated the third heaven and the empyreum, apparently unaware that Paul drew on a tradition that assumed the seat of God in the third heaven.[20]

The painter appears to have been less than entirely happy with the fresco. In a letter of 1666 addressed to a Medici prince he writes: 'But if I had had occasion to produce a great work, with all the necessary help, I would have shown that I am not inferior to anybody alive, because I know what I need in order to execute a well-made work; [but] I was unlucky [even] in the

---

Ikonographie, vol. 8, Rome, Freiburg 1976, cols 128–47 (esp. col. 138). The fact that the fresco depicts Paradise, and its subject demands so, casts doubt on a line of argument found in B. W. Lindemann, *Bilder vom Himmel. Studien zur Deckenmalerei des 17. und 18. Jahrhunderts*, Worms 1994, pp. 48–50. Lindemann argues that since clouds exist only in the sublunar world and not in the empyreum, ceiling paintings can only ever represent the descent of God and the Saints into the cloudy realm near the earth. The example of Cerrini's dome suggests that this argument is too schematic, and that the depicted heavenly views are not necessarily subject to the same conditions that were believed to apply to the heavenly spheres. Unlike a number of Sienese Renaissance paintings that visualise the Lord's descent towards earth as a voyage through the spheres (see, for example, Francesco di Giorgio Martini's *Coronation of the Virgin*, Siena, Pinacoteca Nazionale, 1472–4; L. Bellosi (Ed.), *Francesco di Giorgio e il Rinascimento a Siena 1450–1500*, Milan 1993, pp. 300–5), the glories on baroque ceilings do not demand analysis in such terms. Painters and their public unquestioningly (as far as we can tell today) accepted clouds as a convenient way of framing and supporting sacred figures in heavenly settings, be it Paradise or a vision of saints in the sublunar zone.

[16] Bietenhard 1951 (as in n. 15, above), passim.

[17] Ibid., pp. 3–10; H. W. Hollander and M. de Jonge, *The Testaments of the Twelve Patriarchs. A Commentary*, Leiden 1985, pp. 129–83.

[18] Bietenhard 1951 (as in n. 15, above), pp. 161–8; R. H. Charles (Ed.), *The Book of the Secrets of Enoch*, W. R. Morfill transl., Oxford 1896, pp. 7–8.

[19] See *Poesie* 1656, pp. 20 and 66, where the third heaven is referred to as third sphere.

[20] Ibid., p. 66, Pietro Iacomo Favilla writes: 'Manchi però in un sol: che dipingesti | Si svelato l'eterno, e' sacri Chori, | Ch'in fare il terzo Ciel, l'Empireo festi'.

womb of my mother, and when I painted the dome of the Madonna della Vittoria I firstly did it for nothing and on the ground I was always afraid to be killed by my foes and I never had the opportunity to see from below what effect the said work produced. All these are circumstances that prevented me from doing anything good'.[21] Given the painter's lament, the publication of a book of 83 pages' length containing poems in praise of this work may seem surprising. Cerrini's dome is not, however, the only work celebrated in a collection of poems that did not receive universal praise from contemporaries. The same holds for Francesco Mochi's *St Veronica* in the Vatican.[22] In fact, Giovanni Battista Passeri suggests in his life of Mochi: 'a collection of various poems in his praise ... does not provide sure testimony of the value of a work, because such applause can be earned through begging by those who with the weakness of their works would have earned blame rather than praise'.[23] Passeri is quick to assert that Mochi, a modest man, is above such suspicions. In Cerrini's case, on the other hand, it may well be surmised that the painter or his supporters instigated the publication. That the reasons for assembling the collection of poems may have been polemical, intended to document artistic importance in the face of adverse criticism, is suggested by several poems' references to envy, most overtly in a *canzone* by Michele Stanchi; the

[21] 'Ma se io avessi avuto occasione di fare un'opera grande con asistenza delle cose necessarie averei fatto vedere che io non ero inferiore a nessuno che oggi viva, perché so che cosa mi vole a condurre un'opera assai ben fatta, io sono stato sfortunato nel ventre di mia madre e quando feci la cupola della Madonna della Vittoria in primis la feci per nulla e a tera sempre stavo con timore di non esser ammazzato dai miei nemici né mai ebbi commodità di vedere da basso che effetto faceva detta opera. Tutti questi sono accidenti che mi hanno impedito di fare qualche cosa di buono.' (Firenze, Archivio di Stato, Carteggio Artisti, IX, ins. 16/2, 140), quoted after Borea 1978 (as in n. 10, above), p. 22. The letter is addressed to either Mattia or, more probably, Leopoldo de' Medici.

[22] L. Grignani (Ed.), *La Veronica Vaticana. Del Signor Francesco Mochi. Componimenti poetici*, Rome 1641. On the history of the statue, see M. De Luca Savelli, 'Le opere del Mochi', in *Francesco Mochi 1580–1654*, Florence 1981, pp. 35–85 (esp. pp. 75–6); J. Montagu, *Roman Baroque Sculpture. The Industry of Art*, New Haven, London 1989, pp. 30–5.

[23] The full quotation reads: 'Ne riportò applauso il Mochi da questo suo bel Lavoro, et andò in giro alla Stampa una raccolta di varie poesie in sua lode; ma questo non rende sicura testimonianza del valore d'una operazione, perche questi applausi mendicati possono guadagnarli ancora quelle opere, che si sono fabricate, con le debolezze, più il vilipendio, che la lode. Non dico, che egli lo procurasse, perche era uomo modesto, e sodo; ma delle volte alcuni parziali fanno al galant' uomo piu danno che beneficio con certe lodi sfacciate senza proposito, e senza proporzione.'; J. Hess (Ed.), *Die Künstlerbiographien von Giovanni Battista Passeri*, Leipzig, Vienna 1934, p. 134; also quoted in O. Ferrari, 'Poeti e scultori nella Roma seicentesca: i difficili rapporti tra due culture', *Storia dell'arte*, 90, 1997, pp. 151–61 (esp. pp. 154–5).

very strong wording suggests that more than literary formulae are at work: 'here, with more real modern hate, hell arms itself against a painted heaven'. This modern hate is in the next verse named 'envy', 'L'invidia'. [24] Further evidence in this respect is provided by the engraved frontispiece of the *Poesie* (Pl. 44). It depicts Father Time with an escutcheon bearing an abbreviated version of the title of the book. In the centre of the composition, Fame holds two trumpets; she is accompanied by a putto pointing to a domed church in the background, presumably a reference to S. Maria della Vittoria. Fame's left foot touches the head of a female figure thrown to the ground with her tongue stuck out and vipers for hair; the latter characterize her as Envy. [25]

In his dedication to Archbishop Rospigliosi, the publisher Francesco Moneta uses what we shall recognize as one of the literary devices most widely employed throughout the volume, that is, the *paragone* (both Moneta and the author of one of the poems use this term, which at the time had not yet acquired the specific meaning of comparisons between different arts as it is current today). [26] The dedicatee is compared to Achilles: Achilles chose the harp from the spoils of his enemies, [27] Moneta presents to the Archbishop a publication containing the sounds of numerous harps, 'played by expert hands'. Achilles won his glory with his weapons, the dedicatee triumphed with his harmonious and erudite writings 'spread over a thousand sheets'. [28]

---

[24] *Poesie* 1656, p. 59: 'Mà quì con più verace [more real than ancient stories] odio moderno | Contro un dipinto Ciel s'arma l'Inferno. | L'invidia, a' cui trofei | Son' i trionfi altrui ....' Already Mancini (Pascoli 1992, as in n. 10, above, pp. 123–4) took this poem as indication of the polemical nature of the entire collection of poems.

[25] Compare Y. Okayama, *The Ripa Index. Personifications and their Attributes in Five Editions of the Iconologia*, Doornspijk 1992, p. 143.

[26] *Poesie* 1656, dedication and p. 27 (for the latter text, see n. 52 below). On the early history of the *paragone* between the arts, see C. J. Farago, *Leonardo da Vinci's "Paragone". A Critical Interpretation with a New Edition of the Text in the Codex Urbinas*, Leiden, New York 1992.

[27] Homer, *Iliad* IX.185–8.

[28] Giulio Rospigliosi (1600–69) was given the Archbishopric of Tarsus in 1644, was made cardinal in 1657, and as Pope adopted the name of Clement IX (1667–9); see L. von Pastor, *Geschichte der Päpste seit dem Ausgang des Mittelalters*, vol. 14, 1, Freiburg i. Br. 1929, pp. 527–610. On his literary output, see G. M. de' Crescimbeni, *L'istoria della volgar poesia*, Rome 1698, pp. 160–1 and G. Canevazzi, *Papa Clemente IX poeta (Giulio Rospigliosi – Sec. XVII)*, Modena 1900. Since Moneta refers only to Rospigliosi's literary accomplishments as reason for his dedication, it is most unlikely that the Archbishop was involved as patron in the decoration of the dome, which, as Cerrini's complaint suggests (see n. 21, above), was in any event not lavishly funded. Fabroni attests to Rospigliosi's strong interest in art and close contacts with artists, even before his election; see A. Fabroni, *Vitae italorum doctrina excellentium qui saeculis XVII. et XVIII. floruerunt*, 18 vols, Pisa 1778–99, vol. 2, p. 21; see also pp. 139–42, and C.

Many contributors to the *Poesie* seem to have had literary ambitions even though they were principally engaged in other careers. Among them we find lawyers, secretaries, members of religious orders, academics and artists. We encounter Giovanni Battista Passeri, writer of artists' lives and painter, [29] and Guidobaldo Abbatini, the artist responsible for the fresco in the Cornaro chapel adjacent to Cerrini's dome. [30] His own work, his 'mute Muse', is Abbatini's best witness to document Cerrini's superiority. [31] One of the contributors to the volume is a woman, Maria Porzia Vignoli; her poem is the only one in the collection to betray an interest in the painter's earlier works. [32] The circumstances of one of the authors will have to be considered when addressing the character of encomiastic poetry: the professor of rhetoric, Henricus Chifellius (Kiefel), author of an epigram on the dome written shortly before his death, had been blind for c. 45 years when he wrote his poem. [33]

---

d'Afflitto and D. Romei (Eds), *I teatri del paradiso. La personalità, l'opera, il mecenatismo di Giulio Rospigliosi (Papa Clemente IX)*, Pistoia 2000.

[29] See n. 23 and D. Graf, 'Giovanni Battista Passeri', in *The Dictionary of Art*, vol. 24, London 1996, p. 238, with further literature.

[30] On Abbatini's pictorial work, see C. Guglielmi, 'Abbatini, Guido Ubaldo', in *Dizionario biografico degli Italiani*, vol. 1, Rome 1960, p. 32; A. Sutherland Harris, 'Abbatini, Guido Ubaldo', in *The Dictionary of Art*, vol. 1, London 1996, pp. 20-1, with further literature.

[31] *Poesie* 1656, p. 44: 'Guido Baldo Abbatini. | Per la sudetta Cuppola, presso alla quale sono alcune pitture di mano dell'Autore. | Madrigale | Erger CERRIN vorrei | Con encomi più degni oltre le Sfere | Del tuo Pennel le meraviglie altere; | Mà vani i pensier miei | Ver chi Fabro di glorie erge trofei, | Già la muta mia Musa ivi vicino | Vanta pur troppo il suo Valor divino'.

[32] On Maria Porzia Vignoli (1632-87), see P. Mandosio, *Bibliotheca Romana seu romanorum scriptorum centuriae*, 2 vols, Rome 1682-92, vol. 2, pp. 192-4 (see p. 193 for a reference to her ode 'La Maraviglia', in *Poesie* 1656, pp. 46-54); her best-known work is M. P. Vignoli, *L'Obelisco di Piazza Navona. Idillio. Con la dichiaratione delle statue, animali, piante, e di tutto quello, che si contiene in detto Obelisco*, Rome 1651. In this work Vignoli comments on Bernini's earlier achievements (n.p. [fols 2v-3r]), as the author later did in her Ode on Cerrini (*Poesie* 1656, pp. 50-3). We may therefore recognize such art historical references as characteristic of Vignoli's literary output.

[33] *Poesie* 1656, p. 76. According to F. Sweertius, *Athenae Belgicae sive Nomenclator Infer. Germaniae scriptorum qui disciplinas philologicas, philosophicas, theologicas, iuridicas, medicas et musicas illustrarunt*, Antwerp 1628, pp. 331-2, Kiefel was born in 1583, studied in Louvain, Ingolstadt and Rome, received his doctorate in 1607, went blind in 1610, but was nonetheless employed as professor of rhetoric at the Sapienza in Rome from 1621 to the year of his death, 1656; see E. Conte, *I Maestri della Sapienza di Roma dal 1514 al 1787: I rotuli e altre fonti*, 2 vols, Rome 1991, vol. 1, pp. 191-332 passim. The *Poesie* of 1656 do not yet contain any reference to his death. Kiefel published a number of books or pamphlets between 1604 and 1635. The poem on Cerrini's dome is the only published work of his late years

The collection of poems, like many other such, is a document of the social custom, widespread in the sixteenth and seventeenth centuries, of employing verse in exchanges of social niceties or of information, and in comments on, or more commonly celebrations of, contemporary artistic achievements.[34] Nobody with a reasonable schooling in grammar and the humanities needed to feel excluded from such social use of poetry. Verse allowed authors to display their learning and ingenuity to their peers. Perusal of celebratory poetry could stimulate delight in the display of such ingenuity, a delight that was in turn intended to colour the reader's approach to the celebrated object.

The relation of celebratory poems and their objects is a loose and playful, but not an entirely arbitrary, one. Individual poems may contain praise of the specific work or artist; they may engage with the work or its siting through description, spirited association, or comparison; lastly, they may rehearse the art work's effect of reality, and may do so in hyperbolic ways greatly exceeding the possibilities of the visual arts themselves.

The linguistic strategies characteristic of encomiastic poetry, and of the poems on Cerrini's dome in particular, are well represented by the first poem of the collection, written by a certain Alessandro Bucci. The placing is not necessarily a comment on the distinction of this sonnet; in fact, first the Italian and then the Latin poems are printed in alphabetical order of the authors' Christian names. Bucci's sonnet reads:

Dell'eccelso Saul tù, che pingesti
Il ratto al terzo Ciel, mira tuoi vanti

---

that has come to my notice. On Kiefel, see also L. Allacci, *Apes urbanae, sive de viris illustribus, qui ab anno MDCXXX. per totum MDCXXXII. Romae adfuerunt, ac typis aliquid evulgarunt*, Rome 1633, pp. 128-9; J. Carafa, *De Gymnasio Romano et de eius professoribus ab Urbe condita usque ad haec tempora libri duo, quibus accedunt catalogus advocatorum sacri consistorii, & bullae ad ipsum gymnasium spectantes*, 2 vols, Rome 1751, vol. 2, pp. 320-1; J. Ijsewijn, 'Supplementum "Phoenissis" seu "Thebaidi" Senecanae adiectum ab Henrico Chifellio Antverpiensi', in *Hommages à Jozef Veremans*, F. Decreus and C. Deroux (Eds), Brussels 1986, pp. 161-74 (esp. pp. 162-3).

[34] On the subject of poetry on art, see A. Colasanti, 'Gli artisti nella poesia del Rinascimento. Fonti poetiche per la storia dell'arte italiana', *Repertorium für Kunstwissenschaft*, 27, 1904, pp. 193-220; G. Kranz, *Das Bildgedicht in Europa. Zur Theorie und Geschichte einer literarischen Gattung*, Paderborn 1973; M. Albrecht-Bott, *Die bildende Kunst in der italienischen Lyrik der Renaissance und des Barock. Studie zur Beschreibung von Portraits und anderen Bildwerken unter besonderer Berücksichtigung von G. B. Marinos Galleria*, Wiesbaden 1976; G. Kranz, *Das Bildgedicht. Theorie. Lexikon. Bibliographie*, 3 vols, Cologne, Vienna 1981-7; C. E. Gilbert, *Poets Seeing Artists' Work: Instances in the Italian Renaissance*, Florence 1991; A. Golahny, *The Eye of the Poet. Studies in the Reciprocity of the Visual and Literary Arts from the Renaissance to the Present*, Lewisburg, London 1996.

Immortalarsi, ond'ogni lingua canti,
S'ammirabile fù l'opra, che festi.

Meraviglia non è, s'al Ciel sorgesti,
Ove seggio ei ritien fra gli altri Santi;
Sol per ritrar più vivi i suoi sembianti,
Lassuso in alta mole alhor t'ergesti.

Pomposo aldilui ratto il Ciel gioisce,
Cedendo all'arte la natura istessa,
Che pinto ancor' il senso altrui rapisce.

La Fama al tuo valor encomij intessa
CERRIN', e s'altro Apelle ognun t'ambisce,
Nella Vittoria hai tua Vittoria espressa.[35]

The first quatrain contains a descriptive element in the naming of the fresco's subject; that the painter's immortal fame is the main subject of the sonnet is, however, intimated immediately after this introduction in the second half of this quatrain. The notion of the immortality of Cerrini's fame is no doubt an association derived from the word 'heaven' in the preceding verse; several other poems insist that Cerrini, in depicting heaven, acquires immortality. Giovanni Simone Ruggieri writes:

Emulator de l'immortal soggiorno
Così il CERRINI il proprio nome eterna, ...[36]

Another poem, an elegy by Giovanni Lorenzo Gubernatis, is devoted to voracious time conquered by Cerrini's depiction of heaven. Cerrini's heaven is eternal, and its eternity is shared by the painter.[37]

Bucci's last verse returns to the subjects of success and fame. Creating an associative link with the circumstances of the fresco, in this instance with the place in which it is located, he maintains that Cerrini gained his victory in St Mary of the Victory.

A further association is the memory of ancient art, evoked by the supreme quality of this modern work. Bucci calls the painter a new Apelles, employing one of the most widely used formulae of artistic praise.

[35] *Poesie* 1656, p. 1: 'You, who painted the lofty Saul | ravished to the third heaven, behold how your achievement | is immortalized; may all tongues sing its praises, | so admirable is the work you made. | It is no wonder if you ascended to heaven | where he sits among the other saints; | only so as to be able to portray his features in more lively a manner | when you rose up to this lofty place. | At his ravishment, heaven rejoices in festive delight, | nature herself surrenders to art; | even though painted, heaven ravishes one's sense. | Fame weaves praise of your valour | Cerrini, and as everyone longs for you as a second Apelles, | you have given expression to your victory in the Victory'.

[36] Ibid., p. 29: 'In portraying the immortal residence | Cerrini gives eternity to his own name...'.

[37] Ibid., pp. 14–16.

Most of Bucci's fellow writers sought ways to utilize this association in terms of a *paragone* between ancient and modern achievement. In one of his sonnets, Bernardo Evangelisti maintains that the harmony of Apelles's paintings, and the life with which Lysippus imbued the bodies of the deceased, faint in comparison with Cerrini's art. His art not only ravished earth-bound souls to heaven, it also seized from heaven the ravished St Paul – believing himself to be in heaven, St Paul was in fact seen on earth. The last triplet of Evangelisti's sonnet begins with 'I have erred': the hyperbolic suggestion of the seizing out of heaven gives way to a yet more daring proposition: Cerrini provides proof that one body can be in two places at the same time – whilst he was in heaven, he was also in the church on earth.[38] None of the other poems goes as far in weaving praise out of absurdity, in taking up and playing out the impossibility of the visual experience afforded by this ceiling painting.

A Latin epigram by the same author unfolds the *paragone* between antiquity and Cerrini in a different manner. Zeuxis deceived only men in his image of Helen; in his image of St Paul, Cerrini deceived heaven itself.[39] Even though such extravagant lines of thought are rare in the volume, most authors who draw on the *paragone* between ancient and modern art agree that Apelles and his colleagues, given Cerrini's exalted merit, are well advised to lay down their brushes. The same superiority is maintained in comparisons with mythical artistry of ancient times: the *canzone* by Michele Stanchi concludes with the observation that Prometheus had used the light of the sun to animate mere mortals; Cerrini enlivens saints.[40]

---

[38] Ibid., p. 6: 'Capitano Bernardo Evangelisti | Sonetto | S'Alle tele un'Apel diede i concenti, | Prestò vita Lisippo à corpi estinti, | Fecer creder per ver gl'enti più finti, | Opre degne ben fur di cavi argenti: | Mà che vaglian mirar occhi viventi | Chi rapisca al Motor gli animi avvinti, | Da venereo Epiciclo ancorche cinti; | Opre maggior, degne d'eterei accenti: | CERRINI è quel, che glorie tante afferra | Qual con arte rapì PAOLO rapito, | Che credendosi in Ciel, l'iscorsi in terra. | Errai. Non lo rapì, fù chiaro esempio, | Ch'un sol corpo può star in doppio sito, | Mentre PAOLO era in Ciel, era nel Tempio.' The 'i' as last letter of 'iscorsi' is a manuscript correction found in all five copies of the *Poesie* I have seen (Biblioteca Nazionale, Rome: Misc. B. 1174. 4; Misc. 34. 10. F. 1. 4; Misc. 34. 7. D. 24. 9 [incomplete]; Biblioteca Casanatense, Rome: R. XIII. 49; Biblioteca Vaticana: Racc. I. IV. 1987).

[39] Ibid., p. 70: 'Capitano Bernardo Evangelisti | Epigramma | Infames Zeusis telis animaverat artus, | Vitalesque Helenae iunxerat arte notas | Venali concessa loco tunc Graecia fluxit, | Creditaque est telis vivere Gratia Venus. | Haec concede notis Astro, mirare CERINUS | Expressit telas nobiliore suas. | Iam bene sacrata depinxit fornice PAULUM | Ut vere PAULUM credidit esse Polus. | Erupit quin sponte moras, et praepete penna | Illum ad sidereas abripit iste plagas. | Iam sua iam Zeusis cedat miracla CERINO, | Decipit ille homines, decipit iste Polos'.

[40] Ibid., p. 65: 'E se Prometeo svelse | Dal Sol le fiamme eccelse | Per darne spirto à suo talento a' sassi: | Tù i rai ne traggi à più bell' opre usati, | Quegli animò

Returning to Bucci's sonnet, in the second quatrain we find the suggestion that the painter went up to heaven to give a more lifelike appearance to his portrait of St Paul. The lifelikeness of St Paul is explored in several other poems. For instance, an Ode by Francesco Sbarra intimates that St Paul, killed by the executioner's sword, is brought back to life by Cerrini's brush as a monument to the painter's art.[41] Similar liveliness characterizes the other figures in Cerrini's fresco: with brushes provided by Aurora and Iris, the painter created images which seem to be alive and to breathe; this beautiful version of a very standard homage to figurative painting is found in a sonnet by Bernardo Evangelisti.[42] In another sonnet, the same author expands this formula of praise, maintaining that the absence of voice, usually portrayed as the final barrier painting cannot overcome, is here to be welcomed, as the figures would not be eternal beings, were they to talk.[43] Other poems use the opposite strategy: the painter's merit manifests itself in giving voice to walls, to the depicted figures and to musical instruments.[44]

In the last two lines of an epigram, the blind professor of rhetoric, Henricus Chifellius, draws on the viewer's conflicting responses to repeated experiences of the work in order to characterize its success:

Motum etiam tribuisse putem, ni cuncta revertens
Aspiciam primo fixa manere situ.[45]

Bucci was not the only author to suggest that the painter must be assumed to have had some form of direct access to the object of his depiction. Giovanni Paolo Quintili[46] wonders if Cerrini was himself in heaven, or if he transported heaven down from its heights. More cautiously, a sonnet by Girolamo Garopoli suggests that Cerrini's mind was lifted up to the third heaven.[47] Two poems use mythology to make a similar point: the painter's

---

mortali, e tù Beati'.

41 Ibid., p. 9: 'Nò, che PAOLO non è, non è più morto, | Fatto è del tuo saper vivo Trofeo, | Ch'ove sott'empia spada egli cadeo, | Sul tuo Pennel pietoso hoggi è risorto'.
42 Ibid., p. 2: 'Capitano Bernardo Evangelisti | Sonetto | Pingi, ò dotto CERRIN, gl'eterni Giri, | E forma un PAOLO in fra beati Chori, | Poiche l'Angelo tuo tempra i colori | Col pennello de l'Alba, e quel de l'Iri. | Quindi avvien, che Celeste ognun t'ammiri, | Che s'orni un Ciel di raggi, un Sol di fiori | Sparge la luce quel, questo gl'odori, | Ed' ogn' imago par che viva, e spiri: | Sfronda intanto la Fama, e l'ale spande; | Le sacre Viti, e i Platani adorati, | Per farne al Crine tuo serti, e ghirlande; | E da tepidi Lidi à più gelati | Sona (da tratti tuoi già fatta grande) | Ch'un Pennello divin pinga i Beati'.
43 Ibid., p. 4: 'Manca la voce à dar i sensi interni, | Mà felice mancanza, e chi non vede, | Che parlando non già sariano eterni?'.
44 Ibid., e.g. pp. 29, 33, 38–40, 76.
45 Ibid., p. 76: 'I would believe that the figures were moving, if not, on turning back, | I saw everything remaining firmly in its former place'.
46 Ibid., p. 18.

hand or mind crossed the River Lethe into a world beyond. [48]

A number of poems affirm that Cerrini made Paradise visually accessible within the limited space of the church. None of the authors suggests that the building's restricted space limits the impact of the work. Instead, a verse in the ode by Maria Porzia Vignoli suggests that the painting offers the viewer 'welcome deception'. [49]

Perhaps the most far-reaching claims are made in the first triplet of Bucci's sonnet.

> At his ravishment, heaven rejoices in festive delight
> nature herself surrenders to art;
> even though painted, heaven ravishes one's sense.

Far beyond mere visual deception, the effectiveness of the fresco is dramatised in the *paragone* of nature and art, and is enacted in the mind of the viewer.

A very high percentage of the poems speak of nature and art. In Giovanni Simone Ruggieri's *canzone*, Cerrini, in depicting heavenly splendour, takes from art the 'possible' and from nature 'beauty', [50] a statement written at a time when the connection between art and beauty was not yet perceived as an essential one. [51] The same author maintains in another poem that in Cerrini's fresco nature and art are engaged in a divine *paragone*. [52] Giacinto Fieraboschi in a sonnet goes as far as to ascribe to this new Apelles an almost God-like status; with his brush and colours, the painter is omnipotent. [53]

It is a short step, taken by many of the authors, to ascertain that an art which is able to depict the Lord must in fact outdo nature. [54] And not only nature – Cerrini's art enters a contest with the sky which no longer prides

[47]   Ibid., p. 35.

[48]   Ibid., pp. 7, 27.

[49]   Ibid., p. 49: 'E così ben del Ciel la gloria espressa | Hoggi dal tuo Pennello il Mondo vede; | Che con gradito inganno anco si crede | Mentre l'ammira di goder l'istessa'.

[50]   Ibid., p. 22: 'Spirano quì le mura, | Cui dan vivi colori, e moto, e senso, | Nè divisar ben puoi | S'opra quì sia de l'Arte, ò di Natura | Ciò, ch'in abisso immenso | Di splendori, e di luce, egli apre à noi; | Mentre, che solo hà di rapir qui cura | Destra sì dotta, e scaltra | Il possibil da l'una, e'l bel da l'altra'.

[51]   On the occurrence of the notion of 'Beaux-arts' or 'Belle Arti' first in France in the 1660s, and in the 1670s in Italy, see L. Grassi and M. Pepe, *Dizionario della critica d'arte*, 2 vols, Turin 1978, vol. 1, pp. 73–4.

[52]   *Poesie* 1656, p. 27: 'Meraviglia, e stupore; ecco in CERRINO | Mirasi l'Arte à la Natura unita, | E l'una, e l'altra al paragon divino | Stampano orme d'honor, raggi di vita'.

[53]   Ibid., p. 11: 'Tutto puote il CERRINI, ei novo Apelle | Col pennel, co'i colori, è quasi eguale | Al gran Fabro del Cielo, e delle Stelle'.

[54]   E.g. ibid., p. 49.

itself in its blue.[55] And not only the sky – Cerrini's art enters into a *paragone* with St Paul. Taking up the verse from 2 Corinthians 'and heard words so secret that human lips may not repeat them', numerous poems suggest that Cerrini's brush dared and succeeded where St Paul had to remain silent. A striking madrigal on the subject of *ut pictura poesis* by Giovanni Simone Ruggieri reads:

> Hor sì, che no si dice,
> Che la Pittura sia
> Più muta Poesia,
> Mentre, quel che non lice
> Di spiegare ad'un Huom, ch'il tutto vale
> Con sua lingua immortale,
> Per prodigio novello
> Hoggi spiega il Pennello.[56]

And not only the sky and the Saint are engaged in a *paragone* with art; painting competes with heaven itself. Rutilio Lepidi writes in a sonnet:

> Egli dal Ciel rapito il terzo Giro
> Mirò beato; et io rapito al Polo
> Da divino Pennello Iddio rimiro.[57]

The ecstasy afforded by the brush is more powerful than the seizing by heaven. In a similar vein, Bernardo Evangelisti concludes that the painting not only gives to Rome the souls seized up to heaven that are depicted in the fresco, but also gives to the Lord the thousand others that are transported upwards by the work of art.[58] In a Latin epigram, Pietro Giacomo Favilla – almost blasphemously – asks:

> Quis tamen est melior Raptor, CERRINUS, an Astra?
> Ista ad se PAULUM, ad se rapit Ille Polum.[59]

In the *paragone* of heaven and art, it is within the power of poetry to portray art as the winner.

In an epigram, Evangelisti states more cautiously, taking up the Bible verse in order to leave the matter in suspension:

> Dicite, quis maior Raptus Pietatis, an Artis?
> Non licet haec (PAULO sic referente) loqui.[60]

---

[55] Ibid., p. 20.

[56] Ibid., p. 34: 'Does one not say | that Painting is | mute poetry, | whilst, what must not | be explained by a supreme man | with his immortal tongue, | by novel miracle | the brush now explains'.

[57] Ibid., p. 67: 'He [St Paul] blissfully beheld the third sphere | when ravished by heaven; I, ravished to heaven | by a Divine brush, behold the Lord'.

[58] Ibid., p. 5.

[59] Ibid., p. 82: 'But who ravishes better, Cerrini or the stars? | They ravished Paul, he ravishes Heaven'.

[60] Ibid., p. 72: 'Say, what ravishment is greater, by piety or art? | Such things (so

Only one author, Giovanni Battista Capalli, compares his own poetic activity to St Paul's experience. As the Saint was unable to speak about the secrets of heaven, in like manner the poet's tongue is unable to sing the painter's praises, as art ravishes his spellbound eyes towards the painted heaven.[61] The poet, thanks to the artist's efforts a visionary like St Paul, turns into a new St Paul also in his awe-struck silence, a response as appropriate with regard to heaven as it is beneath this heaven made by art.

A good number of the poems we have discussed, and others in this collection, test the limits of what can plausibly be said, and what can be said without falling into blasphemy, or test the limits of the claims of pictorial illusion. Given the daring of many of the poems, it may be helpful to bear in mind a disclaimer found in a near-contemporary book, the *Rime morali, eroiche, giovanili* by Bartolomeo Tortoletti published in Rome in 1645: 'may nobody wish to make history out of poetry; all [poems] should be considered as exercises and demonstrations of the mind'.[62] Expanding upon Tortoletti's argument, one may say that poetry is not only not history, it is also, more generally, not bound by the strictures applying to most prose texts. The ludic character of poetry allows engagement with levels of the art work inaccessible to prose. Poetry's hugely increased reach has a particular status in poems on art, and in particular on a kind of art that claims to make ecstatic visions accessible to the sense of sight.

In devising responses, the poems we have discussed can be seen as being freely, but not arbitrarily, descriptive. Such description may, however, be more concerned with the iconography than with the artistic appearance of the specific art work. One may assume that most of the authors represented in the *Poesie* had seen Cerrini's fresco, but at least one writer, Chifellius, had access to the dome only through verbal accounts. Encomiastic poems on art have some autonomy with regard to the praised works: even though the collection of poems in its entirety is intended both to document, and to elicit, positive responses to Cerrini's achievement, nothing suggests that individual

---

Paul attests) must not be spoken'.

61   Ibid., p. 78: 'D. Ioannis Baptistae Capalli | Epigramma | Exprimit astriferas aedes CERRINIUS? Umber | Et suprema Poli culmina picta refert? | Ingenuae sunt haec artis miracula. Romae | Lumina vel possunt nostra vedere Polum. | Cernis ut Aligeri extollant ad sydera PAULUM, | Supponant oneri ut lucida terga sacro? | PAULE quid arrectas potuit, dic, ire per aures? | Quid? quod mortali non licet ore loqui. | Angimur, et simili, fas nobis dicere, casu, | Stringuntur nodo labraque nostra pari. | Ars rapit immota ad pictum mea lumina Coelum, | Pictoris laudes lingua referre nequit'.

62   '... della Poesia non gli [i.e. the reader] venga voglia di far' Istoria; ma tutte le consideri, com' esercitationi, e prove d'ingegno ....'; B. Tortoletti, *Rime ... morali, eroiche, giovanili*, Rome 1645, p. 10; also quoted in B. Croce, 'Poesia e realtà', in idem, *Nuovi saggi sulla letteratura italiana del Seicento* (Scritti di storia letteraria e politica, 24), Bari 1949, pp. 307–12 (esp. p. 308).

poems were written to be read underneath the dome; this fact sets them apart from the prose pamphlets that were at least in some instances published to assist viewers during their visits, as is explained in the foreword of the earliest independently-published description of a ceiling in Rome, Rosichino's account of Pietro da Cortona's Barberini ceiling.[63] Written on an art work, the poems assembled in the *Poesie* and in similar collections aim to be considered, and perused, as art works in their own right.

Because they are to some extent independent of the visual fact of the art work, poems are able to verbalise some of its implicit intentions. The poems activate the illusion and the viewer's involvement in it. In superimposing their own art on the painter's, the authors of the poems create images of the fresco in which engagement with illusion does not need to be kept in check by reason. The engagement with the illusion is, to an undefinable extent, generated by poetic convention and the viewing or reading audiences' 'willing suspension of disbelief'. To recognize such engagement is to acknowledge modes of fruition of contemporary works of art by a wide stratum of society that to a large measure did not, and could not, leave traces outside poetry.

---

[63] M. Rosichino, *Dichiaratione delle pitture della sala de' Signori Barberini*, Rome 1640, pp. 3–4.

Ut Sculptura Poesis:
British Romantic Poetry and Sculptural Form

NIGEL WOOD AND ALISON YARRINGTON

We start with a recent and particularly suggestive observation by Alex Potts, that the viewing of sculpture and its position within the academy underwent a radical change in the mid-eighteenth century. For aesthetic theorists such as Johann Gottfried Herder (in his essay *Sculpture. Some Observations on Form and Shape from Pygmalion's Creative Dream* [1778; written 1768–70]) sculpture

> highlights the Pygmalion problem in two ways, firstly because a sculpted figure exists in real space and thus gives one an immediate physical sense of a human presence, and secondly because the image of the represented figure is identical to the inanimate mass of the sculpture; thus the disparity between the illusion of living flesh and the reality of the inert material is more acute in sculpture than in painting.[1]

The desire to remedy this inevitable loss of 'presence' inspired a poetic or painterly appreciation of the material form, a motivation 'to look harder and focus intently on those features of the work ... that momentarily make the fixed shape seem moving and alive'.[2] This observation is pertinent to any discussion of poetry's debt to sculptural form – and *vice versa* – in that the poetic imagination is called upon to piece out an inevitable absence within the actual sculptural body. An erotics of viewing takes over from the more distanced appreciation of ideal form that archaeological classification or cataloguing of the ancient past could provide – as with Herder so also with Reynolds and Winckelmann, as Potts also points out.[3]

It is a central component of Romantic Hellenism, especially within its poetic expression, that the nostalgic glance backwards at the glory that was Athens could only be imagined, never fully enacted. The real, but fragmentary, existence of antiquity in the museums and private collections of the day spawned many draughtsmen to supply an ideal image derived from

---

[1]   A. Potts, *The Sculptural Imagination: Figurative, Modernist, Minimalist*, New Haven, London 2000, p. 35.

[2]   Ibid.

[3]   Ibid., pp. 24–59. For a more detailed discussion of the nature of Winckelmann's interpretation of ancient art and his influence, see A. Potts, *Flesh and the Ideal: Winckelmann and the Origins of Art History*, New Haven, London 1994.

these traces; their efforts are echoed in literary appreciation which aimed to animate the cold marble that survived.

As Malcolm Baker has recently noted, the relative paucity of discussion of contemporary sculpture in the eighteenth century meant that the aesthetic of this period was formed by discourses almost archaeological in inspiration and derived predominantly from the viewing of classical examples. [4] In James Stuart and William Revett's *Antiquities of Athens* (1st. vol., 1762; 2nd. vol., edited by William Newton 1789), one of the earliest projects sponsored by the Society of Dilettanti, the catalogue of Greek remains included graphic examples, in many instances for the first time allowing some visual evidence of individual works to accompany their verbal illustration. The nostalgia of many Romantics, on the other hand, was most certainly not 'neoclassical', but forged a variety of contemporary responses involving a deep sense of loss and the necessity of imaginative recuperation. In this project, poets and sculptors were linked by a relationship of mimicry or cross-media resemblance: poets aspired to present certain poems as if they had the contained mass of sculpture, and sculptors often regarded their own work as 'poetic' – in a variety of senses.

As reported by Alexander Gilchrist in his *Life of William Blake* (first edition 1863), the poet often imaged his rather abstract compositions as capable of taking on a fixed and permanent form, approximating to the sculptural. In conversation with a lady at one of Mr Ader's parties, he recounted a meeting with a 'a fold of lambs'. He admired their 'exquisite pastoral beauty', but had to revise his ideas to some extent when he realised that they were 'no living flock, but beautiful sculpture'. The lady was eager to know where Blake had actually witnessed this scene. '*Here*, madam', Blake is supposed to have answered, 'touching his forehead' (*Life*, 1, 362–3). Blake's refusal to observe a clear distinction between the literal and the imagined may seem teasing, but, in certain contexts, could be seriously intended. It should be remembered that the fountainhead of all artistic inspiration, found in the sculptures of Los's halls in Golgonooza, provided for the poet the first model for the 'Divine Written Law', as found in the Old and New Testaments (*Jerusalem*, 16, 61–9). Blake's reverence for the sculptural is not an isolated example. Several canonical poets of the period turned to this art form for a variety of associated reasons and it is the aim of this paper to examine the grounds and effects of this admiration both for ancient and contemporary works. As with many Romantic symbols, however, the apparently other-worldly can be understood also as code to analyse the – in its widest definition – political aspirations of the period.

If one wished to study the most authoritative and perhaps pervasive view of sculpture within the academy, one might look no further than

[4]   M. Baker, *Figured in Marble: The Making and Viewing of Eighteenth-Century Sculpture*, London 2000, pp. 9–20.

Reynolds's *Tenth Discourse*, the only one reserved for sculpture, delivered in 1780. Here, the very materiality of sculpture, if limiting when compared to painting, could provide sound moral as well as aesthetic principles:

> There is no circumstance which more distinguishes a well-regulated and sound taste, than a settled uniformity of design, where all the parts are compact, and fitted to each other, every thing being of a piece. This principle extends itself to all habits of life, as well as to all works of art.[5]

The chasteness of the sculptural form should provide a sense of 'correctness', and a demonstration of the careful management of art, whereas the poet's use of 'arbitrary and conventional' signs held out a promise of variety and more readily accessible dramatic energy. To convey the ideal, however, the sculptor must suggest as well as construct on the path towards 'faultless form and perfect beauty', for dull conformity misses the vital 'sentiment and character'.[6]

These well-known reflections upon sculpture occupy just one of the fifteen Royal Academy lectures. Where 'imitation' is the end and not merely the 'means' of Art, instruction can usually be limited only to the handing on of technical and workshop tips of the trade.[7] The higher ends of Art can best be exemplified in painting; the attainment of sublimity in sculpted form derives predominantly from placement and context. The required formal perfection does not become evident in the incomplete testimony provided by Classical marbles. Turning to the celebrated late-Hellenistic *Belvedere Torso* (Pl. 45), Reynolds encounters a 'defaced and shattered fragment ... the [relic] of a work on which succeeding ages can only gaze with inadequate admiration'.[8] This shard-like entity prompts an archaeological imagination, and yet he clearly expects a natural response to be one of warm passion, 'as from the highest efforts of poetry'. Here there emerges that innate capacity to reach for what the analyst grasps as 'the perfection of [a] science of abstract form'. John Barrell, pre-eminently, perhaps, has understood this neo-Platonism as derived from an ideology where detail is absorbed into the wider pattern of Grand Style[9] – and yet the broken classical fragment evidences questions implicit in Reynolds's theory: why does this incomplete remnant from antiquity inspire such reverence for Classical form? How can the missing details be re-constructed with any certainty in the instance of the glance?

[5]   J. Reynolds, *Discourses*, P. Rogers (Ed.), Harmondsworth 1992, p. 246.
[6]   Ibid., pp. 235–6.
[7]   Ibid., p. 234.
[8]   Ibid., p. 235. For a history of the reception of the *Torso* see F. Haskell and N. Penny, *Taste and the Antique: The Lure of Classical Sculpture 1500–1900*, New Haven, London 1981, pp. 311–4.
[9]   J. Barrell, *The Political Theory of Painting from Reynolds to Hazlitt: 'The Body of the Public'*, New Haven, London 1986, pp. 102–12.

Sculpture is a problem for Reynolds in the way it rarely manages *in fact* to attain that 'abstract' patterning. The pursuit of novelty led Bernini astray from the true or correct path set by classical antiquity, and for Reynolds for the modern sculptor to ignore the lessons of formal perfection constituted a similarly fatal attraction.[10] This same distrust of Bernini may be found later in Flaxman's *Address on the Death of Thomas Banks* (1805), where he warned of the dangerous influence of the Baroque sculptor's 'taste' that 'infected and prevailed over the Florentine and Roman schools', and exerted a 'baneful' and corrupting influence.[11] In this and his later lectures, delivered as the first Professor of Sculpture at the Royal Academy, Flaxman, as David Bindman has noted, is the first British sculptor 'to talk at length about his own art'.[12] Recognised by his contemporaries for his deeply 'poetic' nature, he provides a useful point of reference for any consideration of connections between Romantic poetry and sculpture, although it has to be recognised that his Reynoldsian view of Bernini was not particularly original. Indeed, in this instance, he could be seen to be confirming a widely-held and long-lasting antipathy towards any sculptural form that strayed away from the straight and narrow path of expressing inner 'truth' into the empty gestures of excessive, external description, thus placing the immediately fashionable above the eternal.

Transposing such sentiments into a consideration of contemporary art the Scottish painter David Wilkie noted the empty rhetoric of sculpture produced in Rome: 'draperies prevail over flesh, and flesh over feature; and sculpture will, like painting, become mere decoration if the inward man does not occupy some share of its attention'.[13] Poetry, given this perspective, seems appealingly free of the contingent and can range more freely due to its obviously abstract medium.

Reynolds's lament at an inevitable disconnection from the past is evident in many Romantic poetic anthologies. For every 'Tintern Abbey', a disquisition on a successful healing of this breach, there is an 'Ozymandias', a poetic fragment about a 'colossal wreck' (v. 13) of a *sculptural* fragment.

[10] See for example his often-quoted verdict on Bernini's *Neptune*, especially the portrayal of the hair 'flying abroad in all directions' and producing 'an entangled confusion ... produced by drapery flying off; which the eye must, for the same reason, inevitably mingle and confound with the principle [sic] parts of the figure'; Reynolds 1992 (as in n. 5, above), p. 241.

[11] J. Flaxman, 'An Address to the President and Members of the Royal Academy on the Death of Thomas Banks, Sculptor', in idem, *Lectures on Sculpture*, London 1881, pp. 275–99 (esp. pp. 282, 284). Flaxman was appointed Professor in 1810.

[12] D. Bindman, 'Flaxman as Professor of Sculpture', in *John Flaxman, R.A.*, D. Bindman (Ed.), London 1979, pp. 131–3 (esp. p. 131).

[13] A. Cunningham, *The Life of Sir David Wilkie with his Journals, Tours and Critical Remarks on Works of Art; and a Selection from his Correspondence*, 3 vols, London 1843, vol. 2, p. 224, letter to Raimbach from Rome dated 10 January 1826.

Published by Leigh Hunt in *The Examiner* for January, 1818, Shelley's poem narrates how a 'traveller from an antique land' (v. 1) summons up the unencompassable size of what we have lost alongside the 'boundless and bare | ... lone and level sands [that] stretch far away' (v. 13–14). The closing isolation of the traveller becomes ours as well, beached on this particular shore of history. This is, however, only one of the sentiments in the poem. Even the fragmentary bears the still living imprint of heart as well as hand of the sculptor. The radical politics of the *Examiner* has been well researched,[14] and Shelley's undoubted agenda at the time of writing, in 1817, made plain. Whereas Reynolds was at pains to track an abstract 'science' of form implied in the antique sculptural fragment, Shelley identifies a once-beating heart, full of a conviction that regal ambition is bound to disappointment *sub specie aeternitatis*. Ozymandias was perhaps the first indication of Shelley's almost macabre nostalgia, amounting to tragedy, at the decay of a colossally conceived grand past, yet his celebration of grand fragments is quite deliberately set in the form of a poetic fragment. Nearly eighteen months later Shelley was to undertake his own sculptural tour of the antique which he wrote up in notebooks published by Thomas Medwin in the *Athenaeum* in 1832 and then in a collected version in the *Shelley Papers* (1833). Not surprisingly Rome and Florence provide for Shelley only glimpses of a grander, and so an idealised, past. His tour through classical antiquity does not introduce particularly radical perspectives on the classical legacy, but the overall effect is one of elegy and of an imagination stirred by the missing dimensions that can only be recaptured in the imagination. In the paper first published in the *Athenaeum* for 22 September 1832 Shelley describes a statue of Minerva. His note exhibits a wrestling with the limitations of words when describing the sculptural ideal. He is drawn to 'the tremendous spirit of superstition' evident only when imagining its original placement on an altar to Bacchus: pleasure and beauty provide an uneasy amalgam, a specifically Greek phenomenon for Shelley: 'only capable of existing in Greece because there alone capable of combining ideal beauty and poetical and abstract enthusiasm with the wild errors from which it sprung'.[15] The climax of the visit to Florence is the poet's encounter with the figure of Niobe, which is reconstructed as the protagonist in an agonistic narrative. Her beauty is a summation of the whole composition, and Shelley's difficulties result from his apparent inability to capture 'the careless majesty which Nature stamps upon those rare master-pieces, of her creation, harmonising them as it were from the harmony of the spirit within'.[16]

---

[14] See especially R. Cronin, 'John Keats and the Politics of Cockney Style', *Studies in English Literature, 1500–1900*, 36, 1996, pp. 785–808.

[15] *The Complete Works of Percy Bysshe Shelley*, R. Ingpen and W. E. Peck (Eds), 10 vols, London, New York 1965, vol. 6, p. 323.

[16] Ibid., vol. 6, p. 332.

What drew the Romantic poets to these often fractured and incomplete antique forms? Why did Shelley bother to note them? Was it merely part of the finishing school of a grand tour, or part of a much larger project where the past figured in sculpture became an active agent informing a perspective on the present?

Perhaps a more symptomatic example is Keats's oft-quoted 'Ode on a Grecian Urn', first published in the *Annals of the Fine Arts*, vol. 15 (January 1820). The urn is the summation of a timeless moment and, simultaneously, its death. It might be 'unravished' (v. 1) at the same time as being a 'Cold pastoral' (v. 45); the Ode in its recursive return to the object itself provides an enactment of the Urn's narrative, 'ever circling', with no start or end point. This is the trope throughout the whole of the *Ode on Indolence*, written in the summer of 1819. Here, the relief figures of Fame, Love and 'Poesy' pass and re-pass before the viewer, initially as s/he scans the 'marble urn' (v. 5), and then as they participate in the reverie of her/his indolent, 'dim dreams' (v. 42). For Keats, the apparent materiality of the object is a preliminary detail, chosen for its facility in evoking dreams and abstract thought. It should be pointed out at this juncture that Keats is not dealing, quite deliberately, with the classical legacy as affected by historical transmission. The urn seems to stand clear of the decay and loss that normally accrues to historical items. Keats's interest in ancient Greek art appears to be a preoccupation with the timeless, yet literary historians have located a precise set of codes and conventions that enlist these works, and the 'more naked and grecian Manner'[17] of his *Hyperion* (1820), as the poet's oblique attempt at a comment on contemporary politics, heavily influenced by the painter Haydon. There is some evidence that any support of Greek art at this time must have inevitably participated in the moral and aesthetic debates surrounding the Elgin Marbles.[18] Their acquisition brought to the fore several associated anxieties about modern culture, such as those surrounding the ethics of appropriation.[19] Unlike Shelley's 'antique traveller', this art lover (Elgin) had packaged up the fragments and anglicised them. Keats took this example much to heart. In two sonnets written no later than March 1817, Keats recounts his own initial encounter with the marbles in Haydon's company. In

[17] Letter to Benjamin Robert Haydon, 23 January 1818, in *Letters of John Keats, a New Selection*, Robert Gittings (Ed.), Oxford, 1970, p. 51. See also I. Jack, *Keats and the Mirror of Art*, Oxford, 1967, esp. pp. 214–24 and M. Aske, *Keats and Hellenism: An Essay*, Cambridge 1985, pp. 182–7.

[18] T. M. Kelley, 'Keats, Ekphrasis, and History', in *Keats and History*, N. Roe (Ed.), Cambridge 1995, pp. 212–37.

[19] Byron's 'The Curse of Minerva', 1811, provides the most trenchant attack on Elgin's project. Minerva addresses the despoilers of the Hellenic heritage: 'Long of their patron's gusto let them tell, | Whose noblest, *native* gusto is – to sell: | To sell, and make – may shame record the day! – the state receiver of his pilfer'd prey.' (v. 170–3).

'On Seeing the Elgin Marbles' he recognises 'the shadow of a magnitude' (v. 14) and in the sonnet addressed directly to Haydon he excuses himself from not speaking 'definitively on these mighty things' (v. 2). Indeed, the object of the sonnets is to celebrate Haydon's friendship rather than to explore sculptural excellence.

Neither Shelley nor Keats share Blake's aspiration toward 'sculptural' symbolism. For both poets, there is an eventual disintegration of certitude and an uncomfortable encounter with the apparently monumental and material. Blake had found sculptural form an incarnation of his thoughts; with Keats and probably Shelley, the reverse was true, as the object dissolves into poetic air. This only appears to be a cue for plangent regret, however, as, just as a sculpture loses its distinctiveness in the poems quoted, it provokes memorable sentiments on temporality and *contemporary* motives for art. As Walter Jackson Bate noted, '... no possible fulfilment exists for the figures on the urn apart from what the responsive mind can give them'. [20] It is the very inscrutability of the antique fragments in *Ozymandias* that renders them so poetic.

Romantic Hellenism has at one and the same time an obvious affinity with the classical past and a less obvious determination to place it within the contemporary. Shelley's observation of classical fragments was less a means of verbal preservation than an investigation into at least two regency preoccupations: on the one hand, a relationship with the past that was under severe strain, and on the other an excursion into the future that was built upon these ruins. The past is inspirationally still there in front of the artist, but as it were under erasure, defaced by the passage of time *and* the need of the artist to break free from the oppressive burden of classical antiquity. Romantic poetry concerned with Hellenistic themes rarely referred back directly to Winckelmann,[21] whose *Reflections on the Painting and Sculpture of the Greeks* (translated by Fuseli in 1765) discovered 'eine edle Einfalt, und eine stille Grösse',[22] in Fuseli's translation, a 'noble simplicity and sedate grandeur'.[23] In the examples quoted above, the mind is anything but still and the sentiments are decidedly complex.

If Flaxman were to be our benchmark when considering Romantic theories of sculpture, we would see far less of that sense of regret for a lost world than a more optimistic hope that a new Greece might soon be born, albeit imbued with Christianity. As Flaxman is supposed to have remarked to Ludwig Schorn when discussing his lectures to the Academy, 'It was my

[20] *John Keats*, Cambridge, Mass.1963, p. 513.
[21] William Hayley, in his *Essay on Sculpture, in a Series of Poetical Epistles to John Flaxman, R.A.*, London, 1800, Epistle 5, lines 483–500, describes Winckelmann as an historian of art 'Who, with enlighten'd love, described the whole, | Each changeful feature, and her inmost soul' (v. 499–500).
[22] *Winckelmanns Werke*, C. L. Fernow (Ed.), 8 vols, Dresden 1808–20, vol. 1, p. 31.
[23] Ibid., vol. 1, p. 30.

purpose [....] to show that art in Christianity can rise higher than in paganism, since Christian ideas are more sublime than pagan ones, and the best that art of Greece and Rome has produced is, to my mind, also contained in Christian ideas'.[24] For Richard Westmacott, in his first lecture as Flaxman's successor as Professor of Sculpture, his predecessor 'not only supported the purity of Sculpture, but carried us within the dominion of Poetry, and taught us its value in art; he boldly passed the barrier which had so long encircled sculpture, and walked freely into the regions of invention'.[25] Flaxman avidly copied details from the Elgin Marbles,[26] and even adopted ideals of poetic unity when describing sculptural excellence. In his sixth RA lecture on 'Composition', he equated the words of the poet with the 'action' depicted in painting and sculpture.[27] Just as the most epic poetic action emphasised the *agon* of an individual, a similar focus was desirable in marble or stone:

> The ancients, who considered simplicity as a characteristic of perfection, represented stories by a single row of figures in the bas-relief, by which the whole outline of the figure or group, the energy of action, the concatenation of limbs, the flight or flow of drapery were seen with little interruption.[28]

'Simplicity and distinctness' governed Greek composition in all the Arts; it comes as no surprise that Flaxman considered this as correct for his and Romantic Hellenic art in general. It should, however, be remembered that the closing and climactic example of 'Modern Sculpture' (as is the case in Reynolds's discourse on sculpture that he delivered to the Academy) derived from 'the sacred writings' and not from sculpture. Instead, he chose Milton's *Paradise Lost*,[29] and in this selection, he had Blake, Fuseli and Keats as companions. The epic similes of Milton's blank verse are shorn of some of their artistic excess and are emphasised as the material of dramatic focus and conflict. Life is given to the soul of action; as William Hayley, Flaxman's friend and promoter,[30] is at pains to point out, this is a common virtue to both Milton and Flaxman: 'Feelings like these the fervent Milton found, | Roving, in studious use, o'er Tuscan ground' (Epistle 1, lines 222–223). This poetic technique was derived for both artists from a thorough grounding in classical precedent. This was no antiquarian spirit, however, as the major

[24] Ludwig Schorn's reminiscences of his visit to Flaxman's studio appeared in *Kunst-Blatt* in 1827 and are translated in Bindman 1979 (as in n. 12, above), pp. 30–2.

[25] 'Extracts from Sir Richard Westmacott's First Lecture, delivered at the Royal Academy, on his Succession to the Chair of Professor of Sculpture after the Death of Flaxman', in Flaxman 1881 (as in n. 11, above), pp. vii–xii (esp. p. ix).

[26] See D. Irwin, *John Flaxman 1755–1826*, London 1979, pp. 174–5.

[27] Flaxman 1881 (as in n. 11, above), p. 151.

[28] Ibid., p. 153.

[29] Ibid., pp. 271–2.

[30] Bindman notes that Hayley's relationship with Flaxman was 'positive', see Bindman 1979 (as in n. 12, above), p. 27.

concern of the more modern artist is to give life to these models 'with attic vigour in an English breast' (Epistle 1, line 207). Hayley's voluminous *Essay on Sculpture* (1800) codified such judgements across six epistles, with Flaxman emerging as the 'First of poetic minds!'[31] Paradoxically, his completed sculptures – if compared with the surface subtleties of Canova's works – were distinctly un-poetic in their execution and it was generally acknowledged that he was not particularly concerned with the niceties of finish but with the generative point of the work, the first sketch and model, and with the composition.[32] This is apparent in a work that takes as its subject a contemporary poet, the plaster sketch model 'Statue of a lady, authoress of "Psyche" a poem' (Pl. 46), the design for the marble monument raised to Mary Tighe at Inistioge, County Kilkenny, where she is buried.[33]

At what level then was Flaxman poetic? It could be argued that this appellation was primarily descriptive, an artist whose international reputation was based upon his outline illustrations to ancient and early modern poetry. As a biographer and foreman of a sculptor's studio – but particularly as a poet – Allan Cunningham could be seen to be the ideal person to assess Flaxman's contribution to these sister arts. Their meeting is recorded by Cunningham as taking place in 1825, at the end of Flaxman's life, when Cunningham was gathering material for his Vasarian project, *The Lives of the Most Eminent British Painters, Sculptors, and Architects*, the volume in which Flaxman's biography appears being published in 1830.[34] Of their meeting in Flaxman's studio, he states their conversation was 'all concerning poetry and poets'[35] and he notes their shared enthusiasm for the poetry of Robert Burns.[36] In defining

---

[31] W. Hayley, Epistle 1, line 303.

[32] M. Webster, 'Flaxman as Sculptor', in Bindman 1979 (as in n. 12, above), pp. 100–11. Webster sees Flaxman's real strengths lying 'in the expression of more intimate piety and of poetry' rather than in the large-scale public sculptures that he was employed upon. She also notes his 'pernicious practice of handing over the entire execution of the marble to workmen in his studio'. Bindman comes to similar conclusions and sees Flaxman's use of assistants very much in the same mode as the draughtsman handing over his drawings for engraving (see D. Bindman, 'Art and Commerce', in Bindman 1979 (as in n. 12, above), pp. 25–29 (esp. p. 28).

[33] For a discussion of these two works, see Webster 1979 (as in n. 32, above), p. 110, who cites Felicia Hemans's enthusiasm for this melancholy site. Tighe's poem, 'Psyche, or the Legend of Love,' was published in 1795. H. Devine Jump, *Women's Writing in the Romantic Period, 1789–1836. An Anthology*, Edinburgh 1997, p. xvi, has pointed out the 'powerful and passionate sensuality' contained in the poem.

[34] Their meeting seems surprisingly late, given that Cunningham had been in London, working since 1814 in Francis Chantrey's studio.

[35] Alan Cunningham, *The Lives of the Most Eminent British Painters, Sculptors, and Architects*, 6 vols, London 1830, vol. 3, p. 356.

[36] Ibid., p. 355: 'Flaxman was an admirer of Burns and a quoter of his poetry'.

Flaxman's 'poetic power' as natural, he points out that 'no causal or accidental inspiration' was involved.[37] Citing Thomas Lawrence's 'Address on the Death of Flaxman', he states that the sculptor's style was 'founded on Grecian art – on its noblest principles – on its deeper intellectual power, and not on mere surface or skill. Though master of its purest lines, he was still more the sculptor of sentiment than of form'.[38] To give this point of view further credence he refers to the view of the poet Thomas Campbell that 'Flaxman is stiff in the workmanship of his marble only – there is much simplicity but no stiffness in his conceptions'.[39] What seems like an excuse for poor workmanship nevertheless points to an understanding in Flaxman's own terms of the 'chaste' nature of sculpture as he conceives it in the true Grecian mode. What was the poetic in sculpture but that which was evoked or imagined, the object merely being the prompt for higher thought?

If during Flaxman's lifetime there were an international contender for the role of the most 'poetic' of sculptors it would undoubtedly be Canova, not only in terms of the sculpture produced but also the verses and prose penned in his praise.

Pindemonte's 'On the Hebe of Canova' (Pl. 47), for example, was translated by one of the most popular English poets of the day, Felicia Hemans:

> O thou, Canova! Soaring high above
> Italian art – with Grecian magic vying!
> We knew thy marble glowed with life and love,
> But who had seen thee image footsteps flying!
>
> Here to each eye the wind seems gently playing
> With the light vest, its wavy folds arraying
> In many a line of undulating grace;
> While Nature, ne'er her mighty laws suspending,
> Stands, before marble thus with motion blending,
> One moment lost in thought, its hidden cause to trace.[40]

Cunningham collected and edited Burns's poetry; see *The Works of Robert Burns; with his Life*, London 1834. *A Catalogue of the Small but Valuable Library of Books, Chiefly Relating to Classical Literature and the Fine Arts, Books of Prints, and Antiquities of John Flaxman, Esq. R.A. Dec. [....] Sold by Auction, by Mr. Christie, June 12th, 1828*, London 1828, p. 4, itemises copies of Burns's *Works*, 5 vols, London 1813 (no. 12) and the poetry of Gray , 'Ossian' (both no. 10) and Cowper's *Milton* (no. 13).

[37] Cunningham 1830 (as in n. 35, above), p. 364.
[38] Ibid., p. 362.
[39] Ibid., p. 367.
[40] *The Poetical Works of Mrs. Hemans Reprinted from the Early Editions with Explanatory Notes, etc.*, London, New York 1887, p. 707. For Pindemonte's poem 'Per l'Ebe del prelodato Scultore', see I. Pindemonte, *Le Poesie originali di Ippolito Pindemonte publicate per cura del Dott. Alessandro Torri con un discorso di Pietro*

In a posthumous account of the Italian's work, published in the year that Cunningham and Flaxman first met, Canova's sculpture was characterised as having 'a certain indefinable charm, diffused over, and emanating from them, – a something altogether ethereal and intellectual that transports the mind, yet mocks the palpable and grosser scrutiny of the senses'.[41] This is likened not to the sense of touch or sound, but to smell: 'Thus, an agreeable perfume, concealed within a precious vase, sheds a balmy atmosphere around that softly steals over the soul, while the sight alone appears delighted by the noble shrine in which the latest sweetness is imprisoned'.[42] The route to this pleasurable engagement with the object is quite distinct: Canova's sculptural sensuality with its seductive, almost voluptuous, surfaces may be seen to be almost in opposition to the chaste remoteness of the works produced by his British counterpart, and yet each required imaginative engagement for the full comprehension of poetic sculptural form. Flaxman's own appreciation of Canova's poetic sculptural style was given public voice at the Academy when he delivered his 'Address ... on the Death of Signor Canova':

> In considering the style of this artist's sculpture, we shall at once acknowledge a poetic fancy which gave a luminous interest to his conversation, equally with his compositions; his figures are graceful, his forms grand, muscle, tendon or bone most naturally distinguished, and the flesh seems yielding to the touch, by an execution as powerful as delicate.[43]

Dal Rio, Florence 1853, p. 421: 'O Canova immortal, che addietro lassi | L'italico scarpello, e il greco arrivi, | Sapea, che i marmi tuoi son molli, e vivi; | Ma chi visto t'avea scolpire i passi? | Spirar qui vento ogni pupilla crede, | E la gonna investir, che frettolosa | Si ripiega ondeggiando, e indietro riede; | E Natura, onde legge ebbe ogni cosa, | Che pietra, e moto in un congiunti vede, | Per un instante si riman pensosa'. An alternative emphasis for the latter sentiments can be found in *The Works of Antonio Canova in Sculpture and Modelling, Engraved in Outline by Henry Moses; with Descriptions from the Italian of the Countess Albrizzi, and a Biographical Memoir by Count Cicognara*, 3 vols, London 1824–28, vol. 1, no. LXVI: 'While Nature's self, whose law the world obeys, | Deceived by mimic art, believes a stone | With motion gifted, swiftly passing on'. For a modern translation, see that provided in the entry in *Antonio Canova*, exh. cat., Venice 1992, p. 264, which gives a history of the four versions of the statue. Vittorio Barzoni's *L'Ebe del Cavalier Antonio che trovarsi nella Casa Albrizzi in Venezia*, Padua 1811, provides a rhapsodic interpretation in prose, 'Bella come l'alba d'un bel giorno' (p. 6). Hebe's sculptural form is analysed: 'Le variazione di tante forme non sono ineguaglianze, ma svariati tuoni d'una melodia celeste' (p. 8).

[41] J. S. Memes, *Memoirs of Antonio Canova with a Critical Analysis of his Works, and an Historical View of Modern Sculpture*, Edinburgh 1825, p. 349.

[42] Ibid., p. 350.

[43] J. Flaxman, 'An Address to the President and Members of the Royal Academy, on the Death of Signor Canova, Marquis of Ischia', in Flaxman 1881 (as in n. 11, above), pp. 300–8 (esp. p. 304).

Flaxman did, however, qualify this statement with the remark that 'we sometimes seek in vain for the severe chastity of Grecian Art', but sees this as partly due to Canova's native artistic environment in which he imbibed 'a strong bias from the imposing and luxurious paintings of the Venetian school'.[44]

Canova's death, as Flaxman's oration suggests, was a moment for retrospective analysis of the man and his work both at home and abroad. In two major English collections of contemporary sculpture, those at Woburn and Chatsworth, the arrangement of the sculpture galleries subtly emphasised his lasting pre-eminence amongst modern sculptors to the viewer. At Woburn the visitor would enter the gallery through an ante-room hung with prints after Canova's works,[45] and, at the far end of the gallery, the Temple of the Graces (containing the sculptor's famous group *The Three Graces*) was heralded by the surtitles of Samuel Rogers's Pindaric ode over its entrance.[46] At the time of Canova's death William Cavendish, 6th Duke of Devonshire was in the process of furnishing a new gallery at Chatsworth to house his growing collection of contemporary sculpture including several important pieces by Canova.[47] The final arrangement emphasised the friendship between the two men with the Duke's bust by Thomas Campbell and Carlo Rinaldi's bust of Canova placed in matching niches high on the wall to either side of the north entrance to the gallery. Below the busts to either side of the doorway were placed full-size copies by Francesco Bengaglia and Rinaldi after

[44]   Ibid., p. 305.
[45]   This arrangement is mentioned by an early visitor to the Temple of the Graces, see 'Private View of the Collection of Ancient and Modern Sculpture, in the Gallery of his Grace the Duke of Bedford, at Woburn Abbey, in the County of Bedford', *Annals of the Fine Arts*, 5, 1820, pp. 415–20, and was still in place when described by P. F. Robinson, *Vitruvius Britannicus. History of Woburn Abbey: Illustrated by Plans, Elevations, and Internal Views of the Apartments from Actual Measurement*, London, 1833, p. 15
[46]   Further testimony to the connections between Canova's works and poetry can be found in the privately-published text by the Duke of Bedford, *Outline Engravings and Descriptions of the Woburn Abbey Marbles*, London 1822, with outline engravings by Henry Moses, in which Foscolo's poem 'Le Grazie' is included along with the description of the much-prized group by Canova. The volume was only privately circulated as G. F. Waagen noted in his *Works of Art and Artists in England*, 3 vols, London 1838, vol. 3, p. 345. For poetic and other responses to the *Graces*, see G. Venturi, 'Grace and the Graces', in *Antonio Canova* 1992 (as in n. 40, above), pp. 69–75.
[47]   The most treasured by the Duke were the *Hebe* (1808–14), a colossal bust of *Napoleon* (1803), *Madame Mere* (1804–7) and, perhaps most precious of all, *Endymion* (1819–22). The collection also includes a bronze copy after his celebrated *Penitent Magdalene*. For an account of the Duke's trip to Italy and his pursuit of the *Endymion*, see J. Lees-Milne, *The Bachelor Duke, a Life of William Spencer Cavendish 6th Duke of Devonshire*, London 1991, pp. 55–7.

Canova's lions from the tomb of Pope Clement XIII (1783–92, marble, Saint Peter's, Rome), commissioned when the Duke made a visit to Rome, having received news of Canova's death. This arrangement, seen across the gallery space when entering from the house, was conceived after Canova's death and thus forms a dedicatory and commemorative note proclaiming Canova's continuing pre-eminence. The 6th Duke's desperate desire to ensure delivery of the much-prized *Endymion,* which he feared would not be released from Canova's Roman studio after the sculptor's death, is another indicator of his passionate engagement with the Italian's sculpture, shared with other members of his family, as evidenced by his stepmother Elizabeth Hervey's proposed monument to the sculptor for the Accademia di San Luca. [48]

For many Canova was the 'second Phidias', no more so than in Italy and in particular in his native Venice, his works having vied successfully with those of antiquity. [49] The emerging cult of Canova, evidence of which is found both in the many poetic tributes paid during his lifetime – of which those by Foscolo, Pindemonte and Missirini are pre-eminent – was intensified by his death and the sense of loss. His post mortem revealed that even his physical self was imprinted by the pressure of the *trapano,* 'an instrument of iron constantly employed by sculptors in working'; he had in effect died for his art. [50] The devotional zeal that followed his death is evidenced by his lying in state at the Academy in Venice; his funeral on 16 October 1822; the encasement of his heart in a porphyry vase to be kept in the Academy; his hand sent to the Accademia di San Luca in Rome; medals struck in his memory; [51] poetic eulogies and written testimonies to his national status; [52] subscriptions for his monument in Venice (to which Byron was a subscriber) [53]

[48] See C. M. S. Johns, *Antonio Canova and the Politics of Patronage in Revolutionary and Napoleonic Europe,* Berkeley, Los Angeles, London 1998, pp. 197–8.

[49] See for example Luigi Zandomenghi's 'Il genio delle Belle Arti incorona il busto di Canova' etching, Padua, Museo Civico, where Canova's bust is raised on a pedestal bearing the inscription 'NEV PHIDIAE | SECUNDO'; see E. Bassi et al., *Venezia nell'età di Canova 1780–1830,* Venice 1978, p. 262. In the context of casts made in England by a Mr. Shout after Canova's works, the Italian sculptor is described as 'our modern Phidias', see *Annals of the Fine Arts,* 3, 1818, p. 632.

[50] Memes 1825 (as in n. 41, above), p. 511. As Memes notes, Canova's death seemed to have been the end result of 'too close an application of professional pursuits; this evidently appeared from an external depression of the right breast, occasioned by bearing against the trapano, – an instrument of iron constantly employed by sculptors in working'.

[51] M. Missirini, 'Dichiarazione delle Medaglie coniate in onore di Antonio Canova', in idem, *Della Vita di Antonio Canova Libri Quattro Compilati da Melchior Missirini,* Prato 1824, n.p.

[52] See Memes 1825 (as in n. 41, above), p. 521, n. 1: 'In Venice, during the course of the Winter following his death, two volumes of poetical tributes, composed on that occasion, were republished in a collected form'. Here Memes is presumably referring to Missirini's *Versi sui Marmi di Canova* which he cites on p. 337.

and the temple raised at his birth place, Possagno.[54] In his poem, 'In Morte di Antonio Canova',[55] Pindemonte used the sculptor's death to convey a sense of nostalgic loss and to affirm his Promethean pre-eminence in sculpture: 'Se un suo di membra tondeggiar, di panni | Se un ondeggiar io miro, | Con gli occhi misurar parmi i miei danni, | E il mirar non é mai senza un sospiro. | Chi alle teste saprà dar più quel giro?'.[56] Pindemonte here constructs Canova's position in terms of sustaining national pride and the poem includes a challenge to Italian sculptors to strive further in their art following Canova's path and not to allow foreign challengers to seize the crown left unclaimed as a consequence of his death: 'E non lasciate a uno scarpello estrano | Quel regno a lungo conservar',[57] and to resist the Goth-like forces that currently threatened their artistic status: 'Ah non ci vinca il Goto | Della pace anco nel tranquillo grembo!'[58] For Wilkie, visiting Canova's now deserted studio in Rome in 1826, the loss of 'presence' (the living body of the sculptor) was palpable; the reputation the sculptor left behind him was apt to inhibit those who followed; his departure was felt intimately.[59]

As Byron's subscription to Canova's monument suggests, the exiled poet was particularly drawn to his work; further evidence to this effect is provided by his celebration 'On the Bust of Helen by Canova' (November

53   *Il Monumento a Canova eretto in Venezia*, Venice 1827, pp. 19–23, provides a complete list of subscribers to the project, amongst which the largest number outside the Italian states were from Britain. This monument, initiated by the Accademia delle Belle Arti, Venice, was raised in S. Maria Gloriosa dei Frari. For further evidence of the various responses to Canova's death, see E. Bassi et al. 1978 (as in n. 47, above), pp. 258–64.

54   For a detailed account of the ways in which Canova's death acted as a political symbol, see Johns 1998 (as in n. 46, above), pp. 195–200.

55   Pindemonte 1853 (as in n. 40, above), pp. 413–7.

56   Ibid., p. 415: 'Whenever I see the rounded forms of a figure, or the fluttering of draperies it is as if I took stock of my pains, and the act of beholding is never without a sigh – who will ever be able to give heads the same turn ?'.

57   Ibid., p. 416. 'And do not let any foreign chisel occupy that realm which he now controls'.

58   Ibid., 'Let not the Goth overcome us even in the calm bosom of peace'. By 1822 the achievements of several northern sculptors were internationally in the ascendant providing a far more correct response to Greek antiquity than Canova's decorative style. In terms of a symbolic resistance to Austrian rule, it could be that here Pindemonte refers to the Austrian sculptor, Franz Anton Zauner, who was professor of sculpture at the Vienna Academy and the sculptor most closely linked with Emperor Joseph II, but as he died in the same year as Canova it is more likely that Pindemonte was thinking of other 'northern' sculptural stars such as Dannecker, Schadow and Thorvaldsen.

59   Cunningham 1843 (as in n. 13, above), vol. 2, pp. 214–6. Canova's Roman studio was open to the public, who could see the plaster models and terracottas on view until they were removed to the Tempio at Possagno in the 1830s.

1816),[60] and his admiration for 'what Nature *could*, but *would not*, do' (v. 3) (Pl. 49). In purely literary historical circles, these are seen as evidence of Byron's yearning for the absolute, and his deep appreciation of the head as 'the most perfectly beautiful of human conceptions', which lay 'far beyond [his] ideas of human execution'.[61] The bust stood distinct for Byron, as he found himself steeped pleasurably in the decay, mystery and sexual decadence of Venice. Canova's work was to provide a moment of magical perfection, and, as the letter to his publisher, John Murray, testifies, was part of an immersion in what he felt were the 'voluptuous feelings' in the salon of the Tuscan-Greek Countess Isabella Teotochi Albrizzi, where he was eventually to view the Head.[62] A few years later, Henry Moses attempted to introduce the 'English reader' to this particular effect by including descriptions of the works penned by the Countess and translated from the Italian alongside his line engravings. In his introduction, Moses directed attention to these texts as 'calculated to produce on the beholder, – effects which no graphic representation can be expected fully to supply'.[63] Consistent with this, and in celebration of her prized possession, the Countess had earlier collected together celebratory poems by contemporary authors, making Byron's response only one amongst many.[64] The Countess's own study of Canova's works (from which Moses had taken his text) had prompted this exquisite gift.[65] For her the *Head of Helen* was the embodiment of 'those ardent but indefinite ideas about Helen's beauty, which are raised in our minds by the reading of the ancient story'.[66] Here the sculptor was 'unfettered by the duty

[60]   'In this beloved marble view | Above the works and thoughts of Man – | What Nature could – but would not do – | And Beauty and Canova can! | Beyond Imagination's power – | Beyond the Bard's defeated art, | With immortality her dower – | Behold the Helen of the heart!'.

[61]   *Lord Byron: Selected Letters and Journals*, L. A. Marchand (Ed.), London 1982, p. 140.

[62]   It is interesting to note that Giannantonio Moschini in his *Guida per la città di Venezia*, 2 vols., Venice 1815, vol. 1, p. 619, includes the *Head of Helen* with details of provenance as one of the important items on view in the vicinity of Sta. Maria Zobenico.

[63]   In *The Works of Antonio Canova* 1824–28 (as in n. 40, above), vol. 1, p. 2.

[64]   See 'Poesie di autori vari in occasione della statua di Elena del Canova', carteggi Albrizzi, in the Biblioteca Civica, Verona. Many of these poems were included in a compilation of writings in various forms by several authors after Canova's death, a monumental work to his memory: *Biblioteca Canoviana ossia Raccolta delle migliori prose, e de' più scelti componimenti poetici sulla vita, sulle opere ed in morte di Antonio Canova*, 4 vols, Venice 1823–4. For commentary upon the wide range of literary responses across Europe to Canova's work and their part in forming the Canova 'myth', see F. Mazzocca, 'Canova: A Myth in his own Lifetime', in *Antonio Canova* 1992 (as in n. 40, above), pp. 77–87.

[65]   I. Teotochi Albrizzi, *Opere di Scultura e di Plastica di Antonio Canova descritte da Isabella Albrizzi, nata Teotochi* (1809), 4 vols, Pisa 1821–24.

of imagination [and] was at liberty to indulge his excited fancy in investing her image with the most exquisite beauty'.[67] The 'Grecian' face she sees as 'animated with a gentle and bewitching smile' and she recognises the duality of the image, the 'dignity of a goddess' combined 'with the expression of human passions'. In the act of gazing upon this marble evocation of antique beauty 'respectful and voluptuous feelings contend within us, but beauty is finally triumphant'.[68] It is clear that Byron knew of her own celebrated *Ritratti* (Brescia 1807, Padua 1808 and Venice 1816), as he praises it alongside her *Opere di Scultura e di Plastica di Antonio Canova descritte* and/or her pamphlet *La Testa d'Elena scolpita in marmo dall'Impareggiabil Canova da esso regalata ad Isabella Albrizzi nata Teotochi* (Pisa 1812) in his letter to Thomas Moore of 24 December 1816.[69] In her own person she was a woman who was seen as an extraordinary individual by many contemporaries, Vivant Denon describing her as having 'dans un même visage, la finesse Gréque, la passion Italienne, l'amabilité Française [...]'.[70] A caricature of Canova in the act of sculpting her bust – his chisel placed between her breasts – entitled 'il vero Ritratto dell'imortal scultore, e pittore Co.e Marc:e Cavaliere Canova. Sortito dal disegno delle belle arti di Venezia .' probably published after 1816,[71] makes witty allusion to the dual nature of the exchange of compliments between sculptor and author with the words 'Amazone Greca', inscribed on the pedestal upon which the bust is placed.

Canova's ability to bring together nuances of nature within apparently antique-like forms came to be regarded as the ultimate in seductiveness as marble became flesh in the imagination. Byron's admirer and biographer, the Irish poet, Thomas Moore, was awakened to this alchemic talent in Rome whilst in the company of Chantrey and Canova. Running their hands and eyes over Paolina Borghese's semi-recumbent sculpted form in a closed room, they sensed an aesthetic and secret act of initiation accessible in this instance only to the select few, where a '... lingering hand would steal | O'er every grace'.[72] Thomas Dibdin visiting Dannecker's Stuttgart studio in 1818

---

[66] *The Works of Antonio Canova 1824–28* (as in n. 40, above), vol. 2 (1824), n.p.
[67] Ibid.
[68] Ibid.
[69] Ibid., p. 149.
[70] 'In the same face, Grecian delicacy, Italian passion, French kindness', letter to Constantino Zacco from Vivant Denon, cited in C. Giorgetti, *Rittrato di Isabella. Studi e documenti su Isabella Teotochi Albrizzi* (Università degli studi di Firenze, Facoltà di Lettere e Filosofia. Quaderni Aldo Palazzeschi, 4), Florence 1992, p. 17. As noted by Romanelli, there was an 'obvious association' between the two Greek-born women, the one from the ancient world, the other from the modern, a nuanced compliment from sculptor to author; see G. Romanelli, 'A Yearning for Home', *Antonio Canova 1992* (as in n. 40, above), pp. 57–8.
[71] Giorgetti 1992 (as above), fig. 9.
[72] *Paolina Borghese as Venus Victorious*, 1805–8, marble, Rome, Galleria Borghese. T.

experienced a similar thrill of engagement with the sculpted object when, under the instruction of the sculptor, he ran his hands across the marble brow of a bust of Schiller, sensing the fount of poetic imagination through its 'almost imperceptible gradations'[73] (Pl. 49).

Byron's own references to marble and sculptural form are very much part of a set of nostalgic themes, part personal, part a comment on a diminished European heritage. Where Canova had managed to capture a complete and finished image of neoclassical beauty, the classical sites to which Byron refers in both *Don Juan* and *Childe Harold's Pilgrimage* provide sculpture that is both neglected and disturbingly fragmentary. This is insistently so in Canto IV of *Childe Harold* (1818), Byron's poetic tour through Italy. Childe Harold has often defied easy categorisation, but the general irony of his pilgrimage is that, in the modern age, a holy destination no longer exists. What remains has been ravaged by recent war and political timorousness. Childe Harold, when visiting the Capitoline Museum in Rome, surveys a figure now identified as the *Dying Gaul*, but then considered a *Dying Gladiator* (Pl. 50).[74] Byron is torn between contending sentiments: that the gladiator should be subjected to such a barbaric spectator sport is an indictment of a decadent classical practice, but the heroism of the figure is at the same time a reproach to contemporary politicians. In stanzas 140 to 141 Byron describes at length a dramatic episode in which he imagines the gladiator to have figured prominently:

140
I see before me the Gladiator lie:
He leans upon his hand – his manly brow
Consents to death, but conquers agony,
And his drooped head sinks gradually low –
And through his side the last drops, ebbing slow

Moore, 'Rhymes on the Road', v. 340-4; these and other connections between Canova, Moore and Chantrey have been explored in A. Yarrington, 'Anglo-Italian Attitudes', in *The Lustrous Trade: Material Culture and the History of Sculpture in England and Italy c. 1700-1860*, C. M. Sicca and A. Yarrington (Eds), London, New York 2000, pp. 132-55.

[73] T. Dibdin, *A Bibliographical Antiquarian and Picturesque Tour in France and Germany*, 2nd ed., 3 vols., London 1829, vol. 3, pp. 52-3; Dibdin, making his visit in 1818, describes Dannecker as 'The Chantrey [rather] than the Flaxman or Canova of Suabia'.

[74] See F. Haskell and N. Penny, *Taste and the Antique. The Lure of Classical Sculpture*, New Haven, London 1981, pp. 224-7, for a more comprehensive note on the provenance of the sculpture and the Byron passage. It is particularly relevant that the piece had only recently been returned to the museum after its enforced removal to Paris, according to the terms of the Treaty of Tolentino (1797). It is tempting to suppose that this sense of contextual dislocation is part of the Byronic allusion.

From the red gash, fall heavy, one by one,
Like the first of a thunder-shower; and now
The arena swims around him – he is gone,
Ere ceased the inhuman shout which hail'd the wretch who won.

141
He heard it, but he heeded not – his eyes
Were with his heart, and that was far away;
He reck'd not of the life he lost nor prize,
But where his rude hut by the Danube lay
There were his young barbarians all at play,
There was his Dacian mother – he, their sire,
Butcher'd to make a Roman holiday –
All this rush'd with his blood – Shall he expire
And unavenged ? – Arise ! ye Goths, and glut your ire !
(IV, 1252–69)

The length of this quotation helps one appreciate a common Byronic technique akin to *ekphrasis*, where an art object provides only a preliminary point of contact and thereafter supplies inspiration for poetic appropriation. It is also tempting to see in this tragic figure something of a confessional strain found in Byron's work in general, a projection of himself as hero far from his own roots and family, isolated and embattled. Don Juan also is an extension of a different side of the alienated personality: accepting and apparently passive yet heroic when called upon. He passes through several adventures as one who keeps his own counsel and records unsparingly. In Canto II (1819), the possibility of staying with Haidee and achieving a permanence otherwise denied him leads Juan to consider abstract beauty. Philosophy reminds him of 'every sacred tie' (Stanza 210, v. 1674) yet his own natural self veers towards inconstancy. He imagines the 'admiration due where nature's rich | Profusion with young beauty covers o'er | Some favoured object' (Stanza 211, v. 1683–5) to 'A lovely statue we almost adore, | This sort of adoration of the real | Is but a heightening of the "beau ideal"' (v. 1686–88). As with Keats, and certainly as with Shelley, Byron exploits a strength in sculpture that poetry is destined to lack. Its materiality, if unravaged by time, eventually beggars accurate literary description. Instead, from the perspective of both personae, it supplies material for poetic questioning. Byron would like to think that beauty could be as real as Canova's *Head of Helen*, and yet he also realises that, pre-emptively, our understanding of the ideal has played no inconsiderable part. At Haidee's death, the parallel with a marble representation also comes to hand:

The ruling passion, such as marble shows
When exquisitely chisell'd, still lay there,
But fix'd as marble's unchanged aspect throws
O'er the fair Venus, but for ever fair;
O'er the Laocoon's all eternal throes,

And ever-dying Gladiator's air,
Their energy like life forms all their fame,
Yet looks not life, for they are still the same.
(Canto IV, stanza 61, v. 481–88)

Here, there is an attempt to console Don Juan by the fact that marble tombs can also celebrate life – and an after-life. The unchanging and constant marble is a resource in commemoration, outstripping poetry's reach. Ancient forms are here no broken testament, but the very reverse.

Byron's language in these passages offers heroism and potential linguistic beauty, but especially in *Don Juan* it is overlaid with an irony that undercuts its claims to full seriousness. There were others who regarded the ancient classical statuary with perhaps more open and unguarded optimism. Felicia Hemans, in her collection *The Domestic Affections* (1812), had provided a rhapsodic treatment of the *Gladiator* that incorporated an undisguised appreciation of the sculptor's art:

> Sculpture, exalt! Thy triumph proudly see,
> The Roman slave immortalized by thee!
> No suppliant sighs, no terrors round him wait,
> But vanquish'd valour soars above his fate! ...
> Yet here, so well has art majestic wrought,
> Sublim'd expression and ennobl'd thought;
> A dying *Hero* we behold, alone,
> And *Mind's bright grandeur* animates the stone!
> (v. 5–8, 33–36)[75]

This is not particularly original praise, and it is highly unlikely that it proceeds from first-hand appreciation. It does, however, testify to the fascination such poets had with the art of statuary, especially where the tropes surrounding death are concerned. One of her translations was indeed of Pindemonte's praise for Canova's *Hebe* cited above. Her love of Chantrey's monuments and statues of children is particularly apparent in works such as 'The Child's Last Sleep, suggested by a monument of Chantrey's', where the frailty of young life, 'as a dewdrop is swept from the bough' (v. 19), is effaced by the sensitive interpretation of nature that Chantrey provides, wherein we

---

[75] The *Dying Gladiator* also makes its way into William Sotheby's celebration of 'Rome' from his collection *Italy and Other Poems*, London 1828. Here, there is the struggle of the 'large life-drops' and the 'sufferance of the pang severe' (Canto II, v. 286, 297) before an inebriate Roman mob. Sotheby finally concludes that, no matter the deep injustice in the historical record, 'all' are now 'swept away' (Canto II, v. 307). Wordsworth in his last collection of poetical works (1849–50) remembers the *Gladiator* as part of his appreciation of the flower 'Love Lies Bleeding' in the poem of that name (composed c. 1842). The sadness of the flower matches the dying form, '(sentient by Grecian sculpture's marvellous power)' (v. 6), in *Wordsworth's Poetical Works*, ed. E. de Selincourt, 2 vols, 2nd ed., Oxford 1952, vol. 2, p. 167.

may 'anchor our fond hearts' (v. 22) (Pl. 51). There is a similar set of consolatory details in her 'The Sculptured Children. On Chantrey's monument in Lichfield Cathedral'[76] and 'The Child and Dove'[77], suggested by Chantrey's *Statue of Lady Louisa Russell*.[78] As with Byron, Shelley and Keats the baroque drama of a Bernini did not represent a highpoint of modern sculpture. On the contrary, it is where consummate modern sculptors deploy the 'ancient' virtues of craftsmanship that the poets had much to praise. It is pertinent to record the degree to which contemporary satirists, perhaps with Lord Elgin in mind, found the grand tourists an almost proverbial form of life. George Daniel contrasts Chantrey's success, in his 'The Modern Dunciad' (1835), with the untutored profligacy that brought to Britain 'The mutilated blocks of Greece and Rome' (v. 429). Pedantry led taste, for

> Heads, noses, arms, our curious eyes engage
> We prize their beauty much, but more their age;
> Not Chantrey's art so wonderful appears,
> It wants the sanction of three thousand years.
> (v. 430–433)[79]

That Chantrey was seen to embody some connection with antiquity is here evident through Daniel's satire, but this notion was also part of a graceful compliment, sincerely meant by a near neighbour of his by the river Sheaf, Ebenezer Elliott, in his poem 'Love' (n.d.). Here the infant prodigy, Chantrey, is encouraged to be 'the Phidias of the second Greece!' (v. 85).[80] Obviously, the poetic taste for 'poetic' sculpture encompassed nostalgia as well as satire.

In a variety of forms and works the parallel between the arts of sculpture and poetry was of especial interest in the years c. 1790–1830. Just as classical pieces were given a fuller archaeological context in works such as Stuart and

---

[76] The work Hemans is responding to is Francis Chantrey's *Monument to Ellen Jane and Marianne Robinson (the Sleeping Children)*, 1817, marble, Lichfield Cathedral. One of Chantrey's most successful works, it was exhibited at the R.A. in 1817 before being installed in Lichfield Cathedral. It prompted much verse which centred upon the youth and innocence of the two girls and the transience of life.

[77] Here, the work that Hemans refers to is Francis Chantrey's *Statue of Louisa Russell*, 1818, marble, Woburn Abbey. The work was made to stand immediately outside the Temple of the Graces and is a pendant to Thorvaldsen's statue of Louisa's sister, Georgiana.

[78] These poems may be found in *The Poetical Works of Mrs Hemans, reprinted from the Early Editions*, London 1887, respectively, pp. 493, 532, 435. See also William Lisle Bowles's poem, 'Chantrey's Sleeping Children' (1826), in *The Poetical Works of William Lisle Bowles*, 4 vols, London 1855, vol. 2, pp. 288–9, for a more orthodox reference to the *ars longa* tradition.

[79] G. Daniel, *The Modern Dunciad, With Notes Critical and Biographical*, 2nd ed., London, 1815, p. 33.

[80] E. Elliott, *The Poetical Works*, 4 vols, London 1876, vol. 1, p. 73.

Revett's *Antiquities*, their relevance in contemporary political and aesthetic comment grew. Poets described statuary and monuments both to demonstrate a certain freedom from their supposed material limitations and also to demand of their own art a monumentality obviously denied them. What was particular to this period, however, was the continuing and controversial traffic in marbles, and their regular transplantation as items of commercial and nationalistic exploitation. Several were fragmentary in their actual form and nomadic in terms of their identity – both tendencies that helped their inclusion in a Romantic poetic canon where individualism and sensibility had become of great interest. Where the solid appeared to melt into air, however, was when an original provenance was discovered, and, to return to the opening of this essay, when that 'real space' suggested by Potts as the attraction for the viewer appeared too much an illusion; what followed was an attempt to re-inscribe the piece as part of an original drama and as a series of connected cultural forms, in part supplied by the imagination. When the noted phrenologist, Sir George Steuart Mackenzie, turned to the sculptural as a site of touch and intimacy (so enthusiastically reported by Moore and Dibdin, see above), he became aware of a certain anxiety that was also part of the encounter with sculpture:

> The contemplation of such an object should stir up discontent, because it is improper to give to marble a character which does not belong to it; and from the total absence of delicacy; and excite a feeling of uneasiness, because force has been employed in its formation. So far, however, from discontent and uneasiness being raised by a statue, it is generally acknowledged that some statues exist, which represent the human figure as more beautiful than is commonly seen in nature.[81]

Much of the poetic comment we have attempted to illustrate in this essay derives from a realisation that statuary has a history of possession and appropriation. The hope remained, however, that art (and its true appreciation) might stand clear of contaminating local forces. The tragedy lay in the degree to which that hope was merely a pious one.

[81]   G. S. Mackenzie, *An Essay on Some Subjects Connected with Taste*, Edinburgh 1817, p. 139.

1. *Giorgione da Castel Franco Pittor Viniziano*, woodcut, in Giorgio Vasari, *Le vite ...*,
1568 (photo: British Library, London).

2. Wenceslaus Hollar, after Giorgione, *Self-portrait as David*, engraving
(photo: Warburg Institute, London).

3. Copy after Giorgione, *Self-portrait*, oil on canvas, 52 x 43 cm, Herzog Anton Ulrich-Museum, Brunswick (photo: Herzog Anton Ulrich-Museum, Brunswick).

4. Copy after Giorgione, *Self-portrait*, oil on canvas, 57.2 x 47 cm, The Royal Collection, Hampton Court (photo: © 2001 Her Majesty Queen Elizabeth II).

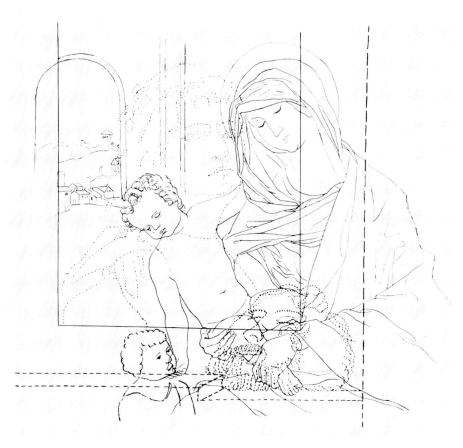

5. Superimposition (from Müller-Hofstede 1957–59) of Pl. 2, Hollar's engraving (dotted lines), over the full composition of the Madonna by Catena revealed by X-rays under Pl. 3. The continuous-line oblong indicates the actual extent of Pl. 3.

6. Anonymous artist in the circle of Giorgione and Titian, *Portrait of a man*, oil on canvas, 76 x 64 cm, National Gallery of Art, Washington, D.C., Kress Collection (photo: National Gallery of Art, Washington).

7. Anonymous artist active in Venice or the Veneto in the early sixteenth century, *Portrait of a man*, oil on canvas, 71 x 57 cm, Pinacoteca di Brera, Milan (photo: Sovrintendenza alle Gallerie, Pinacoteca di Brera, Milan).

8. Giorgione, '*Laura*', oil on canvas, 44 x 33.5 cm (cut down and filled out),
Kunsthistorisches Museum, Vienna (photo: Kunsthistorisches Museum, Vienna).

9. Sebastiano Veneziano, *Salome*, oil on panel, 55 x 44.5 cm, National Gallery, London (photo: National Gallery, London).

10. Titian, '*La Schiavona*', oil on canvas, 118 x 97 cm, National Gallery, London
(photo: National Gallery, London).

11. Titian, *Man with a blue sleeve (Self-portrait)*, oil on canvas, 81.2 x 66.3 cm, National Gallery, London (photo: National Gallery, London).

12. Andrea del Sarto, *Portrait of a man*, oil on canvas, 72 x 57 cm,
National Gallery, London (photo: National Gallery, London).

13. Andrea del Sarto, *Girl with the Petrarchino*, oil on panel, 87 x 69 cm, Uffizi, Florence (photo: Gabinetto fotografico, Soprintendenza per i beni artistici e storici, Florence).

14. Andrea del Sarto, *Girl with the Petrarchino*, detail: page 68 of the 'Petrarchino' with sonnets no. 153 and 154 (photo: Gabinetto fotografico, Soprintendenza per i beni artistici e storici, Florence).

15. Agnolo Bronzino, *Portrait of Lorenzo Lenzi*, oil on panel, 98 x 73 cm, Castello Sforzesco, Milan (photo: Castello Sforzesco, Milan).

16. Agnolo Bronzino, *Portrait of Lorenzo Lenzi*, detail: Lorenzo indicates Varchi's poem illustrating his name (photo: Castello Sforzesco, Milan).

17. Agnolo Bronzino, *Portrait of Ugolino Martelli*, oil on panel, 102 x 85 cm, Staatliche Museen Preußischer Kulturbesitz, Gemäldegalerie, Berlin (photo: Staatliche Museen zu Berlin - Preuischer Kulturbesitz, Gemäldegalerie; Jörg P. Anders).

18. Agnolo Bronzino, *Portrait of Ugolino Martelli*, detail: Ugolino points to *Iliad*, IX, 14
(photo: Staatliche Museen zu Berlin – Preußischer Kulturbesitz, Gemäldegalerie;
Jörg P. Anders).

19. Agnolo Bronzino, *Portrait of a lute-player*, tempera on panel, 94 x 79 cm, detail, Uffizi, Florence (photo: Gabinetto fotografico, Soprintendenza per i beni artistici e storici, Florence).

20. Palma Giovane, *Self-portrait*, oil on canvas, 128 x 96 cm, Pinacoteca di Brera, Milan (photo: Sovrintendenza alle Gallerie, Pinacoteca di Brera, Milan).

21. Former Villa della Torre, south side, Fumane, Verona
(photo: Courtauld Institute, London).

22. Former Villa della Torre, courtyard, Fumane, Verona
(photo: Courtauld Institute, London).

23. Former Villa della Torre, south side, bridge over fishpond, Fumane, Verona (photo: Courtauld Institute, London).

24. Former Villa della Torre, interior, fireplace, Fumane, Verona (photo: Courtauld Institute, London).

25. Frontispiece to the second edition of K. van Mander, *Het Schilderboeck*, 1618
(photo: Warburg Institute, London).

26. K. van Mander, *Het Schilderboeck*, 1618, *Leven*, fols *1v–*2r
(photo: Warburg Institute, London).

Nicola. Iastman. sculp.

IS NOODICH. MENSCH SOECKT VEEL DOCH EEN

Carel Vermander van Molebeke in Vlaenderen, Schilder, ÆTAT. 56.

27 (above). Portrait of K. van Mander, added to the front of K. van Mander, *Het Schilderboeck* in the 1618 edition (photo: Warburg Institute, London).

28 (opposite). Etienne Martellange, *Façade of the Jesuit Church at the Faubourg St. Germain, Paris*, engraving, Bibliothèque Nationale, Paris (photo: Bibliothèque Nationale, Paris).

29. Nicolas Poussin, *St Francis Xavier resuscitating a dead girl at Kagoshima*, oil on canvas, 444 x 234 cm, Louvre, Paris (photo: Agraci).

30. Jacques Stella, *The Child Jesus found in the Temple*, oil on canvas, Notre Dame des Andelys, Les Andelys (photo: Jean Lechortier).

31. Michel Dorigny, after Simon Vouet, *The Madonna of the Jesuits*, engraving (photo: Bibliothèque Nationale, Paris).

Clarissimo Viro   P. Petro le Moyne
è Soc. Iesu Patruo   de se optime merito
hoc grati animi   monumetū consecrabat
Ioan. Bap.te Moyne   regi à consilijs

32. François Poilly, *Pierre Le Moyne*, engraving
(photo: Bibliothèque Nationale, Paris).

33. Column of Trajan, Rome, detail
(photo: Ministero per i beni culturali e ambientali, Rome).

34. Raphael, *Transfiguration*, oil on panel, 405 x 278 cm, detail, Pinacoteca, Vatican
(photo: Alinari).

35. Claude Mellan, after Nicolas Poussin, Bible frontispiece, engraving
(photo: Albertina, Vienna).

36 (above). Meleager-sarcophagus,
detail, Louvre, Paris
(photo: author).

37 (left). *Portrait of St Francis
Xavier*, oil on canvas, Cappellette
di S. Ignazio, Rome
(photo: author).

Religiosissimo Viro Patri Francisco
REGI à Confessionibus. Hanc Apostolici
Imaginem. D.D.C. Addictissimus Cliens

de la Chaise Societatis Iesu Theologo
Viri S. Francisci Xaverij Thaumaturgi
Stephanus Gantrel Metensis.

39 (above). Etienne Gantrel, after Nicolas Poussin, *St Francis Xavier resuscitating a dead girl at Kagoshima*, engraving (photo: author).

38 (opposite). Peter Paul Rubens, *St Francis Xavier*, oil on canvas, 216 x 135 cm, formerly Asscher and Welker, London, destroyed in 1940 (photo: author).

40. Gian Lorenzo Bernini, Four River Fountain, Rome (photo: Conway Library).

41. Gian Lorenzo Bernini, Cornaro Chapel, S. Maria della Vittoria, Rome
(photo: James Austin).

42. Gian Domenico Cerrini, *St Paul ravished to the third heaven*, fresco, S. Maria della Vittoria, Rome (photo: Ministero per i beni culturali e ambientali, Rome).

43. Gerhard van Honthorst, *St Paul ravished to the third heaven*, oil on canvas, 400 x 250 cm, S. Maria della Vittoria, Rome (photo: Ministero per i beni culturali e ambientali, Rome).

44. *Fame conquering Envy*, frontispiece of *Poesie*, 1656, engraving
(photo: Biblioteca Casanatense, Rome).

45. *The Belvedere Torso*, 1st century B.C., marble, Musei Vaticani, Rome
(photo: Conway Library; Dr Nicholas Penny).

46. John Flaxman, *Statue of a lady, authoress of 'Psyche' a poem*, 1814-15, plaster sketch model, University College, London (photo: Conway Library).

47. Antonio Canova, *Hebe*, 1808–14, marble, Devonshire Collection, Chatsworth (photo: Photographic Survey of Private Collections, Courtauld Institute of Art).

48. Antonio Canova, *Head of Helen*, 1818, marble, private collection; this is a second version of the bust owned by Countess Isabella Teotochi Albrizzi, presented to Viscount Castlereagh by the sculptor in 1818 (photo: Conway Library).

49. Heinrich Dannecker, *Friedrich Schiller*, 1794, marble, Staatsgalerie, Stuttgart
(photo: Conway Library).

50. *The Dying Gaul*, 241–197 B.C., marble, Museo Capitolino, Rome (photo: Conway Library; Dr Nicholas Penny).